P9-DEH-350

THE REDUCTION
OF CHRISTIANITY

Other books by Gary DeMar

God and Government:
   A Biblical and Historical Study, 1982

God and Government:
   Issues in Biblical Perspective, 1984

God and Government:
   The Restoration of the Republic, 1986

Ruler of the Nations:
   Biblical Blueprints for Government, 1987

Other books by Peter J. Leithart

A Christian Response to Dungeons and Dragons:
   The New Age Catechism, 1987
   (with George Grant)

THE REDUCTION
OF CHRISTIANITY

Dave Hunt's Theology
of Cultural Surrender

Gary DeMar
and
Peter J. Leithart

DOMINION PRESS • FT. WORTH, TEXAS
AMERICAN VISION PRESS • ATLANTA, GEORGIA

Copyright © 1988 by American Vision, Atlanta, Georgia.

American Vision is a Christian educational and communications organization providing materials to help Christians develop a biblical world view and build a Christian civilization. American Vision believes that the Bible ought to be applied to every area of life: family, church, education, law, medicine, science, music, art, economics, journalism, business, and civil government. American Vision publishes a monthly newsletter, *The Biblical Worldview*, which is edited by Gary DeMar. Consider joining with us to spread the good news that Jesus Christ is Lord and Savior. For more information about American Vision, write: American Vision, P.O. Box 720515, Atlanta, Georgia 30328.

All rights reserved. Written permission must be secured from the publisher to use or reproduce any part of this book, except for brief quotations in critical reviews or articles.

Published by Dominion Press, Ft. Worth, Texas and American Vision, Atlanta, Georgia.

Typesetting by Thoburn Press, Tyler, Texas

Printed in the United States of America

Unless otherwise noted, all Scripture quotations are from the New American Standard Version.

Library of Congress Catalog Card Number 87-073071

ISBN 0-915815-06-0 American Vision edition

ISBN 0-930462-63-7 Dominion Press edition

To Weldon and Kathleen Townsend
Faithful Bereans (Acts 17:11)

TABLE OF CONTENTS

FOREWORD

by Gary North

I was not aware that I had written "books against Dominion Theology." I have made some mention of Dominion Theology in the final chapter of each of my last two books, but I doubt that it would require an entire volume to respond to what I have said.

Dave Hunt[1]

It is a bit perplexing to find how little credit Mr. Hunt wants to take regarding the origin of the widely circulated accusation that "Christian reconstructionists" are implicit theological allies of the New Age Movement. Given the amount of time that at least one television evangelist devotes Sunday evening after Sunday evening to attacking Dominion Theology, and given the fact that he admitted to me personally that he received this information originally from Mr. Hunt's books, this statement by Mr. Hunt was unexpected, to say the least. Like an arsonist caught in the act who insists that he lit only one small match, Mr. Hunt's reluctance to take full credit seems somewhat self-interested.

Mr. Hunt is correct in one respect: it does not require an entire volume to refute what he has said. Refutation is never sufficient; the critic has an obligation to offer a positive alternative. Therefore, it does require an entire volume to show that what Dave Hunt has said rests on a specific view of the Bible, the

---

1. Letter to Gary North, July 20, 1987, in response to an offer to allow Mr. Hunt to read and respond to the first draft of this book.

ix

Church, and the Holy Spirit that has misled millions of otherwise dedicated Christians. It does require a book to present a Bible-based alternative to pessimism concerning the future effects in history of the gospel of Jesus Christ. Mr. Hunt has called into question the power of the Holy Spirit to bring people to the foot of the cross, to transform the lives of lost sinners, and to give them hope that they or their spiritual heirs will be able to see Jesus Christ exalted throughout the world. Mr. Hunt has made it look as though the words of Isaiah will not come true:

> They shall not hurt nor destroy in all My holy mountain, for the earth shall be full of the knowledge of the LORD, as the waters cover the sea. And in that day there shall be a Root of Jesse, who shall stand as a banner to the people; for the Gentiles shall seek Him, and His resting place shall be glorious (Isaiah 11:9-10; NKJV).

But these words *will* come true! The Bible is the very Word of God. It cannot be overcome by God-haters: Communists, New Agers, or any other anti-Christian force in history. Our God's in-spired Word is sure. We Christians can be absolutely confident that some day, "the earth shall be full of the knowledge of the LORD, as the waters cover the sea."

There is an old political slogan: "You can't beat something with nothing." To call Dave Hunt's theology into question is not enough. Gary DeMar and Peter Leithart have done far more than merely show why Mr. Hunt's theology gives too much credit to the satanic God-haters of this world. They show what the Bible offers as an alternative to the humanists' kingdom of man. They show that the Bible offers Christians blueprints for bringing Satan and his forces under the dominion of Jesus Christ. Mr. Hunt be-lieves that this is impossible, even for Jesus Christ Himself, as we shall see. On this point, he has broken with the whole history of the Church, including traditional dispensational theology. This is the peculiar fact: Dave Hunt has written a book, *Beyond Seduction*, that actually teaches that the future millennial reign of Christ will **not** be the kingdom of God on earth, yet hundreds of thousands of dispensationalists have failed to recognize that his book over-throws just about everything that dispensationalists have taught regarding the triumphant premillennial reign of Christ. *The Reduction of Christianity* proves that Dave Hunt has in fact abandoned traditional dispensational theology, and he has substituted something very different in its place—something that inevitably undermines Christians' confidence in the gospel.

The theological issues are clear. You need to think about them. First, does God's Word teach that Satan will be victorious over God's people in history? Second, does the Bible teach that the healing power of the Holy Spirit only affects the soul and not families, schools, businesses, communities, and every area of life? In other words, does Christ offer comprehensive salvation or a very limited salvation? Third, is the Holy Spirit so limited that He is unable to bring millions upon millions of people to Christ? Fourth, does the Holy Spirit empower Christians to obey God's law? Fifth, does obeying the law of God weaken those who obey, and does disobedience to the law of God strengthen those who disobey? Sixth, do we Christians represent Christ on earth in the same way that God-haters represent Satan? Seventh, if we do represent Christ in this way, wouldn't our defeat by Satan's forces in history make Jesus a loser in history?

Do you really believe that the Lord Jesus Christ, the Lord of glory, plans to be a loser in history?

Representative Government

The issue of representation is crucial. Let me ask you a question: Does Satan seek to establish his kingdom on earth? You may think this is a foolish question; of course he does. Millions of Christians even believe that his kingdom is the dominant one in history. But do you also believe that Satan must rule in person, visibly from some nation, in order to establish his kingdom? As far as I know, no theologian has ever argued that Satan must appear in person as a leader of his forces in order to establish his kingdom on earth. He always uses representatives: "the beast," "the antichrist," etc. No Christian commentator ever argues that Satan's use of human representatives is somehow any less of a satanic kingdom. Yet many Christians deny that Christ also rules His earthly forces through human representatives. They deny that *a king normally rules through his representatives*. This is why several of Jesus' parables begin with the story of a king or a landowner who journeys to a far country, but leaves his representatives (stewards) behind to rule in his name.

It is true that Dominion Theology teaches that we can, do, and will have a kingdom of God on earth without Jesus' physical presence in Jerusalem. This is somehow regarded as an outrageous doctrine. One tract-writer says that this is the number-one error of Dominion Theology: "And in this we can isolate the error of hardcore Dominion theology/Reconstruction/postmillennialism. A universal kingdom, but without a personal, physical, literal universal king!"[2] Fine; now would he argue that there is no satanic kingdom either, because Satan is not visible and physically present on the earth? Of course not. Then why does he think that Dominion Theology is necessarily incorrect about the reality of Christ's kingdom reign without His physical manifestation in Jerusalem?

Dave Hunt even denies that Christ's personal, physical reign from Jerusalem is a sign of the kingdom. Yet his supporters think that he is a defender of "the old-time religion."

Dave Hunt vs. Dominion Theology

Let us begin with the words of Jesus: "All power is given unto me in heaven and in earth" (Matt. 28:18; KJV). We should then ask the obvious question: *Where is the earthly manifestation of Christ's power?* Dave Hunt is adamant: only in the hearts of believers and (maybe) inside the increasingly defenseless walls of a local church

---

2. *Q&A With Charles P. Schmitt* (Silver Spring, MD: Foundational Teachings, no date), second page.

or local rescue mission. As he says, in response to an advertisement for my Biblical Blueprints Series: "The Bible doesn't teach us to build society but instructs us to preach the gospel, for one's citizenship is in Heaven (Col. 3:2)."[3]

It seems to me that he could have strengthened his case that we are citizens of only one "country" by citing a modern translation of Philippians 3:20. But this would only have deferred the question: *Why can't Christians be citizens of two countries?* After all, they are *in* the world physically, yet not *of* the world spiritually: John 17:14-16. Christians are, as Hunt (and all Christians) would insist, required to obey national laws, but also obey the Bible. To be required to obey two sets of laws is to raise the question of dual citizenship.

Hunt's dispensationalist gospel is a gospel of the heart *only.* Jesus saves hearts *only*; somehow, His gospel is not powerful enough to restore to biblical standards the institutions that He designed for mankind's benefit, but which have been corrupted by sin. Hunt's view of the gospel is that Jesus can somehow save sinners without having their salvation affect the world around them. He forgets that institutions consist of people (souls). His gospel says: "Heal souls, not institutions."

Hunt separates the preaching of the gospel from the concerns of society. He separates heavenly citizenship from earthly citizenship. In short, he has reinterpreted the Great Commission of Jesus Christ to His followers: "All power is given unto me in heaven but *none* in earth." (A similar other-worldly view of Christ's authority is shared by many amillennialists.)[4] Christ's earthly power can only be manifested when He returns physically to set up a top-down bureaucratic kingdom in which Christians will be responsible for following the direct orders of Christ, issued to meet specific historical circumstances. Such a view has so little

---

3. Dave Hunt, *CIB Bulletin* (Feb. 1987), p. 4.
4. "There is no room for optimism: towards the end, in the camps of the satanic and the anti-Christ, culture will sicken, and the Church will yearn to be delivered from its distress." H. de Jongste and J. M. van Krimpen, *The Bible and the Life of the Christian* (Philadelphia, PA: Presbyterian and Reformed, 1968), p. 27; cited by R. J. Rushdoony, *The Institutes of Biblical Law* (Nutley, NJ: Craig Press, 1973), p. 14n.

faith in the power of the Bible's perfect revelation, empowered by the Holy Spirit, to shape the thoughts and actions of Christians, that Jesus must return and personally issue millions of orders per day telling everyone what to do, case by case, crisis by crisis.

For years, Christian Reconstructionists[5] have argued that such a view of social affairs is inherent in premillennialism. In recent years, premillennial activists have denied this accusation. The intellectual roots of the recent rise of premillennial activism, however, can be traced back to the tiny band of postmillennial Reconstructionists. The premillennial camp is becoming divided, as Dave Hunt has noted. Hunt presents himself (misleadingly) as a representative of the older dispensational premillennialism of the 1925-1975 period: a no-nonsense defender of the earthly defeat of the Church. His book, *The Seduction of Christianity*, has become the number-one Christian best-seller of the 1980s, the biggest selling book on eschatology since Hal Lindsey's books.

Hunt is consistent about his earthly pessimism, even to the point of denying that Jesus' reign on earth will be a manifestation of the kingdom of God. He spells out in no uncertain terms just what his radical brand of dispensationalism necessarily implies. In a taped interview with the publisher of the Canadian newsletter, *Omega-Letter*, Hunt says in response to Christian Reconstructionists: "You're looking forward to meeting Jesus, who when you meet him your feet are planted on planet earth. And He simply has arrived to take over this beautiful kingdom you've established for Him, then you've been under heavy delusion, you've been working for the antichrist and not for the true Christ."[6]

Back in the 1950s, J. Vernon McGee, the pastor of a very large dispensational congregation in Los Angeles, made the following

---

5. Christian Reconstructionists include such Calvinist theologians as R. J. Rushdoony, Greg L. Bahnsen, James Jordan, Ray Sutton, David Chilton, George Grant, and the authors of this book. Christian Reconstructionism was never connected with the pentecostal group of the 1940s called the Manifest Sons of God, a movement that had disappeared before Christian Reconstructionists began writing in the 1960s.

6. *Dominion and the Cross*, Tape #2 of *Dominion: The Word and New World Order*, a 3-tape set distributed by the *Omega-Letter*, Ontario, Canada, 1987.

classic statement about the futility of social reform: "You don't polish brass on a sinking ship." This phrase has become a favorite jibe against dispensational social pessimism and defeatism among Christian Reconstructionists. Rushdoony has quoted it for three decades. It is remarkable that Peter Lalonde, publisher of the *Omega-Letter*, repeats it favorably in his taped interview with Dave Hunt: "Do you polish brass on a sinking ship? And if they're [Reconstructionists] working on setting up new institutions, instead of going out and winning the lost for Christ, then they're wasting the most valuable time on the planet earth."[7]

Thus, *Dave Hunt denies the progressive maturation of Christianity and Christian-operated social institutions in history* (meaning pre-Second Coming history). The millennium ruled by Christ, Hunt says, will be a world in which "Justice will be meted out swiftly."[8] Jesus will treat men as fathers treat five-year-old children: instant punishment, no time for reflection and repentance. Christians today are given time to think through their actions, to reflect upon their past sins, and to make restitution before God judges them. Today, they are treated by God as responsible adults. Not in the millennium! The Church will go from maturity to immaturity when Christ returns in power. And even with the testimony of the perfect visible rule of Jesus on earth for a thousand years, Satan will still thwart Christ and Christ's Church, for at Satan's release, he will deceive almost the whole world, leading them to rebel against "Christ and the saints in Jerusalem."[9]

Dave Hunt vs. the Kingdom of God

In short, Hunt argues, the plan of God points only to the defeat of His Church in history. He is saying that Satan got the upper hand in Eden, and even the raw power of God during the millennium and at the final judgment at the end of history will not wipe

---

7. *Dominion: A Dangerous New Theology*, Tape #1 of *Dominion: The Word and New World Order.*

8. Dave Hunt, *Beyond Seduction: A Return to Biblical Christianity* (Eugene, OR: Harvest House, 1987), p. 250.

9. *Idem.*

out the kingdom of Satan and restore the creation to wholeness. Thus, he concludes, *the kingdom of God will never be manifested on earth, not even during dispensationalism's earthly millennium.* I know of no pessimism regarding history greater than his statement that even the triumphant premillennial reign of Christ physically on earth will end when the vast majority of people will rebel against Him, converge upon Jerusalem, and try to destroy the faithful people inside the city: "Converging from all over the world to war against Christ and the saints at Jerusalem, these rebels will finally have to be banished from God's presence forever (Rev. 20:7-10). The millennial reign of Christ upon earth, rather than being the kingdom of God, will in fact be the final proof of the incorrigible nature of the human heart."[10]

Actually, this is one of the most astounding statements ever written by any Christian author in history. "The millennial reign of Christ upon earth, *rather than being the kingdom of God*, will in fact be the final proof of the incorrigible nature of the human heart."[11] He argues that this rebellion is the final act of history. But if this reign of Christ is *not* the kingdom of God, then just what is it that Jesus will deliver up to His Father at the last day? How do we make sense of the following prophecy? "Then cometh the end, when he shall have delivered up the kingdom to God, even the Father; when he shall have put down all rule and all authority and power. For he must reign, till he hath put all enemies under his feet. The last enemy that shall be destroyed is death" (1 Cor. 15:24-26; KJV). Hunt knows that Christ's destruction of the final satanic rebellion puts down death. So, the kingdom spoken of in this passage *has* to be Christ's millennial reign, whether physical (premillennialism), spiritual (amillennialism), or covenantal (postmillennialism). That he could make a mistake as large as this one indicates that he is a weak reed for dispensationalists to rest on, at this late date, in their attempt to refute Christian optimism

---

10. *Idem.*
11. *Idem.*

regarding the Church's earthly future. The exegetical crisis of pre-millennial dispensationalism is becoming evident, for dispensationalists have failed to recognize the enormous threat to their theological system that Hunt's books have presented. That Dave Hunt, a man with a bachelor's degree in mathematics, is now the most prominent theologian of the dispensational movement, as immune from public criticism by dispensational theologians as Hal Lindsey was in the 1970s, indicates the extent of the crisis. The amateurs give away the store theologically, and the seminary professors say nothing, as if these paperback defenders had not delivered mortal blows to the dispensational system.

He refuses to let go. In Tape Two of the widely distributed three-tape interview with Peter Lalonde, he announces that *God Himself is incapable of setting up an earthly kingdom*!

> In fact, dominion—taking dominion and setting up the kingdom for Christ—is an *impossibility*, even for God. The millennial reign of Christ, far from being the kingdom, is actually the final proof of the incorrigible nature of the human heart, because Christ Himself can't do what these people say they are going to do. . . .

Compare this with Hal Lindsey's comment under "Paradise Restored": "God's kingdom will be characterized by peace and equity, and by universal spirituality and knowledge of the Lord. Even the animals and reptiles will lose their ferocity and no longer be carnivorous. All men will have plenty and be secure. There will be a chicken in every pot and no one will steal it! The Great Society which human rulers throughout the centuries have promised, but never produced, will at last be realized under Christ's rule. The meek and not the arrogant will inherit the earth (Isaiah 11)."[12] Or again, "That time is coming when believers in Jesus

---

12. Hal Lindsey, *The Late Great Planet Earth* (Grand Rapids, MI: Zondervan, [1970] 1973), p. 177.

Christ are going to walk upon this earth and see it in perfect condition. Pollution will be passé. Jesus Christ is going to recycle the late great Planet Earth."[13] All this "kingdom perfection" during the millennium is abandoned by Dave Hunt, in his desperate yet consistent attack on Dominion Theology. He has scrapped traditional dispensationalism's last remaining traces of optimism about history in order to paint a picture of inconceivable despair. Even God cannot set up a kingdom on earth.

Yet we Christian Reconstructionists are criticized by a minority of activist dispensationalists for saying that dispensationalism is inherently a pessimistic worldview. If it isn't, then why did Dave Hunt's books become the best-selling Christian books of the 1980s? *Because his traditional dispensational readers apparently agree with him.* They recognize that today's growing number of dispensational political and social activists are no longer voicing the original theology of dispensationalism, but have adopted Dominion Theology, an implicitly postmillennial worldview.

Dave Hunt has presented to his traditional dispensationalist readers a theology of historical despair, a world forever without any cultural manifestation of the kingdom of God. If this is not a truly consistent version of dispensational theology, then why are all the leaders of dispensationalism silent about his books? If Hal Lindsey rejects Hunt's totally pessimistic cultural conclusions, then why doesn't he say so publicly? Why don't the faculty members at Dallas Seminary and Grace Seminary voice their disapproval? Do they agree with him or not?

Power or Ethics?

Here is Hunt's second message: *the gospel in history is doomed to cultural failure.* (The first message is that God's Old Testament law is no longer binding in New Testament times, which is why he is

---

13. Hal Lindsey, *Satan Is Alive and Well on Planet Earth* (Grand Rapids, MI: Zondervan, 1972), p. 113.

so pessimistic: he no longer rests spiritually on the idea that God blesses His covenant people externally in terms of our faithfulness to His law, nor does He bring His enemies visibly low in history because of their covenantal rebellion.) In both premillennialism and amillennialism, we see the underlying theology of the power religion: the issues of history will be settled in Christ's favor only through a final *physical* confrontation between God and Satan at the end of time (Rev. 20). The history of the Church is therefore irrelevant: the conflict of the ages will be settled apart from the gospel, ethics, and the dominion covenant issued to Adam (Gen. 1:26-28), Noah (Gen. 9:1-17), and the Church (Matt. 28:18-20). The conflict of the ages will be settled in a kind of cosmic arm wrestling match between God and Satan. The Church is nothing more than a vulnerable bystander to this final cosmic event.

Yet we all know who will win in a war based strictly on power. We know that God has more power than Satan. Satan knows, too. What Christians need to believe, now and throughout eternity, is that the earthly authority which comes progressively to Christians as God's reward to His people in response to their righteousness under Christ and under biblical law is greater than the earthly authority progressively granted by Satan to his followers for their rebellion against God. Unfortunately for the history of the gospel during the last century, both premillennialism and amillennialism deny this fundamental truth. Pessimists preach that the power granted to Satan's human followers in history will always be greater than the power granted by God to His people in history (meaning before Jesus' second coming physically). They preach *historic defeat for the Church of Jesus Christ*. Why? Because they have denied the only basis of long-term victory for Christians: the continuing validity of God's Old Testament law, empowered in their lives by the Holy Spirit, the Church's tool of dominion.

The Ultimate Form of Pessimism

Christian Reconstructionists believe that God will steadily transform this world ethically, as He brings people to Himself in grace. Given the depravity of man, He is the only One who can transform this world. But how does He do this? Through demons? No. Through fallen men who are on the side of demons in their rebellion against God? No. So, what is God's historic means of making the world better? *The preaching of the gospel!* This is what postmillennialists have always taught. *And the comprehensive success of the gospel in history is what postmillennialism's critics have always denied.* The critics categorically deny that the gospel of Christ will ever change most men's hearts at any future point in history. The gospel in this view is a means primarily of *condemning gospel-rejecting people to hell*, not a program leading to the victory of Christ's people in history. The gospel cannot transform the world, they insist.

Pessimism regarding the transforming power of the gospel of Jesus Christ in history is what best *defines* pessimism. There is no pessimism in the history of man that is more pessimistic than this eschatological pessimism regarding the power of the gospel in history. The universal destruction of mankind by nuclear war—a myth, by the way[14]—is downright optimistic compared to pessimism with regard to the transforming power of the gospel in history. This pessimism testifies that the incorrigible human heart is more powerful than God in history, that Satan's defeat of Adam in the garden is more powerful in history than Christ's defeat of Satan at Calvary. It denies Paul's doctrine of triumphant grace in history: "Moreover the law entered, that the offence might abound. But where sin abounded, grace did much more abound" (Rom. 5:20; KJV). Does grace struggle so that sin might more abound in history?

Deliberately Deceiving the Faithful?

What do pessimists say in response? They denounce anyone who proclaims eschatological optimism as a heretical preacher of

---

14. Arthur Robinson and Gary North, *Fighting Chance: Ten Feet to Survival* (Ft. Worth, TX: American Bureau of Economic Research, 1986).

utopia. Dave Hunt writes: "A perfect Edenic environment where all ecological, economic, sociological, and political problems are solved fails to perfect mankind. So much for the theories of psychology and sociology and utopian dreams."[15] Here is the key word used again and again by pessimists to dismiss postmillennialism: *utopia*. ("Utopia": *ou* = no, *topos* = place.) In short, they regard as totally mythological the idea that God's Word, God's Spirit, God's law, and God's Church can change the hearts of *most* people sometime in the future. They *assume* (without any clear biblical support) that Revelation 20:7-10 describes a final rebellion in which *most people on earth rebel*, despite the fact that only *one-third* of the angels ("stars") rebelled with Satan, and only *one-third* of the earth is symbolically brought under God's wrath in the Book of Revelation's judgment passages (Rev. 8:7-12; 9:15, 18).

Confidence in Man?

Over and over, pessimists accuse postmillennialists of having too much confidence in man. This is really astounding, when you think about it, because all the primary defenders of modern postmillennialism have been Calvinists and usually followers of Cornelius Van Til. Normally, nobody accuses Calvinists of having too elevated a view of man, what with the Calvinists' doctrine of man's total depravity and fallen man's inability to respond in faith to the gospel without God's predestinating irresistible grace to force conversions.

Postmillennialists never argue for confidence in "mankind as such." They only argue for the increasing long-term influence in history of *regenerate, covenantally faithful* people compared to *unregenerate, covenantally rebellious* people. What the pessimists argue is the opposite: 1) the steadily increasing long-term authority in history of unregenerate, covenantally rebellious people, and 2) the declining cultural influence of regenerate, covenantally faithful

---

15. *Beyond Seduction*, p. 251.

people. It is not "confidence in man" that is the basis of postmillennial optimism; it is *confidence in the covenantal faithfulness of God* in rewarding covenant-keepers (Deut. 28:1-14) and punishing covenant-breakers (Deut. 28:15-68).[16] Listen to the words of Professor Thomas Sproull over a century ago regarding the coming period of millennial blessings:

> In order to accomplish this, the presence of the humanity of Christ is not necessary. The destruction of the kingdom of Satan cannot be done by a nature, but by a person. It is the work not of humanity, but of divinity. That kingdom extends over the whole world, and requires for its overthrow an omnipresent power. It received its death-blow when our Lord by his resurrection was "declared to be the Son of God."—*Rom* 1:14. In his ascension "he spoiled principalities and powers, and made a show of them openly."—*Col*. 2:15. His manifestation in the flesh was necessary, that he might make atonement for sin; but by his incarnation he received no increase in strength, for vanquishing his enemies. It is indeed the God-man that gains the victory; not by human, but by divine power.[17]

How much plainer could he be? The basis of millennial blessings in history is the power of God in history, not the power of man in history. Yet our opponents for over a century have boldly and unconscionably distorted the postmillennialists' explanation of the millennium. These leaders have not been ignorant men; they have been able to read. They have simply and deliberately preferred to mislead their followers. It is not an intellectual defect on their part; it is a moral defect.

Dave Hunt has gone one step beyond. He not only rejects postmillennial optimism, he even implies that to hold such a view of the future is to give aid to the New Age Movement.

---

16. Ray R. Sutton, *That You May Prosper: Dominion By Covenant* (Tyler, TX: Institute for Christian Economics, 1987), chapter 4.

17. Rev. Thomas Sproull, *Prelections on Theology* (Pittsburgh, PA: Myers, Shinkle, & Co., 1882), p. 411.

Dominion Theology and the New Age Movement?

Christianity is the source of the idea of progress in the history of mankind. Other groups have stolen this vision and have reworked it along anti-Christian lines, from the Enlightenment[18] to the Social Gospel movement to the New Age Movement, but this does not mean that postmillennial optimism is the cause of the thefts. It only means that Satan recognizes the motivating power of *orthodox* Christian theology. It surely does not mean that eschatological pessimism is in any way an effective shield against humanism, New Age philosophy, or socialism. New Age social theorist Jeremy Rifkin is proof enough. He is a pessimist who appeals for support to eschatological pessimists within the Christian community.[19]

What is even more galling is that Dave Hunt has tried to link the Christian Reconstruction movement with the New Age Movement, simply because Christian Reconstructionists, as dominion theologians, proclaim the legitimacy of social action along biblical lines.[20] What angers traditional premillennialists is that Reconstructionists say that the world is *not* going to hell in a handbasket. Satan's world is going there, but not the kingdom of God, which does have manifestations on earth.

I wrote the first Christian book exposing the theology of the

---

18. Robert A. Nisbet, "The Year 2000 and All That," *Commentary* (June 1968).

19. Jeremy Rifkin (with Ted Howard), *Entropy: A New World View* (New York: Bantam New Age Books, [1980] 1981) and *The Emerging Order: God in the Age of Scarcity* (New York: Ballantine, 1979). For a refutation of Rifkin, see my book, *Is the World Running Down? Crisis in the Christian Worldview* (Tyler, TX: Institute for Christian Economics, 1987).

20. "Closely related in belief are several other groups: the Reconstructionists such as Gary North et al, as well as Christian socialists such as Jim Wallis (of *Sojourners*), Tom Sine et al whose major focus is upon cleaning up the earth ecologically, politically, economically, sociologically etc. They imagine that the main function of the Church is to restore the Edenic state—hardly helpful, since Eden is where sin began. Many groups are beginning to work together who disagree on some points but share with the New Agers a desire to clean up the earth and establish the Kingdom." Dave Hunt, *CIB Bulletin* (Feb. 1987), front page.

New Age Movement in 1976, *None Dare Call It Witchcraft*,[21] years before Dave Hunt wrote anything about it. Yet the cassette tape-buying public is tantalized by the *Omega-Letter* advertising piece for its three-tape interview with Hunt, in which the copywriter asks some legally safe but preposterous leading questions:

> Is Dominion Theology placing the church in allegiance with the New Age and Globalist groups who are trying to build a New World Order of peace and prosperity?
>
> Does Dominion Theology represent a rejection of the finished work of the cross?

Dave Hunt, citing 2 Peter 3:11 (and erroneously attributing to Peter the words of Isaiah 34:4), states categorically that theological optimism toward the gospel's power to transform this earth is a stepping stone to humanism. Instead, we should turn totally from this earth. Hunt separates heaven from earth so completely that the earth must show no signs in history of God's healing power. This is an explicit, self-conscious defense of the theology that undergirds that old line, "He is so totally spiritual that he's no earthly good." Hunt implicitly denies Jesus' required prayer: "Thy kingdom come. Thy will be done in earth, as it is in heaven" (Matt. 6:10; KJV).

> Now you would say, boy, that's a pretty hopeless thing, well, but Peter didn't say that. He said, "Seeing that these things will all be dissolved, what manner of persons ought you to be in all holy conversations and godliness?" He said, "The day of the Lord is coming in which the heavens will be rolled up like a scroll. The elements will melt with a fervent heat," and so forth. And *that* in fact, Peter says, ought to motivate us to holy living, to turn *totally*

---

21. Gary North, *None Dare Call It Witchcraft* (New Rochelle, NY: Arlington House, 1976). This has been updated as *Unholy Spirits: Occultism and New Age Humanism* (Ft. Worth, TX: Dominion Press, 1986). See especially Chapter 11 for a critique of Dave Hunt's eschatology.

from this world, from the materialization and all of the ambitions, and so forth, to a hope in the heavenlies, in a new creation, and it ought to motivate us to *godliness*. But these people are saying "no, the motivation we need is the desire to build, to reconstruct planet earth, to realize that ecologically we've got problems." I mean we should be concerned about all that. I'm not denying that, but that's not our hope; that's not the primary goal of the church: social transformation. But the primary goal is to save souls, and to bring men to the cross of Jesus Christ, and I feel—I don't feel, I'm *convinced*—that the kingdom-dominion teaching is playing into the hands of the very lie that turns us from the cross and from the gospel and the true solution to a humanistic idea, but all done in the name of Jesus Christ, and for good cause.[22]

Even the idea of cleaning up the earth is a socialistic New Age deception, in Dave Hunt's view. He is quite specific about the link between the New Age Movement and ecology:

But forgetting that for the moment, people will say, "Well I mean, you know, whether we are going to be taken to heaven, or whether the kingdom is on this earth, or, you know, whether we are going to be raptured, or whether we are not going to be raptured, those are future events. Let's not worry about that; let's unite in our common concern for our fellow man," and so forth. That opens the door to a very deceptive lie which literally turns us from heaven as our hope to this earth, which is at the heart of the kingdom-dominion teaching, that we—man—was given dominion over this earth, and the problem is that he lost the dominion to Satan, and the big thing is that we need to regain the dominion. . . . But it opens the door to a marriage with New Age beliefs, as you know, with humanistic beliefs, so that we will all be joining together in working for ecological wholeness, working for peace, working for prosperity, because we are not concerned about heaven, or the return of Christ, or the Rapture, but we

---

22. *Dominion and the Cross*, Tape #2, in *Dominion: The Word and New World Order*.

have got to be concerned about earth, the threat of ecological collapse, the threat of a nuclear holocaust.[23]

Here we have the continuing historical theme in all traditional Christian pessimism: the radical separation of heaven and earth, which necessarily implies the increasing connection between hell and earth. The pessimists are promoting the spread of Satan's imitation New World Order when they protest the validity of Christ's New World Order, which He established definitively with His death, resurrection, and the sending of the Holy Spirit at Pentecost. Pessimism delivers the world to Satan and his followers *by default*, and all in the name of biblical orthodoxy.

Whose New World Order?

Now, let me say right here: I believe in the New World Order of Jesus Christ, inaugurated at Calvary and visibly sanctioned in history by the resurrection and ascension of Christ to the right hand of God, where He now reigns in power and glory. What I reject is the imitation New World Order of humanism. But there *is* a biblical New World Order. There is a *new creation in Christ.* "Therefore, if anyone is in Christ, he is a new creation; old things have passed away; behold, all things have become new" (2 Cor. 5:17; New King James Version). This new creation was established *definitively* at Calvary. It is being established *progressively* in history. And it will be established *finally* at the day of judgment.

We cannot expect to beat something with nothing. We cannot expect to defeat the humanists' New World Order with a theology of guaranteed historical defeat, the theology of traditional pessimistic eschatologies. We must fight theological hellfire with theological heavenfire, just as God fought it at the destruction of Sodom. The Sodomites lost that confrontation, not Lot, and certainly not Abraham. Pessimists forget this. Nevertheless, just because Christian Reconstructionists preach victory for the Church in history, we are now being linked to the New Age Movement—a

---

23. *Dominion: A Dangerous New Theology*, Tape #1.

movement that I led the fight against long ago.

We have seen this strategy before. The Pharisees said that Christ was in league with Satan because He successfully cast out demons.

> Then was brought unto him one possessed with a devil, blind, and dumb: and he healed him, insomuch that the blind and dumb both spake and saw. And all the people were amazed, and said, Is not this the son of David? But when the Pharisees heard it, they said, This fellow doth not cast out devils, but by Beelzebub the prince of the devils (Matt. 12:22-24; KJV).

The Pharisees could not deny that Christ had achieved a visible victory over a demon. The blind man saw. Mute before, he could now speak. This called into question the *narrow, Palestine-bound religion of the Pharisees.* It meant that the son of David, the promised Messiah, had come among them. This was a threat to their nationalistic religion. It was a threat to their working alliance with the humanist Roman Empire. They had bowed the knee politically to Rome's humanist empire, and now Christ's manifestation of power was calling their compromise into question. The alliance between the Pharisees' escapist religion and Rome's power religion was being challenged by Christ's dominion religion. The escape religionists resented this, as they always do. Christ was challenging their theology of an exclusively *internalized* kingdom of God in the midst of a hostile, all-powerful kingdom of political humanism.

Christ replied in kind, showing them a new theology about the kingdom of God on earth:

> And Jesus knew their thoughts, and said unto them, Every kingdom divided against itself is brought to desolation; and every city or house divided against itself shall not stand. And if Satan cast out Satan, he is divided against himself; how shall then his kingdom stand? And if I by Beelzebub cast out devils, by whom do your children cast them out? Therefore they shall be your

judges. But if I cast out devils by the Spirit of God, then the kingdom of God is come unto you (Matt. 12:25-27; KJV).

How do we know that *the kingdom of God is now on earth*? Because of this verse, among others. Jesus *did* cast out devils by the Spirit of God. He *did* use the power of God to overcome Satan. He *did* heal the sick. And He *will* conquer His enemies, through His Church, in history, before He comes again in final judgment. He *now* reigns in heaven, at the right hand of God (Eph. 1:19-22). He reigns now, both in heaven and on earth (Matt. 28:18-20). Because He cast out demons by the Spirit of God, we know that the kingdom of God has come unto us. We also have that same Holy Spirit. The victory in principle is behind us: "For he *hath* put all things under his feet" (1 Cor. 15:27a; KJV).

Anyone who denies this *denies the cross of Christ*. This is why it is preposterous to see the defeat-preachers ask: "Does Dominion Theology represent a rejection of the finished work of the cross?" No, Dominion Theology affirms *Christ's definitive victory over Satan at Calvary.* What outrages the escape religionists is that postmillennialists also preach *Christ's progressive victory over Satan in history, through His Church.* Hunt categorically and self-consciously denies victory in history for the Church of Jesus Christ. He affirms that Christ's chosen people are losers in history.

This is exactly what the Pharisees taught the Jews: that until the Messiah came, the Jews would be losers in history. This was the basis of the Pharisees' political compromise with the Roman Empire. Victory could not come until the Messiah came. Victory was always in the future. Victory was always on Messiah's shoulders, and always far ahead in time. And indeed, victory *was* on Messiah's shoulders, which was what Christ's miracles announced. But this meant that the Pharisees had to bow to Christ rather than Rome, that they would have to start preaching gospel victory and training redeemed people to exercise dominion. This was unacceptable to the Pharisees. It meant political trouble with Rome. It also meant that they would be responsible for working out in history the Bible's principles of social transformation, and on a worldwide scale, for they would have to begin preaching a comprehensive gospel of total healing.

The Pharisees refused to accept this responsibility. They hated the very idea of worldwide responsibility. They wanted peace with Rome. But the Church believed Christ, *which is why Christ's Church took the gospel to the world in power*, while the Jews were scattered by the Romans in a series of historic defeats, beginning with the fall of Jerusalem and the destruction of the temple.[24]

The postmillennial Christian Reconstructionists unquestionably teach that there will be a future era in which the gospel heals the souls of large numbers of people, and these healed people will then work to subdue the earth to the glory of God. But this is the offense, in Hunt's eyes. This optimism about visible manifestations of God's kingdom on earth, he says, is what the New Age Movement is all about.

Conclusion

Although Dave Hunt denies that he has called postmillennial Christian Reconstructionists "New Agers," there can be no doubt that he hints at this supposed relationship. His followers have picked up the accusation, and I have letters in my files that prove this.

We should not make eschatology the test of being a "fellow traveller" of the New Age Movement. The New Age Movement's three key doctrines are all anti-Christian: 1) reincarnation, 2) the divinization of man, and 3) techniques of "higher consciousness" as a means to divinization. There are optimistic New Agers, and there are pessimistic New Agers. Jeremy Rifkin is the most influential New Age social philosopher, and he is self-consciously pessimistic, and he self-consciously targeted premillennialists as those Christians closest to his worldview. I could make a far better case for Dave Hunt as a secret New Ager than he has been able to make concerning me. But either argument, and either innuendo,

---

24. David Chilton, *The Days of Vengeance: An Exposition of the Book of Revelation* (Ft. Worth, TX: Dominion Press, 1987).

would be equally wrong, both morally and factually. Orthodox Christianity is inherently opposed to New Age doctrines. The early Christian creeds were statements of faith drawn up when proto-New Age theologians began to mislead Christian believers.

Gary DeMar and Peter Leithart argue that the worldview of Dave Hunt leads to a shortened view of time, a minimal view of Christians' authority in history and their responsibility in history. Dave Hunt is a self-conscious cultural retreatist. He has raised the white flag in the name of "true Christianity." Where views such as his predominate, the Church becomes temporarily what he says it will be in the future: a loser.

When Christians start winning in history, as they surely will, they will look back in amazement that anyone calling himself a Christian could have such a low view of the Church in history and such a low view of the civilization-transforming power of the gospel in history. They will be amazed that any Christian could have believed that God would voluntarily transfer more power to Satan in history than to the Holy Spirit. They will perhaps be most amazed that millions of those Christians who are most vocal in their preaching of the Holy Spirit, meaning pentecostals and charismatics, have also preached some version of traditional dispensationalism. Thousands of them have read and approved of Dave Hunt's *Seduction of Christianity*. Such a view of the Church's future is totally inconsistent with their view of the Holy Spirit, as Gary DeMar and Peter Leithart demonstrate clearly in *The Reduction of Christianity*.

I have made a series of very serious accusations. I have said that pessimists believe that the Christian gospel that saves men's souls will have no long-term positive effects in society at large. They therefore are forced to deny that the progressive sanctification of Christians in history will produce positive results in society that will then lead to the long-term social transformation of society at large. They therefore deny the cause-and-effect relationship between Christians' progressive faithfulness and the progressive healing of society.

Pessimists look forward to the millennium as a period of reduced personal responsibility for Christians, for Jesus will issue orders to people and rule with an iron hand. They tend to see the historical battle between Christ and Satan in terms of cosmic power, not human ethics. This is because they reject the continuing validity of Old Testament law today. They therefore have to adopt "neutral" concepts of "natural law" that are shared by covenant-breakers and covenant-keepers.

In contrast, Christian Reconstructionists believe that God can and will transform social institutions for the better in the future. They believe that God will use Christians to achieve this improvement. They affirm the historic power of the Church, the Holy Spirit, and God's law. They therefore believe in the culture-transforming power of the gospel in history. Christian Reconstructionists have little confidence in man as such, but they do have confidence in the Lord as He works through redeemed, faithful men.

For those who persist in accusing Christian Reconstructionists of being heretical, let alone cult members, because of the supposed connection between Reconstructionism and something called the Manifest Sons of God, let me refer you to the conclusions of the Christian Research Institute, whose director is Walter R. Martin, author of *The Kingdom of the Cults*. In its newsletter of November 2, 1987, CRI subscribers were correctly informed that "the 'dominion' or 'kingdom now' teaching which has developed from the 'positive confession' and 'manifest sons of God' movements is different from reconstructionism" (p. 4). With respect to Christian Reconstructionism's five central points — Calvinism, covenant theology, biblical law ("theonomy"), presuppositional apologetics (Vantilianism"), and postmillennialism — the report distinguished the Reconstructionist system from *some* of the positions of CRI, but assured its readers that these doctrines are not heretical. Let theological critics less well-versed in cultism than Dr. Martin be forewarned. A word to the wise should be sufficient. (The not-so-wise probably won't be satisfied with an entire book, but I have decided to publish this one anyway.)

PREFACE

by Gary DeMar

Why *The Reduction of Christianity*? There are at least three reasons. First, defensive necessity; second, to set forth a positive agenda for Christians to influence their world with the life-transforming effects of the gospel; and third, to show that as we approach the end of the 20th century the "full purpose of God" has been *reduced* to a shadow of its former glory.

Let me reflect for a moment on this third point, which accounts for the title of this book. Dave Hunt, to whom we are responding, has brought to light a real problem by exposing the demonic side of the New Age Movement. It is a widespread and culturally accepted revival of paganism. Eastern mysticism is no longer counter-culture, as it was in the '60s, but mainstream culture. The New Age Movement needs to be confronted and battled. Mr. Hunt has provided much valuable ammunition to help Christians deal with New Age seduction.

In order to battle the New Age, however, we must have a full arsenal. And it is in this respect that we differ with Mr. Hunt. He has discerned a problem, but has no solution. In fact, one of the thrusts of his books is that there is really no solution. He sees no way to combat a growing cultural malaise because he is operating with a *reduced* gospel and a *reduced* Christianity. Hunt has no *comprehensive* Christian view of life to offer. He has no philosophy of historical progress rooted in the sovereign operation of the Spirit of God. And he cannot motivate Christians to action, because he believes that there is no hope of *comprehensive* earthly success for the gospel of the Lord Jesus Christ. Thus, he has robbed the

Christian faith of much of its breadth, depth, and power. Mr. Hunt is not alone in this. In fact, all those who interpret the present cultural collapse as a sign of the end side with Mr. Hunt. Their reduction of Christianity is no match for New Age humanism. In this book, we will provide the outlines of a solution, a *comprehensive* Christianity, one for which the New Age is no match.

The Background of *Reduction*

I do a number of seminars each month on a variety of topics: from abortion and economics to the Constitution and education. So many people had questions about the New Age Movement, dominion theology, kingdom theology, and Christian reconstruction, and I have had to spend so much time trying to define terms, that I was often unable to get to the substance of my seminars.

I decided that *The Reduction of Christianity* needed to be written when I received a phone call from a concerned Christian who wanted me to present a seminar to clear up some of the confusion that many of her friends were experiencing about the philosophical relationship of dominion theology, Christian activism, and New Age humanism. It seems that Dave Hunt, author of *The Seduction of Christianity* (1985) and *Beyond Seduction* (1987), had just been in town. He had maintained that any attempt to effect social change was doomed to fail because all Christians will see a great apostasy that will signal the appearance of the Antichrist. In fact, it almost sounded as if any attempt to change the world for the better was playing into the hands of the Antichrist.[1]

My caller asked: How could Christians reconcile their interest in stopping abortion, changing present political policies, mandat-

---

1. Hunt has said that "dominion theology" "opens the door to a marriage with New Age beliefs, as you know, with humanistic beliefs, so that we will all be joining together in working for ecological wholeness, working for peace, working for prosperity, because we are not concerned with heaven, or the return of Christ, or the Rapture, but we have got to be concerned about earth, the threat of ecological collapse, the threat of a nuclear holocaust." *Dominion: A Dangerous New Theology*, Tape #1 of *Dominion: The Word and New World Order*. This tape is available from Omega Letter, Box 744, North Bay, Ontario, Canada, P1B 8J8.

ing lower taxes, establishing Christian schools, helping the poor, and a whole host of other so-called "worldly" concerns with the belief that there is no hope of changing anything long-term? It seems that everybody is asking the same question. Pretribulational dispensationalist author David Schnittger asks it:

> [Gary] North and other postmillennial Christian Reconstructionists label those who hold to the pretribulational rapture position pietists and cultural pessimists. One reason these criticisms are so painful is because I find them to be substantially true. Many in our camp have an all-pervasive negativism regarding the course of society and the impotence of God's people to do anything about it. They will heartily affirm that **Satan is Alive and Well on Planet Earth**, and that this must indeed be **The Terminal Generation**; therefore, any attempt to influence society for Christ is ultimately hopeless. They adopt the pietistic platitude: *"You don't polish brass on a sinking ship."* Many pessimistic pretribbers cling to the humanists' version of religious freedom; namely Christian social and political impotence, self-imposed, as drowning men cling to a life preserver.[2]

This writer understands the issues. Christians are starting to talk, walk, and act like humanists. The humanists do not want Christians involved in the affairs of this world, and neither do many popular Christian writers. "Christian social and political impotence" rules the day and is advocated by Christians *and* humanists. I never thought I would see the day when Bible-believing Christians would be lining up with People for the American Way. But it is happening. Of course, the reasoning is different, but the results are the same: Humanists rule while Christians reduce their influence in the world.

Unjustified Fears

Arguing that Christians should be worried that the Antichrist is just around the corner is a very strange argument. Why? Be-

---

2. David Schnittger, *Christian Reconstruction from a Pretribulational Perspective* (Box 1144, Oklahoma City, OK: Southwest Radio Church, 1986), p. 7.

cause pretribulational dispensationalism has always taught that the Antichrist is supposed to come only *after* the rapture! First the rapture, then the Antichrist, and finally the tribulation. Dispensational theologians have always maintained that the Antichrist will come to power only *after* the rapture.[3] Hal Lindsey wrote these words in his best-selling book, *The Late Great Planet Earth*: "There would be no earthly advantage in being alive when the Antichrist rules. We believe that Christians will not be around to watch the debacle brought about by the cruelest dictator of all time."[4]

So why is Mr. Hunt going around the country warning Christians about the imminent appearance of the Antichrist? Why bother ourselves about the Antichrist? If pretribulational dispensationalism is true, not one Christian alive today will be around to identify the Antichrist, let alone serve him. All Christians will be raptured *before* Antichrist makes his appearance. This is why Hal

---

3. Post-tribulational dispensationalists do have a legitimate worry about the appearance of the Antichrist, but Mr. Hunt is not generally recognized by his readers as a post-tribulationist, nor are most of his readers. Hunt, as far as we have been able to determine, has never explicitly called himself a "pretribber." It is clear from his book, *Peace Prosperity and the Coming Holocaust* (Eugene, OR: Harvest House, 1983), that he does not believe that Christians will go through the tribulation. In that book, Hunt proposes a "contrary scenario" in response to the "gloom-and-doom and frightening forecasts" of other premillennialist writers (p. 18). Jesus will return to a prosperous, peaceful, wealthy, and utterly corrupt world. The prophecies of Jesus' Second Coming are "hardly indicative of either a worldwide financial collapse or a nuclear holocaust" (p. 18). Thus, it seems clear that Hunt believes in a pretribulational rapture.

Or is it? Certain portions of Hunt's other books are difficult to reconcile with this position. In *The Seduction of Christianity*, for example, Hunt and T. A. McMahon lament the "growing rejection within the church of [the] fundamentalist scenario as negative, 'gloom-and-doom' eschatology" (p. 216). What is the fundamentalist scenario (which appears to be the authors' own)? This view stresses that "the world is heading for a great tribulation climaxing in the Battle of Armageddon" (p. 216). Of course, it may be possible to reconcile this with Hunt's rejection of the "gloom-and-doom" scenario. But it appears to us a wee bit inconsistent. We assume in this book that Hunt is a pretribber, though we must admit that we are not quite sure what his position on the rapture is.

4. Hal Lindsey, *The Late Great Planet Earth* (Grand Rapids, MI: Zondervan, [1970] 1973), p. 113.

Lindsey warns that "we must not indulge in speculation about whether any of the current figures is the Antichrist."[5] It is just one more nonexistent problem for Christians to worry about. Gary North writes: "This needless fear of the antichrist is paralyzing Christians' required fear of God; God tells us to serve as prophets who are required to confront a sinful civilization with the ethical demands of God's covenant, but the Jonahs of this age are too busy packing for their trip to the heavenly Tarshish. 'Antichrist fever' is being added to 'rapture fever.'"[6]

This misguided belief in the power of the Antichrist certainly puts a damper on any long-term program that expects success in turning back the tide of evil in our society. Of course, we want to be faithful to Scripture, and, if Mr. Hunt is correct, we shall have to change our views. But if he is wrong, then we must sound a different warning to the church, a warning to wake up and get busy with the work at hand.

The Advance of Christianity

Question: Is it possible that the Bible teaches that the gospel will have worldwide success, that nations will be discipled, and that we will see the Word of the Lord cover the earth as the waters cover the sea *before* Jesus returns in glory to rapture His saints? (Isa. 11:9). But even if this were not possible, is it possible that the Antichrist will come to power before the rapture? Pretribulational dispensationalists have always said no, until Mr. Hunt came along.

The tragic thing is this: well-meaning dispensational Christians upset themselves about a problem that the leading teachers of dispensational theology have always insisted is not a problem at all. They are worried about something that is a non-event as far as pretribulational dispensationalism is concerned.

---

5. *Idem.*
6. Gary North, *Is the World Running Down? Crisis in the Christian Worldview* (Tyler, Texas: Institute for Christian Economics, 1987), p. 288.

The Christian Legacy

The Reduction of Christianity is not designed to be negative, although it may appear that way to many readers. While we do disagree with a number of people on a variety of issues, our goal is to present a *biblical* and *historical* case that throughout church history, there have been many Christians who believed that the world could be changed and had been changed through the preaching of the gospel and the application of the Word of God to every area of life. In this sense, *The Reduction of Christianity* is a hopeful book. It was hope that motivated the great missionary enterprises of the last few centuries, a hope that has been reduced in the light of prophetic speculation.

A hope which led to such world-wide results is surely worth examining. In the light of history we can hardly say that matters prophetic are too secondary to warrant our attention. The fact is that what we believe or do not believe upon this subject will have continual influence upon the way in which we live. The greatest spiritual endeavors and achievements in the past have been those energized by faith and hope. By comparison how small are our efforts! And can we disregard the possibility that this stands related to the smallness of our anticipations and to the weakness of our faith in the promises of God?[7]

Christians affirm that Jesus sits on the throne, ruling from heaven. They affirm that the Holy Spirit is working effectively on the earth. This means that the devil's kingdom is in constant disrepair. The church has believed these doctrines since the dawn of the gospel. Paul wrote to the church at Rome, "And the God of peace will soon crush Satan under your feet. The grace of our Lord Jesus be with you. Amen" (Rom. 16:20, 27b). But today's Christians no longer shout "Amen!" to Paul's prophetic word. It is only since the people of God have believed the lie of the devil—that the

---

7. Iain Murray, *The Puritan Hope* (London: Banner of Truth Trust, 1971), p. xxii. For a comprehensive study of how an optimistic eschatology affected cultural progress, see *The Journal of Christian Reconstruction*, "Symposium on Puritanism and Progress," ed., Gary North, Vol VI, No. 1 (Summer, 1979).

church is impotent in history—that the church has ceased to be salt and light to a world that has the stench of moral and cultural decay and the darkness that comes from spiritual blindness.

Rather than trying to convince Christians of a new position, we will attempt to show them that there are other positions that try to be equally faithful to Scripture. Mr. Hunt's books leave the impression that his view is the only view that the church has ever believed. R. J. Rushdoony writes:

> One of the intellectual curiosities of the twentieth century is the unwillingness of scholars and Christian leaders to admit the existence of a major school of Biblical interpretation. Although postmillennialism has a long history as a major, and perhaps the central, interpretation of Biblical eschatology, it is summarily read out of court by many on non-Biblical grounds. According to [Merrill F.] Unger, "This theory, largely disproved by the progress of history, is practically a dead issue." This note resounds in the critical literature, the appeal, not to Scripture but to history to read postmillennialism out of court.[8]

The question must also be raised: "History as interpreted by whom?" How can a Christian speak of the "progress of history" and not also affirm the progress of Christ's church—creeds, missions, Bible translating, and electronic communications? Where does this "progress of history" come from? From Satan? From evildoing? Surely it must come from the healing effects of the gospel in history. Surely it must be the work of the Holy Spirit.

While this book tries to persuade, it also has a broader purpose: to help Christians understand what other brothers and sisters in Christ believe. Before we hurl theological stones at one another, let us first try to understand what we believe and why we believe it. We may all learn something in the exchange.

Yes, *a new age has dawned*. This new age began with the entrance of the King of glory into history: "Do not be afraid; for behold, I bring you good news of a great joy which shall be for all

---

8. "Introduction" to J. Marcellus Kik, *An Eschatology of Victory* (Nutley, NJ: Presbyterian and Reformed, 1971), p. vii.

the people; for today in the city of David there has been born for you a Savior, who is Christ the Lord" (Luke 2:10, 11). This new age was extended when He died, rose again, and ascended into heaven. It reached us Gentiles through the power of the Holy Spirit that was first displayed at Pentecost. Yet there are many Christians who are so worried about a satanic imitation of the New Testament's new age that they are afraid even to think about the transformation Christ's work and the Holy Spirit have produced. They act as though they believe that Christ's new age is only a shadow of the so-called New Age Movement. They forget Christ's announcement:

> All authority has been given to Me in heaven and on earth (Matt. 28:18).

Though we have endeavored in this book to be fair to Mr. Hunt and others, and have avoided inflammatory rhetoric, this book necessarily has a somewhat negative tone because it is predominantly a response to and critique of another man's theology. Thus, we must stress at the outset that our purpose is not to divide further the grievously divided church of Jesus Christ. We consider Mr. Hunt and other critics of dominion theology and Christian reconstruction mentioned in this book to be brothers in Christ.

We hope and pray that this book will promote further discussion of the issues that Mr. Hunt has raised and thereby contribute to the strengthening of the Church of our Lord Jesus Christ.

1

ORTHODOXY: SETTING THE
RECORD STRAIGHT

The Reduction of Christianity is a response particularly to two books written by cult watcher Dave Hunt, *The Seduction of Christianity* and *Beyond Seduction*. Mr. Hunt, moreover, has been joined by David Wilkerson,[1] Hal Lindsey,[2] Jimmy Swaggart,[3] and a growing list of others in a struggle against what they perceive to be dangerous and even heretical tendencies in modern churches. As we explain more fully throughout this book, they believe, for example, that Christians who support social and political involvement with any chance of long-term success are leading people astray. Dave Hunt does make passing reference to the Christian's responsibility to be involved in what are typically described as "social issues."[4] But in all of his writings and in the writings of those who support his theological position of impending eschatological disaster, there is the denial that any of these activities can ever be successful. In effect, Christians are wasting their time trying to fix what can never be fixed this side of heaven.

More particularly, we wish to respond to Mr. Hunt's implica-

---

1. Wilkerson, *Set The Trumpet to Thy Mouth* (Lindale, TX: World Challenge Inc., 1985) and "The Laodicean Lie!" (Lindale, TX: World Challenge Inc., n.d).

2. Hal Lindsey's criticisms have come from radio and television debates on the subject.

3. "The Coming Kingdom," *The Evangelist* (September 1986), pp. 4-12. Rev. Swaggart has had Dave Hunt on his daily Bible study program "A Study in the Word."

4. Dave Hunt, *Beyond Seduction: A Return to Biblical Christianity* (Eugene, OR: Harvest House, 1987), pp. 247-48.

tion that those who teach that Christianity will be victorious in history and on earth before the rapture are on the verge of apostasy. With this we enter the area of eschatology, the study of the "last things." While the church has always believed that Jesus will come again to judge both the "quick and the dead," Mr. Hunt and others tend to make a specific eschatological position a test of orthodoxy.

In addition, there is the implied association of Christian reconstruction and various strains of "dominion theology" with the atheistic views of the New Age Movement. As we will demonstrate, this accusation is clearly false and borders on the absurd. As we will show in this chapter and subsequent chapters, Christian reconstructionists have led the way in fighting against secular humanism and New Age humanism. The writings of Christian reconstructionists give clear indication that they have had a real understanding of these movements long before they became an issue in the broader Christian community. This is why we are shocked to read in books and periodicals that somehow Christian reconstructionists are being seduced by the stupidity and silliness of the New Age Movement.

Moreover, we will address a subtle current in the writings and interviews of those who criticize the theology of Christian reconstructionists. With the radical division these men make between the Old and New Testaments, law and grace, and Israel and the Church, there is no objective *ethical* standard that the world can use to make societal transformation possible. They believe something like the following:

> While there is a *personal* ethic for the Christian, there is no *universal* ethical standard for the nations. While a Christian can run for political office, he cannot, for example, bring his biblical views regarding civil affairs with him into the law-making process. The law was for Israel. There is no longer a universal *biblical* law that applies to Christians *and* non-Christians. For Christians, the law has been internalized.

We will spend considerable time refuting this viewpoint.

Finally, this book is not a defense of all those who call themselves "Christian reconstructionists." There are many people who
claim the name but know very little about its theological characteristics. Neither do we defend all advocates of "dominion theology" since many wear the label without understanding its distinctives as they relate to Christian reconstruction.

The Goals

The Reduction of Christianity is also designed to accomplish several
other things. First, we want to show the importance of creeds and
their usefulness in disagreements over doctrinal positions. Second,
we want to set the record straight by defining terms. What do
Christian reconstructionists really believe?[5] Third, we clearly show
that Christian reconstructionists have always distanced themselves
from the distinctives of New Age humanism and all movements
that teach any degree of human autonomy, that is, that man is a
law unto himself, independent from the rule of God in his life. This
is so clear in the writings of prominent reconstructionists that it
hardly needs to be mentioned in another book, but mention it we
will. Fourth, we hope to show that the eschatological view of postmillennialism held by most Christian reconstructionists is in the
theological mainstream and has been for centuries.[6] A study of
church history will make this crystal clear. Christian reconstructionists are not teaching a new view as some might suppose. Fifth,
while we differ with a number of Christians on various theological
issues, we have not designed this book to be an attack on any man's
relationship with Jesus Christ. This is an intramural debate, a dispute within the "household of the faith" (Gal. 6:10). This will be

---

5. R. J. Rushdoony, a noted reconstruction scholar, responded to an article in
the Fall 1986 issue of *Policy Review* that misrepresented his position with these
words: "I was amazed to read 'Apocalypse Now?' in *Policy Review*. I learned things
about myself from reading the article that I never knew!" *Policy Review*, Winter
1987, p. 88. Rev. Rushdoony went on in his letter to clear up the points of mis-
information.

6. George M. Marsden, *Fundamentalism and American Culture: The Shaping of
Twentieth Century Evangelicalism: 1870-1925* (New York: Oxford University Press,
1980), pp. 85-92.

hard for some people to see because there are a good number of references to the critics of Christian reconstruction. Since Dave Hunt's books have precipitated *The Reduction of Christianity*, some will see our critique as being directed at him personally. This is not our intent, and we believe that a careful reading of this book will show that we have done our best to separate the man from his message.

Creeds and the Unity of the Church

The church has been marked by division since its inception. The Apostle Paul writes that "there must also be factions among you, in order that those who are approved may have become evident among you" (1 Cor. 11:19). The purpose of these "debates" is to sort out what we believe and then assess whether these beliefs are in accord with the Bible.[7] Again, these debates are not new to the church. The church has been fighting theological battles for centuries. But how did the early church go about solving its serious theological differences? We can learn a lot from earlier attempts to unify the church under the banner of the truth of God's Word.

In the midst of mounting secularism and odd religious sects, Mr. Hunt has issued a courageous call for a much-needed "return to Biblical Christianity."[8] Most of what he says is very accurate and needed to be said. He has recognized the seemingly heretical implications of statements made by some recognized charismatic leaders and non-charismatic "self-esteem" advocates, and his description of biblical Christianity is generally accurate. Mr. Hunt's books, however, raise an important series of questions. What are the central doctrines of biblical Christianity? How do we know what those doctrines are? How do we decide who is within the Church and who is outside? Where do we draw the lines? Who decides? Can individual Christian writers declare other Christians to be heretical? If so, on what basis?

---

7. In a letter to the authors, dated August 6, 1987, Dave Hunt agrees: "I appreciate your sincerity and fairness [in sending me a copy of the manuscript before publication] and assure you that I am as determined to see this discussion through as you are."

8. Hunt, *Beyond Seduction*, chapter 1.

Mr. Hunt's books thus raise the broader issue of Christian unity. On what basis are Christians united with one another? Should we be striving for greater unity? Or, is unity something that will be achieved only in the millennium?

The Reality of Unity

We could describe the unity of the Church from several different perspectives. Ultimately, we are united with one another because all of us who are Christ's are united to Christ, and Christ is not divided (1 Cor. 1:13). Christians are also united sacramentally, because we all participate in the one baptism (Eph. 4:4-6), and we all eat of the one loaf (1 Cor. 10:17), and drink of the same Spirit (1 Cor. 12:12-13). Thus, there are several senses in which all Christians are *already* united with one another. Most Christians, however, see unity in terms of doctrinal beliefs. Those who hold the same beliefs are unified. This is the basis of denominationalism. Denominations often start over a disagreement on one doctrinal variance. Many consider the proliferation of denominations as evidence that unity does not exist. Others, despising denominationalism, suppose that they can escape it by being "independent." Independency is nothing more than single-church denominationalism.

The issue, then, is whether this unity should take on visible form. Obviously, Christians must strive for visible unity, because the Lord of the church prayed for a unity that the world could see (John 17:21). This does not, however, solve all the problems. What form should this unity take? Should denominations dissolve their boundaries and unite in a single administrative structure? Or, should Christians simply cooperate across denominational lines, without any formal union?

Truth and Unity

These are complex questions, and we do not provide a full treatment of them here.[9] Rather, we simply wish to make several

---

9. See the discussion in James B. Jordan, *The Sociology of the Church* (Tyler, TX: Geneva Ministries, 1986), pp. 60-82. For a scriptural exposition of unity see D. Martyn Lloyd-Jones, *The Basis of Christian Unity: An Exposition of John 17 and Ephesians 4* (Grand Rapids, MI: Eerdmans, 1962).

observations about the basis for Christian cooperation and unity. When the question of unity is raised, many conservative Christians immediately object that unity can only be on the basis of truth. We have no quarrel with this, but it is a distortion of the biblical position to set truth and unity in opposition to each other. The church is to be characterized by both, because it is both the pillar and ground of truth (1 Tim. 3:15) and the *one* body of Christ (Eph. 4:4). We believe that it is sometimes necessary to break ties of cooperation and fellowship as when a church has become apostate. But this raises again the question of how to determine when a church is apostate.

How can the church faithfully hold fast to the truth and still be unified in the faith? One important way to do this is to determine which doctrines are *essential* to the Christian faith. In one sense, of course, every doctrine of Scripture is necessary, and distortion of one leads to a distortion of all. Yet, the church has always recognized that some doctrines are closer to the core of biblical religion. Certain doctrines are absolutely foundational. Thus, we can cooperate with those who profess the same essentials, while recognizing that there are many, often important, issues on which we may disagree and debate. This has been the vision of the church for centuries: In necessary things, unity; in doubtful things, liberty; in all things, charity.[10] This does not mean that we ignore our differences, nor should we be indifferent to them. We should strive for unity in all doctrine, "until we all attain to the unity of the faith, and of the knowledge of the Son of God" (Eph. 4:13). In the meantime, though, we should not break fellowship with other Christians over non-essentials.[11]

By What Standard?

But, again we must raise the practical question, what standard do we use to determine what doctrines are essential to the

---

10. Attributed to Philip Melanchthon (1497-1560).

11. It is important to distinguish between breaking fellowship and breaking denominational ties. It may be advisable to break denominational ties over less central doctrines, though this should not lead to a loss of fellowship and cooperation. We should refuse fellowship and cooperation only with churches and individuals that have abandoned orthodoxy.

Christian faith? Historically, the boundaries of orthodox teaching have been established by the Christian creeds. Historian J. N. D. Kelly notes that the creeds that were formulated by church councils in the 4th century were "tests of the orthodoxy of Christians in general" and "touchstone[s] by which the doctrines of Church teachers and leaders might be certified as correct."[12] This is true ecumenism, which, one author notes, is defined in some dictionaries as " 'the doctrine or theology of the ecumenical councils.' "[13]

Today many churches claim to be creedless. But in fact, every church, whether it admits it or not, has a creed. As John Frame writes,

> If we have the Bible, why do we need a creed? That's a good question! Why can't we just be Christians, rather than Presbyterians, Baptists, Methodists, and Episcopalians? Well, I wish we could be. When people ask what I am, I would like to say, quite simply, "Christian." Indeed, I often do. And when they ask what I believe, I would like to say with equal simplicity "the Bible." Unfortunately, however, that is not enough to meet the current need. The trouble is that many people who call themselves Christians don't deserve the name, and many of them claim to believe the Bible. . . . We must *tell* people what we believe. Once we do that, we have a creed.
>
> Indeed, a creed is quite inescapable, though some people talk as if they could have "only the Bible" or "no creed but Christ." As we have seen, "believing the Bible" involves applying it. If you cannot put the Bible into your own words (and actions), your knowledge of it is no better than a parrot's. But once you do put it down into your own words (and it is immaterial whether those words be written or spoken), you have a creed.[14]

---

12. J. N. D. Kelly, *Early Christian Creeds* (New York: David McKay, 1972), p. 205. Doctrine is not, of course, the only mark of a true church. An organization may be theologically conservative, but if it does not administer the sacraments, it is no church. Our emphasis here is on *doctrinal* orthodoxy, but we believe that ortho*praxy*—biblical practice—is equally important.

13. J. Marcellus Kik, *Ecumenism and the Evangelical* (Philadelphia, PA: Presbyterian and Reformed, 1958), p. 2.

14. John Frame, *The Doctrine of the Knowledge of God* (Phillipsburg, NJ: Presbyterian and Reformed, 1987), pp. 304-5. Frame's entire discussion on tradition and creeds is helpful (pp. 304-314).

A creedless faith opens the door to all types of theological aberrations and the unwelcome necessity of books like *The Seduction of Christianity* and *Beyond Seduction*. Why should we be surprised when we find heretical doctrines littering the theological roadside? In the attempt to abandon the creeds, we have opened Pandora's box and let loose a whole host of false doctrines. The issue, therefore, is not "creed or no creed," but "*which* creed."

A call to return to biblical doctrine must take its cue from the creeds. We should not call our contemporaries to line up with our particular brand of Christian doctrine. Rather, we all—from Dave Hunt to the Positive Confession movement to Kingdom Now teachers to reconstructionists—must line up with what the church has historically believed and taught concerning the orthodox faith, as the Spirit has led the church through the centuries. This is neither because the church is infallible nor that the creeds and confessions are substitutes for Scripture or even equal with Scripture. Rather, it is because the creeds deal with issues that are central to the Christian faith.[15] If an article of the creed is denied, the foundations of the faith are destroyed. Practically, the creeds have dealt with the doctrines of God and of Christ, in other words, those teachings on which the Christian faith stands or falls.[16]

Background to the Creeds and Confessions

Some of the disciples were put to death because they believed certain truths over against the prevailing views of the day (e.g.,

---

15. There might be those who want to maintain that the Bible is our standard and the creeds are designed by men who are fallible. This is indeed true. But every book written and every sermon preached is someone's view of what the Bible teaches. The creeds are the work of many men who have labored countless hours and studied the issues thoroughly to arrive at what they believe the Bible teaches. If there is a disagreement with a creedal formulation, then let that disagreement be made public for the Christian world to see. Let the biblical reasons also be attached. Of course, this too will be a creed. Even Dave Hunt's books are creedal formulations.

16. See Harold O. J. Brown, *Heresies: The Image of Christ in the Mirror of Heresy and Orthodoxy from the Apostles to the Present* (Garden City, NY: Doubleday, 1984), pp. 2-3; and R. J. Rushdoony, *The Foundations of Social Order: Studies in the Creeds and Councils of the Early Church* (Fairfax, VA: Thoburn Press, [1968] 1978).

Acts 7:54-60). These truths were based on what had been "seen and heard" (Acts 4:20). The Apostle Paul calls the basic tenets of the Christian faith "trustworthy" or "faithful" sayings: "It is a trustworthy statement, deserving full acceptance, that Christ Jesus came into the world to save sinners . . ." (1 Tim. 1:15). Each time Paul stood before a civil official he would confess what he believed (Acts 22-26). The Apostle was often sneered at because of his *creed* (e.g., Acts 17:32). His confession consisted of the basic tenets of the Christian faith. He followed the example of Jesus who "testified the good confession" (1 Tim. 6:13). The Latin word *credo*, from which we get the word creed, means simply, "I believe."

But what are creeds, how did they develop, and what help can they be for the church today? There is always a desire to distill and systematize the faith, to make it easy to communicate to others. This systematizing usually revolves around what the Bible says about God, Jesus, man, sin, death, and judgment. The doctrine of the millennium is also very important, but as we shall see, it has never been made a test of orthodoxy—a test governing access to baptism and the Lord's Supper—by the historic church. While the doctrine of time (eschatology) is certainly important, the church has not been able to settle on a single position.

Confession and Creed

The "good confession" of the new creature in Christ centers on what it means to be a Christian: "If you confess with your mouth Jesus as Lord, and believe in your heart that God raised Him from the dead, you shall be saved; for with the heart man believes, resulting in righteousness, and with the mouth he confesses, resulting in salvation" (Rom. 10:9-10). There is no sharp distinction here between confession and belief. A person cannot truly confess what he or she does not believe.

The church was immediately hit with contrary creeds. For some, the gospel of grace was not enough. Good works had to be added to the sacrificial death of Christ. The Apostle Paul was "amazed" that the Galatians were "so quickly deserting Him who called" them "by the grace of Christ" (Gal. 1:6). It was a "different gospel" that in reality was no gospel. Paul then proceeds, in his letter to the Galatians, to outline once again the basics of the gospel message reminding them that "if righteousness comes through the Law, then Christ died needlessly" (2:21). Justification by grace through faith was a test of one's orthodoxy. You could not claim the name of Christ and deny justification by the grace of God. A denial of it meant the repudiation of the faith. Not even "an angel from heaven" has any authority to preach and thus alter the gospel message (1:8).

Paul's disciples at Galatia were not alone in their confusion of what the Christian message was all about. All those who claim Christ should be aware of false doctrine. The Apostle John warns the church with these words:

> Beloved, do not believe every spirit, but test the spirits to see whether they are from God; because many false prophets have gone out into the world. By this you know the Spirit of God: every spirit that confesses that Jesus Christ has come in the flesh is from God; and every spirit that does not confess Jesus is not from God; and this is the spirit of the antichrist, of which you have heard that it is coming, and now it is already in the world (1 John 4:1-3).

So then, a creedless Christianity will not do. In fact, a creedless Christianity is a contradiction, an impossibility. There must be a constant appraisal of what the Bible teaches about itself and about what it means to be a Christian. We are to "test" everything by the standard of truth. Confessions and creeds are expressions of unity, demonstrations of a common faith that help the church gather around truth and fight against error. What a person professes to believe about Jesus Christ separates him from all competing faiths. Without a creed there is no difference between belief and unbelief, saved and lost, truth and error, and salvation and damnation. A creedless church is no church at all since it has nothing to distinguish it from the rest of what the world believes. Church historian Philip Schaff writes that the Christian church has never been without a creed, for it has never been without con-

fession of faith in Christ. There has never been a time in which
church members were not required to say, *credo*, "I believe."

> There would have been creeds even if there had been no doc-
trinal controversies. In a certain sense it may be said that the
Christian Church has never been without a creed (*Ecclesia sine
symbolis nulla*). The baptismal formula [Matt. 28:19-20] and the
words of institution of the Lord's Supper [1 Cor. 11:23-34; cf.
15:1-8] are creeds; these and the confession of Peter [Matt. 16:16]
antedate even the birth of the Christian Church on the day of
Pentecost. The Church is, indeed, not founded on symbols, but
on Christ; not on any words of man, but on the word of God; yet
it is founded on Christ as *confessed* by men, and a creed is man's
answer to Christ's question, man's acceptance and interpretation
of God's word.[17]

Councils and Creeds

The early church encountered doctrinal controversy that was
broader than its battle with apostate Judaism. The Judaizers were
dealt with through letters and councils which clarified doctrinal
controversies for the first-century church (Acts 15:1-35). As the
church extended its boundaries throughout the pagan world, it
faced additional challenges to the faith that had to be answered.
The Pharisees questioned Jesus' claim that He was the promised
Messiah. Here we find the seeds of controversy that were settled
in a number of very important creedal formulations. How could
God become man? Were the natures of Jesus mixed? Were there
two natures present within the one person?

Christians in A.D. 325 met in what has been called the Ecumenical Council of Nicea to settle the question raised by the Arians:[18]

---

17. Philip Schaff, *The Creeds of Christendom: With a History and Critical Notes*, 3
vols. (6th ed.; Grand Rapids, MI: Baker [1931] 1983), vol. 1, p. 5.

18. The Arian heresy shows itself in nearly every cult. In fact, you can test a
suspicious religious movement by asking its members what they think of Jesus. Is
He God in human flesh, the Second Person of the Godhead (Trinity)? Or is He
"a god" or just a great spiritual teacher? Cornelius Van Til was correct when he

Was Jesus really God or was He a creature, albeit the greatest of God's created beings? The Nicene Creed[19] stated emphatically that Jesus was "very God of very God, begotten, not made, being of one substance with the Father." But there were still questions and disputes. The Council of Constantinople assembled in A.D. 381 to take up the question of Jesus' complete humanity. At this council the true, complete humanity of Jesus was maintained over against Apollinaris of Laodicea who insisted that Jesus was God but denied that He was also man. But the issue of the relationship between Jesus' divinity and humanity was still not solved. Nestorianism maintained that the divine and human natures in Christ constitute two persons. This was condemned by the Creed of the Council of Ephesus in A.D. 431. The opposite heretical belief was Eutychianism, which insisted that the divine and human natures are so united in Christ that they form but one nature. This was condemned by the Council of Chalcedon, A.D. 451. The conclusion of these debates resulted in the belief that Jesus has *two natures* in *one person*. Orthodoxy was measured by these creedal formulations. The orthodox churches have unified around these essential beliefs about the person and work of Jesus Christ for centuries.

---

argued that all heresies in the church have begun with *subordinationism*: making Jesus less than God the Father in His very being or essence. Van Til, *The Defense of the Faith* (rev. ed.; Philadelphia, PA: Presbyterian and Reformed, 1963), p. 25.

The Jehovah's Witnesses have made the Arian heresy famous with their belief that Jesus is "a god" based on a very strained interpretation of John 1:1 and various other verses. To support this conclusion they create a Greek verb tense, the "perfect indefinite" tense, to deaden the effect of Jesus' comments to the Pharisees when He told them: "Truly, truly, I say to you, before Abraham was born, I AM" (John 8:58), an obvious reference to His divinity (Ex. 3:14). "I AM" becomes "I have been." You will find this "Scripture twisting" in the 1950 edition of their *New World Translation of the Christian Greek Scriptures*, now out of print and nearly impossible to locate.

Colossians 1:16-20 states very clearly that Jesus created "all things." But if Jesus is a creature (a "thing"), how can Scripture say that He created *all* things? Very simple. The Jehovah's Witnesses' own *New World Translation* inserts the word "other" in brackets before the word "things." So now they have Jesus creating "all [other] things" since as a created being He too would be a "thing."

19. See Appendix A.

Little confusion would have arisen in the church today if the creeds had only been read and studied. The all-important doctrines of the Trinity and Christology (the study of the person and work of Christ) were hammered out and settled long ago. What we are encountering today is nothing new. The same errors have resurfaced. Christians need a good dose of theology in every generation to equip them to fight against "every wind of doctrine" that seems to blow every which way.

Danger: Going Beyond the Creeds

Hunt is, from what we can tell from his books, an entirely orthodox Christian. He does not deny any article of the historic creeds. We object, however, to his tendency to test orthodoxy by something more than the creeds demand. We believe that Hunt is generally calling for a return to a sound biblical Christianity. But in the area of eschatology (the doctrine of the end times), he implies that, in order to be orthodox, Christians must subscribe to a particular millennial position. He recognizes that many Christians are turning from the traditional fundamentalist eschatology. He claims that "The views of many Christians concerning the future of the world are beginning to have more and more in common with the humanistic hope that mankind can really 'find itself.'"[20] He fails to inform his readers that many Christians are returning to a biblically-based, historically-held belief that the kingdom of God operates in the world and that Christians are to live in terms of its ethical requirements (Matt. 6:33).

Mr. Hunt rejects both the optimistic socialism of the evangelical left and the optimistic prosperity gospel of many charismatics.

> From their increasingly isolated corner, the fundamentalists warn that neither will succeed because the world is heading for a great tribulation climaxing in the Battle of Armageddon, which will involve the return of Christ to rescue Israel, to stop the destruction, and to set up His kingdom. . . . Whether it appeals to

---

20. Dave Hunt and T. A. McMahon, *The Seduction of Christianity: Spiritual Discernment in the Last Days* (Eugene, OR: Harvest House, 1985), p. 215.

our generation or not, the fact remains that the Bible does predict in unequivocal language great judgment from God coming upon planet Earth, and gives us the reasons for this judgment.[21]

Mr. Hunt believes that this change in eschatology indicates that the "great delusion" is just around the corner. In fact, Hunt and McMahon explicitly equate the "New Age Movement" with the "great delusion" that they believe will occur near the end of the world: "What is happening seems to fit the very pattern prophesied for the period of time just before the return of Christ for His own."[22]

It is difficult to say how important these eschatological views are to Hunt's argument. Some reviewers have suggested that Hunt's entire diagnosis of New Age seduction is based on his eschatology.

> It may or may not be that the "great delusion" is upon us. But there are . . . major problems with the way Hunt and McMahon approach this. First, because the field of end times study is filled with controversy among *orthodox* interpreters, to assume that all Christians should agree with Hunt and McMahon's pretribulational, dispensational eschatology is unwarranted. *Seduction's* eschatological presentation is simplistic to the point of error. A majority of biblical Christians throughout history have held different views of the "end times" than the view represented in *Seduction*. Hunt and McMahon have centered their whole argument around a view—pretribulational dispensationalism— which, in spite of its present popularity, had no real place in church eschatology for almost eighteen and a half centuries![23]

In other words, these reviewers think that Hunt's books are basically premillennial tracts, on the order of Hal Lindsey's *Late Great Planet Earth* and *Satan Is Alive and Well on Planet Earth*. His eschatology gets in the way of objective evaluation.

---

21. *Ibid.*, p. 216.

22. *Ibid.*, p. 213.

23. Bob and Gretchen Passantino, Review of "Seduction of Christianity," *Forward* (Fall 1986), p. 28. For a study of the recent arrival of the pretribulational rapture doctrine see Dave MacPherson, *The Great Rapture Hoax* (Fletcher, NC: New Puritan Library, 1983) and *The Incredible Cover-Up* (Medford, OR: Omega Publications [1975] 1980).

On the other hand, it is possible that Hunt is only secondarily concerned with eschatology. His second book, *Beyond Seduction*, in fact, has little to say about the "great delusion" and the end of the world. The emphasis of the second book is on heaven as the ultimate hope of Christians. Perhaps Hunt is simply calling Christians back to creedal orthodoxy, and his preoccupation with the end of the world is secondary to this aim. If this is the case, we have little quarrel with his diagnosis of the New Age Movement or of aberrant teaching in the church.

Regardless of whether eschatology is intended to be a primary or secondary theme in Mr. Hunt's analysis, we believe that his eschatology does affect his understanding of the current state of the church, and it plays an especially important role in his reaction to other eschatological positions. By making his premillennial and dispensational eschatology an important part of his analysis, Hunt has, perhaps unintentionally, made eschatology an implicit test of orthodoxy. He implies that anyone who adopts an optimistic eschatology is moving toward a humanistic view of the future.

Creeds and Eschatology

It is important to recognize that the historic creeds of the church do not include anything about the millennium, the rapture, the Antichrist, or the great tribulation. The creeds mention "individual eschatology," such as the resurrection of the body and everlasting life. They also say that Christ will return again in judgment. Yet, as far as the creeds are concerned, the timing of Christ's second coming is a matter of doctrinal freedom: The creeds did not bind any believer to a particular millennial position. Harold O. J. Brown observes:

> The orthodox doctrine of the person and natures of Jesus Christ is one on which there has been a very large degree of agreement throughout the Christian world for more than fifteen centuries. The doctrine of the return of Christ, called eschatology or the doctrine of the Last Things, by contrast, is one on which Christians have never come to substantial agreement. Orthodox believers all recognize that the Scripture teaches and the creeds

affirm that Christ shall "come again to judge the living and the dead." But the time of his coming, and the signs that are to precede it, have been interpreted in several different ways. Through the centuries, there have been any number of premature alarms.[24]

Throughout history, there have been differences of opinion on the meaning of the millennium. Even more detailed confessions, such as the Westminster Confession of Faith and its catechisms,[25] which have been the doctrinal standards of the Presbyterian churches, avoid binding statements on the precise details of eschatology.[26] Up to the present time "the doctrine of the millennium

---

24. Brown, *Heresies*, p. 447.

25. Work on the Westminster Confession of Faith began on July 1, 1643. The Shorter Catechism was completed on November 5, 1647, and the Larger Catechism on April 14, 1648. The Assembly of men who participated in this monumental project were some of the finest minds the church of the 17th century had to offer. "The Westminster Confession consists of 33 chapters. Chap. I includes 10 articles which in a very clear manner affirm the authority of Holy Scriptures and divine inspiration. . . . A Latin translation of the Confession and Catechism appeared at Cambridge in 1656. More than 200 editions appeared in Britain and about 100 in America. As early as 1648 it was translated into German. Altogether it was translated into 17 languages. *As a confession it is professed by more Protestants than any other.*" P. J. S. De Klerk, "Confessions and Creeds," *The Encyclopedia of Christianity*, gen. ed., Philip E. Hughes, 4 vols. (Marshallton, DE: The National Foundation for Christian Education, 1972), vol. 3, pp. 116-17.

26. See Appendix B. The Westminster Confession contains six substantial paragraphs on the "last things" without binding Christians to a particular millennial perspective. Like the ancient creeds, the chapters on eschatology deal only with "individual eschatology" and the Final Judgment. Question 191 of the Westminster Larger Catechism deals in more detail with the future of the church, but this statement can be affirmed by amillennialists, premillennialists, and postmillennialists. In fact, the authors of the confession purposely left the language somewhat ambiguous to gain unanimity on this point.

Robert L. Dabney, a postmillennialist of the last century, makes this important point regarding the absence of any representative millennial position set forth in the Westminster Confession of Faith: "[W]e note the caution of the Assembly concerning the millennium. They were well aware of the movement of the early Millennarians, and of the persistence of their romantic and exciting speculations among several sects. Our divines [who drafted the WCF] find in the Scriptures the clearest assertions of Christ's second advent, and so they teach it most positively. They find Paul describing with equal clearness one resurrection of the saved and the lost just before this glorious second advent and general judg-

has never yet been embodied in a single Confession, and therefore cannot be regarded as a dogma of the Church."[27] If we use creeds to mark the boundary between orthodoxy and heresy, as the church has always done, we have no basis for making one's millennial view a test of his orthodoxy. And, if we don't use the creeds, what shall we use? Creeds are not infallible, because they were written by fallible men. Thus we can and should reform the creeds as necessary, or write new ones. Until that time, we must depend on existing creeds. One of the purposes of this book is to show that the eschatological views that Mr. Hunt criticizes are well within the bounds of historic orthodoxy. One's millennial position is important, but we should not say that those who disagree with us are heretical.

Conclusion

Since the turn of the century, Christians have looked for ways to identify other orthodox Christians. Prior to this time creeds and confessions did the job. With the rise of denominationalism, a divided institutional body of Christ, and the proliferation of divergent unorthodox doctrines, the church has worked to unify under some doctrinal standard. An attempt was made to articulate the "fundamentals" of the Christian faith with the publication of twelve volumes called *The Fundamentals* (1910-15). But with divergent organizational ties, there still was no way to initiate a single expression of Christian orthodoxy. Today, with the neglect of the creeds and historic confessions, individual Christians have been drawing the lines of Christian orthodoxy on their own. It's

---

ment. So they refuse to sanction a pre-millennial advent. But what is the nature, and what the duration, of that millennial glory predicted in the Apocalypse? Here the Assembly will not dogmatize, because these unfulfilled prophecies are obscure to our feeble minds. It is too modest to dictate a belief amidst so many different opinions." "The Doctrinal Contents of the Confession: Its Fundamental and Regulative Ideas, and the Necessity and Value of Creeds," *Memorial Volume of the Westminster Assembly*, eds., Francis R. Beattie, et al. (Richmond, VA: Presbyterian Committee of Publication, 1897).

27. Louis Berkhof, *The History of Christian Doctrines* (London: Banner of Truth Trust, [1937] 1969), p. 264.

been fashionable to despise church tradition because it tends to be absolutized by some. But this real potential for abuse should not stop the Church of Jesus Christ from drawing on the experiences and wisdom of our Christian brethren of past generations. Can we honestly say that we are any wiser?

2

LET'S DEFINE OUR TERMS

"How do you define reconstructionism?" This question was asked of Dave Hunt by Peter Waldron, host of the syndicated radio program, "Contact America," on August 12, 1987. Dave Hunt's response may astound some of our readers:

> *I haven't defined that term.* We barely touch on it in the last two chapters of those last two books.[1] In fact, I had to really work hard to get the publisher to allow it in, because the publisher said, "We don't think this is really part of the topic. We think it ought to be left out."[2]

In response to his publisher's reaction, Hunt said, "Wait a minute. This is very important." Yes, it is important. But it deserves separate treatment in a full-length book.

Consider what Mr. Hunt has said. He comments on a significant theological movement that has world-wide appeal and respect,[3] but it has only been since August 12, 1987, that he has ac-

---

1. The last chapter of *The Seduction of Christianity* and the last chapter of *Beyond Seduction*.

2. As this chapter and other chapters will show, the publisher was correct. Any mention of Christian reconstruction within the context of Dave Hunt's critique of the New Age Movement and particular theological errors within certain popular Christian groups is a serious mistake. Hunt's readers assume guilt by association.

3. Some might argue that the familiar version of Christian reconstruction was completed with R. J. Rushdoony's book, *The Institutes of Biblical Law* (Nutley, NJ: Craig Press, 1973). The groundwork of Rushdoony's ideas can be seen in his first published work in 1958, *By What Standard?: An Analysis of the Philosophy of Cornelius Van Til* (Nutley, NJ: Craig Press, 1958).

19

tually defined what he and others have already criticized. This is where most of the confusion lies with those who had never even heard of Christian reconstruction until they read Dave Hunt's books, listened to him on a three-tape interview with Peter Lalonde, or watched him on Rev. Jimmy Swaggart's television program "A Study in the Word." Those who link Christian reconstruction with the New Age Movement, Manifest Sons of God, and aberrant theological views that are coming from the fringes of charismatic teaching do not have a definitional handle on what reconstructionists believe. Because reconstructionists are sometimes listed with these other groups solely because of their victory-oriented gospel message, it's assumed that agreement can be found on *many* points.[4] This simply is not true. There is no organizational or common theological tie. Even Dave Hunt belatedly agrees that Christian reconstructionists should not be linked with these groups.

Peter Waldron in his interview with Dave Hunt wants to drive home this important point for his listeners. Hunt criticized the views of certain leaders in segments of the charismatic movement, but Waldron interrupted:

Peter Waldron: "Let's be careful. I am familiar with Dr. Rushdoony. He's not teaching this."

Dave Hunt: "Right."

Peter Waldron: "Gary North is not teaching that."

Dave Hunt: "Right."

Peter Waldron: "Neither is Gary DeMar or any of the other people who are often identified as the philosophical foundation of the reconstruction movement."

Dave Hunt: "Right. Right."

Before evaluation takes place, terms must be defined. Many critics take the straw man approach to debate, that is, forming "an argument against a view that the opponent does not actually hold, which, perhaps, no one actually holds."[5] Albert James Dager, for

---

4. For example, Albert James Dager, "Kingdom Theology, Part II," *Media Spotlight* (July-December 1986), pp. 8-20.

5. John Frame, *The Doctrine of the Knowledge of God: A Theology of Lordship* (Phillipsburg, NJ: Presbyterian and Reformed, 1987), p. 324.

example, builds his straw man from a remarkable misreading of Christian reconstructionist literature. He maintains that reconstructionists want to "establish the Kingdom of God through politics and other societal strategies."[6] He does not quote one book or article to prove his assertion. In fact, if Mr. Dager would read any of the approximately one hundred books and scholarly journals plus the two decades of newsletters written by Christian reconstructionists, he would quickly learn that reconstructionists believe just the *opposite*.

One of the distinctives of Christian reconstruction is its aversion to the use of politics as the method to bring about social change. In reconstructionist social theory, politics plays a *minor* role.[7] We've made this clear with our writings on government.[8] But why all the attention to politics in reconstructionist literature, and, we might add, in the literature of many evangelical and

---

6. Dager, "Kingdom Theology: Part II," p. 19.

7. R. J. Rushdoony has insisted that the Bible teaches a "minimal State," that is, government means more than the State and politics. He writes: "Tragically, today when we say *government* we mean the state, the federal government, or some other form of civil government. And, more tragically, civil government today claims to be *the* government over man, not one government among many, but the one over-all government. Civil government claims jurisdiction over our private associations, our work or business, our schools and churches, our families, and over ourselves. The word government no longer means self-government primarily and essentially; it means the state." *Law and Liberty* (Fairfax, VA: Thoburn Press, 1971), p. 59.

8. The assertion that government is broader than the State and politics is developed in Gary DeMar, *God and Government*, 3 vols. (Atlanta, GA: American Vision, 1982-86) and *Ruler of the Nations* (Atlanta, GA: American Vision, 1987). Jimmy Swaggart Ministries purchased 1,500 copies of volumes 1 and 2 of *God and Government* and offered them for sale in its 1984 "Gift Selection" catalog accompanied by the following advertising copy: "Finally here is a series that will give you an understanding about the foundation of our country on God and His Scriptures. The God and Government Series contains two [now three] workbooks (over 400 pages [now over 650 pages]) divided into easy-to-understand lessons. Also included is a dramatized cassette and workbook that detail America's spiritual foundations. This is the best series for you to learn about this all-important area. Every Christian needs to understand about America's spiritual history . . . and future."

charismatic groups?[9] The answer is very simple. Politics has become the savior of the people. Reconstructionists write about politics and civil government in order to call Christians and non-Christians back to their only Savior, the Lord Jesus Christ, because the State is not "the order of man's salvation."[10] We will quote Gary North, a prominent Christian reconstructionist to make our point:

> Because the humanists have made the State into their agency of earthly salvation, from the ancient Near Eastern empires to the Greeks to Rome's Empire and to the present, Christians need to focus on this battlefield, but we must always remember that political battles are important today primarily because *our theological opponents have chosen to make their first and last stand on the political battlefield.* Had they chosen to fight elsewhere, it would not appear as though we are hypnotized with the importance of politics. Christian reconstructionists are not hypnotized by politics; humanists and pietists are hypnotized by politics. Nevertheless, we are willing to fight the enemy theologically on his chosen ground, for we are confident that God rules every area of life. He can and will defeat them in the mountains or on the plains (1 Kings 20:28), in politics and in education, in family and in business.[11]

This emphasis runs through all Dr. North's writings. But Mr. Dager creates a caricature of Christian reconstruction and dominion theology when he writes that the "central doctrine of all, how-

---

9. "The Bible is replete with references to government and its rightful place under God, with Daniel noting that God 'removeth kings and setteth up kings' (Dan. 2:21) and appointeth over it [i.e., the kingdom of man] whomsoever he will' (5:21). . . . Is the Lordship of Jesus Christ in American Government a dream? Not if I can help it!" Donnie Swaggart, "The Lordship of Jesus Christ in American Government," *Judgment in the Gate*, ed., Richie Martin (Westchester, IL: Crossway Books, 1986), pp. 80 and 89.

10. R. J. Rushdoony, *The Nature of the American System* (Nutley, NJ: Craig Press, 1965), p. vii.

11. North, "Editor's Introduction," in George Grant, *The Changing of the Guard: Biblical Principles for Political Action* (Tyler, TX: Dominion Press, 1987), p. xx.

ever, is that Jesus cannot or will not return to the earth *until the Church has taken control of at least a significant portion of human government and social institutions.*[12] He leaves the impression that Christian reconstructionists equate the kingdom with political advances. This is patently false. He goes on to write that the goal of dominion theology advocates is the "subjugation of individual secular states to the authority of the Church."[13] Where is this doctrine found in the many writings of Christian reconstructionists? Christian reconstructionists are looking for the *transformation* of all of society, including families, churches, business establishments, the legal profession, education, economics, journalism, the media, *and* civil government through personal redemption and adherence to the Bible as the standard for godly rule. This is a far cry from calling for the "subjugation of individual secular states to the authority of the Church."[14]

Clearing Up the Confusion

Mr. Hunt's books take issue with some of the teachings of several loosely organized "movements." These are known by various names: dominion theology, kingdom theology, and Christian reconstruction. The best way to handle these topics is to begin with definitions. A lot of confusion can be cleared up by the simple exercise of defining terms. As with all attempts to describe something, however, there is the danger of leaving out some aspect of the position that some people might hold or adding a distinctive that others do not. We have tried to stay with the foundational elements of these beliefs, as we understand the concepts. Of course, we are speaking for ourselves, and so the definitional limitations lie with us.

---

12. Albert James Dager, "Kingdom Thology: Part III," *Media Spotlight*, Vol. 8, No. 1 (January-June 1987), p. 8. Emphasis added.

13. *Idem.*

14. Mr. Dager is describing an "ecclesiocracy." See pages 321-25 for a definition of the term and the different uses of the term "church."

Dominion Theology

Dominion theology is best understood by first looking at the dominion that God, through Jesus Christ, exercises in the world. Jesus has dominion because he is "the King of kings, and Lord of lords" (Rev. 19:16). A synonym for dominion is lordship.[15] The Bible states in numerous places that dominion belongs to Jesus: "Now to Him who is able to keep you from stumbling, and to make you stand in the presence of His glory blameless with great joy, to the only God our Savior, through Jesus Christ our Lord, be glory, majesty, dominion, and authority, before all time and now and forever. Amen" (Jude 24-25). Those who hold to a dominion theology believe the Bible when it states that the dominion of Jesus is *before all time* and *now* and *forever.*" God exercises His dominion *now.* His lordship is over all things, in time and in eternity.

Because Jesus has dominion, His people, who are united to Him by faith, also have dominion. The Bible says we are adopted "children of God" and "fellow-heirs with Christ" (Rom. 8:17). As Christians, created in the image of God and restored in Jesus Christ, we inherit what was given to Jesus. We therefore share in His dominion.

But the exercise of this dominion is *ethical.* It does not come automatically, nor is it imposed top-down by a political regime or by an army of Christians working frantically to overthrow the governments of the world.[16] Such a concept of dominion is rather the essence of secular humanism: the religion of revolution.[17] God's people exercise dominion in the same way that Jesus exercised dominion — through sacrificial obedience and faithfulness to

---

15. For an extended discussion of dominion, see Gary DeMar, *God and Government: Issues in Biblical Perspective* (Atlanta, GA: American Vision, 1984), chapter 3.

16. Gary North, *Moses and Pharaoh: Dominion Religion Versus Power Religion* (Tyler, TX: Institute for Christian Economics, 1985). Rushdoony writes: "Those who render unto God the things which are God's, believe rather in regeneration through Jesus Christ and the reconstruction of all things in terms of God's law. In such a perspective, a tax revolt is a futile thing, a dead end, and a departure from Biblical requirements." R. J. Rushdoony, "Jesus and the Tax Revolt," *The Journal of Christian Reconstruction*, ed., Gary North, Vol. II, No. 2 (Winter 1975), p. 141.

17. David Chilton, *Productive Christians in an Age of Guilt-Manipulators* (3rd rev. ed.; Tyler, TX: Institute for Christian Economics, 1985), pp. 3-16.

the commandments. Dominion comes through service. The Gentiles, those outside of Christ in Jesus' day, "lord it over" the people, looking to the power of the State to grant favors and protection to loyal subjects (Luke 22:25). It's something of a master-slave relationship. As a result, these lords are described as "benefactors." They, through force, work to "benefit" some of the people for their own political ends. This is not the way the dominion-oriented Christian rules with Christ. Again, service is the prescription for dominion: "But not so with you, but let him who is greatest among you become as the youngest, and the leader as the servant. For who is greater, the one who reclines at table, or the one who serves? Is it not the one who reclines at table? But I am among you as the one who serves" (vv. 26, 27). It is idolatrous to seek dominion primarily by political means, whether by domination or anarchic revolution.

When Christians "serve" the world, they will be seen as "benefactors," wanting nothing in return but to bring glory to God. Dominion will then be established progressively over time, not through oppression, but through faithful service. Notice the goal in Jesus' statement. He does not say that Christians should not have authority, that they should not be the leaders. To the contrary, He asserts that Christians ought to do things differently in order to reach results that are much better than anything the Gentiles can offer. The task for the Christian is to be "light" in a world of darkness. How does he do this? Again, he serves. For what purpose? To extend the dominion of the Lord Jesus Christ into every area of life, a dominion that is His by divine right, a dominion that He shares with His subordinates.

The dominion of Christians is a benefit to the world only because Christ works in and through them. The benefits do not come ultimately from Christians, those who do the nitty gritty work of service in the world, but from Christ. How then are non-Christians pointed to Jesus as their true "Benefactor"? Through our works of service: "You are the light of the world. A city set on a hill cannot be hidden. Nor do men light a lamp, and put it under the peck-measure, but on the lampstand; and it gives light to all who are in the house. Let your light shine before men in such a way that *they may see your good works, and glorify your Father who is in heaven*" (Matt. 5:14-16, emphasis added). David Chilton comments on the service aspect of dominion and its relationship to work:

> The biblical method of attaining dominion is through diligent labor. When Adam rebelled, he chose instead to have dominion by playing god, rejecting God's leadership over him. He wanted power over the creation, not legitimately, through God-ordained work, but by becoming his own god. The world doesn't work that way, of course; and man was driven into slavery, losing domin-ion. But sinful men still seek power outside of the pattern God has commanded.[18]
>
> An important principle is at work in history. It is this: *God is continually at work to destroy unbelieving cultures and to give the world over to the dominion of His people.* (That, by the way, is what is meant by those verses about God uprooting the rich; see Leviticus 20:22; Deuteronomy 28; Proverbs 2:21-22; 10:30). God works to over-throw the ungodly, and increasingly the world will come under the dominion of Christians — not by military aggression, but by godly labor, saving, investment, and orientation toward the future. For a time, ungodly men may have possessions; but they are disobedient, and become dispossessed [Job 27:16-17; Prov. 13:22; Eccl. 2:26].[19]

The effects of the gospel go beyond the individual and his per-sonal relationship with Jesus. Those who hold to a dominion the-ology believe that there are cultural or societal effects to the gos-pel. The world is affected by the lordship of Jesus as Christians take personal dominion and seek to live in all facets of life in obe-dience to Christ and in the power of the gospel. The transforma-tion that takes place in the individual believer has an effect on family, church, education, entertainment, business, law, journal-

---

18. *Ibid.*, pp. 35-6.
19. *Ibid.*, pp. 94-5.

ism, the media, art, music, civil government, communication, publishing,[20] economics, and every and any good gift created by God (cf. Gen. 1:31).

All Christians agree that Jesus' finished work on the cross has freed us from the dominion of sin in our lives: "For sin shall not have dominion over you: for ye are not under the law, but under grace" (Rom. 6:14, KJV).[21] Sin is no longer our master, our lord. We have a new Master who has broken the bonds of sin and death, who has freed us from the curse of the law. The language in Romans 6 is very important. The New American Standard Version uses the word "master" instead of "dominion": "Sin shall not be *master* over you" (Rom. 6:14). We are no longer "slaves of sin" (v. 17). We have been "freed from sin" (v. 18) and have been made "slaves to righteousness" (v. 19). Paul says it differently in Colos-

---

20. Some of the most ardent critics of dominion theology are using the fruits of dominion to get their views across. Think where the church would be without the audio cassette, satellite television, and the growing Christian publishing industry. How would the spread of the gospel fare if we decided that the airplane and automobile were products of a demonized religion? This is dominion in action, dominion that did not flourish in a religious vacuum. These inventions developed in the Christian West. For example, it was Gutenburg's printing press that energized the Reformation of the 16th century. The first work to come off Gutenburg's press was the Bible. See Gary North, *Dominion and Common Grace: The Biblical Basis of Progress* (Tyler, TX: Institute for Christian Economics, 1987).

21. Many Christians misunderstand the meaning of Paul's statement, "For you are not under law, but under grace." Paul is not saying that the Christian is no longer obligated to keep the law. Rather, he is telling us that the law no longer condemns those who are in Christ, who took upon Himself the condemnation of the law: "Christ redeemed us from the *curse of the Law*, having become a curse for us" (Gal. 3:13). The law still remains as a standard of judgment *and* righteousness for Christians and non-Christians. This statement in Romans 6:14 "is widely taken to mean that the authority of the law has been abolished for believers and superseded by a different authority. And this, it must be admitted, would be a plausible interpretation, if this sentence stood by itself. But, since it stands in a document [the Book of Romans] which contains such things as 3.31; 7.12, 14a; 8.4; 13.8-10, and in which the law is referred to more than once as God's law (7.22, 25; 8.7) and is appealed to again and again as authoritative, such a reading of it is extremely unlikely. The fact that [under law] is contrasted with [under grace] suggests the likelihood that Paul is here thinking not of the law generally but of the law as condemning sinners." C. E. B. Cranfield, *The International Critical Commentary on the Epistle to the Romans*, 2 vols. (Edinburgh: T. & T. Clark Limited, 1975), vol. 1, pp. 319-20.

sians but with the same intent: "For He delivered us from the domain of darkness, and transferred us to the kingdom of His beloved Son, in whom we have redemption, the forgiveness of sins" (1:13-14).

Sin no longer has dominion over the Christian. Sin is no longer *master*. We are no longer *enslaved* to sin. We are now in a new kingdom, the kingdom of God's beloved Son. The devil does not reign. The world is not his turf. Jesus has plundered the enemy and freed the captives (Luke 11:14-28). He is the King, and we are His subjects.

Now, this is the important part, *personal dominion extends throughout the kingdom and includes every aspect of life.* Personal dominion becomes kingdom-wide. All of life should be transformed by the liberating effects of the gospel.[22] *"Grace dethrones sin. It destroys sin's lordship and enables the believer to offer himself, and whatever pertains to him, in loving service to God!"*[23] If we believe that the work of Jesus dethroned the curse of sin so that it no longer has dominion over the believer, then why is it so hard to believe that millions of Christians should not work to have dominion over sin in every area of life? This is the essence of dominion theology. As we will show elsewhere, dominion theology is neither perfectionist nor utopian. Sin is still with us, but with Jesus' help and the power of His Spirit, it does not have to master us or this world.

R. J. Rushdoony has an extended discussion of dominion in *The Institutes of Biblical Law.* Dominion begins with the new man in Christ. There is no dominion without Christ:

> Clearly, there is no hope for man except in regeneration. . . .
> The salvation of man includes his restoration into the image of God and the calling implicit in that image, to subdue the earth and to exercise dominion. Hence, the proclamation of the gospel was also the proclamation of the Kingdom of God, according to all the New Testament.[24]

22. Gary North, *Liberating Planet Earth: An Introduction to Biblical Blueprints* (Ft. Worth, TX: Dominion Press, 1987).

23. William Hendriksen, *Exposition of Paul's Epistle to the Romans*, 2 vols. (Grand Rapids, MI: Baker, 1980), vol. 1, p. 203.

24. Rushdoony, *Institutes*, p. 449.

The church of today has reduced Christianity to regeneration (being born again) alone. For many Christians there is nothing more. Few ask the question: "Regeneration for what?" When the question is asked, the answer that usually comes back is: "Regeneration for heaven and only heaven." Reconstructionists believe that dominion begins with regeneration and should encompass all of life. Christians should keep in mind that dominion cannot be denied. Rushdoony again writes:

> Dominion does not disappear when a man renounces it; it is simply transferred to another person, perhaps to his wife, children, employer, or the state. Where the individual surrenders his due dominion, where the family abdicates it, and the worker and employer reduce it, there another party, usually the state, concentrates dominion. Where organized society surrenders power, the mob gains it proportionate to the surrender.
>
> This fact poses the problem, which for an Orwell, who saw the issue clearly, is impossible to answer. Fallen man's exercise of dominion is demonic; it is power for the sake of power, and its goal is "a boot stamping on a human face — forever." Its alternative is the dominion of anarchy, the bloody and tumultuous reign of the momentarily strong.[25]

Dominion is a fact. For Christians, it is a lost legacy that must be regained as we move into the 21st century. If the clocks of the prophetic speculators are running fast, then it is imperative that we begin now to recapture the biblical doctrine of dominion under the lordship of Jesus Christ. Dominion cannot be avoided.

Kingdom Theology

Kingdom theology grows out of the dominion concept. In fact, the terms are often used interchangeably. The phrase kingdom theology is widely used in certain charismatic circles. It has not been used by those who advocate a dominion theology, although there are many points of agreement. Basically, kingdom theology deals with the timing and nature of the kingdom. Is the kingdom

---

25. *Ibid.*, pp. 448-49.

only future? Or is the kingdom both now and future? Does the kingdom only have reference to heaven? Or does the kingdom manifest itself on earth? Is the kingdom solely internal? Or does the kingdom manifest itself externally as well?

These questions may sound technical. To clarify them, let us ask them in a personal way. Is your personal salvation only future? Or is it both now and future? Does your personal salvation only have reference to heaven? Or does it manifest itself on earth? Is your personal salvation solely internal? Or does it manifest itself externally?

All of a sudden, the light dawns. These are *false choices*, aren't they? Well, it's an equally false choice regarding the kingdom of God. Mr. Hunt has created an unnecessary choice between the kingdom of God in heaven and the kingdom of God on earth, between the kingdom of God in people's hearts and the kingdom of God in people's behavior.

The first chapter of Colossians describes God's reign as including things "visible and invisible, whether thrones or dominions or rulers or authorities" (Col. 1:16). Jesus has reconciled "all things to Himself . . . whether things on earth or things in heaven" (v. 20). This is not something that *will* happen; it *has* happened.

The Reduction of Christianity seeks to explain the issues raised by proponents and opponents of dominion and kingdom theology. Much of the discussion in this book will center on the timing and nature of the kingdom. It is enough to say at this point that the kingdom is both present and future, internal and external, visible and invisible.[26]

Christian Reconstruction

Christian reconstruction is not a movement in a strict sense.[27]

---

26. For a helpful discussion on the kingdom see Greg L. Bahnsen, "This World and the Kingdom of God." Appendix D.

27. "The term 'Christian Reconstruction' was coined by Gary North for use with the *Journal of Christian Reconstruction*, which began publication in 1974." James B. Jordan, "The 'Reconstructionist Movement,'" *The Geneva Review*, No. 18 (March 1985), p. 1. This essay is available from Geneva Ministries, P.O. Box 131300, Tyler, TX 75713.

There is no central director, no overall, tightly controlled strategy. What unites "reconstructionists" is their commitment to certain distinctive doctrines. There are several "think tanks" that promote reconstructionist distinctives, including Geneva Ministries, the Chalcedon Foundation, and the Institute for Christian Economics. Several of these institutions have publishing wings. The "reconstructionist movement" embraces numerous scholars and writers as well as many pastors and teachers who are also sympathetic to the main thrust of Christian reconstruction. Many of the teachings of "Christian reconstructionists" are developments of particular Reformed doctrines that find their best expression in the confessional standards of the Westminster Confession of Faith.

In particular, reconstructionists believe in the sovereignty of God as it relates to personal salvation and all aspects of the created order,[28] hold to the old Puritan belief in the continuing significance of the Old Testament case laws[29] and a victorious view of the future progress of the kingdom of God,[30] and advocate

---

28. Loraine Boettner, *The Reformed Faith* (Phillipsburg, NJ: Presbyterian and Reformed, 1983); *The Reformed Doctrine of Predestination* (Philadelphia, PA: Presbyterian and Reformed, 1969); R. C. Sproul, *Chosen by God* (Wheaton, IL: Tyndale, 1986); Michael Scott Horton, *Mission Accomplished* (Nashville, TN: Thomas Nelson, 1986); Robert A. Morey, *The Saving Work of Christ: Studies in the Atonement* (Sterling, VA: Grace Abounding Ministries, 1980); Arthur C. Custance, *The Sovereignty of Grace* (Grand Rapids, MI: Baker, 1979); Walter J. Chantry, *Today's Gospel: Authentic or Synthetic* (London: Banner of Truth Trust, 1970); A. W. Pink, *The Sovereignty of God* (rev. ed.; London: Banner of Truth Trust, 1968); J. I. Packer, *Evangelism and the Sovereignty of God* (Downers Grove, IL: InterVarsity Press, 1973).

29. Greg L. Bahnsen, *Theonomy in Christian Ethics* (rev. ed.; Phillipsburg, NJ: Presbyterian and Reformed, [1977] 1984); *By This Standard: The Authority of God's Law Today* (Tyler, TX: Institute for Christian Economics, 1986); R. J. Rushdoony, *The Institutes of Biblical Law* (Nutley, NJ: Presbyterian and Reformed, 1973); James B. Jordan, *The Law of the Covenant* (Tyler, TX: Institute for Christian Economics, 1984).

30. David Chilton, *Paradise Restored: A Biblical Theology of Dominion* (Ft. Worth, TX: Dominion Press, 1985) and *The Days of Vengeance: An Exposition of the Book of Revelation* (Ft. Worth, TX: Dominion Press, 1987).

the presuppositional apologetic methodology and philosophy of
the late Cornelius Van Til (who was not a "reconstructionist").[31]

Moreover, "reconstructionists" have a broad understanding of
the church's mission in the world. They believe that the gospel
commission involves not only saving individuals, which is fundamental and primary, but also the "discipling" of the nations,
bringing the nations under the authority of Christ through sacrificial service and the application of Scripture (Matt. 28:18-20).

Reconstructionists have drawn from a rich history of thought
in the development of their ideas. Some of these distinctive
elements can be found in the literature of the early church fathers,
although in a less systematic form. The reconstructionist emphasis on a biblically-based view of life goes back at least to the
Puritans. Leland Ryken notes that the Puritans held firmly to the
inerrancy of Scripture and trusted its authority in every area of
life.

> According to William Perkins, the Bible "comprehendeth
> many holy sciences," and when he began to list them, they in-
> cluded "ethics . . . , economics (a doctrine of governing a fam-
> ily) . . . , politics (a doctrine of the right administration of a
> common weal) . . . , academy (the doctrine of governing schools
> well)." According to another source, the Bible is so broad in its
> application that all subjects "in schools and universities" can be
> related to it.[32]

For the Puritans, all work was holy, because it was done in

---

31. *The Defense of the Faith* (3rd rev. ed.; Philadelphia, PA: Presbyterian and
Reformed, [1955] 1967). Van Til did show appreciation for R. J. Rushdoony's
work: "Your continued interest in all my works is always encouraging." Van Til's
response to Rushdoony's "Van Til and the One and the Many," *Jerusalem and
Athens: Critical Discussions on the Philosophy and Apologetics of Cornelius Van Til*, ed.,
E. R. Geehan (Nutley, NJ: Presbyterian and Reformed, 1971), p. 348.

32. Leland Ryken, *Worldly Saints: The Puritans as They Really Were* (Grand
Rapids, MI: Zondervan, 1986), p. 143.

obedience to the Lord and for His glory. The American Puritan preacher John Cotton said,

> A true believing Christian . . . lives in his vocation by his faith. Not only my spiritual life but even my civil life in this world, and all the life I live, is by the faith of the Son of God: He exempts no life from the agency of his faith.[33]

The Puritans were not, however, abstract theorists who sat idly in their towers spinning abstract philosophies.

> Puritanism was *a reform movement.* Its identity was determined by its attempts to change something that already existed. At the heart of Puritanism was the conviction that things needed to be changed and that "business as usual" was not an option. . . . Of all the key terms used by the Puritans, the foremost were *reform,* *reformation,* or the adjective *reformed.* These terms were not the coinage of later historians but were the words on everyone's lips during the Puritan era itself. It was an age in which rulers were urged "to reform their countries," churchmen to effect "the reformation of religion," and fathers "to reform [their] families." At a more personal level, the Puritan impulse was to "reform the life from ungodliness and unrighteous dealing."[34]

The Puritans' vision "was nothing less than a totally re-formed society based on biblical principles." In short, the Puritans "were activists to the very core of their being."[35] Significantly, as we shall see in detail in chapter 13, the Puritans were confident that their efforts would succeed.

Thus, we find in the Puritans many of the distinctive qualities of the "reconstruction movement": commitment to the authority

---

33. Quoted in *ibid.,* p. 26.
34. *Ibid.,* p. 11.
35. *Ibid.,* p. 212.

of Scripture in every area of life, an emphasis on the importance and significance of work and service, an activist, reformist spirit, and optimism about the future.

These emphases were not lost with the Puritans. They reappeared in a somewhat different form and in a very different cultural context in 19th-century America. Like the Puritans, American Calvinists of the last century believed that the Bible should be used in every area of life and thought. In political theory, for example, they rejected the theories of popular and State sovereignty and insisted instead that God was sovereign over all nations.

> Though they supported the separation of church and state, Calvinists and many other evangelicals living in the late nineteenth century proclaimed that religion should not and could not be divorced from politics. Underlying all governments were central presuppositions that either supported or undermined Christianity; there was no intermediate option.[36]

They also insisted that the Bible be central to all education. They argued "that religious substance could not simply be tacked on to a neutral curriculum by Bible reading and prayer; rather, a biblical world and life view must undergird and inform the study of all subjects in the public schools."[37]

Again like the Puritans, American Calvinists worked for comprehensive reform. The Calvinist understanding of the kingship of Christ was especially important.

> William Greene [professor at Atwater and Princeton Seminaries] emphasized that the doctrine of God's sovereignty in history and salvation stimulated Christians to serve God through their vocations, homes, and statecraft in order to bring the affairs of society under the rule of Christ. Calvinists, who believed that

---

36. Gary Scott Smith, *The Seeds of Secularization: Calvinism, Culture, and Pluralism in America, 1870-1915* (Grand Rapids, MI: Christian University Press/Eerdmans, 1985), pp. 55-56.

37. *Ibid.*, p. 78.

biblical principles should guide all human activities, denounced efforts to confine the influence of Christianity to the church and family life.[38]

Some Reformed groups, such as the National Reform Association, sought to implement Christ's rule through legislation. Most, however, believed that evangelism and service were more important for reforming American society according to biblical principles.[39]

Many of these teachings, particularly the idea that Christianity applies to every area of life, found a brilliant expositor in the 19th-century Dutch theologian and statesman, Abraham Kuyper (1837-1920). Two writers have said that Kuyper's brand of Calvinism was the "only modern exception"[40] to the tendency of Christians either to abandon social action in favor of piety or to abandon piety in favor of social action. Kuyper himself was an incredibly active and prolific figure. After earning a doctorate in theology from the University of Leiden in 1862, Kuyper held pastorates in Beesd, Utrecht, and Amsterdam. During his Amsterdam pastorate, Kuyper also edited a church newspaper and became increasingly involved in politics. Together with a group of politically active Christians, Kuyper helped to organize and strengthen the Anti-revolutionary Party, which had been started a few years earlier by Guillaume Groen van Prinsterer. Kuyper was elected to the Dutch Parliament in 1873 and eventually rose to the position of Prime Minister (1901-1905). Meanwhile, he edited a political journal and wrote editorials that eventually numbered over 16,000. In the late 1870s, Kuyper devoted his vast energies to the founding of the Free University of Amsterdam, where he also taught several diverse subjects.[41]

---

38. *Ibid.*, p. 144.
39. *Ibid.*, pp. 142-48.
40. Irving Hexham and Karla Poewe, *Understanding Cults and New Religions* (Grand Rapids, MI: Eerdmans, 1986), p. 126.
41. Frank vanden Berg, *Abraham Kuyper: A Biography* (Ontario, Canada: Paideia Press, 1978).

Kuyper was obviously a man of action, but he was also a significant scholar and theologian. In 1898, Kuyper gave a series of lectures at Princeton Theological Seminary.[42] These lectures on Calvinism developed Kuyper's thesis that Calvinism is more than a system of doctrine. It is a full-orbed world and life view. Calvinism provides distinctive teachings on man's three-fold relationship: to God, to other men, and to the world. Kuyper showed how the principles of Calvinism worked out in the church, in politics, science, and art, and insisted that only Calvinism could provide an antidote to the life-system of modernism.[43] Kuyper's ideas formed much of the basis for Henry Van Til's *The Calvinistic Concept of Culture*,[44] and was one of the inspirations behind the apologetic works of Cornelius Van Til. And, it is from Cornelius Van Til that reconstructionists derive their basic philosophical position. Of course, Kuyper's original ideas were modified over the decades, but reconstructionists still look to Kuyper as one of their key intellectual forefathers.

The "Kuyperian" tradition "was at once pious and socially influential."[45] But there is one significant difference between Kuyper and reconstructionists. Kuyper was an amillennialist; he really did not believe that Christian efforts at reform would prove successful. In fact, he believed that all ideologies, including atheism, should be considered as viable options for the nation. All views should be allowed to compete without any single view claiming the *only* right and true view. There can be no earthly victory for the gospel because the game is rigged in favor of the other guy. In time, Christianity was squeezed out by the competing options. When we consider that Amsterdam has become a major

---

42. Gary Smith, *Seeds of Secularization*, pp. 42-49.

43. Abraham Kuyper, *Christianity as a Life System: The Witness of a World-View*, abridged from the Kuyper Stone Lectures, (Memphis, TN: Christian Studies Center, 1980). Available for $4.00 from American Vision, P.O. Box 720515, Atlanta, GA, 30328.

44. Philadelphia, PA: Presbyterian and Reformed, (1959) 1972.

45. Hexham and Poewe, *Understanding Cults and New Religions*, p. 126.

European center for drugs and pornography, we can begin to better understand that ideas, especially eschatological ideas, have consequences.

This brief historical overview helps to place the Christian reconstructionists in historical perspective and shows that their ideas have a rich and broad heritage in the Reformed churches.

Millennial Views

This book focuses on the "eschatological" issues that Dave Hunt raises in his books. Eschatology is that part of theology that deals with the end times. The question is: The "end times" of *what*? Old Testament Israel? The Church Age? The great tribulation? The restored Israel of the millennium? We believe that this is one of the most significant differences between ourselves and Mr. Hunt. In order to help the reader understand the terms that will be used throughout the book, let us briefly describe different general views of the "end times."

Traditionally, eschatological views have been categorized according to different views of the thousand year period of Revelation 20. Each of these views has been held by orthodox and conservative theologians. All three have coexisted in the church, often in the same congregation. Though some denominations hold to a particular millennial position, the various denominations are not agreed on eschatology, as they are, for example, on the doctrine of the Trinity.

Using one text of Scripture to categorize one's eschatology is clearly not the best way to describe the differences between various positions. After all, in a sense the entire New Testament is about eschatology.[46] Also, the terms are of fairly recent origin and were not used by the theologians of earlier centuries. Thus, it is somewhat anachronistic to talk about the millennial position of, say, Luther or Augustine.

---

46. See Geerhardus Vos, *The Pauline Eschatology* (Phillipsburg, NJ: Presbyterian and Reformed, [1930] 1986).

Finally, there are numerous variations of these views. Not every premillennialist will agree with every other premillennialist. In fact, not every dispensational premillennialist agrees with all other premillennial dispensationalists.[47] Therefore, any insistence on making millennial views a test of orthodoxy will only create greater divisions in the church. Still, these categories help to distinguish in a general way the different positions that Christians have taken with respect to the future.

Premillennialism

The "premillennial" view,[48] as the name suggests, says that Christ will return physically *before* the millennium begins. Christ's return will be preceded by "the preaching of the gospel to all nations, a great apostasy, wars, famines, earthquakes, the appearance of the Antichrist and a great tribulation."[49] Thus, Christ returns physically to a world in turmoil and sets up His kingdom on earth for a thousand years. At the end of the millennium, there will be a final, cataclysmic battle, followed by the final judgment

---

47. Gleason L. Archer, Jr., Paul D. Feinburg, Douglas J. Moo, and Richard R. Reiter, *The Rapture: Pre-, Mid-, or Post-Tribulational?* (Grand Rapids, MI: Zondervan/Acadamie, 1984).

48. The historic premillennial position was supported by many of the early church fathers, including Justin Martyr, Irenaeus, and Tertullian. There is a distinction between "historic" premillennialism and "dispensational" premillennialism. Prior to the 20th century nearly all premillennialists were historic premillennialists. Francis A. Schaeffer, Carl F. H. Henry, George Eldon Ladd, Alan Johnson, Carl McIntire, and J. Barton Payne would be classified as historic premillennialists. When dispensationalists claim the Mathers, for example, they often fail to mention that their 17th-century brand of premillennialism is not the 20th-century dispensational variety. One of the elements that distinguishes historic premillennialism from dispensational premillennialism is the timing of the rapture. For the dispensational premillennialist, the rapture occurs *before* a period of intense persecution of the church known as the Great Tribulation. In effect, Jesus actually comes two times: *for* His saints before the Tribulation and then *with* His saints after the Tribulation. For the historic premillennialist, Jesus will return in a single event after a period of intense persecution of the church known as the Great Tribulation.

49. Robert G. Clouse, ed., *The Millennium: Four Views* (Downers Grove, IL: InterVarsity Press, 1977), pp. 7-8.

and the resurrection. In broad terms, the premillennialist does not believe that Christianity will triumph over all other systems on earth without Christ's sudden intervention.

One particular brand of premillennialism has been called "dispensational premillennialism."[50] As a general system, dispensationalism is distinguished by several emphases. First, dispensationalists claim to rely on what they consider to be a literal interpretation of the text of Scripture. Second, the dispensationalist distinguishes sharply between Israel and the church. They are two separate peoples of God. God has different purposes for these two peoples. The church is God's "heavenly people," while Israel remains, even after Christ's first advent, God's "earthly people."[51]

In addition to these more general differences, the dispensational premillennialist differs from the historic premillennialist on several details of the "end times." Dispensationalists, for example, relying on a literal interpretation of Ezekiel 40-48, conclude that "in the millennium, the Jewish temple will be rebuilt and the entire sacrificial system reinstituted."[52] Furthermore, the dispensationalist interpreter has a clear idea of God's purposes for ethnic Israel during the millennium. On the other hand, there are some overriding similarities between the two forms of premillennialism. Like historic premillennialism, dispensationalism teaches that Christ will return physically to establish His millennial kingdom on earth. Both, furthermore, believe that the church will be vic-

---

50. In the past century, most popular American premillennialists have been dispensationalists, including William E. Blackstone, Dwight L. Moody, C. I. Scofield, Alva J. McClain, Herman A. Hoyt, Charles Ryrie, Dwight Pentecost, Hal Lindsey, H. A. Ironside, and John Walvoord.

51. Charles Ryrie, *Dispensationalism Today* (Chicago, IL: Moody Press, 1965), pp. 44-47. Ryrie lists a third distinctive feature of dispensationalism: that the underlying purpose of God is His own glory. He compares this to what he perceives to be covenant theology's emphasis on salvation. It is hard to see how Ryrie might come to this conclusion about covenant theology. The covenantal Westminster Shorter Catechism's first question says that man's chief end is "to glorify God and to enjoy Him forever." It has always been a hallmark of covenant theology to emphasize the centrality of bringing glory to God.

52. Clouse, *Meaning of the Millennium*, p. 26.

torious only by direct divine intervention and thus are pessimistic about the church's future during the present age.

Amillennialism

The "amillennial"[53] view teaches that the millennium is not a literal thousand years. The name literally means "not millennial." Many amillennialists prefer the term "realized millennium,"[54] which calls attention to their belief that the millennium is not exclusively future, but present after the outpouring of the Holy Spirit at Pentecost. For the amillennialist, the thousand years of Revelation 20 is a reference to the entire period of the church's historical mission.[55] Christ returns at the end of this indefinite period of time. During this time, the church grows slowly, and so does the kingdom of Satan. The signs of the final coming of Christ, though present throughout this period, will intensify as the time of Christ's coming approaches. The church will survive and may be influential until Jesus returns, but it will not rise to pre-eminence among the kingdoms of the world.[56]

Despite their differences, there is a significant similarity between amillennialism and the different forms of premillennialism. Both deny that the church will be victorious in history and on earth prior to the millennium. Both deny that the nations will be converted to Christ before the second coming. They tend to define "victory" solely in terms of "souls saved" or *personal* "victory over sin." They claim that their positions are victorious in the sense

---

53. Amillennialism first became widely accepted with Augustine, though, as we shall see, there are some apparently "postmillennial" elements in Augustine. Many of the reformers would be classified as amillennial. Today, amillennialism is advocated in the writings of Louis Berkhof, William Hendriksen, Jay Adams, Leon Morris, G. C. Berkhouwer, and Cornelius Van Til. The Lutheran tradition is also amillennialist.

54. Jay Adams, *The Time is at Hand* (Phillipsburg, NJ: Presbyterian and Reformed, 1970).

55. The use of "thousand" in the Bible usually means more than a thousand (Deut. 1:10, 11; Isa. 30:17; 60:22; Psalm 50:10; 84:10; 90:4).

56. See Anthony Hoekema, *The Bible and the Future* (Grand Rapids, MI: Eerdmans, 1979), chapter 14.

that ultimately Christ will triumph during the millennium and the final judgment. Culturally and historically, however, both tend to be pessimistic about the church's earthly future. We would like again to remind the reader that a study of history will show that the church was not preoccupied with the end of all things. The great advances in civilization came because Christians believed that God gave them time as a gift to bring glory to God in their work. The more orthodox believers—whether premillennial, amillennial, or postmillennial—faithfully carried out God's directive to "subdue" the earth by gospel proclamation and adherence to the ethical law of God.

Postmillennialism

"Postmillennialism"[57] teaches that Christ will return after the millennium. The millennium itself is variously interpreted. Some postmillennialists equate the millennium with the present age, as Christ rules from His heavenly throne and graciously saves men and nations through His church. This is similar to the amillennial view; in fact, it may also be labeled "optimistic amillennialism." This position differs from that of many amillennialists, however, in the fact that the postmillennialist believes that Christ will triumph over His enemies during the present age through His redeemed people. True, the forces of Satan become more satanic, but Satan does not dominate the world. Before Christ returns, the nations will have been converted to Him.

Other postmillennialists interpret the millennium as a future stage of history. Though the kingdom is already inaugurated, there will someday be a greater outpouring of the Spirit than the

---

57. Postmillennialism has been taught by Loraine Boettner, Charles Hodge, W. G. T. Shedd, B. B. Warfield, Marcellus Kik, John Jefferson Davis, Roderick Campbell, John Murray (in his commentary on Romans, chapter 11) as well as by "reconstructionist" writers such as R. J. Rushdoony, Gary North, Greg Bahnsen, James B. Jordan, and David Chilton. You can also find strains of postmillennialism in the writings of the great English Baptist preacher of the 19th century, Charles Haddon Spurgeon. See Iain Murray, "C. H. Spurgeon's Views on Prophecy," in *The Puritan Hope* (London: Banner of Truth Trust, 1971), pp. 256-65.

church has yet experienced. In either view, the postmillennialist views the future with confidence that Christ's kingdom will triumph on earth and in history.

There is another, more subtle distinction among postmillennialists. Some emphasize that the victory of Christ will be manifested in the conversion of more and more people to Christ. Thus, the victory of the church will be seen in the salvation of many individuals. Others, while not denying or de-emphasizing the central importance of conversion, teach in addition that there will be a transformation of society and culture, resulting from the conversion of vast multitudes of peoples and nations. "Reconstructionists," without denying the other postmillennial distinctives, generally fall into this latter group. As we shall see in a later chapter, this is not distinctive to "reconstructionists." What is distinctive about "reconstructionists," however, is their consistent emphasis on the necessity of preaching the gospel and adherence to the Bible as the standard and means of advancing the kingdom on earth.

Conclusion

When "fundamentalism" first came on the scene, there was great misunderstanding and misrepresentation of its beliefs. In fact, if you pick up the literature that was written about fundamentalism and substitute "Christian reconstruction" where you find "fundamentalism," you will notice that similar misconceptions exist. The influential scholar and writer J. I. Packer describes the difficult time fundamentalists had in having their position properly understood. He writes:

> 'Fundamentalism' has recently grown notorious. Three factors seem to have caused this: Billy Graham's evangelistic crusades, the growth of evangelical groups in schools and universities, and the increase of evangelical candidates for the ministry. A long correspondence in *The Times* in August 1955, coupled with strong words from bishops, headmasters and other responsible persons, made 'Fundamentalism' a matter of general interest. Since then, 'anti-fundamentalism' has become a widespread fashion. The debate continues, and shows no sign of abating yet.

It must encourage evangelical Christians to find so much notice taken of their position. The fact that those who differ from them can no longer ignore them marks a real increase of their position.[58]

What was true of fundamentalism is now true of reconstructionism. The number of books, journals, articles, and newsletters that come from reconstructionist writers is staggering. And there seems to be a disproportionate amount of reconstructionist influence compared to their small number. But alas, the misrepresentations and caricatures continue to flow from the pens of those who do not show a real understanding of what reconstructionists believe.

---

58. Packer, *'Fundamentalism' and the Word of God* (Grand Rapids, MI: Eerdmans, 1958), p. 9.

3

CRYING WOLF?

The New Age Movement is a hot topic in conservative Christian circles these days. New Age humanism was first discussed in detail from a Christian perspective by Dr. Gary North in Chapter Nine of his 1976 book *None Dare Call It Witchcraft* (updated in 1986 as *Unholy Spirits*).[1] Constance Cumbey later wrote a best-selling book on the topic in 1983, *The Hidden Dangers of the Rainbow.*

The basic ideas of the New Age Movement are ancient: cosmic evolution, the self-transcendence of man into God through "higher consciousness" techniques (e.g., yoga), and reincarnation (karma). The New Age groups are numerous, but they are quite small. They possess nothing like the membership of, say, the Southern Baptist Association. They are having a growing influence in the media, however, which makes them appear to be more influential than they actually are.

Why should the New Agers appear, seemingly overnight, in the 1970s and exert even greater visibility in the 1980s? One reason is that what social commentator Tom Wolfe called the "Me Generation" continues into the '80s. The primary focus of concern for most New Agers is internal uplift, personal spiritual evolution, and escape from "the rat race." Some New Agers are power-seekers, but not the vast majority. The cultural retreat and quietism of Hindu mystics is representative of the New Age Movement. New Agers much prefer getting in tune with cosmic waves than designing hydro-electric power systems. In short, the New

---

1. Ft. Worth, Texas: Dominion Press.

Agers were and are "in sync" with the present-oriented, humanistic "Me Generation," despite all their rhetoric about cosmic evolution.

The New Age Movement should not be taken lightly, but neither should we cringe in its presence. This book is designed to put present events, both good and evil, into biblical and historical perspective. We believe that the New Age Movement is humanism becoming more and more consistent with its foredoomed attempts to rebel against God. As with all those who oppose the Lord and His law, "they will not make further progress" (2 Tim. 3:9).

Why Such Visible Progress?

Weeds advance when little effort is expended to remove them from a carefully prepared, once-vibrant garden. *Anti-Christian systems progress because the church does very little to challenge them.* More often than not, we find the church retreating from battle instead of leading the charge "against the schemes of the devil" (Eph. 6:11). As we will show, this program of cultural retreat has not been the position of the church down through the centuries. The advance of civilization came with the advance of Christianity.

God has always called Christians to set the agenda, to be a light in a world where there is darkness. Those outside of Christ are to see our "good works" so they can glorify God who is in heaven (Matt. 5:16). The redeemed in Christ are to act as signposts to point the lost to Christ. In Jesus' day, miracles were used. Today, God calls on His new creations to perform the task through the fruit of gospel works. It is our contention that this vision has been lost in a day when the church is preoccupied with signs it believes point to the end of the world. Today, there is a new agenda. The church has taken a defensive posture, fighting battles when the war is just about over. If God has given us time, then we should get busy with the work at hand. Idleness is apt to give the devil an "opportunity" (Eph. 4:27).

In this chapter we will explore the impact of the notion that we are the last generation before Jesus returns. Is the so-called prophetic clock of Daniel ticking once again? Are our present troubles an indication that Jesus will return in *"our* generation,"[2] or are we misusing the events of history to form a strained view of Bible prophecy? "For centuries, various Christian and other groups have tried to attach dates to these prophecies, with spectacularly little success."[3] Will modern prophetic writers suffer a similar fate?

Hunt's Challenge

Dave Hunt's books have been helpful in many ways. They expose dangerous trends in theological thinking. Many of today's "new theologies" thrive because there is little familiarity with the Bible and the centuries of theological debate during which the basics of orthodoxy were developed. This is most clearly evident, for example, in the teaching by some that Christians are "little gods." An experienced cult watcher like Dave Hunt immediately saw the dangers inherent in such thinking. Dr. Gary North, whose *None Dare Call It Witchcraft* (1976)[4] exposed the festering sore of New Age humanism in the mid-seventies, points out that today

> there is no doubt that some of [the "positive confession" preachers] have not come to grips with the Bible's teaching on Christology: that Jesus Christ in His incarnation was alone fully God and perfectly human. Some of them have verbally equated Christian conversion with becoming divine. This is unquestionably incorrect. At conversion, the Christian *definitively* has imputed to him Christ's *perfect humanity* (not His divinity), which he then *progressively* manifests through his earthly lifetime by means of his progressive ethical sanctification. But their confusion of language is a testimony of their lack of theological understanding; they *mean* "Christ's perfect humanity" when they say "Christ's divinity." Those who don't mean this will eventually drift away from the orthodox faith.[5]

---

2. Ed Dobson and Ed Hindson, "Apocalypse Now?: What Fundamentalists Believe About the End of the World," *Policy Review* (Fall 1986), p. 18.

3. *Idem.*

4. New Rochelle, New York: Arlington House, 1976.

5. Gary North, "The Attack on the 'New' Pentecostals," *Christian Reconstruction* (Jan./Feb. 1986), p. 3. Published by the Institute for Christian Economics, P.O. Box 8000, Tyler, Texas 75711.

These cautions are necessary. If a segment of the church of Jesus Christ is drifting into the swift currents of doctrinal error, then life rafts must be sent out to rescue them. Doctrinally mature Christians should call the immature back to the truth, not sink them in their struggle.

But Hunt's books must be read on two levels. On the first level he critiques "positive and possibility thinking," "healing of memories," "self-help philosophies," and "holistic medicine," and their association with sorcery, scientism, shamanism, and aspects of the burgeoning New Age Movement. Most of what Hunt writes about these errors is quite accurate and should be taken to heart.

It is possible, however, that many of those who hold these views are not consciously rejecting the orthodox faith.[6] Of course, this does not lessen the damage that can be done. A number of these ministers have little theological training.[7] Moreover, they are rarely students of the history of theological debate. Their "no creed but Christ" has gotten them into doctrinal hot water.[8] Other

---

6. Robert Schuller, however, is one who self-consciously rejects the reformational understanding of sin and grace. He tells us that to preach about sin and man's need of redeeming grace is part of the "old reformation." Today, he says, we need a gospel where man has a higher view of himself. Man needs a better self-image and more self-esteem. This perspective is worked out in his view of ethics. On "The Larry King Show," he told the viewing audience that he knows of no Bible verse that condemns homosexuality. See Gary DeMar, "Homosexuality: An Illegitimate, Alternative Deathstyle," *The Biblical World View*, Vol. 3, No. 1 (January 1987).

7. This is not to demean their ministries. The observation arises from their evident lack of familiarity with well-known and respected Bible scholars, historians, and theologians. Seminary training has ruined many a fine and eager minister of the gospel, but there is a corpus of literature available that seems to be ignored by a large segment of the church. We pray that this book will introduce this material to a larger audience.

8. The "little gods" controversy would not have arisen if time had been taken to study the Council of Chalcedon (A.D. 451). R. J. Rushdoony writes: "The Council of Chalcedon met in 451 to deal with the issue as it came to focus at the critical point, in Christology. If the two natures of Christ were confused, it meant that the door was opened to the divinizing of human nature. If the human nature of Christ were reduced or denied, His role as man's incarnate savior was reduced or denied, and man's savior again became the state. If Christ's deity were reduced, then His saving power was nullified. If His humanity and deity were not

critics of Hunt's sweeping indictment believe that he failed to raise the possibility that these men are mistaken, but are not consciously perpetuating false doctrine. Doug Groothuis, a well-published expert on the New Age Movement, states that Hunt's analysis is "[s]ometimes too heavy-handed."[9] In a review of *The Seduction of Christianity* he warns that

> the reader should be careful, though, to assess each person separately. Some of those cited have strayed far from the truth; others have committed only minor errors. Unfortunately, the authors have not drawn careful distinctions.
>
> This is the greatest flaw in *Seduction*. It is indeed a blast of the trumpet and lacks the clarity of sharply, individual notes of warning.
>
> Offenders are sometimes lumped together unfairly. For example, Hunt and McMahon are critical of Christians who call for an exercise of dominion over the earth and concern for society. They have succumbed to a selfish "we can do it" attitude, according to the authors. Many Christians who pursue social renewal, however, are doctrinally sound. They look to God, not self, to turn the world right side up again. The late Francis Schaeffer was a shining example.[10]

The Apostle Paul reminded the early church leadership that false doctrines will find their way into the fellowship of the saints. Even with the apostles still preaching and teaching, the early church was not immune to false doctrine. Paul writes about those who will "fall away from the faith, paying attention to deceitful spirits and doctrines of demons" (1 Tim. 4:1). He even mentions some by name:

> This command I entrust to you, Timothy, my son, in accordance with the prophecies previously made concerning you, that

---

in true union, the incarnation was then not real, and the distance between God and man remained as great as ever." *The Foundations of Social Order: Studies in the Creeds and Councils of the Early Church* (Nutley, NJ: Presbyterian and Reformed, 1968), p. 65.

9. Douglas R. Groothuis, *Unmasking the New Age* (Downers Grove, IL: InterVarsity Press, 1986), p. 192.

10. Douglas R. Groothuis, "Guarding Pure Doctrine," a review of *The Seduction of Christianity*, in *Moody Monthly* (January 1986), pp. 63-5.

by them you may fight the good fight, keeping faith and a good conscience, which some have rejected and suffered shipwreck in regard to their faith. *Among these are Hymenaeus and Alexander, whom I have delivered over to Satan, so that they may be taught not to blaspheme* (1 Tim. 1:18-20, emphasis added).

Our analysis, however, does not focus on the sections in Hunt's books where he critiques "psychotherapy, visualization, meditation, biofeedback, Positive Confession, Positive or Possibility Thinking, hypnosis, Holistic medicine, and a whole spectrum of self-improvement and success/motivation techniques."[11] Rather, *The Reduction of Christianity* deals with the second level of Hunt's work.

Dave Hunt and others believe that New Age humanism and what we believe is the theological imprecision of a number of "positive confession" preachers is nothing less than the prelude to the "great apostasy" predicted in the Bible. It is Dave Hunt's opinion that we are living in the "last days." The Great Tribulation is almost upon us, and Jesus should be returning to planet earth in the very near future. Thus, in Hunt's opinion, those who teach that the church is headed for victory are on the edge of apostasy. In short, Hunt's own eschatological (end times) viewpoint influences his evaluation of a group of theologians, scholars, pastors, and writers who preach and teach a position that has been called "dominion theology."[12]

---

11. Dave Hunt and T. A. McMahon, *The Seduction of Christianity: Spiritual Discernment in the Last Days* (Eugene, OR: Harvest House, 1985), p. 8. Having concurred with Dave Hunt that these are humanistic mind techniques, we should be careful not to throw out the baby with the bath water. For example, meditation is not evil, although what one meditates on can be evil. Scripture tells us that the blessed man delights "in the law of the Lord, and in His law he *meditates* day and night" (Psalm 1:2). John Oliver, senior pastor of the First Presbyterian Church in Augusta, Georgia, describes the confusion over "meditation": "Meditation. The psalmist commends it to us. Pagan religionists practice it. 'New Age' cultists frighten us with it. Many Christians misunderstand it or ignore it." Oliver, "Meditation: A Biblical Command with a Bad Reputation," *RTS Bulletin*, VI (Summer 1987), p. 12. For a very fine discussion of biblical meditation see Edmund P. Clowney, *CM: Christian Meditation* (Nutley, NJ: Craig Press, 1979).

12. See chapter 2 for a definition of this term.

The Shift in Eschatology

Apostasy has marred the church for centuries, and the church has dealt with it time after time without the world coming to an end. We suggest that the present preoccupation with the end of the world may be a false alarm pulled by the devil to keep the church from working at its full mission. The devil leads Christians to believe that changing the world is hopeless. One "dominion theology" critic tells us "God's Word is clear that before Jesus returns tremendous evil will encompass the governments of the world (Matthew 24, Mark 13, Revelation 6 & 7). We might not like that prospect, but God's Word is without error."[13] The Bible is used to support this position, as we would expect. This is the devil's greatest tactic. He convinces Christians that they are being faithful to the Word of God by doing nothing to resist culturally while they watch the world "collapsing" around them. What a great demonic tactic!

The anti-dominionists' argument runs approximately as follows. The Bible predicts the inevitability of evil's progress. Today's visibly advancing evil is a prelude to the Second Coming of Christ, where Jesus will rapture the saints, defeat the Antichrist, and establish His earthly millennial rule. Any discussion about long-term victory for the church does not match up with what the Bible predicts concerning the end of the world. All talk about "noble ideas of bringing about a transformation of society through which righteousness will be manifested are doomed to failure."[14]

---

13. Albert James Dager, "Kingdom Theology: Part II," *Media Spotlight* (July-December 1986), p. 18.

14. *Idem.* Mr. Dager does go on to write: "But that does not mean we cannot use the information on politics and other fields of human endeavor that notable Reconstructionists provide. Their analyses of world affairs from a Scriptural perspective are often intelligent and well-documented, and can be of significant help to Christians who wish to be informed on current events. (Just beware the leaven.)

"Nor does it mean we shouldn't continue to wage spiritual warfare and take authority wherever God grants it to us." For what end? These efforts "are doomed to failure." The church can only sit back and take note of the collapse of culture; it supposedly can do nothing to stop its inevitable demise.

We should not be surprised to learn that the secular humanists are delighted with the doctrinal system espoused by Dave Hunt, David Wilkerson, and others. Long-term, Christians who do not see any societal change coming from Christians are not seen as a threat to the humanist agenda. Christians have no plans for planet earth. The humanists have comprehensive plans, and with the present climate of prophetic speculation, they do not fear fatalistic and immobilized Christians.[15] What they fear are Christians who are confident of the church's earthly victory. A number of articles have appeared in humanist publications that show how mobilized Christians are a threat to the humanist cause. Here's an example:

> And it is precisely this change in thinking, from premillennialism to postmillennialism, under the influence of Christian Reconstructionism, that has made possible the religious right and the political mobilization of millions of otherwise fatalistic fundamentalists.[16]

Now, this should not disturb the humanists unless there is a perceived threat to their man-centered agenda, and, not only a threat, but the distinct possibility of Christians scoring major cultural victories. The humanists, it seems, have more regard for the effect Christians can have in and on the world than do some notable Christian leaders and writers.

---

15. There are humanists who consider the end times scenario described by some prophetic speculators as "scary." The dust jacket copy to *Prophecy and Politics* is indicative of their concern: "Militant TV evangelists are preaching that a nuclear holocaust is inevitable, and their message is influencing top level governmental leaders in the U.S., Israel and elsewhere.

"Reaching an estimated 60 million Americans, charismatic war-minded evangelists insist that they have the right and power to help orchestrate not only their End of Times, but doomsday for all the rest of the species." Grace Halsell, *Prophecy and Politics: Militant Evangelists on the Road to Nuclear War* (Westport, CT: Lawrence Hill & Company, 1986).

16. Frederick Edwords and Stephen McCabe, "Getting Out God's Vote: Pat Robertson and the Evangelicals," *The Humanist* (May/June 1987), p. 10.

A Deafening Silence

A shift in eschatology has taken place. In general terms, there has been a shift from pessimism to optimism.[17] For most of the twentieth century, orthodox Christians who have held a premillennial position have remained relatively silent regarding social issues. One reason is that, as John Walvoord, former president and now chancellor of Dallas Theological Seminary, writes, they "know that our efforts to make society Christianized are futile because the Bible does not teach it."[18] Much of this attitude has to do more with current events than with interpreting the Bible. There is also a reaction to 19th-century theological liberalism that spawned the "Social Gospel" era. It too was optimistic. Today, some dispensational premillennialists equate postmillennialism with liberalism and the "Social Gospel."

Hal Lindsey writes of postmillennialism:

> *There used to be a group called "postmillennialists."* They believed that the Christians would root out the evil in the world, abolish godless rulers, and convert the world through ever increasing evangelism until they brought about the Kingdom of God on earth through their own efforts. Then after 1000 years of the institutional church reigning on earth with peace, equality, and righteousness, Christ would return and time would end. These people rejected much of the Scripture as being literal and believed in the

---

17. "Pessimism" and "optimism" may not be the best terms to describe the Christian's hope. These words are sometimes used to describe a view of the future that is based solely on the trends of the present. Thus, an optimist turns pessimist when disaster strikes. By contrast, we mean by the phrase "optimistic Christian" a Christian who, trusting in the promises of Scripture, is confident that Christian civilization will triumph visibly and institutionally in history. A "pessimistic Christian" is one who believes that Scripture does not promise an earthly and historical victory for God's people. Because we are in the midst of a transition, however, many Christians are optimistic about the future, but have not yet formulated an eschatology that matches their outlook and activism. In time, these Christians will conclude that the Bible promises long-term victory to the church, or they will drift back into pessimism.

18. "Our Future Hope: Eschatology and Its Role in the Church," *Christianity Today* (February 6, 1987), p. 5-I. But does the Bible teach that our efforts to Christianize society are futile? This has not been proven biblically to our satisfaction.

inherent goodness of man. World War I greatly disheartened this group and World War II virtually wiped out this viewpoint. *No self-respecting scholar who looks at the world conditions and the accelerating decline of Christian influence today is a "postmillennialist."*[19]

Let's rephrase Mr. Lindsey's assertion in the light of Numbers 13-14 and Joshua 2:8-14: "No self-respecting Israelite who looks at the land of Canaan and the decline of Israel's faithfulness can ever believe that we can take the land because 'we became like grasshoppers in our own sight, and so we were in their sight' " (Num. 13:33).

In the minds of many students of eschatology, postmillennialism[20] was stripped of the centrality of the gospel message and became the darling of the purveyors of the "Social Gospel." The reaction of many Christian leaders was to repudiate not only theological liberalism but also postmillennialism and the social dimension of the gospel.[21] This is a mistake and a misreading of history.

Now, the formerly withdrawn church is emerging from the sanctuary of the cave to take on the world of unbridled secularism (see Judges 6:1-18). Many who have moved to earthly optimism

---

19. Hal Lindsey, *The Late Great Planet Earth* (Grand Rapids, MI: Zondervan, [1970] 1973), p. 176. Emphasis ours.

20. See Greg L. Bahnsen, "The *Prima Facie* Acceptability of Postmillennialism" and James B. Jordan, "A Survey of Southern Presbyterian Millennial Views Before 1930," ed., Gary North, *The Journal of Christian Reconstruction*, Symposium on the Millennium, Vol. III, No. 2 (Winter 1976), pp. 48-121.

21. Since 19th-century postmillennialism spoke of "progress" (the result of obedience) and early 20th-century liberalism spoke of progress ("in terms of rational and scientific planning by an intellectual elite"), postmillennialism became suspect. Progress was equated with liberalism. While the ideals seemed similar, the ways of getting there were quite different. This was guilt by association. "[S]ince the publication of H. Richard Niebuhr's *The Kingdom of God in America* (1937), it has been widely assumed that postmillennialism led to the social gospel. . . . The heart of the problem, however, has been a simplistic confusion in the minds of many that historical succession means necessary logical connection and succession. Hence, it is held, because postmillennialism was the original kingdom of God idea in America, the social gospel idea of the kingdom of God is a logical and necessary product of postmillennialism. This 'proves' too much." R. J. Rushdoony, "Postmillennialism Versus Impotent Religion," *Journal of Christian Reconstruction*, Symposium on the Millennium, p. 122.

have not formally rejected their dispensational premillennial views. All they know is that they are tired of getting their heads kicked in by the humanists, and they are willing to work to change things, no matter when Jesus returns. Their children are being propagandized in the public schools,[22] abortion is making them feel guilty for doing little if anything about the issue in 1973 during the infamous *Roe v. Wade* pro-abortion decision, and they sense the constant ridicule in the press for their deeply held religious convictions.[23]

"No More Mr. Nice Guy!"

For these energized Christians, it's no more Mr. Nice Guy.[24] Jerry Falwell is a good example of someone who had shifted his emphasis from quietism in 1965 to action beyond the four walls of the church. In a sermon delivered in 1965, entitled "Ministers and Marchers," Falwell said:

> . . . as far as the relationship of the church to the world, [it] can be expressed as simply as the three words which Paul gave to Timothy—"Preach the Word." This message is designed to go right to the heart of man and there meet his deep spiritual need. Nowhere are we commissioned to reform the externals. We are

---

22. Paul C. Vitz, *Censorship: Evidence of Bias in our Children's Textbooks* (Ann Arbor, MI: Servant Publications, 1986).

23. In Greenville, Tennessee, a group of Christian parents wanted alternative textbooks for their children. Here's what a syndicated columnist had to say about them: "These poor children are being denied the most basic of childhood's freedoms, the right to imagine and learn. Someone should remind their parents the law of this land still requires we educate our children in qualified schools with qualified teachers. That a sound education involves free exploration of ideas and fact. That they may rant and rave against humanism and feminism and any other 'ism' on Sunday, but come Monday the children belong in school.

"It is time for someone to remind [Christians who want to have a say in what their children learn] that a majority in this country believe in God, but only a fanatic few feel their beliefs exempt them from laws written by the people in this democracy." Rheta Grimsley Johnson, "'People' vs. Fundamentalists," *The Marietta Daily Journal* (September 2, 1986), p. 4A.

24. Stephen Brown, *No More Mr. Nice Guy!: Saying Goodbye to "Doormat" Christianity* (Nashville, TN: Thomas Nelson, 1986).

not told to wage war against bootleggers, liquor stores, gamblers, murderers, prostitutes, racketeers, prejudiced persons or institutions or any other existing evil as such. Our ministry is not reformation, but transformation. The gospel does not clean up the outside but rather regenerates the inside.

While we are told to "render unto Caesar the things that are Caesar's," in the true interpretation we have very few ties on this earth. We pay our taxes, cast our votes as a responsibility of citizenship, obey the laws of the land, and other things demanded of us by the society in which we live. But at the same time, we are cognizant that our only purpose on this earth is to know Christ and to make him known. Believing the Bible as I do, I would find it impossible to stop preaching the pure saving gospel of Jesus Christ, and begin doing anything else—including fighting Communism, or participating in civil-rights reforms.[25]

Fifteen years later, Dr. Falwell repudiated his earlier remarks calling them "false prophecy." In *Listen, America!* Rev. Falwell outlines his new agenda: "I am seeking to rally together the people of this country who still believe in decency, the home, the family, morality, the free enterprise system, and all the great ideals that are the cornerstone of this nation. Against the growing tide of permissiveness and moral decay that is crushing our society, we must make a sacred commitment to God Almighty to turn this nation around immediately."[26]

Many have noticed the shift. Dave Hunt, David Wilkerson, Jimmy Swaggart, and others have noticed. As the earlier quotation from *The Humanist* shows, the humanists are also aware of it, and they are not happy with the turn of events. Paul G. Kirk, Jr., chairman of the Democratic National Committee, labeled conservative, Bible-believing Christians who are involved in politics as "an extremist faction." He is most concerned about the presidential candidacy of Pat Robertson. Kirk makes the following points:

---

25. Quoted by James A. Speer, *New Christian Politics* (Macon, GA: Mercer University Press, 1984), pp. 19-20.

26. Jerry Falwell, *Listen, America!* (New York: Doubleday, 1980), p. 244. Falwell has slowly drifted back to his pre-1965 views, although he has not stopped training "champions for Christ" at his future-oriented Liberty Baptist University.

1. The idea that a Christian like Pat Robertson may run for President is "very frightening."

2. Pat Robertson is "an ultrafundamentalist." The emphasis is on extremism. He's not just a fundamentalist; he's an *ultra*fundamentalist.

3. Pat Robertson is "one of the most radical right-wing leaders in America." Notice the term "radical."

4. Pat Robertson is *"one of the most powerful public figures in America today."* Is power evil?

5. According to Mr. Kirk, "Pat Robertson is beginning to worry the leaders of *both* the Democratic and Republican parties."

After listing the impact that Pat Robertson has through his donor list, television network, and the recently disbanded Freedom Council, Mr. Kirk makes this statement: "But his greatest threat is not his powerful organization. It is the enormous political muscle of the Religious Right." So then, Pat Robertson is not the only perceived threat. All Christians who hold to certain fundamental beliefs are the enemies of the political faith. The real issue is *Christian* involvement. Pat Robertson is just a visible target, someone to raise funds by shooting at. If a representative of a perceived monolithic movement can be shot down, then the movement itself is immobilized.

It is not our purpose to endorse Pat Robertson, nor to criticize his desire to seek the presidency. Neither is it our purpose to judge Democrats. We are firmly convinced that there are Republicans who hold similar views. The point we are trying to make is that Christian involvement is seen as a threat by some very powerful people. We have to ask why.

The Heresy of the Faithful

The humanists are opportunists. They go after weak points. One significant weak point that they have exploited is the fling that many Christians have with Manichaean[27] and Neo-

---

27. Mani, a Babylonian philosopher born around A.D. 216, was the founder of the Manichaean school of philosophy. Mani taught that only the spiritual realm is good, while material things are inherently evil. There is an eternal struggle between Good and Evil, which are equally powerful. Man is a mixture of the

Platonic[28] world views. While the Bible addresses only "spiritual" issues such as prayer and Bible reading,[29] we are told that it has little if anything to say about "secular" matters such as economics and politics, unless we're dealing with the tithe and church government. Sin and the power of the devil make it nearly impossible for Christians to effect any real and permanent societal changes, we are assured. The church's only recourse is to retreat to the "spiritual" dimension. R. J. Rushdoony has called this the "The Heresy of the Faithful":

> Many people excuse the extensive apostasy in the Church by pointing to original sin. Man is so great a sinner, we are told, that we should not be surprised at the extensive sway of unbelief in the very hearts of the faithful, let alone the world. We are reminded that the heart of man "is deceitful above all things, and desperately wicked: who can know it?" (Jer. 17:9). This is true, but the Scripture is not a Manichaean document. It does not assert that Satan and sin have a power equal to or greater than God and His grace. On the contrary, "God is greater than our hearts" (I John

---

spiritual and material, and seeks salvation by denying his material nature. Mani's principal ideas are found in many Christian groups, who teach that the only significant part of man is his soul. As a result, political and social concerns are not considered to be significant for the Christian.

28. Neoplatonism was a modification of Plato's philosophy that was first systematized by Plotinus in the 4th century A.D. Like Manichaeanism, Neo-Platonism often involves a low view of the material world. For the Neo-Platonist, the world of sense objects—the world that can be seen and felt—is a dim reflection of the true world of ideas. The world of sense is therefore less real and less important than the realm of ideas. Neo-Platonic thought has deeply influenced the church. See R. J. Rushdoony, *The Flight From Humanity* (Tyler, TX: Thoburn Press, 1973).

29. Prayer and Bible reading are foundational to any real reformation. Prayer and Bible reading are not ends in themselves but are means for the greater work of the kingdom. When thirty-six men were killed in the battle with the men of Ai, Joshua and the elders prayed to the Lord. But that was not the end of things: "So the LORD said to Joshua, 'Rise up! Why is it that you have fallen on your face? Israel has sinned, and they have also transgressed My covenant which I commanded them'" (Joshua 7). For a full discussion of the "privatization" of prayer and Bible reading see R. J. Rushdoony, "Sanctification and History," in *Law and Society* (Vallecito, CA: Ross House Books, 1982), pp. 227-30.

3:20), and "greater is he that is in you, than he that is in the world" (I John 4:4). Great and almighty is our sovereign and triune God, and we cannot limit His power without sinning, nor can we ascribe the helplessness of the church to the greater power of sin and Satan. Rather, we must ascribe it to the heresy and laziness of believers, who limit God in their unbelief.

Related to this acceptance of apostasy, which is an implicit acceptance of the superiority of Satan, is the surrender of this world to Satan and to unbelievers.[30]

For those who see no hope for this world this side of heaven, God is seen as orchestrating the events of history for the imminent "rapture" of the saints, to deliver them from the mess of history. At the same time, the devil is marshalling his forces of evil against the people of God. This is an old, old story, repeated century after century when external events begin to press in on Christians.[31] These two events are necessary and inevitable, say the proponents of earthly defeat, just prior to the rapture of the saints. We supposedly should expect the advance of evil and the decline of those things explicitly Christian. One author goes so far as to say that America will be "destroyed by fire! Sudden destruction is coming and few will escape. Unexpectedly, and in one hour, a hydrogen holocaust will engulf America—and this nation will be no more."[32]

---

30. R. J. Rushdoony, *The Biblical Philosophy of History* (Nutley, NJ: Presbyterian and Reformed, 1969), p. 139.

31. "[A]ll the scripture texts claimed as proof that the coming of Jesus Christ must now be close at hand have also been confidently so used in former generations. Not a few Christians in the past have been erroneously convinced that their age must witness the end. When the Teutonic barbarians overturned Rome and reduced a stable world to chaos in the fifth century A.D., many in the Church despairingly drew the wrong conclusion that the world could have no future. Even larger numbers did so at the approach of the year 1000, believing that the closing millennium would end the world. In the gloom of the fourteenth century such tracts appeared as *The Last Age of the Church*, and in terms very similar to that old title a great number have written since." Iain Murray, *The Puritan Hope* (London: Banner of Truth Trust, 1971), p. xix.

32. David Wilkerson, *Set the Trumpet to Thy Mouth* (Lindale, TX: World Challenge, Inc., 1985), p. 1. Wilkerson's assessment of the current state of the Church is correct, but his conclusions in our opinion, are flawed. For decades the Church has taught that the world *must* get worse and worse. "One common reason

Charles Haddon Spurgeon (1834-1892), the great Baptist preacher and evangelist of the 19th century, shows how pessimism robs the church of its vitality and stunts its growth.

> David was not a believer in the theory that the world will grow worse and worse, and that the dispensation will wind up with general darkness, and idolatry. Earth's sun is to go down amid tenfold night if some of our prophetic brethren are to be believed. Not so do we expect, but we look for a day when the dwellers in all lands shall learn righteousness, shall trust in the Saviour, shall worship thee alone, O God, *"and shall glorify thy name."* The modern notion has greatly damped the zeal of the church for missions, and the sooner it is shown to be unscriptural the better for the cause of God. It neither consorts with prophecy, honours God, nor inspires the church with ardour. Far hence be it driven.[33]

For nearly a hundred years, Christians have been in retreat.[34] Through the adoption of pagan ideas about the world, some Christians have concluded that matter (this world) is of little value while spiritual things (heaven) are the only real focus of a Christian's attention. While Christianity became more and more pietistic[35]

---

for believing that the world must grow worse and worse has always been the evidence of abounding moral decay. Confronted by this evidence it has too often been supposed that the only work left for God is judgment. Yet the history of revivals should teach us that even in the midst of prevailing evil it is possible to form precisely the opposite conviction. For example, when John Wesley arrived in Newcastle-upon-Tyne in May, 1742, he wrote these memorable words: 'I was surprised; so much drunkenness, cursing and swearing (even from the mouths of little children) do I never remember to have seen and heard before in so small a compass of time. Surely this place is ripe for Him who "came not to call the righteous, but sinners to repentance".'" Murray, *The Puritan Hope*, pp. xix-xx.

33. *The Treasury of David: An Expository and Devotional Commentary on the Psalms*, 7 vols. (Grand Rapids, MI: Guardian Press, [1870-1885] 1976), vol. 4, p. 102.

34. Douglas W. Frank, *Less Than Conquerors: How Evangelicals Entered the Twentieth Century* (Grand Rapids, MI: Eerdmans, 1986).

35. We must distinguish between "piety" and "pietism." Originally, a "pious" person was one whose whole life was ordered by his relationship to God. Today, piety is generally used to describe one's personal devotional life, such as prayer, Bible study, fellowship with the Lord, and so forth. In both these senses, piety is essential to Christian living. By contrast, we are using the term "pietism" to describe the belief that there is nothing to the Christian life except personal piety. A "pietistic" Christian says that Christians should not become involved with political and social issues, but should devote themselves entirely to personal devotional practices.

and retreatist, secularism became (because of little opposition
from dominion-oriented Christians) aggressive and dominating.[36]
At last, Christians are beginning to fight back. This is why Hunt
and many others are upset. This confident and optimistic vision of
the future, according to Hunt, indicates that we are in the final
apostasy. The idea of cultural victory by Christians is *anathema* to
Dave Hunt. The idea of cultural defeat is pure orthodoxy—the
"old time religion" of 1830.

Is This Really the End?

Hunt concludes that 1 Timothy 4:1 addresses this very situation: "But the Spirit explicitly says that in *later times* some will fall
away from the faith." The advocates of the near-end-of-the-world
scenario of future events want to project Paul's warning into what
would have been the distant future when Paul wrote his epistle.
Little thought is given to the possibility that the "later times" that
Paul had in mind were in the early church's *near* future, the end of
the Jewish age just prior to A.D. 70. We use similar language with
little if any confusion. A politician might remark that he will an-
nounce his candidacy at a "later time." The audience understands
this as "in the near future." He is biding his time, but not for nine-
teen hundred years.

In fact, there have always been Christians who have been preoccupied with the end of the world and the return of Christ. The
sack of Rome by the Vandals (A.D. 410) was supposed to bring on
the end; the birth of the Inquisition (1209-1244) prompted many
well-meaning saints to conclude that it was the beginning of the
end; the Black Death that killed millions was viewed as the

---

36. "At the turn of the century, political and conspiratorial elites began a long-
term program to 'capture the robes' of American culture. They recognized the
importance of judges, professors, and ministers. I remember hearing a speech by
a former Communist, Karl Prussion, in 1964, in which he told of the assignment
he received from the Party. He became a theology student at Union Theological
Seminary in New York. The Party knew what it was doing." Gary North,
Backward, Christian Soldiers? (Tyler, TX: Institute for Christian Economics, 1984),
p. 60.

prelude to the demise of the world (1347-1350).[37] Martin Luther
"frequently expressed the opinion that the End was very near,
though he felt it was unwise to predict an exact date. Christians,
he said, no more know the exact time of Christ's return than 'little
babies in their mothers' bodies know about their arrival.' "[38] This,
however, did not stop him from concluding that the end was not
too far off. In January 1532, he wrote, "The last day is at hand.
My calendar has run out. I know nothing more in my Scriptures."[39]
As it turned out, there was a lot more time to go after 1532. Many
other disasters, natural and political, gave rise to the same speculation, century after century. Disasters on the front page of their
newspapers send far too many Christians scurrying to the back
pages of their Bibles. Such fears and delusions become grist for the
humanist historians' mill:

> Contemporary events like the Lisbon earthquake of 1755
> were interpreted as evidence of the fulfillment of biblical prophe-
> cies. Above all, the French Revolution excited a spate of inter-
> pretations on both sides of the Atlantic designed to show that the
> world was entering upon the last days. Millennialism was widely
> espoused by leading scholars and divines. In America the names
> of Timothy Dwight (President of Yale), John H. Livingston

---

37. The plague disrupted society at all levels. Giovanni Boccaccio wrote a
vivid description of how some people responded. Much of it reads like the
prelude to the end: For some "debauchery was the road to salvation, or, if there
was to be no salvation [from the plague], to happiness in the few days that remained. These profligates abandoned all work and drifted from house to house,
drinking, stealing, fornicating. 'People behaved as though their days were numbered,' Boccaccio wrote, 'and treated their belongings and their own persons with
equal abandon. Hence most houses had become common property, and any
passing stranger could make himself at home. . . . In the face of so much affliction and misery, all respect for the laws of God and man had virtually broken
down. . . . Those ministers and executors of the laws who were not either dead
or ill were left with so few subordinates that they were unable to discharge any of
their duties. Hence everyone was free to behave as he pleased." Quoted in Otto
Friedrich, *The End of the World: A History* (New York: Coward, McCann &
Geoghegan, 1982), p. 116.
38. Mark Noll, "Misreading the Signs of the Times," *Christianity Today*
(February 6, 1987), p. 10-I.
39. Quoted in *idem*.

(President of Rutgers) and Joseph Priestly come to mind: in Britain, George Stanley Faber, Edward King, and Edward Irving. A spate of pamphlets and sermons by Church of England clergy and orthodox American ministers poured forth from the 1790s; and there was constant reference back to the prophetical studies of Sir Isaac Newton, Joseph Mede, and William Whiston. The usual method of interpretation was some variant of the year-day theory, by which days mentioned in the prophecies were counted as years, weeks as seven-year periods, and months as thirty years. There was general agreement in the late eighteenth century that the 1,260 days mentioned in Revelation 12:6 were to be interpreted as 1,260 years, and that this period was now ended. An alternative theory, which became increasingly popular after 1800, emphasized the importance of the 2,300-year period of Daniel 8:14 and the 'cleansing of the sanctuary' which would fall due some time in the 1840s. The fulfillment of the time prophecies meant that mankind was living in the last days, that the 'midnight cry' might soon be heard, and that the coming of the messiah might be expected shortly. Such beliefs had an influence far beyond the members of explicitly adventist sects. They were part and parcel of everyday evangelical religion.[40]

In the 20th century, there has been wild speculation that the end of the world is just around the next world disaster. The onslaught of World War I led many to conclude that Armageddon was at hand: "We are not yet in the Armageddon struggle proper, but at its commencement, and it may be, if students of prophecy read the signs aright, *that Christ will come before the present war closes*, and before Armageddon. . . . The war preliminary to Armageddon, it seems, has commenced."[41] The war he is talking about is *World War I*.

---

40. J. E. C. Harrison, *The Second Coming: Popular Millennarianism, 1780-1850* (New Brunswick, NJ: Rutgers University Press, 1979), p. 5.

41. *The Weekly Evangel* (April 10, 1917), p. 3. Quoted in Dwight Wilson, *Armageddon Now!: The Premillenarian Response to Russia and Israel Since 1917* (Grand Rapids, MI: Baker, 1977), pp. 37-38. Emphasis added. This book is "must" reading by anyone who believes that today's front page headline is proof of Christ's imminent return. What about front page headlines two generations ago? Apocalyptic dispensational expectations have made public fools in retrospect out of generations of Bible expositors.

Benito Mussolini,[42] Adolf Hitler, Henry Kissinger, and the Papacy[43] have been mistakenly identified as *the* "Antichrist." In Scripture, the word "Antichrist" is often plural, and it refers to anyone who denies that Christ came in the flesh to save His people (see 1 John 2:18, 22). Taken out of its historical context, almost anyone can be *the* Antichrist. Hal Lindsey is correct: "However, we must not indulge in speculation about whether any of the current figures is the Antichrist."[44]

Predictions of the near end of the world have been a prominent feature of recent evangelical thought. Looking back, we can say with confidence that *they were wrong*. Of course, this does not mean that current predictions are automatically wrong because they have been wrong in the past. It does mean, however, that we should be careful when it comes to analyzing the Bible in terms of contemporary events, in what one writer has described as "newspaper exegesis."[45] Historian Mark Noll again writes: "The verdict of history seems clear. Great spiritual gain comes from living under the expectation of Christ's return. But wisdom and restraint are also in order. At the very least, it would be well for those in our age who predict details and dates for the End to re-

---

42. "Many will recall widespread preaching during the World War II era that Mussolini or Hitler was the Antichrist. Since the slogan VV IL DUCE was widely used by Mussolini, and because the Roman numeral value of the slogan/title is 666, many were sure of positive identification." David A. Lewis, "The Antichrist: Number, number, who's got the number?" (no publishing information).

In a popular tract that was circulated during World War II, Mussolini was supposed to be the Antichrist: "Someone has to be the Anti-christ. Why not Mussolini? In his life, death, and his exhumation he has fulfilled 49 prophesies. Why not consider him?" From the pamphlet *Mussolini . . . The Antichrist* by McBirnie.

43. Samuel J. Cassels, *Christ and Antichrist or Jesus of Nazareth Proved to be the Messiah and the Papacy Proved to be the Antichrist* (Philadelphia, PA: Presbyterian Board of Publication, 1846); Ralph Woodrow, *Great Prophecies of the Bible* (Riverside, CA: Ralph Woodrow Evangelistic Association, 1971), pp. 148-200.

44. Hal Lindsey, *The Late Great Planet Earth* (Grand Rapids, MI: Zondervan, [1970] 1973), p. 113.

45. Greg L. Bahnsen, "The *Prima Facie* Acceptability of Postmillennialism," pp. 53-55.

member how many before them have misread the signs of the times."[46]

The historical landscape is filled with the failed prophetic pronouncements by some of the best-intentioned biblical expositors. It seems that every disaster and every deviation from orthodox doctrine is heaped upon piles of wild prophetic speculation to prepare (and culturally paralyze) another generation of anxious Christians to meet Jesus in the air.

The back cover of David Hunt's *The Seduction of Christianity* notes that the adoption of "fashionable philosophies" by prominent Christian leaders and their loyal following is symptomatic of a "great Apostasy [that] *must* occur before Christ's Second Coming." Notice two things. First, Hunt has now placed the "great Apostasy" *before* the rapture, a major departure from traditional pretribulational dispensational theology. Second, the church has been seduced before. Rampant immorality stalked the church prior to the reformational awakening of the 15th and 16th centuries. Doctrinal error overshadowed even the most basic message of the gospel. Was that the end of the world? In a way it was. The end of the Renaissance world came, and a powerful gospel message emerged from the struggles of the Reformation. Was the church seduced prior to Luther and Calvin? Most certainly. Were these great Christian leaders able "to choose between the Original and the counterfeit"?[47] Did they and millions more "escape the Seduction of Christianity"?[48] Yes. Is it possible that the present heresies are not a sign of the end but a sign of a new reformation?[49]

But there is even more at stake here. For decades, the preoccupation with speculative prophecy has embarrassed and immobilized the church. As children we learned Aesop's fable of the "Shepherd Boy and the Wolf":

---

46. Noll, "Misreading the Signs of the Times," p. 10-I.
47. Back cover of *The Seduction of Christianity*.
48. *Idem.*
49. We do not mean Robert Schuller's "New Reformation" of "self-esteem." See Jay E. Adams, *The Biblical View of Self-Esteem, Self-Love, & Self-Image* (Eugene, OR: Harvest House, 1986).

A mischievous lad was set to mind some sheep, used, in jest, to cry "Wolf! Wolf!" When the people at work in the neighboring fields came running to the spot, he would laugh at them for their pains. One day the wolf came in reality, and the boy this time called "Wolf! Wolf!" in earnest; but the men, having been so often deceived, disregarded his cries, and the sheep were left at the mercy of the wolf.

Of course, if you cry long enough, you just might be the one to get it right, but by then there might not be anyone listening. Preaching about the end of the world has long been used by religious groups as a way of pleading with the lost to commit themselves to Jesus Christ before He returns. Such a motivating device can backfire on even the most well-intentioned evangelist. What happens if a listener shouts out, "Preachers like you have been telling us for decades that the world is coming to an end. Why should we believe you now?"[50]

Those who are sure that the end is near should heed the warning from someone who does believe that Jesus is returning soon:

> The date-setters will have a heyday as the year 2000 approaches. It will be a fever. It will sell pamphlets and books by the millions. But if Jesus does not come back by the year 2000, it is hard to imagine any credibility being left for the Bible prophecy message unless we begin a strong program right now to offset the heresy of date-setting.
>
> Ignoring it will not make it go away. Only by preaching the true and dignified message of the Lord's return and by strongly denouncing date-setting can we hope to maintain confidence in the Bible message of Jesus' return.[51]

---

50. The New Testament does use the imminent coming of Jesus in judgment as a way of spurring the church on to greater works. But the imminent judgment spoken of in Scripture is the destruction of Jerusalem in A.D. 70. Peter writes: "The end of all things *is at hand*; therefore, be of sound judgment and sober spirit for the purpose of prayer" (1 Peter 4:7). In Luke's gospel we read these words of Jesus: "But keep on the alert at all times, praying in order that *you* may have strength to escape all these things that *are about to take place*, and to stand before the Son of Man" (Luke 21:36). John writes in his first epistle: "Children, it is the *last hour*; and just as you heard that antichrist is coming, *even now many antichrists have arisen; from this we know that it is the last hour*" (1 John 2:18).

51. David Lewis, "The Dating Game," *The Pentecostal Evangel*, no page or month, 1975.

Conclusion

In the past decade, Christians have begun to fight back against the humanistic establishment. Many also have rediscovered the hope that the visible church of Jesus Christ will be victorious on earth because Christians in every area of life will be victorious. Many people, both Christians and non-Christians, are troubled by this resurgence. Dave Hunt and others see it as a sign of impending judgment, a fulfillment of biblical prophesies about the last days. We believe, on the contrary, that it may be a sign of an impending reformation. But keep in mind that even reformation takes time. It does not come "in an instant."

4

WHAT IS NEW AGE HUMANISM?

Although it is possible that Christians have been seduced by New Age concepts, yet it is wrong to identify someone as a New Age humanist simply because he or she uses terminology stolen by New Age advocates. After all, it's equally possible that some Christians who believe in a "kingdom theology" are not being seduced because they may fully understand that New Age humanism is man-centered, while "kingdom theology" is Christ-centered in the most biblical sense. They also know, as we hope to demonstrate, that New Age humanism is a counterfeit of the kingdom of God.

What, then, would someone have to believe in order to be labeled a New Ager? We've chosen four foundational presuppositions of New Age philosophy, but there are many more New Age concepts that we will not critique.[1]

One New Age principle that seems to get tremendous attention in this debate is an optimistic view of our earthly future. Since this is a crucial topic for Dave Hunt, a number of our later chapters are devoted exclusively to the subject. Optimism is not, however, a prerequisite for someone to be a New Ager, although it is a prominent strain in the movement.[2] There are plenty of pessimists who are part of New Age humanism. Jeremy Rifkin is

---

1. See Douglas Groothuis, *Unmasking the New Age* (Downers Grove, IL: Inter-Varsity Press, 1985), pp. 13-36 for a detailed description of New Age presuppositions.

2. "This reality, this 'New Consciousness,' is hoping to bring about a 'New Age' of hope and human fulfillment." *Ibid.*, p. 16.

one of them.³

The following New Age "criteria" separate the New Agers from the broad spectrum of evangelical Christianity.

1. *Monism, pantheism*: God is an impersonal undifferentiated oneness, not separate from creation.
2. *Divinization*: Humanity, like all creation, is an extension of this divine oneness and shares its essential being. Thus, humanity is divine.
3. *Higher consciousness*: Transformation of humanity is brought about through techniques that can be applied to mind, body, and spirit.
4. *Reincarnation, karma*: Salvation is a multi-lifetime process of progression or digression.

Anyone who holds all four of these doctrines has adopted the New Age religion. You cannot believe these four doctrines and remain an evangelical Christian. On the other hand, *if you do not believe in any of these doctrines, you cannot possibly be a New Ager.* We hope to force the debate beyond the rhetoric of New Age humanism and get down to biblical specifics. The debate is being obscured by the constant reference to New Age seduction.

1. Monism, pantheism: God is an impersonal undifferentiated oneness, not separate from the creation.

This one identifying mark sets off the orthodox Christian from the "orthodox" New Ager. The Christian believes in a *personal* God who is separate from His creation. This is called the Creator-creature distinction. In contrast to many Eastern religions, which teach that God is part of the creation, Christianity teaches that God did not create the world out of Himself, using the "stuff" of His own being to bring the universe and man into existence.⁴ "By

---

3. Gary North, *Is the World Running Down? Crisis in the Christian Worldview* (Tyler, Texas: Institute for Christian Economics, 1987).

4. Pagan creation myths abound with this notion. According to one Babylonian account, Marduk, the great stone god, "killed the dragon Tiamat and split her body in half. The upper half was made into the sky, and the lower half the earth." John J. Davis, *Paradise to Prison: Studies in Genesis* (Grand Rapids, MI: Baker, 1975), p. 69.

faith we understand that the worlds were prepared by the *word of God*, so that what is seen *was not made out of the things which are visible*" (Heb. 11:3; cf. Gen. 1:1, 2).

The Creator-Creature Distinction

One of the distinguishing marks of Christian reconstruction is the Creator-creature distinction.[5] Cornelius Van Til, whose apologetic methodology is the foundation for much of Christian reconstruction's thinking, makes this concept abundantly clear in his introductory work on apologetics, *The Defense of the Faith*:

> So I point out that the Bible does contain a theory of Reality. And this theory of Reality is that of two levels of being, first, of God as infinite, eternal, and unchangeable and, second, of the universe as derivative, finite, temporal, and changeable. A position is best known by its most basic differentiation. The meanings of all words in the Christian theory of being depend upon the differentiation between the self-contained God and the created universe.
>
> The history of non-Christian philosophy shows that it is built upon a monistic[6] assumption. It has no place in its thought for the basic differentiation that is fundamental to a true Christian metaphysic. Greek philosophers, together with all men, were descendants of Adam. . . . As sinners they were as anxious to suppress the Creature-creature distinction as are all other sinners. They simply assumed that all Reality is at bottom one, that is, they assumed that God does not have incommunicable attributes. When Thales said that *All* is Water, he gave evidence of this monistic assumption.[7]

The Creator-creature distinction is a theological pillar in the

---

5. For a popular study of this concept see Richard L. Pratt, Jr., *Every Thought Captive: A Study Manual for the Defense of the Faith* (Phillipsburg, NJ: Presbyterian and Reformed, 1979), pp. 10-18.

6. Monism, the idea that "all is one," is essential to New Age thinking. See Groothuis, *Unmasking the New Age*, pp. 18-20; and Arthur F. Holmes, *Contours of a World View* (Grand Rapids, MI: Eerdmans, 1983), pp. 8-10.

7. Cornelius Van Til, *The Defense of the Faith* (Phillipsburg, NJ: Presbyterian and Reformed, 1955), pp. 235-36.

writings of Dr. Greg L. Bahnsen,[8] Rev. Ray Sutton,[9] David
Chilton,[10] R. J. Rushdoony,[11] and Dr. Gary North,[12] all of whom
hold to an optimistic eschatological position called "postmillennialism," and all of whom could be identified as "reconstructionists." There is nothing in any of their writings that would suggest
that man ascends the great "chain of being" and becomes one with
God or that the creation in some way is a part of God. Gary North
writes about the Creator-creature distinction in these terms:

> There is a basic difference between God and the universe,
> between God and man. Man is a created being. No man stands
> alone. No man stands independent of God. No man merges into
> God, either. God tells us very specifically that "my thoughts are

---

8. "The Reformation of Christian Apologetics," *The Foundations of Christian
Scholarship: Essays in the Van Til Perspective*, ed., Gary North (Vallecito, CA: Ross
House Books, 1976), p. 210.

9. "Biblical transcendence means there is a fundamental distinction between
the Creator's Being and the creature's being. . . . God's Being is uncreated, and
man's is created. God is original, and man is derivative. . . . God is independent
(aseity) and man is dependent. God is God, man is man, and the latter is never
able to become God, although God did become man in Jesus Christ. Furthermore, God is 'near' by means of the covenant." Ray Sutton, *That You May Prosper:
Dominion By Covenant* (Tyler, TX: Dominion Press, 1987), pp. 24-26.

10. "Ethical Theology teaches that my relationship with God is covenantal and
legal; that my salvation has taken place objectively in Another, Jesus Christ. In
salvation I am not metamorphosed into a higher level of reality; rather, God
saves me from my sins and conforms me ethically to the image of Christ, so that I
am restored to the purpose for which God originally created man: godly dominion over the earth. This means that the Christian life is *primarily* to be defined in
terms of personal communication with God and obedience to God's word. Rap-
turous experiences are not discounted, but they must be recognized as of secondary importance. More than this, those subjective experiences must be interpreted in the light of the objective word of God, the Bible. *No* experience makes
me anything more than a finite creature. I will *always* be a finite creature, and
nothing more. Salvation is not deification." David Chilton, "Between the Covers
of Power for Living," in *Biblical Economics Today*, Vol. VII, No. 2 (Feb./Mar.,
1984), p. 4.

11. Rushdoony, *By What Standard? An Analysis of the Philosophy of Cornelius Van
Til* (Tyler, TX: Thoburn Press, [1958] 1983), pp. 122-26, 130-31, 150-64; *The One
and the Many: Studies in the Philosophy of Order and Ultimacy* (Fairfax, VA: Thoburn
Press, [1971] 1978), pp. 58-60, 132-33, 168-70, 190-97, 259-60.

12. North, *Unholy Spirits: Occultism and New Age Humanism* (Ft. Worth, TX:
Dominion Press, 1986), pp. 58-61.

not your thoughts, neither are your ways my ways" (Isaiah 55:8). Why not? "For as the heavens are higher than the earth, so are my ways higher than your ways, and my thoughts than your thoughts" (Isaiah 55:9).[13]

Having said all of this, we should not forget that God is also immanent. He is present *with* His creation. While God is not a part of creation as in pantheism, He has not removed Himself from the created order, as in deism. God came to meet with Moses on the mountain, to give him the commandments: "Thus you shall say to the house of Jacob . . . 'Now then, if you will indeed obey My voice and keep My covenant, then you shall be My own possession among all the peoples, for all the earth is Mine'" (Ex. 19:3, 5). The Psalmist writes: "Where can I go from Thy Spirit? Or where can I flee from Thy presence? If I ascend to heaven, Thou art there; if I make my bed in Sheol, behold, Thou art there. If I take the wings of the dawn, if I dwell in the remotest part of the sea, even there Thy hand will lead me, and Thy right hand will lay hold of me" (Psalm 139:7-10; cf. Jer. 23:23-24). God is specially present with His people: "For what great nation is there that has a god so near to it as is the Lord our God whenever we call on Him?" (Deut. 4:7). Jesus took on human flesh and "dwelt among us" (John 1:14), promising that He would be with us "always, even to the end of the age" (Matt. 28:20). Of course, the Holy Spirit "came from heaven" to be with us (Acts 2:2). In effect, God is with us — *immanent* — in the Person of the Holy Spirit. "Our physical bodies serve as the temple of the Holy Spirit (I Cor. 6:19; II Cor. 6:16)."[14] God is so near that He can hear our words and judge our actions. Peter accused Ananias of lying to the Holy Spirit (Acts 5:3). He went on to say: "You have not lied to men, but to God" (v. 4).

The transcendence (God is *distinct from* us) and immanence

---

13. Gary North, *Unconditional Surrender: God's Program for Victory* (2nd ed.; Tyler TX: Institute for Christian Economics, 1983), pp. 11-12.

14. Gary North, *The Dominion Covenant: Genesis* (Tyler, TX: Institute for Christian Economics, 1982), p. 433.

(God is *near to* us) of God are not contradictory concepts.[15] Immanence is consistent with God's transcendence, omnipresence, and omnipotence. John Frame writes:

> These two attributes do not conflict with one another. God is close *because* he is Lord. He is Lord, and thus free to make his power felt everywhere we go. He is Lord, and thus able to reveal himself clearly to us, distinguishing himself from all mere creatures. He is Lord, and therefore the most central fact of our experience, the least avoidable, the most verifiable.[16]

Escape from God's Judgment

The New Ager must keep a personal God out of his world. A personal God who sees and judges what man does is banned by those who want to live independent, autonomous (self-legislating) lives, free from the restrictions of a holy God. He is defined out of existence. When King David was confronted by Nathan with his sin, David's confession brought him back to reality: God sees and judges all things. There is no escape from the gaze of God: "Against Thee, Thee only, I have sinned, and done what is evil in Thy sight, so that Thou art justified when Thou dost speak, and blameless when Thou dost judge" (Psalm 51:4a).

> Here David acknowledges the reality of that guilt and notes two very important factors. First he notes that the sin is *ever* before him. It hounds him and pursues him. He sees it wherever he goes. He cannot rid himself of the memory. Like Lady Macbeth, the spot is indelible. Second, he notes that he has done evil in the sight of God. Thus, David not only sees his sin but he realizes it has not escaped the notice of God.[17]

---

15. Sutton, *That You May Prosper*, chapter 1.

16. "God and Biblical Language," *God's Inerrant Word: An International Symposium on the Trustworthiness of Scripture*, ed., John Warwick Montgomery (Minneapolis, MN: Bethany Fellowship, 1974), p. 173.

17. R. C. Sproul, *The Psychology of Atheism* (Minneapolis, MN: Bethany Fellowship, 1974), pp. 128-29.

Most Americans will not give up God, or at least their view of God. So how do the New Agers allow for God and at the same time deny Him? How do they recruit millions of "God-fearing" Americans to the New Age world view? One way is to identify the creation and/or the creature with God. "Yes, there is a god. In fact, you are a god. You become the judge and the lawgiver. You, as a god, know what's best for you. In a sense you can have your god and deny Him too." Rudyard Kipling's quip that "East is East and West is West, and never the twain shall meet"[18] is obsolete in the world of New Age. The impersonal god of the East has come West.

2. Divinization: Humanity, like all creation, is an extension of this divine oneness and shares its essential being. Thus, humanity is divine.

New Agers believe in some form of "chain of being" or "continuity of being,"[19] the idea that man and God are one essence, and

---

18. Kipling, "The Ballad of East and West."

19. "The universe was conceived as a 'great chain of Being,' starting with the completely real being, the One, or God, or the Idea of the Good, whose very nature overflowed into lesser realms of being, such as the world of Ideas, human beings, animals, inanimate objects, down to matter, 'the last faint shadow of reality. . . .'

"In this theory, the aim of human existence was seen as an attempt to move up the ladder of existence, to become more real. To accomplish this, men were to direct their interests and attention to what was above them on the 'great chain of Being.' By philosophizing they could liberate themselves from the sense world, and become more and more part of the intelligible world. The more one could understand, the more one would become like what one understood. Ultimately, if successful, one would reach the culmination of the 'journey of the mind to God,' by a mystical union with the One. Thus the final end of seeking to understand the nature of reality would be to become absorbed by what is most real, and to lose all of one's individuality which merely represents lesser degrees of reality. Through philosophizing, through art, and through mystic experience of unity with the One, [an individual found] the path to human salvation, and of liberation from the lesser reality of sensory and material worlds." Avrum Stroll and Richard H. Popkin, *Introduction to Philosophy* (2nd ed.; New York: Holt, Rinehart and Winston, 1972), pp. 100-101.

that in time, through an evolutionary process or reincarnation, man becomes divine. Writes Ray Sutton:

> Life according to this system is a *continuum*. At the top is the purest form of deity. At the very bottom is the least pure. They only differ in *degree*, not in kind. God is a *part of* creation. Man, who is somewhere in the middle of the continuum, is god in another "form." In other words, god is just a "super" man, and man is not a god . . . yet![20]

This is an old pagan belief. Modern New Age humanism did not pull it out of thin air. It is the revival of the mythical Olympian gods of ancient Greece. Sutton continues: "Such gods were not truly divine in the Biblical sense. They were not distinct from the creation. They married, committed adultery with other gods, came down to earth and committed more adultery with people, and so on. They were just an extension of man."[21] We also see this extension of divine oneness in the "familiar *totem pole* image, the organizing symbol of the American Indians, which is found in most religions of the world in some form or another."[22]

Again, those who espoused a "dominion theology" long before the positive confession movement began to pick up the language of visible victory have spoken against the idea of a "chain of being," "continuity of being," or a "little gods" theology. As was pointed out, the language of some of the positive confession preachers is at best sloppy. But on this "little gods" doctrine, no one can accuse Christian reconstructionists of being anything but forthright: they do not believe that man is a little god, that he can

---

20. *That You May Prosper*, p. 37.
21. *Ibid.* Mormonism is a modern revival of these pagan myths. Mormon doctrine teaches that man, with the proper striving, will one day become a god: "God was once as we are now, and is an exalted man. . . . Here then, is eternal life—to know the only wise and true God; and you have got to learn how to be Gods yourselves, and to be kings and priests to God, the same as all Gods have done before you." Joseph Smith, Jr., *King Follett Discourse*, pp. 8-10. "As Man is, God was, As God is, Man may become." *Ibid.*, p. 9, note by Lorenzo Smith. These Mormon references are from Josh McDowell and Don Stewart, *Handbook of Today's Religions* (San Bernardino, CA: Here's Life Publishers, 1983), pp. 69-70.
22. Sutton, *That You May Prosper*, p. 36 .

become a god, or that man is "an exact duplicate of God." Reconstructionists have taught over and over again that there is a fundamental Creator/creature distinction.

The Meaning of "Deification"[23]

We should, however, at least examine how these men use these terms. Some of the most orthodox church fathers used similar phrases but meant something different from the way present New Agers use them. They too spoke of the "deification" of man in Christ. Athanasius,[24] in a famous statement from his classic work, *On the Incarnation of the Word of God,* wrote: "The Word was made man in order that we might be made gods." David Chilton makes this point:

> The Christian doctrine of *deification* (cf. Ps. 82:6; John 10:34-36; Rom. 8:29-30; Eph. 4:13, 24; Heb. 2:10-13; 12:9-10; 2 Pet. 1:4; 1 John 3:2) is generally known in the Western churches by the terms *sanctification* and *glorification*, referring to man's full inheritance of the image of God. This doctrine (*which has absolutely nothing in common with pagan realistic theories of the continuity of being, humanistic notions about man's "spark of divinity," or Mormon polytheistic fables regarding human evolution into godhood* [emphasis ours]) is universal throughout the writings of the Church Fathers; see, e.g., Georgios I. Mantzaridis, *The Deification of Man: St. Gregory*

---

23. For a detailed discussion of deification, the reader is encouraged to study Robert M. Bowman, Jr., "Ye Are Gods?: Orthodox and Heretical Views on the Deification of Man," *Christian Research Journal* (Winter/Spring 1987), pp. 18-22.

24. Athanasius (c. 296-373) led the theological battle against Arianism, a heresy that denied the eternality of Jesus Christ the Son of God as the Logos. Arianism taught that Jesus was only a subordinate being, that He was not the Second Person of the Trinity. Athanasius challenged Arius and the Arians during most of the fourth century by teaching the eternal Sonship of the Logos (Jesus, John 1:1), the direct creation of the world by God (Gen. 1:1; Col. 1:17-23), and the redemption of the world and men by God in Christ. A good dose of the Athanasian Creed would go a long way in helping present day cultists. See Appendix C.

Palamas and the Orthodox Tradition, Liadain Sherrard, trans. (Crestwood, NY: St. Vladimir's Seminary Press, 1984).[25]

The term "deification" was used by some in the early church to mean *sanctification* and *glorification.* Athanasius, one of the most orthodox church fathers, in using "deification," did not mean that man becomes a god or evolves into God. He did not suffer persecution, decade after decade, from the heretical Arian party because he believed in "man into God." He was persecuted because he believed that Jesus was the *only* God-Man over against the Arians who held that Jesus was only man. There was never any consideration that Athanasius ever taught that man evolved into a god.

Man, as a new creature in Christ, reflects Jesus' perfect *humanity.* Man was created as the image of God, to reflect His glory. When Adam fell, the image of God was disturbed, though not completely lost. In Christ, we are restored to the image of God, and through our lives we reflect more and more the image of God. We more and more reflect the *glory* of God. This increasing reflection of the image of God is called glorification, or, in the language of the church fathers, "deification."

The quotations found in Hunt's book under the sections, "The Deification of Man," "Exact Duplicates of God?," "A Lie Whose Time Has Come," and " 'Ye are gods,' "[26] show how negligent some popular teachers and preachers have been. But is Dave Hunt's interpretation of Psalm 82:6 and John 10:34 correct? First, we will look at his interpretation, and then we will compare it with numerous Bible scholars who have written extensive commentaries on the texts in question.

---

25. David Chilton, *The Days of Vengeance: An Exposition of the Book of Revelation* (Tyler, TX: Dominion Press, 1987), p. 278n.

26. Dave Hunt and T. A. McMahon, *The Seduction of Christianity: Spiritual Discernment in the Last Days* (Eugene, OR: Harvest House, 1985), pp. 80-90.

Hunt on "Little Gods"

Mr. Hunt gives a very good analysis of how man rebelled against God, and in his rebellion desired to become a god unto himself. Jehovah's status as God was rejected, Hunt tells us, and man, taking his cue from Satan, established himself as a rival to God's Word. But is this really the point of the passages in Psalm 82:1-6 (especially v. 6) and John 10:22-39 (especially vv. 34-38)? Hunt thinks so:

> If man is not intended to be a god, then why did Jesus quote Psalm 82:6 to His accusers? He was doing two things: 1) demonstrating that they didn't understand their own Scriptures, so were in no condition to condemn Him for saying that He was God; and 2) showing them the depths and horror of their rebellion.[27]

Nearly everything that Mr. Hunt says in this passage concerning what Jesus was saying is correct, and we agree with him. As a general analysis of man's rebellion and his attempt to shake off his own creaturehood and sin, Hunt's appraisal of Jesus' statement is quite good. But Hunt's subsequent analysis of the *meaning* of Jesus' remarks does not fit the context of Jesus' discussion with the Pharisees in John 10:34-36 and His use of Psalm 82:6.

> Jesus was not complimenting the Jews of His day, but reminding them of their rebellion against the true God. Indeed we are gods, just as Jesus said, but it isn't good. Through rebellion man has broken free from God and is now a little god on his own. It is a terrible thing to be called "gods," to be identified with demons who have rebelled against God and are seeking to reign in His place.[28]

Jesus was discussing His deity with the Pharisees, something which they denied. He was using a comparison: If something is true in the lesser case, then it stands to reason that it is true in the greater case. He was saying, "If you Pharisees really believe the

---

27. *Ibid.*, p. 87.
28. *Idem.*

Bible when it states that God ordained rulers under the Old Covenant as 'gods, to whom the word of God came' (John 10:35), then
how can it be blasphemy for the 'Word' who 'became flesh and
dwelt among us' to be called God?" (John 1:1, 14). Jesus was *not*
answering the Pharisees on what they thought of *themselves*. Hunt
obscures the meaning of Jesus' battle with the Pharisees. The
issue was *Jesus'* divinity, not the supposed divinity of the
Pharisees. Again, Jesus was dealing with who *He* is, based on
what the *rulers in the Old Testament* had been. Hunt even hints at
this when he writes: "Psalm 82 does not say, 'Ye shall *become* gods,'
as Mormons hope, but 'Ye *are* gods.' So whatever is meant by this
statement, it refers to something that humans already *are*, not to
some new status that we will eventually *attain*."[29] Jesus did not say,
"They *said*, 'We are gods.' " It was *God* who called them "gods . . .
sons of the Most High." This is quite different from the passage
Hunt quotes to support his interpretation: "*I* [Satan] will make
myself like the Most High" (Isa. 14:14). Here Satan declared what
he wanted to become. The passage in Psalm 82 describes what
already *is* an established fact: *some* men are *elohim*, gods. The
crucial question is: Who and what kind of gods are they? Something is going on in this passage that Mr. Hunt fails to see.

I wonder how Dave Hunt would respond to Charles
Spurgeon's comment on Psalm 82:6? Spurgeon wrote: "The greatest honour was thus put upon them; they were delegated gods,
clothed for a while with a little of that authority by which the Lord
judges among the sons of men."[30] No one would accuse Spurgeon
of Mormonism, demonism, or New Age philosophy.

---

29. *Ibid.*, p. 86.
30. *The Treasury of David: An Expository and Devotional Commentary on the Psalms*, 7
vols. (Grand Rapids, MI: Guardian Press, [1870-1885] 1976), vol. 4, p. 41.
Spurgeon goes on to comment: "This was their *ex-officio* character, not their moral
or spiritual relationship. There must be some government among men, and as
angels are not sent to dispense it, God allows men to rule over men, and endorses
their office, so far at least that the prostitution of it becomes an insult to his own
prerogatives. Magistrates would have no right to condemn the guilty if God had not
sanctioned the establishment of government, the administration of law, and the execution of sentences. Here the Spirit speaks most honourably of these offices, even
when [He] censures the officers; and thereby teaches us to render honour to whom
honour is due, honour to the office even if we award censure to the office-bearer."

It seems that the Hebrew term for "gods" (*elohim*) in Psalm 82:6 is a reference to those who *exercise judicial authority in God's name*. Keep in mind that *Yahweh*, God's personal name, is not used here. It is quite clear by Charles Spurgeon's extended comments on the Psalm that this is what he understood the text to mean. It's an interpretation that Hunt fails even to mention. His readers are left with the impression that no other interpretation is even possible than his own, namely, that becoming a "god" in this sense is a wicked thing, a sign of man's rebellion. In fact, nearly every commentator we consulted on Psalm 82 understands that "gods" has reference to civil magistrates. H. C. Leupold translates the Hebrew *elohim* ("gods") as "rulers." He goes on to comment:

> This is the last statement God is represented as saying in the assembly of God. What He had said to the judges or rulers was in effect that they were "gods." The same word is used which was employed in v. 1. That is, He had given them a position that was analogous to His in that He made them administrators of justice, His justice.[31]

If we re-read the quotations from the alleged "New Age seducers" cited by Dave Hunt in *The Seduction of Christianity* in the light of Leupold's comments and the comments to follow, it's at least *possible* that these "positive confessionists" were describing how Christians ought to rule in God's name.[32] Keep in mind that we are not defending these men. We are equally suspicious of what they mean. The reference to "gods" in Psalm 82:6 is very specific and any use beyond the limits of the Psalm is inappropriate and borders on the heretical.

Too often we fail to scrutinize the Bible for its own interpretation. Experienced Bible commentators draw on the use of a term and how it is used throughout Scripture to reach their conclusions on what a passage means. Dave Hunt has not done this with respect to Psalm 82:6. Nowhere does he justify his interpretation,

---

31. Leupold, *Exposition of Psalms* (Grand Rapids, MI: Baker, [1959], 1969), p. 595.
32. Groothuis, *Unmasking the New Age*, pp. 147-48.

either by quoting similar Scripture passages or by quoting Bible expositors who are well respected in the Christian community. Therefore, we should not be too quick to look for a novel interpretation, when so many capable and gifted men throughout the centuries have understood "gods" to mean civil magistrates who rule in God's name. Thomas Scott,[33] F. S. Delitzsch,[34] J. J. Stewart Perowne,[35] David Dickson,[36] Joseph Addison Alexander,[37] William S. Plumer,[38]

---

33. "The rulers of Israel, as immediately appointed by JEHOVAH to be his representatives, to judge according to his law, and to be types of his Anointed, were especially honoured with this high title, 'Ye are gods.'" Scott, *The Holy Bible Containing the Old and New Testaments, According to the Authorized Version; With Explanatory Notes, Practical Observations and Copious References,* 3 vols. (New York: Collins and Hannay, 1832), vol. 2, p. 182.

34. "[T]hey are really *elohim* [gods] by the grace of God." C. F. Keil and F. S. Delitzsch, *Commentary on the Old Testament: Psalms,* 3 vols. (Grand Rapids, MI: Eerdmans, 1980), vol. 2, p. 404.

35. "He declares that it was He Himself who called them to their office, and gave them the name, together with the dignity which they enjoy. (This interpretation falls in readily with our Lord's words in John x. 34.)" Perowne, *The Book of Psalms,* 2 vols. (Grand Rapids, MI: Zondervan, [1878] 1966), vol. 2, pp. 106-7.

36. "Princes, magistrates, chief rulers, and judges, have allowance from God, of honour, power, and strength, tribute and revenues, for the better discharge of their office under him: *I have said, Ye are gods, and all of you are children of the most High*; that is, I have put the image of my superiority on you, and given you pre-eminence of place, power, and gifts, over others in my name." Dickson, *Psalms,* 2 vols. (London: Banner of Truth Trust [1653-5] 1959), vol. 2, p. 62.

37. "Their sin did not consist in arrogating to themselves too high a dignity, but in abusing it by malversation, and imagining that it relieved them from responsibility, whereas it really enhanced it. They were God's representatives, but for that very reason they were bound to be pre-eminently just and faithful." Alexander, *The Psalms Translated and Explained* (Grand Rapids, MI: Baker [1873] 1975), pp. 350-51.

38. "The office of the magistrate was as dignified and awful [full of awe] as any of them claimed it to be. They were invested with the character of representatives of God. Therefore they acted under the highest responsibility. Their name was dreadful; so was their position; and, if their power was abused, their doom should be dreadful also." Plumer, *Psalms: A Critical and Expository Commentary with Doctrinal and Practical Remarks* (Edinburgh: Banner of Truth Trust, [1867] 1975), p. 782.

John Calvin,[39] Matthew Henry,[40] Matthew Poole,[41] and Woodrow Michael Kroll[42] all take the position that "gods" in Psalm 82:6 refers to civil magistrates who rule in God's name. There was only one commentator among those we consulted who took a different view. He offered three possible interpretations, none of which reflected Dave Hunt's view.[43]

New Testament commentators interpret John 10:22-39 in a similar way: "The passage refers to the judges of Israel, and the expression 'gods' is applied to them in the exercise of their high and God-given office."[44] This is not an isolated interpretation.

---

39. "God has invested judges with a sacred character and title. This the prophet concedes; but he, at the same time, shows that this will afford no support and protection to wicked judges." Calvin, *Commentary on the Book of Psalms*, 5 vols. (Grand Rapids, MI: Baker, 1979), vol. 3, p. 334.

40. "The dignity of their character is acknowledged (*v.* 6): *I have said, You are gods.* They have been honoured with the name and title of gods. God himself called them so in the statute against treasonable words Exod. xxii. 28, *Thou shalt not revile the gods.*" Henry, *Matthew Henry's Commentary on the Whole Bible*, 6 vols. (Old Tappan, NJ: Fleming H. Revell, [1712] n.d.), vol. 3, p. 552.

41. "*I have said, Ye are gods*; I have given you my name and power to rule your people in my stead. *All of you*; not only the rulers of Israel, but of all other nations; *for all powers are ordained by God*, Rom. xiii. 1. *Children of the Most High*; representing my person, and bearing both my name and lively characters of my majesty and authority, as *children* bear the name and image of their parents." Poole, *A Commentary on the Whole Bible*, 3 vols. (Edinburgh: Banner of Truth Trust [1685] 1972), vol. 2, p. 132.

42. "But even though these men have held lofty positions, they must not forget that great men die, just as common men do. Even God's representatives in judgment must one day die and face judgment themselves (Heb. 9:27)." Kroll, "Psalms," *Liberty Bible Commentary*, Old Testament (Lynchburg, VA: The Old Time Gospel Hour, 1982), pp. 1086-87.

43. "The crux for the interpreter is the repeated reference to 'gods,' who are reprimanded for injustice. Our Lord's reference to verse 6 in John 10:34f. leaves their identity an open question." Derek Kidner, *Psalms 75-150: A Commentary* (Downers Grove, IL: InterVarsity Press, 1975), p. 296.

44. Leon Morris, *The Gospel According to John* (Grand Rapids, MI: Eerdmans, 1971), p. 525. Elohim "is translated 'the judges' in the Authorized Version [King James Version] in Exodus xxi. 6, xxii. 8, 9, 9, and in the margin of Exodus

Homer Kent, who writes from an eschatological perspective similar to Hunt's, is a representative of the position articulated by the Old Testament commentators listed above:

> Jesus based his answer on such passages as Psalm 82:6 and Exodus 4:16 and 7:1, where God's spokesmen who minister his word are called "gods." His point was that if Scripture can term such men "gods" because they were the agents to interpret divine revelation, how could Christ be a blasphemer by claiming the title "Son of God" when he was sent from heaven as the very revelation of God himself?[45]

In all of our discussion thus far, we have shown that the term "gods," *elohim* in the Hebrew, refers *solely* to magistrates, rulers, and judges. The reference is to a God-ordained *office*. It is not a position that *all* Christians hold. In this sense, it is inappropriate and exegetically improper to apply this text to *all* Christians. Thus, since there is so much confusion today over what the Psalmist meant in Psalm 82:6 and what Jesus meant in John 10:34, 36, Christians from all camps should avoid the use of the terms "deification," "little gods," or anything else that smacks of Mormonism and New Age philosophy. Those within the positive confession camp should work on their Christology and anthropology before they get into any more semantic trouble.[46]

---

xxii. 28, while the singular is employed in I Samuel ii. 25. In all these passages except the last the Revised Version reads 'God' in the text and 'the judges' in the margin, while in the last the marginal reading is in the singular, 'the judge.' *There does not seem much doubt but that the judicial processes are envisaged in all these passages, however we translate the term. Nor need we doubt that the judicial process is seen as something of a high dignity and to be performed only as in the sight of God.*" Leon Morris, *The Biblical Doctrine of Judgment* (Grand Rapids, MI: Eerdmans, 1960), pp. 33-4. Emphasis added. See his entire discussion, pp. 33-36.

45. Homer A. Kent, Jr., *Light in the Darkness: Studies in the Gospel of John* (Grand Rapids, MI: Baker, 1974), p. 144.

46. This is being done. See Bowman, "Ye Are Gods?," p. 22, note 14.

Rightly understood, however, Psalm 82:6 shows us that God delegates dominion to some men to rule in His name. The church has always held this position. It has been only in recent decades that the church has abandoned this belief, one of the most basic of biblical doctrines: dominion *under* God. George Hutcheson, a Scottish Puritan scholar of the mid-17th century, drawing out the implications of John 10:36 (and Psalm 82:6), gets to the heart of the issue when he writes:

> Albeit magistrates be but men like their brethren, yet in respect of their office they have the glorious title of gods conferred upon them, as being his vicegerents [deputies of a king or magistrate], and as bearing some stamp of his authority and dominion; therefore saith the scripture, I said, ye are gods. This should both engage them to see to their qualifications and the exercise of their power; and others, to reverence and honour them.[47]

Rulers must never forget that they must not abandon God as they exercise dominion. The majestic title of Elohim does not allow God's subjects to be a law unto themselves, ruling independent of His lordship over all men and creation. The religion of humanism places man at the center of the universe as an independent sovereign, ruling and overruling according to his self-made law. The Psalmist declares their just end: " 'Nevertheless you will die like men, and fall like any one of the princes.' Arise, O God, judge the earth! For it is Thou who dost possess all the nations" (Psalm 82:8). No exalted title will save them.

3. Higher consciousness: Transformation of humanity is brought about through techniques that can be applied to mind, body, and spirit.[48]

---

47. *The Gospel of John* (Edinburgh: Banner of Truth Trust [1657] 1972), p. 215.
48. Examples of such techniques include meditation, yoga, chanting, creative visualization, hypnosis, and submission to a guru.

This is where much of contemporary Christianity falls into error. We mentioned that Dave Hunt's books should be read on two levels. The first level is his critique of the methods some prominent ministers are using to help Christians "get closer to God" or to "take dominion" through verbal authority.[49] Man does not speak anything into existence; God did that during the creation week. The basis of dominion under God is *ethics*, not magic; obedience, not vocalization. We agree with Dave Hunt when he writes:

> We do not believe the leaders of the Positive Confession movement are deliberately involved in sorcery. However, the terminology, while sounding biblical, promotes concepts that cannot be found in the Bible, but are found in occult literature and practice. Moreover, some of the Positive Confession leaders not only admit but teach that the methods, laws, and principles they use are also used successfully by occultists. Nowhere in the Bible does it indicate or even imply that the people of God are to use the same methods or powers as the pagans.[50]

Dispensationalism's Revolt Against Biblical Ethics

We admit that their practices border on the mystical rather than the ethical. But this may not be the result of seduction by a New Age philosophy. The law of God as the standard for a Christian's sanctification has not been popular with the church for over a century. When the law of God is jettisoned, some other standard fills the void. David Chilton writes that when an objective standard outside of man is no longer available, man then "relates to God by using magic or manipulative techniques. Metaphysical Theology is man-centered, humanistic theology, or, more pre-

---

49. Language is central to dominion. Adam "named" the animals (Gen 2:19). Judges "pronounce" sentences. They "speak" (*diction*) judgment (*juris*). Of course, this is quite different from using words to create out of nothing.
50. Hunt and McMahon, *The Seduction of Christianity*, p. 101.

cisely, *anthro*pology. This is why there is such an emphasis on individual experience, and why what goes on under the name of evangelism is often more concerned with the subjective feelings of the believer than with the objective gospel of Jesus Christ. . . ."51

One of the most prominent doctrines of "dominion theology" and Christian reconstruction is the belief that the whole Bible is applicable for the Christian today; that man pleases God through obedience; that dominion comes through God's grace, giving us the ability and will to obey His law in love for Him and service to man. There are dozens of books written by reconstructionists of one variety or another that support this claim.

There is a curious bit of irony here. For nearly a century, dispensational premillennialists have been telling us that the Christian is no longer obligated to keep the law of God. As one dispensational writer tells us, "the Bible does give us broad commands to do good to the general public."52 But broad commands are not enough. Christians are looking for specifics. Keep telling Christians that the law does not matter, and they will find novel ways to please God. The Bible tells us that we show our love to God by keeping His commandments. Dave Hunt, Hal Lindsey, and Jimmy Swaggart are all dispensationalists. They do not believe that the law of God as outlined in all the Bible is appropriate for the Christian to use today. They make a radical division between law and grace,53 Old and New Testament, and Israel and the Church.54

---

51. Chilton, "Between the Covers of Power for Living," p. 4
52. John Walvoord, "Our Future Hope: Eschatology and Its Role in the Church," *Christianity Today* (February 6, 1987), p. 6-I.
53. The real distinction is between "works" and "grace," or the "works of the law" and "grace."
54. The Bible assures us that gentile believers were brought into the already existing church (Eph. 2:11-22; Rom. 11). The church existed in the wilderness: "This is he [Moses], that was in the church [Gr., *ekklesia*] with the angel which spake to him in the mount Sinai and with our fathers: who received the lively oracles to give unto us" (Acts 7:38, KJV).

Millions of Christians were raised on this teaching. The chickens have now come home to roost, and they have now laid some colossal theological eggs. If a person does not keep the law to please God, then he must look elsewhere. So, then, the seduction of Christianity has not come so much from the New Agers, who were little known as recently as 1976, when Gary North's *None Dare Call It Witchcraft* first appeared. The seduction of Christianity has been in the midst of the camp of those who are New Age humanism's most vocal critics.

Hal Lindsey, a critic of "dominion theology," has a chapter in his best-selling book *Satan is Alive and Well on Planet Earth* (1972) that describes "legalism" as the Christian's obligation to keep the law. He goes on to write:

> Legalism—seeking to live for God by the principle of the law —is the first and the worst doctrine of demons. It is the dent in your armor at which Satan will chip away until he has a hole big enough to drive a truck through. I don't know another doctrinal distortion that has been more devastating to believers. The awful thing is that it can sidetrack a mature believer as well as a young one. In fact, this demonic doctrine seems to find especially fertile soil in the life of a growing believer who is intent upon pleasing God in this life.[55]

Now, if Mr. Lindsey means by "legalism" that an individual is justified on the basis of keeping the law, then his warning is justified. But he seems to go beyond this traditional interpretation of the term. If he means that the Christian is not obligated to keep the objective, inscripturated law as a standard of righteousness for holy living, then he is out of accord with the testimony of Scripture.[56]

---

55. Hal Lindsey, *Satan is Alive and Well on Planet Earth* (Grand Rapids, MI: Zondervan, 1972), pp. 168-9.

56. Greg L. Bahnsen, *Theonomy in Christian Ethics* (rev. ed.; Phillipsburg, NJ: Presbyterian and Reformed, [1977] 1984); *By This Standard: The Authority of God's Law Today* (Tyler, TX: Institute for Christian Economics, 1985).

Lindsey tells us that "Grace emphasizes love as a motivation for obedience and service, but law uses a fear-threat motive."[57] This is only partially true. Perfect love does cast out fear (1 John 4:18), but this is no open door for lawlessness or the abandonment of the law of God found in Scripture as the standard of righteousness. "The fear of the Lord is the beginning of wisdom" (Psalm 110:11; see Prov. 1:7). We are not given a license to sin that "grace might increase" (Rom. 6:1). Jesus tells us how we can know if we are loving Him: "If you love Me, you will keep My commandments" (John 14:15). Remember, the law is not the way we are *justified* by God. The law is, however, an *objective standard* to which we conform our thoughts, words, and deeds. Paul describes love in Romans 13:8-10 in terms of obedience to the law. One way that you know if you are loving your neighbor is by looking at the law. Paul writes in another place that through faith "we establish the law" (Rom. 3:31).

But Lindsey is not officially lawless. He tells us that "[t]he answer to a righteous and obedient life is to walk in the Spirit and walk by faith in His ability to produce God's righteousness and obedience to His laws within you."[58] What are these "laws within you"? Where did these laws come from? How are they different from God's inscripturated laws? Lindsey is correct in telling us that it cannot be the conscience, for conscience is not a "reliable standard of conduct" because "it can easily be seared."[59] Rather, it is the immediate guidance of the Holy Spirit. Lindsey even goes beyond traditional dispensational theology by never telling the Christian that at least he is obligated to keep New Testament commands over against Old Testament commands. Greg Bahnsen describes this as *"Spiritual* antinomianism," a view that teaches

---

57. *Ibid.*, p. 179.
58. *Ibid.*, p. 177.
59. *Ibid.*, p. 171. For a discussion of the conscience as an inadequate standard of authority see Gary DeMar, *God and Government: The Restoration of the Republic* (Atlanta, GA: American Vision, 1986), pp. 47-51.

that the Christian needs guidance for the holy living expected by
God, but it would deny that such guidance comes from a written
(or verbally defined) code. Ethical direction is rather found in the
internal promptings of the Holy Spirit. . . . Quite expectedly,
such thinking leads quickly to *subjectivism* in Christian ethics, with
each man doing whatever he claims "the Spirit" has prompted
him to do—despite the fact that it conflicts with what the Spirit
has prompted others to do and (worse) with what the Spirit has
revealed once-for-all in the Scriptures. The Bible teaches us that
the Spirit works through *the word*, not speaking or directing from
Himself (John 16:13-15). The Spirit works to fulfill *the law* in us
(Rom. 8:4-9). The abiding of the Spirit in believers brings obedience to God's *commandments* (1 John 3:24).[60]

Denying an Objective Standard

Some positive confession preachers unwittingly have opened
themselves to the subjectivism of the human potential movement,
just as Dave Hunt and others have opened themselves to the
pessimism that abounds among the humanists. Why? Because
neither group has had an objective standard to measure righteousness. Rushdoony makes this observation: "To deny the permanence of God's
law is to fall . . . ultimately into Manichaeanism."[61] Dispensationalists have been telling Christians for over a century and a
half that the law of God as found in the Old Testament and the
gospels no longer applies to the church today. So, where does the
church get its law? What objective law-word does the church have
for the State, meaning civil government?

For some, law is based on feelings. The individual has internal
promptings that guide him. He looks to himself for direction, to
the movement of the Holy Spirit on his or her spirit. Law becomes
subjective. What's right for one person might not be right for
someone else. The end of such a philosophy is that old slogan, "If

---

60. Bahnsen, *By This Standard*, p. 299.
61. R. J. Rushdoony, *The Institutes of Biblical Law* (Nutley, NJ: Craig Press,
1973), p. 654.

it feels good, do it." Or "do your own thing." It should not surprise us that some have turned to the subjectivism of the "positive thinking" movement: think and grow rich, the power of positive thinking, possibility thinking, etc. Furthermore, with this internal-only view of law the church cannot address the world on social issues.

Dispensationalists also do not have an objective law-word for church and society. This is why they have abandoned the world to humanism's power-seekers. They have no standard by which the Christian ought to live as he moves in the realms of education, law, politics, and economics. God's law no longer speaks today. It will speak once again only in the Jewish millennium. The church must be content with a "natural law" ethic.[62] This is evident in dispensational social ethics. Consider the position of Dr. Norman Geisler, a well respected representative of dispensational theology, a professor at Dallas Theological Seminary, one of dispensationalism's leading academic institution:

> While premillennialists, especially dispensationalists, do not believe that Christians are living under the Old Testament Law today, this in no way means they are antinomian. To be sure, dispensational premillenarians insist that the Old Testament Law was given only to the Jews and not to the Gentiles. And they argue that the Old Testament Law has been done away by Christ (2 Cor. 3:7-13; Gal. 3:24-25). However, most premillenarians recognize that God has not left Himself without a witness in that He has revealed a moral law in the hearts[63] and consciences of all

---

62. For a popular critique of natural law see Gary DeMar, *Ruler of the Nations: Biblical Principles for Government* (Atlanta, GA: American Vision, 1987), pp. 47-51.

63. This is not what Romans 2:14-15 says. It specifically states that Gentiles "show the *work* of the Law written in their hearts" (2:15). The context is explicit: Those who do not have the law as Israel did cannot deny that they are guilty before God. The law works on their conscience; therefore, they have no excuse for their sin even though they do not have the details of law before them. This use of the law tells a person whether he is guilty or not guilty before God. John Murray writes: "Paul does not say that the law is written upon their hearts. He refrains from this form of statement apparently for the same reason as in verse 14 he had said that the Gentiles 'do the things of the law' and not that they did or fulfilled the law. Such expressions as 'fulfilling the law' and 'the law written upon the heart' are reserved for a state of heart and mind and will far beyond that

men (Rom. 2:14-15). . . . Government is not based on special revelation, such as the Bible. It is based on God's general revelation to all men. . . . Thus civil law, based as it is in natural moral law, lays no specifically religious obligation on man.[64]

Is it any wonder that the church has been on the outside looking in? Why are Christians surprised that the world aborts millions of unborn babies every year? Nothing objective is thought to rule the world, least of all God. For the Christian, dispensationalists have preached for over a century, the only thing that really matters is the "spiritual." Heaven is all-important. Christians therefore have retreated from this world psychologically in the face of their declining cultural influence, as they wait for the rescue from history promised in the rapture. This pessimism regarding the future of their own earthly efforts has reinforced modern Christians' antinomianism, meaning the rejection of God's law as binding in this dispensation. Again, Rushdoony comments:

Antinomianism, having denied the law, runs into mysticism and pietism. As it faces a world of problems, it has no adequate answer. To supply this lack, antinomianism very early became

---

predicated of unbelieving Gentiles." *The Epistle to the Romans*, 2 vols. (Grand Rapids, MI: Eerdmans, 1959), vol. 1, pp. 74-75.

Dr. Geisler wants to maintain that this single verse is grounds for establishing that the "work of the Law" is sufficient for the *unbeliever* to build an entire social ethic independent of the Bible. Nations, whether Christian or non-Christian, establish governments. Does this mean that nations are free to establish the standard by which they will rule? What are the limits of power? How much tax should be collected? Should the State control education? Is homosexuality a crime? If it is, what should the punishment be if two men are caught in the act? Is bestiality wrong? How about abortion? It's convenient to say that "government is not based on special revelation," but it is not much help when you must deal in particulars. General revelation does not give answers to specific ethical dilemmas.

Of course, Geisler's argument falls to pieces if the Gentiles mentioned in Romans 2 and 3 are *believing* Gentiles. See the insightful discussion by James B. Jordan in *The Sociology of the Church: Essays in Reconstruction* (Tyler, TX: Geneva Ministries, 1986), pp. 107-10.

64. "A Premillennial View of Law and Government," *The Best in Theology*, gen. ed., J. I. Packer (Carol Stream, IL: Christianity Today/Word, 1986), p. 259.

premillennial; its answer to the problems of the world was to postpone solutions to the "any moment return" of Christ. Antinomianism thus led to an intense interest in and expectation of Christ's return as the only solution to the world's problems, Christ's law being denied the status of an answer.[65]

Dave Hunt and other critics of dominion theology and Christian reconstruction have become pietists, retreating from the social problems of this world. Some positive confession adherents have been seduced by elements of mysticism. What do Dave Hunt and those he criticizes have in common? *A denial of the law of God as a standard for righteous living.*

But many of the positive confession preachers are escaping from this antinomian trap. (Dave Hunt's attacks on them are important motivations in this defection from dispensational antinomianism to Christian reconstruction.) The law of God is being accepted for what it is: the law of *God*. The whole Bible is accepted as the standard for righteous living for individuals, families, churches, and civil governments. This is what Christian reconstructionists have been saying for a number of years, long before New Age humanism became popular and Dave Hunt began to write on the subject.[66]

4. Reincarnation, karma: Salvation is a multi-lifetime process of progression or digression.[67]

New Age humanism makes its "leap of being" from mere man to god through raising the state of consciousness, evolutionary development, reincarnation, or some combination of the three.

---

65. Rushdoony, *Institutes of Biblical Law*, p. 654.

66. Rushdoony, *Institutes of Biblical Law*, 1973; *Law and Society* (Vallecito, CA: Ross House Books, 1982); *Law and Liberty* (Tyler, TX: Thoburn Press, 1971); James B. Jordan, *The Law and the Covenant: An Exposition of Exodus 21-23* (Tyler, TX: Institute for Christian Economics, 1984); Greg L. Bahnsen, *Theonomy in Christian Ethics* and *By This Standard.*

67. "If one accumulates good karma, positive benefits accrue in later lives. Bad karma produces future punishments. Eventually one may leave the cycle of birth and rebirth entirely through the experience of enlightenment." Groothuis, *Unmasking the New Age*, p. 150.

Reincarnation has been popularized over the years through the writings of Edgar Cayce[68] and most recently, Shirley MacLaine. The Eastern variety of reincarnation would never have been accepted in the Christian West if it had not been stripped of the hideous concept of the "transmigration of the soul."

Reincarnation as it is usually understood in Hinduism states that all life is essentially one (monism): plant, animal, and human life are so interrelated that souls are capable of "transmigrating" from one form of life to another. A person could have been an animal, plant, or mineral in some previous existence. This version, however, is unpalatable to American tastes, so the movement of human souls is in the newer version limited to human bodies.[69]

Modern proponents of reincarnation have cleaned up the Eastern variety. You don't hear Shirley MacLaine telling people that she was a rock or a slug in a former life. The typical reincarnationist usually believes that he was once some exotic personality. This is not true reincarnationism. This is "I've always been a star" reincarnationism.

There are enough able Christian evaluations already on the subject.[70] Suffice it to say that Christian reconstructionists do not believe in any form of reincarnation (Heb. 9:27-28). And this is just the point. No one we know even hints at believing in reincarnation. Dave Hunt nowhere accuses anyone of believing in it. Yet reincarnation is foundational to New Age humanism. If recon-

---

68. For an insightful analysis and critique of Cayce's views see: Gary North, *Unholy Spirits: Occultism and New Age Humanism* (Ft. Worth, TX: Dominion Press, 1986), pp. 193-225. Cayce was an avid Bible student. It is reported that he tried to read through the Bible once each year. He tried to reconcile his occultism with the Bible and failed, ignoring Hebrews 9:26-27. See Phillip J. Swihart, *Reincarnation, Edgar Cayce & the Bible* (Downers Grove, IL: InterVarsity Press, 1975).

69. John Snyder, *Reincarnation vs. Resurrection* (Chicago, IL: Moody Press, 1984), p. 19.

70. Mark Albrecht, *Reincarnation: A Christian Critique of a New Age Doctrine* (Downers Grove, IL: InterVarsity Press, 1987); Robert A. Morey, *Death and the Afterlife* (Minneapolis, MN: Bethany House, 1984), pp. 182-3, 264-5; Pat Means, *The Mystical Maze* (San Bernardino, CA: Campus Crusade for Christ, 1976), pp. 238-40.

structionist theologians are being seduced by New Age humanism, then why haven't they adopted any of its central planks?
Why haven't they adopted monism (pantheism) or evolutionism?

Who's Really an Ally of the New Age?

It's possible that those who hold to a pessimistic earthly world
view can be seduced by some New Age premises. New Age humanists believe, as John Naisbitt says, that it is possible to re-
invent "the world we live in."[71] Christians who fail to counter this
secularized, man-centered, power-oriented religion will find
themselves unsuspecting allies with numerous militant humanist
groups. As we have already noted, the humanists fear Christians
oriented toward dominion far more than Christians oriented toward defeat.[72]

Christians may also be unwitting allies of the New Age in
another sense. If Christians retreat from the cultural issues of the
day, who will, humanly speaking, visibly control the future course
of history? If Christians won't, humanists will. Thus, Hunt's vision of the future becomes the worst kind of self-fulfilling prophecy when it is taken seriously by Christians. Christians retreat
because there is no hope. As more Christians retreat, there is less
hope. Finally, the whole cultural field is left to humanists who insist on taking us down the road to an international statist utopia.

Hunt's critique of Christian reconstruction and dominion theology is curiously one-sided. This is partly because his view of the
New Age is one-sided. Hunt concentrates on the upbeat, optimistic side of New Age humanism. But there is a pessimistic side
as well. Douglas Groothuis quotes from a California Democratic

---

71. Naisbitt, *Megatrends: Ten New Directions Transforming Our Lives* (New York:
Warner Books, 1982), p. ix.

72. See Frederick Edwords and Stephen McCabe, "Getting Out the Vote: Pat
Robertson and the Evangelicals," *The Humanist*, Volume 47, Number 3 (May/June
1987), pp. 5-10, 36; and *CovertAction*, Special Issue on the Religious Right, Number 27 (Spring 1987). We don't know who publishes *CovertAction*, but it's indexed
in the "Alternative Press Index." We don't want to fall prey to guilt by association,
but we think that tells us something about the publisher's political preferences.

platform whose wording was based on a New Age "Transformation Platform" (1982):

> Ultimately, all humanity must recognize the essential interconnectedness and interdependence of all human beings and all of nature—humanity has no other choice if we are to stop world annihilation.[73]

This apocalyptic and pessimistic strain of New Age thinking comes out in some aspects of the thought of Jeremy Rifkin, who is, according to Gary North, largely responsible for New Age infiltration into Christian circles.[74] Rifkin says that the law of Entropy "destroys the notion of history as progress." Rifkin describes the ecological crisis faced by people in the industrialized countries.

> We look around us only to find that the garbage and pollution are piling up in every quarter, oozing out of the ground, seeping into our rivers, and lingering in our air. Our eyes burn, our skin discolors, our lungs collapse, and all we can think of is retreating indoors and closing the shutters.[75]

Rifkin is hostile to the dominion mandate of Genesis.

> The fact is, we made a mistake. Our parents made a mistake and so did theirs. It began a long time ago when God said to the first of our kind, "You shall have dominion over the fish of the sea and over the birds of the air and over every living thing that moves upon the earth." We thought God meant for us to subdue the earth, to become its master.[76]

As a result, Christians have been responsible for the exploitation of the earth's resources, and have brought us to the mess we are now in. Of course, Rifkin is optimistic that things can change,

---

73. Groothuis, *Unmasking the New Age*, p. 122.

74. North, *Is the World Running Down? Crisis in the Christian Worldview* (Tyler, TX: Institute for Christian Economics, 1987).

75. Jeremy Rifkin, *Entropy: A New World View* (New York: Viking, 1980), p. 3.

76. Rifkin, *Declaration of a Heretic* (London: Routledge and Kegan Paul, 1985), p. 107.

once people stop trying to maintain the existing order and adopt the Entropy world view. But there is certainly a pessimistic thread to his argument. In fact, his whole point is to encourage people to adopt his world view in order to prevent ecological and political disaster.[77] As Gary North says, "Rifkin's outlook, *if we believe what he says about entropy and the universe,* leads to pessimism and retreat, not revolution."[78] Later, North describes him as a man without legitimate hope.[79]

Now, what happens when Rifkin comes to pessimistic premillennialists, telling them that the only way to turn things around is a "new economics" and a "new social order" and a "new politics"? Will all the pessimists be discerning enough to see the evil solutions that Rifkin proposes? It is at least possible that dispensational premillennialism will have prepared conservative Christians to capitulate to Rifkin's New Agism.

Conclusion

First, the Creator-creature distinction is foundational to Christian reconstruction. This is a radically anti-pantheistic doctrine. The idea that man could ever evolve into God is nowhere hinted at in any of the literature published by Christian reconstructionists.

Second, Dave Hunt's analysis of Psalm 82 and John 10 is in error. It is not supported by any Bible commentator that we know

---

77. There are some interesting connections here that Hunt, in his concentration on victory-oriented reconstructionists, has missed. Rifkin's book is endorsed by Senator Mark Hatfield, a left-wing evangelical Senator. Hatfield says,

> *Entropy: A New World View* explains, with sometimes disarming simplicity, the breakdown of the existing world order. It has compelled me to re-evaluate much of the safe and comfortable thinking which governs our day to day lives. This is an inspiring work. (Back of book jacket)

Hatfield is not a reconstructionist. In fact, he would doubtless be quite adamantly opposed to reconstruction. Yet, Hatfield has endorsed a New Age book, while no reconstructionist has done so. Will the real New Age sympathizer please stand up?

78. North, *Is the World Running Down?*, p. xxxiv.

79. *Ibid.*, chapter 5.

of. The texts that some apply to all Christians actually refer to man as a magistrate who represents God in the exercise of his high office.

Third, Dave Hunt sees no hope for the world because he does not have an objective standard by which to evaluate the world; thus the world cannot be directed in the areas of righteousness.

5

NEW AGE HUMANISM:
A KINGDOM COUNTERFEIT

In a stunningly brief period of time, a new and powerful world religion has swept across America and the entire planet. Popularly called the New Age Movement by its own leaders, this new religion is rapidly and dramatically reshaping man's views of God and the universe.[1]

The "New Age" is upon us! So say a good number of contemporary social-thinkers, Christian cult experts, and radio and television evangelists. The New Age Movement, we are told, will be used by the Antichrist to establish a "New World Religion." Much of the world will be duped by this "masterful political genius and leader."[2] But more than this, he will be considered a great "*spiritual teacher*."[3] In fact, "[s]omewhere, at this very moment, a man is perhaps being groomed for world leadership. He is to be Satan's man, the Antichrist. His number will be 666."[4] God's kingdom will fail during the so-called "Church Age," while Satan's kingdom will succeed. God's work is viewed as a failure. The power of God's Spirit manifested in millions of Christians throughout the world will not be enough to push back the advances of New Age humanism, an operation energized by the devil himself. Only the personal appearance of the Lord Jesus Christ and His reign on the earth will subvert the designs of the devil—or postpone them, in Hunt's view.

---

1. Texe Marrs, *Dark Secrets of the New Age: Satan's Plan for a One World Religion* (Westchester, IL: Crossway Books, 1987), p. 11.
2. *Ibid.*, p. 261.
3. *Idem.*
4. *Idem.*

This scenario of the "last days" is typical of many of the books that have come out criticizing the sinister designs of New Age humanism. It seems that this new form of secular humanism[5] is the final satanic conspiracy that will bring on the Great Tribulation, the rise of Antichrist, and the rapture of the saints.

Is there another explanation for these new humanistic expressions? Is it possible that, although New Age humanism is demonic, it really is no long-term threat to a healthy church? Could God, in fact, be using New Age humanism to spur His people on to kingdom work?

Instead of fearing New Age humanism, Christians should be working for the advancement of God's kingdom through the preaching of the gospel and the application of God's law to every area of life. The advances of New Age humanism are the result of Christians acting as if no good can be accomplished before Jesus returns to establish His millennial kingdom. The same could be said for the advances of the Social Gospel, communism, Islam, secular humanism, scientism, evolutionism, atheism, and every other "ism" that works to counter the effects of the gospel and copies the ideals of God's kingdom. We tend to blame the devil for our neglect. We should recall that paganism did not advance in Israel until Israel denied God.

In this chapter, we will show that the threats of New Age humanism are real. At the same time, we hope to demonstrate that *New Age humanism is simply a perverse counterfeit of biblical Christianity.* New Age humanism has advanced because the modern church has not been a diligent teacher of sound biblical doctrine, and at the same time, the modern church has not been receptive to the primary tenets of the Christian faith. This has led many Christians to adopt a smorgasbord view of religion. The counterfeit nature of Satan's kingdom cannot be recognized because few Christians realize the nature of the genuine kingdom now present and operating in the world.

---

5. "The New Age and secular humanism are more like cousins than strangers, and the competition between the two world views is more of an in-house feud than a dispute between opposites. A better metaphor might be to view the One as taking the baton from a once robust but now failing secular humanism so that the race to win Western civilization might be won by a new kind of humanism — cosmic humanism." Douglas Groothuis, *Unmasking the New Age* (Downers Grove, IL: Inter-Varsity Press, 1986), p. 52; also pp. 53, 161-63.

New Age Realities

John Naisbitt of *Megatrends*[6] fame sees a new age dawning at the corporation level. Old industrial structures must be dismantled to compete in the information society of the future. "Look at how far we have already come. The industrial society transformed workers into consumers; the information society is transforming employees into capitalists. But remember this: Both capitalism and socialism were industrial systems. The information society will bring forth new structures. And the companies re-inventing themselves are already evolving toward that new reality."[7] But there's more!

Mark Satin has described a *New Age Politics*[8] that will "heal self and society."

Fritjof Capra, author of *The Turning Point*,[9] sees changes in science that will affect society and culture.

Marilyn Ferguson, whose *The Aquarian Conspiracy*[10] is considered by many as the manifesto of the New Age Movement, describes "a new mind—a turnabout in consciousness, a network powerful enough to bring about radical change in our culture."

Much of this literature is rooted in Eastern and occult philosophy, emphasizing oneness (monism): the one, the unity and interdependence of all things. There is a clever mix between Eastern religious philosophy and Western religious forms. The '60s counter culture brought the esoteric music and religious ideology of the East into the West. The Beatles made Eastern music popular when George Harrison introduced the Indian sitar music of Ravi

---

6. Naisbitt, *Megatrends: Ten New Directions Transforming Our Lives* (New York: Warner Books, 1982). Marilyn Ferguson, author of *The Aquarian Conspiracy*, writes of *Megatrends*: "In such turbulent times, we prize those among us who see clearly. John Naisbitt offers a dramatic, convincing view on the changes already under way. This is a book for everyone who wants a sense of the near future."

7. John Naisbitt and Patricia Aburdene, *Re-inventing the Corporation* (New York: Warner Books, 1985), p. 252.

8. New York: Dell, 1979.

9. New York: Simon and Schuster, 1982.

10. Los Angeles, CA: J. P. Tarcher, Inc., 1980.

Shankar on their "Rubber Soul" album.[11] Transcendental Meditation was also popularized by the Beatles. Some of those in the ecology movement base their concern for the environment on the inherent "oneness" of the universe.[12] Man and nature are one in essence. Man is not much different from the animals. He is only higher on the great scale of being. The environment should be protected, not as a stewardship under God, but because we are all god, nature included.

The advance of Eastern thought was gradual, but layer upon layer of this mix eventually made it stick like epoxy. As Christianity steadily lost its hold on the heart and mind of the nation, softer forms of religious beliefs were more easily embraced. Christianity's drift into an emphasis on experience over objective, written revelation has made it easy prey for the pure subjectivism of Eastern thought.

Os Guinness wrote about the meeting of East and West in 1973, in what has become a standard Christian analysis of the decline of secular humanism, *The Dust of Death*. He tells us that the "swing to the East has come at a time when Christianity is weak at just those points where it would need to be strong to withstand the East."[13] He goes on to show the three basic weaknesses within the church that open it up to Eastern influences.

> The first is its compromised, deficient understanding of revelation. Without biblical historicity and veracity behind the Word of God, theology can only grow closer to Hinduism. Second, the modern Christian is drastically weak in an unmediated, personal, experiential knowledge of God. Often what passes for religious experience is a communal emotion felt in church services, in meetings, in singing or contrived fellowship. Few Chris-

---

11. Gary North, *Unholy Spirits: Occultism and New Age Humanism* (Ft. Worth, TX: Dominion Press, 1986), p. 6.

12. Francis Schaeffer, *The Complete Works of Francis A. Schaeffer: A Christian World View*, 5 vols.: *Pollution and the Death of Man: The Christian View of Ecology* (Westchester, IL: Crossway Books, [1970] 1984), vol. 5, pp. 3-76.

13. Os Guinness, *The Dust of Death: A Critique of the Establishment and the Counter Culture—and a Proposal for a Third Way* (Downers Grove, IL: InterVarsity Press, 1973), p. 209.

tians would know God on their own. Third, the modern church is often pathetically feeble in the expression of its focal principle of community. It has become the local social club, preaching shop or minister-dominated group. With these weaknesses, modern Christianity cannot hope to understand why people have turned to the East, let alone stand against the trend and offer an alternative.[14]

Western Christians have a faith that is "extremely blurred at the edges."[15] This opens them up to any and all spiritual counterfeits.

Many New Agers seem to say some good things, but the philosophy behind their emphases is out of accord with biblical Christianity. They talk about decentralization, building from the bottom up, networking, and the importance of the individual and his involvement in the corporate and political processes. The emphasis on changing the individual, usually through raising the consciousness, which results in the metamorphosis of peripheral institutions like the family, church, business, and civil governments at the local, state, and national level is also a prominent feature of New Age humanism.

So why are many Christians afraid of New Age humanism? The answer is obvious: New Age humanism is anti-Christian to the core. It is a utopian dream built on a flawed understanding of man's nature and a devotion to a westernized Eastern philosophy where God is nothing more than a cosmic Idea. The copy on the dust jacket to Ferguson's *The Aquarian Conspiracy* shows that the Christian's fears are justified: "A leaderless but powerful network is working to bring about radical change in the United States. Its members have broken with certain key elements of Western thought, and they may even have broken continuity with history." With all their seemingly "good" emphases, the New Age Movement is at heart humanistic (man is the center of the universe), materialistic (self-actualization is all-important), and anti-God (the God of the Bible is dismissed in favor of self-deification). The American public, with its inability to distinguish biblical truth from anti-

---

14. *Idem.*
15. *Idem.*

Christian religious subtleties, is easily sucked in by the seemingly harmless religious and cultural goals of New Age humanism.

It seems that everybody is on the New Age bandwagon. This fact alone makes it difficult to speak against it. New Age terminology and thought have been woven into the warp and woof of American culture. There are New Age health food stores, New Age music, New Age medicine, and New Age politics. The pantheon of pagan gods has been dropped, but there is enough Eastern baggage to do us much harm.

Political Counterfeits

Politics is not immune to New Age thinking, just as it is not immune to secular humanism. Politics is energized by religious tenets. Even secular humanism, which claims to be non-religious, is steeped in religious assertions.[16] "Political vision stems from our deepest beliefs concerning reality and value. Politics follows faith."[17]

In general, the history of non-Christian politics has been the quest for political salvation. For example, the early Roman State presented itself as the savior of the people. "By the time of Domitian (81-96), it had become common to address him as *dominus et deus*, 'my Lord and God.'"[18] The coins in Domitian's day, like the coins in our day that reflect a once-Christian past, were a daily reminder of the divinity of the State. The coin brought to Jesus in Matthew 22:15-22 had the following inscription: "'TI[berius] CAESAR DIVI AUG[usti] F[ilius] AUGUSTUS,' or, in translation, 'Tiberius Caesar Augustus, son of the deified Augustus.'"[19]

---

16. The two editions of the *Humanist Manifesto* are written in creedal form. The most recent version (1973) states: "We *believe* . . . that traditional dogmatic or authoritarian religions that place revelation, God, ritual, or creed above human needs and experience do a disservice to the human species." The word "believe" comes from the Latin word *credo* from which we get the word creed. Every humanistic organization has some creed that members must subscribe to. To be an atheist, one must *believe* there is no God.

17. Groothuis, *Unmasking the New Age*, p. 111.

18. Herbert Schlossberg, *Idols for Destruction: Christian Faith and its Confrontation with American Society* (Nashville, TN: Thomas Nelson, 1983), p. 185.

19. Merrill C. Tenney, *New Testament Times* (Grand Rapids, MI: Eerdmans, 1965), p. 152.

The symbolic meaning is clear: a new day is dawning for the world. The divine saviour-king, born in the historical hour ordained by the stars, has come to power on land and sea, and inaugurates the cosmic era of salvation. Salvation is to be found in none other save Augustus, and there is no other name given to man in which they can be saved. This is the climax of the Advent proclamation of the Roman empire.[20]

Rome's kingdom and king were counterfeits of God's kingdom and King. Rome hoped to establish a New Age outside the redemptive work of Jesus Christ. Even the unbelieving Jews fell for it. In rejecting their promised Messiah, they cried out: "We have no king but Caesar" (John 19:15). Modern American politics has not shaken Rome's preoccupation with statist salvation, although its forms are much more subtle.[21]

The Smorgasbord Mentality

Many entertainers believe that they are the nation's conscience and its only guiding light. Shirley MacLaine is an example. Her popular books and movies present a nicely camouflaged occult world view. What would have been thought ridiculous twenty years ago, today is considered to be "normal." Shirley MacLaine "claims that her book *Out on a Limb* was indirectly inspired by an extraterrestrial named 'the Mayan.'"[22]

---

20. Ethelbert Stauffer, *Christ and the Caesars* (Philadelphia, PA: Westminster Press, [1952] 1955), p. 88.

21. "In the United States, federal tax policy illustrates the government's unconscious rush to be the god of its citizens. When a provision in the tax laws permits the taxpayer to keep a portion of his money, the Internal Revenue Service calls this a 'tax expenditure,' or an 'implicit government grant.' This is not tax money that the state has collected and expended but money it has allowed the citizen to keep by not taking it. In other words, any money the citizen is permitted to keep is regarded as if the state had graciously given it to him. Everything we have is from the state, to which we owe gratitude. In fact, we are the property of the state, which therefore has the right to the fruit of our labor." Schlossberg, *Idols for Destruction*, p. 187. The chapter, "Idols of Power," along with the entire book, is worthy of study.

22. Groothuis, *Unmasking the New Age*, p. 24. MacLaine's two books, *Out on a Limb* and *Dancing in the Light* were national bestsellers. Her ideas were so well-received by the general public that ABC aired a two-part, five-hour mini-series based on *Out on a Limb*.

No one seems to blink at such an assertion.[23] Why? Spiritual discernment is at a minimum. For example, a "1982 Gallup Poll claimed that twenty-three percent of the American public believed in some form of reincarnation."[24] This does not count those people who merely "tolerate" such a view in light of our religiously pluralistic culture but do not embrace it as a personal belief. People are so confused about what is true that they tend to believe *anything* and *everything*. Doug Groothuis has called this "The Smorgasbord Mentality." This leads to the proliferation of counterfeits:

> Pluralism refers to a diversity of religions, worldviews, and ideologies existing at one time in the same society. We are socially heterogeneous. One religion or philosophy doesn't command and control the culture. Instead, many viewpoints exist. We have Buddhists and Baptists, Christian Reformed and Christian Scientist—all on the same block, or at least in the same city. This can have a leveling effect on religious faith.[25]

Our nation is steeped in pluralism, tolerance, diversity, freedom, and the "democratic spirit."[26] All lifestyles are permitted. Homosexuality is tolerated because we live in a "diverse society." Abortion is legal because "you cannot impose your morality on someone else who has a different set of moral standards." The only view that is not tolerated is the view that does not tolerate all views. Christianity came on the scene with Jesus saying, "I am the way and the truth and the life; no one comes to the Father but by Me" (John 14:6). How intolerant of Him to exclude Mayan spirits, the Buddha, and reincarnationists!

23. Some of the better cartoonists have provided considerable amusement, however. A February 10, 1987, "Far Side" cartoon by Gary Larson pictured two iguanas on a rock, with one saying to the other, "There it is again . . . a feeling that in a past life I was someone named Shirley MacLaine."

24. Groothuis, *Unmasking the New Age*, p. 150.

25. Douglas Groothuis, "The Smorgasbord Mentality," *Eternity* (May 1985), p. 32.

26. See Gary DeMar, *Ruler of the Nations* (Atlanta, GA: American Vision, 1987), pp. 22-23; and *God and Government: A Biblical and Historical Study* (Atlanta, GA: American Vision, 1982), pp. 82-83 for a definition of "democracy" and its inherent instability.

.Modern pluralism presents one prevailing opinion about Jesus Christ. Like all great religious leaders, he is special but not unique; and he is certainly not exclusive. That would be closed- and narrow-minded. He is classed with the multitude of masters, grouped with the gurus, but not exalted as supreme. He is tucked into a comfortable corner of the religious pantheon so as to dis- turb no one.The assumption is that Jesus just couldn't have claimed to be the only way; that's undemocratic! So instead of facing Christ's challenge as it stands, the whole idea is dismissed as anti-pluralistic, and closed-minded.[27]

As a result, our ability to distinguish the real thing from the counterfeit is lost. We have been told over and over again that Christianity is just one religion among many. We've sent our chil- dren to public (government or State) schools where religion is taught as a matter of personal preference, with "no preference" being preferable. There is supposedly no true religion over against all false religions. Christianity is *a* religion but not *the* re- ligion. The Bible can *sometimes* be taught as fictional literature like Shakespeare, but it cannot be taught as the Word of God. This would offend Moslems, Buddhists, Mormons,[28] and most cer- tainly atheists. Our children are then open to any and all philoso- phical gurus who are ready, willing, and seemingly able to lead the way to a new vision for the future. New world views are a dime a dozen. Those best able to express their views get the great- est following.

In an interview with film director and producer Francis Ford Coppola, the aggressive nature and comprehensive effects of a new world view come to light:

> My dream is that the artist class—people who have proven
> through their work that they are humanists and wish to push for
> what Aldous Huxley called the desirable human potentialities of
> intelligence, creativity and friendliness—will seize the instru-

---

27. Groothuis, "The Smorgasbord Mentality," p. 33.

28. While Mormons may accept the Bible as authoritative, they also maintain that *The Book of Mormon, The Pearl of Great Price, Doctrine and Covenants*, and the continuing authority of the church apostles are equally trustworthy.

ment of technology and try to take humanity into a period of history in which we can reach for a utopia. Of course, it is possible for the technology to be misused—we could end up with a Big Brother—but we could also have a balanced society, with an artist class leading the culture toward something approximating a happy family or tribe.

At the moment, the nation is in a fog, and we've got to put our headlights on. Artists—those who rely on their intuition—can be the nation's headlights.[29]

Coppola's world view comes on bold and bright through the larger-than-life silver screen. He doesn't set out to tell you: "This is my world view; God does not matter." Rather, he describes and promotes his world view by creating a world that leaves out Jesus Christ. Yes, Jesus is often mentioned in film, but only as an obscenity. Most audiences don't really note the expletives on film because Jesus has been trivialized in life. He was a great man. He may have been god-like, but we all have a similar "spark of divinity." In a sense, we're all god-like but to a different degree.

Since no religion prevails in society, young people are susceptible to the latest attractions. There is no future. They are being told this by those advocating unilateral disarmament in the face of the threat of nuclear annihilation,[30] and by those Christians who say "you cannot polish brass on a sinking ship."[31] The sinking boat

---

29. "A Conversation with Francis Coppola," *U.S. News & World Report*, (April 5, 1982), p. 68.

30. Ronald J. Sider and Richard K. Taylor, *Nuclear Holocaust & Christian Hope* (Downers Grove, IL: InterVarsity Press, 1982).

31. *Dominion: A Dangerous New Theology*, Tape #1 of *Dominion: The Word and New World Order*. Peter Lalonde comments: "It's a question, 'Do you polish brass on a sinking ship?' And if they're [advocates of dominion theology] working on setting up new institutions, instead of going out and winning the lost for Christ, then they're wasting the most valuable time on the planet earth right now." Souls can be lost because of pressure from institutions that have abandoned the faith. How many young people have lost their faith through the humanistic university system, a system that was at one time Christian? "If God has decreed that the world's future is one of a downward spiral, then indeed Christian reconstruction is futile. As a prominent premillennial pastor and radio preacher, the Rev. J. Vernon McGee, declared in the early 1950s, 'You don't polish brass on a sinking ship.' If the world is a sinking ship, then efforts to eliminate prostitution, crime, or any

reference to Western civilization has been around a long time. If it had been taken seriously every time someone used it, we would be in worse shape than we are now. The Rev. John Newton, the once infamous slave trader who wrote the classic Christian hymn "Amazing Grace," used the sinking ship metaphor in the 19th century in addressing a minister who believed that the Bible applied in some measure to politics.

> Allow me to say, that it excites both my wonder and concern that a minister, possessed of the great and important views expressed in your two sermons, should think it worth his while to appear in the line of a political writer, or expect to amend our constitution or situation, by proposals of a political reform. When I look around upon the present state of the nation, such an attempt appears to me no less vain and unseasonable, than it would be to paint a cabin while the ship is sinking, or a parlour when the house is already on fire.[32]

Newton's words are curious in light of his kind words for William Pitt, of whom he said, "I cannot but think that the providence of God raised up Mr. Pitt for the good of these kingdoms, and that no man could do what he has done, unless a blessing from on high had been upon his counsels and measures."[33] Where would the abolition of slavery have gone without the work of Wilberforce? Keep in mind that it was *Christians* who worked to put an end to the evil trade by which Newton once gained his living. There was no civil war in England. It was done with peaceful means, unlike America's experience. There was the genuine belief that when the gospel and God's law are applied to all aspects of life, society changes.

---

kind of social evil, and to expect the Christian conquest of the social order, are indeed futile. It must be noted, however, that it was such premillennial opinions that united with Unitarianism in the early 1800s to replace Christian schools with state schools, so that the church could retreat to a minimal program, revivalism." R. J. Rushdoony, *God's Plan for Victory: The Meaning of Post Millennialism* (Fairfax, VA: Thoburn Press, 1977), p. 9-10.

32. Newton, *The Works of the Rev. John Newton*, 4 vols. (London: Nathan Whiting, 1824), vol. 4, pp. 579-80.

33. *Ibid.*, p. 582.

Those who propose a sinking ship scenario project no hope for an earthly future prior to the millennium. There is no possible chance to change things for the better. People like Coppola paint a picture of glamor for those without hope. It's no wonder that we are losing our future to those who offer at least the temporal vision of hope.

Phoney as a Three Dollar Bill

The average American and most Christians have grown up with this "smorgasbord mentality," so they no longer can tell the real from the counterfeit. The writer to the Hebrew Christians describes this mind-set. He stops in mid-thought, wanting to explain the priesthood of Jesus and how it is similar to the priesthood of Melchizedek. He recognizes that their spiritual discernment makes what he wants to write "hard to explain" (Heb. 5:11).

What had happened to these converts? They had become "dull of hearing" (Heb. 5:11). By this time in their Christian walk they should have matured, advancing from "milk" to meat (1 Cor. 8:1-2; 1 Peter 2:2). Instead of progressing from the basics and becoming "teachers" (Heb. 5:12), they are in need of someone once again to teach them "the elementary principles of the oracles of God" (v. 12). As a result, their senses were not trained to discern good [the real] and evil [the counterfeit] (v. 14). When something like the New Age Movement comes along, we have no reason to think that Christians and the typical American religionist will be able to tell the difference between the real and the counterfeit, unless they have progressed to "solid food."

What is a counterfeit? A counterfeit is an illicit copy of an original designed to be passed off as the real thing. We're most familiar with the counterfeiting of United States currency. The important thing to remember about counterfeiting is that there is a genuine article that is being copied. If there is no genuine article, then there can be no counterfeit. If someone handed you a three dollar bill, you would know immediately that it wasn't real. You might, however, be hard pressed to spot a counterfeit ten dollar bill.

We do not often consider "theological counterfeiting" as a way the devil might hide the truth from Bible-believing Christians. Yet the Bible shows us that there are counterfeit Christs (Matt. 24:5; Acts 5:36-37), counterfeit prophets (Matt. 7:15; 24:11), counterfeit miracles (Ex. 7:8-13), counterfeit angels (2 Cor. 11:14), counterfeit gods (Gal. 4:8; Acts 12:20-23), counterfeit good works (Matt. 7:15-23), counterfeit converts and disciples (1 John 2:19), counterfeit spirits (1 John 4:1-3), counterfeit doctrines (1 Tim. 4:3), counterfeit kings (John 19:15), counterfeit names (Rev. 13:11-18; cf. 14:1), and counterfeit gospels (Gal. 1:6-10). Why should we be surprised if there are counterfeit kingdoms (Dan. 2; Matt. 4:8-11; Acts 17:1-9) and a counterfeit new age (Rev. 13:11-18)? The New Age Movement is a counterfeit. It wants the *fruit* of Christianity without the *root*.

What should this tell us? When Jesus came to earth to do the work of His Father, there was heightened demonic activity. Satan's purpose was to counterfeit the work of Christ, to confuse the people. The devil knew his time was short (Rev. 12:12; Rom. 16:20). He was making a last-ditch effort to subvert the work of the kingdom. Satan gathered his "children" around himself to call Jesus' mission into question (John 8:44). At one point, Jesus was even accused of being in league with the devil (Luke 11:14-28). As Jesus moved closer to establishing peace with God for us through His death and resurrection (cf. Rom. 5:1), the power of the devil was grounded, made impotent (Luke 10:18). But through Jesus' disciples the world was turned upside down (Acts 17:6). Satan's kingdom was spoiled and left desolate (Luke 11:20; Acts 19:11-20). The Apostle Paul then tells the Roman Christians that God would "*soon crush Satan,*" the great counterfeiter, under their feet (Rom. 16:20).

Religious corruption was Satan's new strategy for subverting God's kingdom work. Jesus' battles were with the *religious* leaders of the day. The scribes and Pharisees were scrupulously theological in their evaluation of Jesus. The law was quoted, but certainly misapplied. Jesus was always accused of not keeping the law, of not following Moses. The devil had the Pharisees convinced that

Jesus' view of reality was false, the counterfeit, while their view was true, the original. In order for the Pharisees to keep up the charade, they needed to get rid of the Original. Their counterfeit would no longer be considered a counterfeit because there would be no original around with which to compare it.

The Counterfeit Kingdom

Jesus came to install His kingdom through His marvelous grace. The kingdom was God's good news that sinners would be saved. The political savagery of Rome's kingdom and its promise of peace and salvation would die as God's kingdom flourished in the light of His unfathomable grace. John the Baptist was its forerunner: "Repent, for the kingdom of God is at hand" (Matt. 3:2). God's grace made repentance a reality. Without grace repentance would mean nothing. So entrance into the kingdom is God's doing: "Truly, truly, I say to you, unless one is born of water and the Spirit, he cannot enter into the kingdom of God" (John 3:5).

But the King demands obedience. First, the sinner must repent, bow before God in humble submission to Him, in effect, to surrender unconditionally to God's demands.[34] Second, the new man or woman in Christ must live in terms of the King's demands. His life must reflect *righteousness*: "For the kingdom of God is not eating and drinking, but righteousness and peace and joy in the Holy Spirit" (Rom. 14:17; cf. Matt. 6:33). For Jesus, the kingdom was established by fulfilling "all righteousness" (Matt. 3:15). This meant that He had to submit Himself to the demands of His Father. This is why His Father could say at Jesus' baptism: "This is My beloved Son, in whom I am well pleased" (Matt. 3:17).

Satan offers a similar program. Entrance into his kingdom comes through unconditional surrender to *his* "ethical system": "The devil took Him to a very high mountain, and showed Him all the kingdoms of the world, and their glory; and he said to

---

34. Gary North, *Unconditional Surrender: God's Program for Victory* (2nd. ed.; Ft. Worth, TX: Dominion Press, 1987).

Him, 'All these things will I give You, if You fall down and worship me'" (Matt. 4:8-9). Satan wanted Jesus to give up the real for the counterfeit. Jesus' finished work of obedience and sacrifice leads John to write: "The kingdom of this world *has become* the kingdom of our Lord, and of His Christ; and *He will reign forever and ever*" (Rev. 11:15). The Kingdom belongs to Jesus. It's His now! With this fact established, John writes that "He will reign forever and ever." Because of Jesus' obedience, "becoming obedient to the point of death, even death on a cross, . . . God highly exalted Him, and bestowed on Him the name which is above every name, that at the name of Jesus every knee should bow, of those who are in heaven, and on earth, and under the earth, and that every tongue should confess that Jesus Christ is Lord, to the glory of God the Father" (Phil. 2:8-11).

New Age, New Names: Babel Revisited

God has a present, operating kingdom in the world that Satan has been trying to duplicate for centuries. Counterfeiting the kingdom of God has been going on since the building of Babel. These kingdom rebels wanted to supplant God's "name" with a "name" of their own. In the Bible naming something is a mark of dominion.[35] God names Himself (Ex. 3:14); thus, man has no

---

35. In Scripture naming is not arbitrary. Generally, to give a name to something is to say what something truly is. Names are given to *interpret*. Where Adam named the animals, he tells what those animals really *are*. When God changes the name of Abram to Abraham, He gives him a name which has redemptive historical significance, that he will be a father of a multitude. Naming is also an act of *power*; it is to declare and claim *authority over* the thing that is named. When someone would encounter a city, sometimes he would change the name over that city. For example, Jacob changed the name of Luz to Bethel, "the house of God" (Gen. 28:19). The act of man naming the animals is not only man interpreting, telling what the animals are, but because he is the one who shows who the animals are, he is showing his sovereignty and displaying his dominion over all the lower creatures. Adapted from lecture notes on Ethics by John Frame, Professor of Ethics and Systematic Theology, Westminster Theological Seminary, Escondido, California.

claim on God except when and how God permits him. God names Adam because he was formed from the dust of the ground (2:7), a reminder to all of us that God created and sustains us (cf. Acts 17:24-28). Man did not create himself, and neither did he evolve through random changes in the cosmos.[36] God has dominion over man. We find that Adam named Eve "woman [Heb., *Ishshah]* because she was taken out of Man *[Ish]*" (Gen. 2:23). Adam has authority over Eve (Eph. 5:22), and God has authority over Adam and Eve for they are both named "Adam" (Gen. 5:2; cf. Eph. 5:23). Adam and Eve name their children, showing their authority over their offspring (Gen. 4:1-2). Cain built a city "and called the name of the city Enoch, after the name of his son" (Gen. 4:17). It was Cain's desire to extend dominion through his seed.

The building of the tower at Babel is a corruption of God's kingdom work. Where God is sovereign, man claims sovereignty for himself. God's kingdom is supplanted by man with horrendous consequences. "Let *us* make a *name* for *ourselves*" (Gen. 11:4). God's name would be rejected. A New Age would dawn with man as master. Francis Schaeffer described the tower of Babel as "the first declaration of humanism."[37] Babel grew out of man's desire to control and overrule the designs of God's kingdom where the creature rules *under* the Creator as a subordinate. "Here is the theology that Satan offered to Adam: autonomous man's way to heaven. The tower was a link between heaven and earth, but one which men built, not God. The pinnacle of the tower represented the seat of power, the link between evolving man and the gods."[38]

The Babylon of Daniel's time is a continuation of the Babel theme of Genesis 11. Babel and Babylon were built in the "land of Shinar" (Gen. 11:2 and Dan. 1:2). We should expect the sover-

---

36. The Hebrew word for "ground" is *adamah*. Being called "man" is a constant reminder of our origin; it was *God* who made us out of dirt. In death we return to the ground from which we came. There is no transmigration of the soul, no reincarnation, no elevation into a new essence. It is only through Christ that we will be raised "imperishable" (1 Cor. 15:42).

37. Schaeffer, *Genesis in Space and Time* (Downers Grove, IL: InterVarsity Press, 1972), p. 152.

38. Gary North, *Unconditional Surrender*, p. 143.

eignty and dominion theme to continue. Nebuchadnezzar had shown Judah that he was the new sovereign by taking the vessels of the house of God and bringing them "to the house of his god" (Dan. 1:2).

How did Nebuchadnezzar extend his dominion? He took the best of the young men and *indoctrinated* them with a Babylonian conception of kingship, "to enter the king's personal service" (1:5). The leadership, the best in Israel, would be used to direct the nation in Babylonian ways. This is the dream of all tyrants and totalitarian regimes. Notice, however, that dominion is the goal in the names. Humanism, the belief that man is the center of the universe, is the new faith. Daniel and his three friends easily spotted the counterfeit. Many of the Israelites did not.

Nebuchadnezzar expressed his sovereign claim by renaming them with Babylonian names. These young children had distinctly covenantal names with a common characteristic: the name of God was attached to each of them. The suffix of each name either has the general name of God, *el* (a shortened version of "Elohim"), or the personal name of God, *yah* (a shortened version of "Yahweh"). Daniel means *God has judged* or *God is my judge*; Hananiah, *Jehovah has been gracious*; Mishael, *Who is what God is?*; Azariah, *Jehovah has helped*. The new names pointed the people to the new sovereign, the gods of Babylon. Sovereignty was transferred and dominion was continued, but under the name of the new sovereign. Kingship and kingdom are not denied, they are only reinterpreted.

New Age humanism is no different. While New Agers do create new terms, they are more apt to redefine old and familiar ones.[39] This is an act of rebellion and an expression of autonomy

---

39. "Deceit and evil always go hand in hand, and our own age finds them wedded once more. For example, think of the abuse of language today. 'Choice' has come to mean death. 'Government assistance,' control of the population. 'Liberal,' an indefinite intolerance of everyone and anything, *except* those who disagree about issues on the basis of moral principle. 'Pluralism' no longer means that men may differ in their views of truth, but that truth does not really exist, outside the limited sphere of science.

because renaming and redefining are sovereign acts. Like the counterfeiter who hopes to grow rich through his engraving techniques, New Agers who fill biblical words and concepts with occultic content do so in hopes of possessing the bounty of God's order through magic. Words like "God," "holistic," "meditation," and "healing" are emptied of their biblical meaning and are then filled with New Age concepts with the intention of deceiving the unsuspecting.

The kingdom of Christ is counterfeited to meet the needs of man. It is Babel revisited. We see this with Nebuchadnezzar's attempt to counterfeit God's kingdom by building a *golden* statue of a *man*. In the king's mind there would be no end to his reign (a gold statue endures), and man would be the focal point. God had shown the king in a dream that any kingdom built on the shaky foundation of man is doomed to failure and judgment (Dan. 2:19-45). On the other hand, God's kingdom is a "kingdom which will never be destroyed" (Dan. 2:44). The issue, therefore, is not whether there is a kingdom; rather, it is whose kingdom will rule all other kingdoms.

Denying the Real Thing

Dave Hunt assumes that an operating *earthly* kingdom does not exist.[40] He does not recognize that New Age humanism is a

---

"Think of the use of labels to categorize political activity. Some labels are used to neutralize the actions of certain groups; others denote being 'one of us,' acceptable.

"The words 'right wing,' 'fundamentalist,' 'pro-life,' 'absolutist,' and 'deeply religious' are put-downs more than categories. Conversely, think of the unspoken pat on the back and blessing that the following words convey: 'moderate,' 'pluralistic,' 'liberal,' 'civil libertarian,' 'pragmatic,' and 'enlightened.'" Franky Schaeffer, *A Time for Anger: The Myth of Neutrality* (Westchester, IL: Crossway Books, 1982), p. 15.

This is also the tactic of Liberation Theology and Process Theology. See Emilio A. Núñez C., *Liberation Theology*, trans. Paul E. Sywulka (Chicago, IL: Moody Press, 1985); Ronald Nash, ed., *On Process Theology* (Grand Rapids, MI: Baker, 1987).

40. Other critics of Christian reconstruction make similar assumptions. This is why some declare that Christian reconstructionists are working at "establishing the Kingdom of God." Albert James Dager, "Kingdom Theology: Part III," *Media*

counterfeit of God's progressive kingdom activity on earth, in time and in history, because he has no conception of an earthly manifestation of the kingdom. For Hunt, then, the kingdom that is being counterfeited is heaven itself because God's kingdom does not even find expression in the earthly millennium. He writes: "The millennial reign of Christ upon earth, *rather than being the kingdom of God*, will in fact be the final proof of the incorrigible nature of the human heart."[41] But this does not conform to Scripture. In Isaiah 65:17-25, there is a description of what all Christians would certainly describe as kingdom-like conditions: "No longer will there be in it an infant who lives but a few days, or an old man who does not live out his days; for the youth will die at the age of one hundred and the one who does not reach the age of one hundred shall be thought accursed" (v. 20). This cannot be a description of heaven, since people will not die in heaven. Houses will be built, vineyards will be planted (v. 21), and the "wolf and the lamb will graze together," and "the lion shall eat straw like the ox" (v. 25).

For the traditional premillennialist, Isaiah 65:18-25 is describing conditions during the earthly millennium—the "kingdom age." Most premillennial commentators see this as the millennial reign of Christ on the *earth*. In Jerry Falwell's *Liberty Bible Commentary*, which is described in the Preface as "*Eschatologically Premillennial*" without "many of the excessive divisions of extreme dispensationalism," Edward F. Hindson comments on Isaiah 65:18-20:

> In this kingdom to come, time itself shall begin to fade away; and both the *infant* and the *old man* shall have *filled* (lived to fulfill) their days. The phrase, the *child shall die a hundred years old*, means

---

Spotlight, Vol. 8, No. 1 (January-June 1987), p. 8. The kingdom of God is operating in the world now. There is no kingdom to establish. Mr. Dager creates a false impression for those who have not read much Christian reconstruction literature. If the kingdom is a present reality, then as kingdom-subjects, Christians and non-Christians are responsible to live in terms of the King's demands. Christian reconstructionists believe that as King, Jesus calls all men everywhere to repent (Acts 17:30), to obey His commandments (John 14:15), and to recruit additional kingdom members through the proclamation of the gospel (Matt. 28:18-20).

41. Hunt, *Beyond Seduction: A Return to Biblical Christianity* (Eugene, OR: Harvest House, 1987), p. 250. Emphasis added.

that if someone were to die at a hundred, he would be considered a mere child. However, by contrast, death shall cut off the *sinner* without hesitation. While amillennial commentators attempt to relate this promise to eternity, it is an utter impossibility to do so. Here we have the blessedness of the millennial kingdom of Christ in view. It is a time when men shall have the potential of living for a thousand years; hence, anyone who shall die at a hundred shall be looked upon as a mere child.[42]

The Kingdom is Now!

Hunt, with his anti-kingdom theology, Hindson and other premillennialists, with their millennial-kingdom theology, and amillennialists, with their heavenly-kingdom theology, all miss the point of Isaiah 65 because they fail to fully comprehend the meaning of God's words when he says, "For behold, I create a new heavens and a new earth" (v. 17).

Hindson tells us that the prophet "looks down beyond the church age, the Tribulation Period, and the millennial kingdom, to the *new heavens and a new earth* (cf. Rev 21:1ff.)," of what he calls the "eternal state."[43] But there is no mention of the eternal state. This must be read into the text. Hindson assumes that "the new heavens and a new earth" of verse 17 *must be* the eternal state because it *cannot mean* the gospel age.

New Heavens, New Earth, New Birth

We believe that Isaiah 65:17-25 describes what the world will look like as the gospel message is faithfully preached and acted upon. This condition is described in "new creation" language. Thomas Scott comments:

> [T]he context requires us to interpret the words, in this place, of that state of the church on earth, which shall most resemble the world of glory, in knowledge, holiness, and felicity, and which will terminate in it. By the

---

42. (Lynchburg, VA: The Old-Time Gospel Hour, 1982), p. 1421.
43. *Idem.*

new-creating power of God, the circumstances of the church, and the character of men, shall be so altered, that it will appear as entirely a new world; so that the former confusions, iniquities, and miseries of the human race, shall be no more remembered or renewed.[44]

The new heavens and new earth are parallel to the *new birth*. New creatures will mean a new creation. As Christians are renewed in Christ, so the world is renewed in Christ. Paul says of the new birth: "Therefore if any man is in Christ, *he is a new creature* [creation]; the old things passed away; behold, new things have come" (2 Cor. 5:17). This parallels what God says in Isaiah 65:18. When the "new heavens and a new earth" come ("new creation"), "the former things shall not be remembered or come to mind" ("old things passed away"). The new birth brings on such radical changes that a person "in Christ" is described as a "new creation." In Galatians 6:15, Paul reminds us that neither circumcision nor uncircumcision is of any value when it comes to the new birth. What is needed is "a new creation." This "new creation" is God's doing: "For we are God's workmanship, *created in Christ Jesus* for good works, which God prepared beforehand, that we should walk in them" (Eph. 2:10).

When does the Christian become a "new creation"? The Bible

---

44. Scott, *The Holy Bible, Containing the Old and New Testaments, According to the Authorized Version; with Explanatory Notes, Practical observations and Copious Marginal References*, 3 vols. (New York: Collins and Hannay, 1832), vol. 2, p. 552. Emphasis added. John Calvin makes a similar point: *"For, lo, I will create new heavens and a new earth.* By these metaphors he promises a remarkable change of affairs; as if God had said that he has both the inclination and the power not only to restore his Church, but to restore it in such a manner that it shall appear to gain new life and to dwell in a new world. These are exaggerated modes of expression; but the greatness of such a blessing, which was to be manifested at the [first] Coming of Christ, could not be described in any other way. Nor does he mean only the first coming, but the whole reign, which must be extended as far as to the last coming, as we have already said in expounding other passages.

"Thus the world is (so to speak) renewed by Christ; and hence also the Apostle (Heb. ii. 5) calls it 'a new age,' and undoubtedly alludes to this statement of the Prophet." Calvin, *Commentary on the Book of the Prophet Isaiah*, 4 vols. (Grand Rapids, MI: Baker, [1850] 1979), vol. 4, pp. 397-98.

says that it *has happened*. He *is* a new creature. The old things *have passed away*.[45] Does the Christian progress after he has become a new creation? Yes. Is this "new creation" a perfect creation? No. But the important thing to keep in mind here is that the language used for the change that happens to anyone who comes to Christ is absolute and comprehensive. He or she is spoken of as being a "new creature" or a "new creation." He or she is "born again" (John 3:3), which is new creation language.

Now, what is true of the individual is also true of the cosmos. Jesus' redemptive work was for the "world" (John 3:16). Why should we be surprised when the new covenant order is described as the recreation of heaven and earth?[46] The kingdom of God reflects this "new creation" idea. John the Baptist comes on the scene describing the coming of the Messiah in cosmic terms: "Make ready the way of the Lord, make His paths straight. Every ravine shall be filled up, and every mountain and hill shall be brought low; and the crooked shall become straight, and the rough roads smooth; and all flesh shall see the salvation of God" (Luke 3:4-6).

But doesn't the kingdom of God need the *presence* of the Savior to operate? This question is at the heart of the anti-kingdom position. The most prevalent belief among premillennial evangelicals today is that Jesus must be *physically* present on the *earth* before we will see the kingdom manifested. But, as the New Testament shows, the Spirit of God is here. Because the Spirit is here, Christ Himself is with us; the Spirit is the Spirit of Christ (Acts 16:7).

John 14:15-21 is a prophecy of the coming of the Spirit. Jesus tells His disciples that He will return to them, which, in the context, is not a prophecy of the end of the world, but of Pentecost. He did not leave us orphans (John 14:18), but sent His Spirit to be

---

45. The tense of the verb is aorist, which, in the context, refers to past time.

46. For a comprehensive treatment of what Peter means by "new heavens and a new earth" (2 Pet. 3:10, 12), see David Chilton, *The Days of Vengeance: An Exposition of the Book of Revelation* (Ft. Worth, TX: Dominion Press, 1987), pp. 537-45; John Owen, *Works*, 16 vols. (London: Banner of Truth Trust, 1965-68), vol. 9, pp. 134-35.

another Comforter (14:15; cf. 1 John 2:1). Paul goes so far as to say that in the resurrection, the Last Adam has become a "life-giving Spirit" (1 Cor. 15:45). In fact, Jesus' *absence* is necessary for the work of the church: "But I tell you the truth, it is to your advantage that I go away; for if I do not go away, the Helper shall not come to you; but if I go, I will send Him to you" (John 17:7). Jesus goes on to say that the Spirit will guide them into "all the truth" (v. 13).[47] Thomas Sproull, addressing the presence of Christ during the millennium, wrote a century ago:

> [T]he immediate power of God is never employed in administering the affairs of his kingdom, when the end can be accomplished through subordinant instrumentality.[48]
>
> [Dealings] with the humanity of Christ when on earth was necessarily limited to those who had access to his bodily presence. It was not till after his ascension and the Comforter was sent, that the circle of fellowship was widened to embrace all who in every place call on his name. To have [dealings] with the humanity of Christ would now be no help, but a hindrance to communion with him. This gives meaning and force to the apostle's declaration: "Though we have known Christ after the flesh, yet henceforth know we him no more."—II *Cor.* 5:16.[49]
>
> This same truth he taught to Mary shortly after his resurrection: "Touch me not, Mary, for I am not yet ascended to my Father."—*John* 20:17. The condition of the presence of the Comforter on earth, is the presence of Christ's humanity in heaven: "If I go not away, the Comforter will not come to you."—*John* 16:7. Through him, and not through sensible intercourse with the hu-

---

47. See the excellent discussion of the connection between Pentecost and Christ in Richard B. Gaffin, *Perspectives on Pentecost* (Phillipsburg, NJ: Presbyterian and Reformed, 1979), pp. 14-20.

48. Thomas Sproull, *Prelections on Theology* (Pittsburgh, PA: Myers, Shinkle & Co., 1882), p. 410.

49. Philip Edgcumbe Hughes, in commenting on this verse, shows what difference the Spirit made at Pentecost: The disciples' "knowledge of Christ *in* the flesh, pregnant with blessing though it was, was far from being unmixed with knowledge of Him *after* the flesh. It was not until the great enlightenment of Pentecost that they at last came to know Him fully after the Spirit. Then we find them no longer dull of understanding, cowardly, despondent, of little faith, but wise in the things of God, bold, outspoken, and full of joy and power." *Commentary on the Second Epistle to the Corinthians* (Grand Rapids, MI: Eerdmans, 1962), p. 201.

manity of Christ, will the communion on earth be carried on between the Head and the members. And to me it seems to be nothing else than slighting the Comforter, to expect the enjoyment of the blessedness of which he is the appointed channel of communication, from visible association with the humanity of Christ.[50]

Jesus shows us in His own words that He is present with His people now! "For where two or three have gathered together in My name, *there I am in their midst*" (Matt. 18:20). The Holy Spirit was poured out at Pentecost and is now in the world, and Jesus is in the midst of His church. Christians should start acting like they believe these most fundamental truths. Who knows, we might see things change for the better.

The Devil's Tactic

How can there be such a thing as a New Age energized by the devil unless there is a New Age energized by God? Hunt seems to assume that Satan has *not* borrowed from the Christian world view, that he has created this New Age philosophy from scratch. But we know that Satan cannot create. He must steal to keep his world view running. Satan is the greatest counterfeiter in the universe. Many Christians have never considered such a possibility. They believe there is no way they could be tricked by the devil, at least not on this point. They don't want to believe that there could ever be another explanation for why we are seeing New Age thinking at this time in history. The devil wants us to believe that he is not what he is. He wants us to impute power to him, to make him more than what he is by nature. The devil then uses this imputed power against us: We believe he can accomplish all these feats using his own supposed inherent creative powers. He doesn't want us to think that there might be another explanation for the New Age Movement. He wants the Christian to believe that anyone who stresses earthly victory is apostatizing. He wants those outside of Christ to believe that a New Age can be implemented with man as the central figure. C. S. Lewis, in his immortal book, *The Screwtape Letters*, addresses this very issue. Speaking to his ap-

---

50. Sproull, *Prelections on Theology*, pp. 411-12.

prentice devil Wormwood about his Christian "patient," senior devil Screwtape writes:

> By the very act of arguing, you awake the patient's reason; and once it is awake, who can foresee the result? Even if a particular train of thought can be twisted so as to end in our favour, you will find that you have been strengthening in your patient the fatal habit of attending to universal issues and withdrawing his attention from the stream of immediate sense experiences. *Your business is to fix his attention on the stream. Teach him to call it "real life" and don't let him ask what he means by "real."*[51]

The devil wants us to believe that he is in control of the world, that the church is weak, that God cannot use His redeemed and transformed people through the power of His Spirit to advance His purposes in time and in history. He hypnotizes us with the unbiblical assertion that *he* is in control of the world, that God's plans are on hold until *God personally* intervenes in history to reign over the earth. But even this is not enough, for Dave Hunt tells us that "the millennial reign of Christ upon earth, rather than being the kingdom of God, will in fact be the *final proof of the incorrigible nature of the human heart.*"[52] Sin then is greater than God's efforts. The devil, in principle, wins the game. Satan can laugh at God's efforts through eternity, always reminding Him that as long as the devil is around, He just can't succeed.

Building a New Civilization

When we as Christians advocate the building of a Christian civilization, much of what we say and write seems to be similar to what advocates of New Age humanism are espousing. But in fact we are not imitating New Agers. They are imitating God and His kingdom. The New Age kingdom is the counterfeit kingdom. In effect, the New Age kingdom is a Johnny-come-lately kingdom that cannot be sustained because man is its foundation (Dan. 2-3). Postmillennialism was the prevalent eschatological view of

---

51. (New York: Macmillan, 1946), p. 12. Emphasis added.
52. Hunt, *Beyond Seduction*, p. 250. Emphasis added.

the Puritans who came to these shores to establish "a city on a hill." Of course, the inception of a "New World Order" or a "New Age" began with Jesus' earthly ministry, was proclaimed at His "Great Commission" (Matt. 28:18-20), empowered at Pentecost (Acts 2), and was visibly manifested at the fall of Jerusalem in A.D. 70. The "New Age" of Jesus' Kingdom is worked out by faithful Christians throughout history.

As Christians we should not be fooled by the New Age Movement, and neither should we fear it. We understand human nature (man is a sinner); God's program for history (God works in history to accomplish His purposes and to defeat the works of the devil); the importance of this "age" (God's kingdom is now, and all competing kingdoms are being relegated to the dust bin of history); the biblical emphasis on decentralization (no one earthly institution has all power and authority; all authority comes from God); and an optimistic vision of the future (God's enemies cannot win no matter how strong they might *seem* to be).

We are seeing the battle lines being drawn once again, because the church is steadily advancing, storming the very gates of hell (Matt. 16:18). It seems that nearly everybody is talking about victory. But the secularist's version of the New Age cannot last. There is nothing original in it. Anything it has that is of any use has been stolen from the pattern of Christ's kingdom. As soon as Christians realize that the theft has taken place, they will abandon their lethargy and pessimism. What are God's people waiting for? We have God's infallible and inerrant word, the power of the Holy Spirit, and the ministry of the gospel. The New Agers have counterfeits. Yet we're supposed to believe that the church cannot extend the boundaries of the kingdom beyond a few souls "plucked from the burning." We suspect that many people in the church are not even willing to try. What if this generation of Christians refuses even to try, believing that it *cannot* be done? Then G. K. Chesterton's words cease to be an observation and become an indictment: "The Christian ideal has not been tried and found wanting. It has been found difficult; and left untried."[53] The New Agers are just a testimony to these words: "The sons of this age are more shrewd in relation to their own generation than the sons of light" (Luke 16:8).

The philosophy and actions of the New Age Movement should shame Christians. New Agers at least believe that change can come, yet they only have confidence in man, or at most, some cosmic impersonal force. We have the Lord of Glory, the Ruler of the kings of the earth, God Almighty. For too long, Christians have had only a bleak earthly future to offer the lost. Even today, many Christians do not believe there is an earthly future. The world is despised and rejected. The secularists are doing what we should have been doing. Although they have done a terrible job, they are in visible control, for now. No wonder things look bad. What do we expect when we turn the world over to people who deny God and the power of His gospel?

It's time for Christians to present alternatives to the bankrupt New Age philosophy without jettisoning the realities of a Christian civilization. We can either react in despair or compete head to head and win the battle through excellent kingdom work (Zech. 1:18-21).

Conclusion

The ideology of the New Age is satanic and humanistic. It is a result of the influx of Eastern religious thought into the West. It is, therefore, a dangerous movement that must be resisted by Christians. In order to resist the movement effectively, we must recognize New Age humanism for what it is: a counterfeit of the true New Age and the true kingdom, which were both inaugurated by the life, death, and resurrection of Christ. New Age humanism cannot be resisted by retreating, hopeless Christians. In fact, a Christian retreat will aid and abet the New Age's program. Instead, Christians must resist confidently, knowing that the true King fights with and for them.

---

53. "The Unfinished Temple," *G. K. Chesterton: Collected Works*, 28 vols. (San Francisco, CA: Ignatius Press, 1987), vol. 4, p. 61

6

HERE A CONSPIRACY,
THERE A CONSPIRACY

The term "New Age" is certainly not new. The Bible distinguishes between "this age" and the "age to come" (Matt. 12:32). By implication, the "age to come" is new, while "this age" will pass away and become old.[1] The term "New Age" has been used quite freely by some very orthodox Christian theologians. There is nothing in their writings that would indicate that they have been seduced by New Age humanism as espoused by present-day occultists.

A cursory reading of major theological works will show that the term "New Age" was used quite freely without any hint of hidden occultic meaning:

> We need to recognize that eschatology does not pertain exclusively to the future. Jesus did introduce a *new age*, and the victory over the powers of evil has already been won, even though the

---

1. The "age to come" refers to the era of the new covenant provisions set forth in the book of Hebrews. The reference is not to heaven. The Old Covenant ended with the destruction of Jerusalem in A.D. 70. The new covenant began with the ministry of Jesus. The 40 year period between Jesus' ministry and Jerusalem's destruction was an overlap period of the two covenants. The "age to come" is the new age just on the other side of the end of the Jewish dispensation that had its significance in old covenant structures. Many Bible students do not understand "age," sometimes translated "world," in this way. The book of Hebrews begins with these words: "God, after He spoke long ago to the fathers in the prophets in many portions and in many ways [old age], in these last days [new age] has spoken to us in His Son, whom He appointed heir of all things, through whom He made the world" (Heb. 1:1-2).

struggle is still to be enacted in history.[2]

The new age has already been ushered in. . . . . the New Testament believer was conscious that he was living in the last days and the last hour. . . .[3]

Among biblical writers no one has laid so much stress on the fact that Christ has ushered us into a new age as has the Apostle Paul. In Colossians 1:13 he says that God "has delivered us from the dominion of darkness and transferred us to the kingdom of his beloved Son," implying that we have been delivered from the power of the old aeon [age] of sin (cf. Gal. 1:4).[4]

There was a new age after the fall of man, an age of sin and death. The new age brought on by Adam's sin became the old age after the coming of the second Adam, Jesus Christ (2 Cor. 5:17). The New Christian Age is also described as the "new covenant" (Jer. 31:27-34; Heb. 8:8-12).

Jesus' New Age

Long before the "New Age" became identified with pagan occultic practices, the term was used to describe the new age that Jesus inaugurated through His death, resurrection, and ascension. One such book that expresses this view is Roderick Campbell's *Israel and the New Covenant*, originally published in 1954 by Presbyterian and Reformed Publishing Company and recently reprinted.[5]

---

2. Millard J. Erickson, *Christian Theology*, 3 vols. (Grand Rapids, MI: Baker, 1985), vol. 3, p. 1164. Emphasis added.

3. Anthony A. Hoekema, *The Bible and the Future* (Grand Rapids, MI: Eerdmans, 1979), p. 30.

4. *Idem.*

5. Presbyterian and Reformed Publishing Company (P&R) is nothing but orthodox. They have published books by Jay Adams, Cornelius Van Til, and Henry Morris. In fact, it was P&R that brought Whitcomb and Morris' *Genesis Flood* into print when a number of evangelical publishers would not. While P&R does not push a single eschatological position, the books they have published or distributed on the subject have been either amillennial (William Hendriksen, William Cox, and Jay Adams) or postmillennial (R. J. Rushdoony, Marcellus Kik, and Loraine Boettner). Boettner's *The Millennium* had gone through thirteen printings by 1984.

The Foreword to *Israel and the New Covenant* was written by O. T. Allis, who was for seven years Professor in the Old Testament Department of Westminster

Chapter 12 is titled "The New Age," and contains this passage:

> The following are a few significant phrases or titles which are based upon references in the New Testament to this most revolutionary of all transformations. In each of them the context from which they are derived demands that they be understood as applicable either to the transition from the Old to the New Covenant age, or to the consequent transformation which is being or will be effected in this present age:
>
> (1) The Restoration of All Things (Mat. 17:11).
> (2) The Regeneration (Mat. 19:28).
> (3) Times of Refreshing (Acts 3:19).
> (4) The Times of the Restitution of All Things (Acts 3:21).
> (5) The Time of Reformation (Heb. 9:10).
> (6) New Heavens and a New Earth (Rev. 21:1).
> (7) All Things New (Rev. 21:5).[6]

The present humanistic New Age advocates have taken these biblical concepts and have secularized them. On the other hand, much of the church has denied these rich biblical truths and has instead taught a doctrine that denies the people of God any earthly victory through the preaching of the gospel and the indwelling

---

Theological Seminary, Philadelphia, Pennsylvania. Why was Dr. Allis chosen to write the Foreword? His book *Prophecy and the Church* was an incisive critique of dispensational premillennialism, the eschatological position presently advocated by Dave Hunt, Hal Lindsey, David Wilkerson, et al. Campbell's work was a positive presentation of the kingdom. Allis wrote *Prophecy in the Church* in 1945. The subtitle tells it all: "An examination of the claim of dispensationalists that the Christian church is a mystery parenthesis which interrupts the fulfillment to Israel of the kingdom prophecies of the Old Testament." Allis writes of Campbell's position that it is not novel: "It is to be carefully noted that Mr. Campbell does not claim to be presenting a new interpretation, but rather a teaching which has been widely held in the past and by able scholars, an interpretation which can only be called novel, because it has been largely obscured by the quite different teachings which are so popular today. This is made clear by the footnotes which form a valuable addition to and confirmation of the argument presented in the text" (pp. viii-ix). Allis was a traditional postmillennialist of the "Princeton Seminary" variety, not an amillennialist.

6. Roderick Campbell, *Israel and the New Covenant* (Philadelphia, PA: Presbyterian and Reformed, [1954] 1983), p. 105.

and transforming work of the Holy Spirit. O. T. Allis makes a very timely observation as he seems to anticipate the present controversy. Speaking of Campbell and *Israel and the New Covenant*, Allis writes:

> He does not accept what he calls the "easy" solution of the problem [of the duty and destiny of the church], according to which we are to accept the failure of the church to win the world for Christ as evidence that this is not really the task of the church, and that we are to expect the Lord by His coming and visible reign to accomplish the task of establishing His kingdom upon earth. He tells us very definitely that this task is assigned to the church; and he challenges her to bestir herself for its achievement. For he believes, that it is only when the church has accomplished the task assigned her, that she can expect her Lord to say unto her, "Well done good and faithful servant," and to receive her unto Himself. This is the reason that the constant emphasis in the book is on the present task of the church as the ambassador of Christ to a needy, sin-cursed world.[7]

Again, the *term* "New Age" is empty by itself. We should ask about its content: What *concept* is carried by the phrases "New Age" or "New World Order"? Some writers and thinkers might use the phrases quite innocently. In Christian love we first should seek to understand what these people mean before we start accusing them of being something they may not be. Not everyone who believes in the Christianization of this world and the transformation of its institutions according to the renewing work of the gospel through the empowering of the Holy Spirit is "seduced" by New Age propaganda.

Modern "Newspeak"

As we all know, words can mean different things to different people in different times. Our society is notorious for giving new meanings to old words. Since we find comfort in what is familiar,

---

7. O. T. Allis, "Foreword" to *Israel and the New Covenant*, p. viii.

words are used by various non-Christian groups and then filled with new and sometimes sinister content. First it was sodomy, then it became homosexuality, now a sodomite is described as being "gay." Being "gay" takes the verbal edge off the descriptive and negative "sodomite." The semantic abuse in the abortion debate is even more clear. Abortionists do not call themselves "pro-death." Rather, they choose words that bridge religious and political lines of thought. Most Americans believe that they ought to have the right to make their own choices without interference from government. The pro-abortionists chose "pro-choice" to put the best face on their bloody business. The majority of Americans who really do not know what happens during an abortion are often fooled because the word pro-choice is so American.[8] The Communists' use of the words "peace" and "détente" are other examples.

The words "humanist" and "humanism" were chosen centuries ago by pagan philosophers and scientists to present a world view that few people could disagree with by only hearing the words. Most people equate "humanism" with humanitarianism or the humanities. Historically, a humanist was someone whose studies included "classical" learning.[9] So then, today, being anti-humanistic means you must be anti-humanitarian, and you despise the humanities. This is a very clever tactic. Find a word that has broad

---

8. Let's assume that Christian parents wanted to describe their desire to put their children in alternative schools as a "pro-choice" decision. Is their use of the word different in content from that of the pro-choice abortionists? Of course. The pro-choice abortionists are using their choice to snuff the life out of a defenseless human being. Christian parents are asking for the freedom to choose so their children will not be denied training in a comprehensive biblical world view that the public schools deny them.

9. "The secular humanism that we meet today is not the same thing as the Renaissance humanism which one sees in such men as Erasmus and Leonardo da Vinci. (Renaissance humanism, despite some murky streaks, was in essence a plea for a rich and robust Christian culture.) Nor should we equate secular humanism with the humanism professed by those who teach the humanities professionally; nor should we confuse it with the spirit of sympathetic concern for others' welfare which is often called humanism in these days." J. I. Packer and Thomas Howard, *Christianity: The True Humanism* (Waco, TX: Word Books, 1985), p. 16.

appeal and then fill it with new content. The unsuspecting will be drawn into the new world view without warning. But in fact, humanism is much more sinister than the word would suggest. Francis Schaeffer writes:

> The term *humanism* means Man beginning from himself, with no knowledge except what he himself can discover and no standard outside of himself. In this view Man is the measure of all things, as the Enlightenment expressed it. In other words, mankind can only look to itself for solutions to its problems and never looks to God either for salvation or for moral direction. Humanism can be seen, then, as the ultimate attempt to pull one's self up by one's own bootstraps.[10]

The New Agers are equally adept at choosing the right words. What if the present New Age Movement used phrases that really expressed what they believe? They would call their movement "The anti-God, Man is god, we are god Movement." Or perhaps, "I'm all god, you're all god." This would immediately turn off millions of people who are normally quite naive when it comes to spiritual things.

A head-on, frontal attack is unwise if your goal is to capture the mood and mind of the unsuspecting. "New Age" seems so optimistic and upbeat. Who doesn't want to be part of a new age, the "Age of Aquarius" as it was described in the 1960s? The aging traditional New Deal liberal, Max Lerner, in the Foreword to Marilyn Ferguson's *The Aquarian Conspiracy*, captures the author's hopeful prognosis for the future: "She describes with excitement the world of those who have strained to see past the blinders on the human spirit and have thrown them off, and she matches her own mood to their sense of optimism. 'I bring you good news' is her message."[11] Such an appeal is attractive to people with little or no theological training. The Christian knows that the gospel is the

---

10. Francis A. Schaeffer, "The Secular Humanist World View Versus the Christian World View and Biblical Perspectives on Military Preparedness," in *Who is For Peace?* (Nashville, TN: Nelson, 1983), p. 13.

11. (Los Angeles, California: J. P. Tarcher, Inc., 1980), p. 12.

true "good news": "And the angel said to them, 'Do not be afraid; for behold. I bring you good news of great joy which shall be for all the people; for today in the city of David there has been born for you a Savior, who is Christ the Lord'" (Luke 2:10-11). Any other claim to "good news" is a counterfeit gospel.

Christians must insist that content is what is really important. In this age of creedless Christianity, sloppy theology, and blind ecclesiastical unity, the church is easily thrown onto the mat by the masters of verbal jujitsu, or persuaded by artful slight of hand. Some newly initiated dominion thinking Christians are now confused because "dominion," "kingdom theology," and "Christian reconstruction" are being linked to the anti-God, man-is-god, we-are-all-god world view of New Age humanism. The devil couldn't be happier. The church, after basking in the light of God's promises of victory for the faithful, now seems to be retreating back to the seemingly comfortable surroundings of their previously occupied caves waiting for Jesus to rapture them home. No such rescue will take place. The rapture is a sign of victory for the church, not defeat.[12]

Is There a New Age Conspiracy?

Conspiracy.[13] The word strikes a note of terror (or excitement) in the heart of the little guy. What can a few Christians do when

---

12. No one we know denies the rapture, the ascension of the saints, although critics often accuse us of such a denial. The question of the rapture is one of timing. Even dispensationalists disagree on when the rapture will occur. Will it happen before the tribulation (pre-trib), in the midst of the tribulation (mid-trib), or after the tribulation (post-trib)? Postmillennialists hold that the rapture will occur *after* the millennium. Since it is in the distant future for the postmillennialist, some have seen this as a denial of its existence.

13. "Normally conspiracy suggests something sinister. But [Marilyn] Ferguson intends it to mean a breathing together of like-minded individuals in the spirit of the age, which she contends is the Age of Aquarius, characterized by the 'symbolic power of the pervasive dream in our popular culture: that after a dark, violent age, the Piscean, we are entering a millennium of love and light—in the words of the popular song, "The Age of Aquarius," the time of "the mind's true liberation."'" Irving Hexham and Karla Poewe, *Understanding Cults and New Religions* (Grand Rapids, MI: Eerdmans, 1986), p. 37.

the whole world is controlled by a liberal media, international bankers, and the Council on Foreign Relations, especially when they are in league with one another and the devil? Of course, the natural response is that we can't do much. Dave Hunt states that "it is no longer a question of *whether* but *when* humanity will be united both economically and politically under a one-world government."[14] He goes on to quote from the *Washington Post*'s evaluation of the Carter administration:

> If you like conspiracy theories about secret plots to take over the world, you are going to love the administration of President-elect Jimmy Carter. At last count 13 Trilateralists had gone into top positions . . . extraordinary when you consider that the Trilateral Commission only has about 65 American members.[15]

The Biblical View

The Bible has something to say about the conspiracies of men: "You are not to say, 'It is a conspiracy!' In regard to all that this people call a conspiracy. And you are not to fear what they fear or be in dread of it" (Isa. 8:12). Basically, God is saying that the conspiracies of men mean nothing in the long run. First, we should not call everything conspiratorial just because a number of anti-Christian groups think alike and often work in the same areas. The anti-Christian "conspirators" often look to Christian groups and make the same assessment. There are hundreds of Christian ministries that are not officially related, but their common beliefs and goals give the impression that they are working together, conspiring to bring an end to humanism wherever it is found. There are times when many of these Christian groups might work together on common projects to display a show of force. Usually, when the battle is finished, each group goes back to its original

---

14. Dave Hunt and T. A. McMahon, *The Seduction of Christianity: Spiritual Discernment in the Last Days*, (Eugene, OR: Harvest House, 1985), p. 49.

15. January 16, 1977, cited in *Idem*.

chartered goals.[16]

To his credit, Hunt does tell us that "these organizations [Trilateralists, Masons, Illuminati, and New Age networks] are only pawns in the real game. . . . The mastermind behind the scenes is Satan himself, and the world takeover is his move."[17] Isn't it at least *possible* that the "world takeover" is *God's* move? With what we know about God and His infinite power, and what we know about the devil and his limited power, what leads Hunt and others to conclude that there is no hope for the world?[18] Doesn't Scripture tell us that "greater is He that is in you than he who is in the world"? (1 John 4:4). Gary North writes:

> Why is it that Satan's earthly followers, who violate God's principles for successful living, supposedly will remain in control of the world until the Rapture? Are we supposed to believe that Satan's principles produce personal failure but cultural success, while biblical principles produce personal success but cultural failure? Does this make sense to you? It doesn't to me.[19]

---

16. The Coalition on Revival is one such group. Nearly 100 Christian leaders meet once a year to discuss the content of 17 world view documents. Some Humanists consider this conspiratorial: "The drive for unity has brought a variety of shepherding streams together under one umbrella organization, the California-based Coalition on Revival (COR). The groups represented in COR are the most politically active and, therefore, *the most worthy of our attention.*" Sara Diamond, "Shepherding," *CovertAction*, Number 27 (Spring 1987), p. 20. Nearly the entire issue of *CovertAction* is designed to counter the "conspiratorial" strategies of Christians groups that *seem* to be aligning themselves to overthrow pro-humanist organizations.

17. Hunt and McMahon, *Seduction of Christianity*, p. 50.

18. The Bible says that Satan is defeated, disarmed, and spoiled (Col. 2:15; Rev. 12:7ff.; Mark 3:27). He has "fallen" (Luke 10:18) and was "thrown down" (Rev. 12:9). He was "crushed" under the feet of the early Christians (Rom. 16:20). He has lost "authority" over Christians (Col. 1:13). He has been "judged" (John 16:11). He cannot "touch" a Christian (1 John 5:18). His works have been destroyed (1 John 3:8). He has "nothing" (John 14:30). He "flees" when "resisted" (James 4:7). He is "bound" (Mark 3:27; Luke 11:20). Surely Satan is alive, but he is not well on planet earth. Because of the present status of the devil, Scripture tells us that as Christians actively involve themselves in this world, the gates of hell "shall not overpower" the advancing church of the Lord Jesus Christ (Matt. 16:18).

19. "A Letter to Charismatics," *Christian Reconstruction* (July/August 1985), Institute for Christian Economics, P.O. Box 8000, Tyler, Texas, 75711.

Paranoia for Jesus

Second, preoccupation with conspiratorial designs leads to paranoia and immobility, even if the devil is orchestrating the whole mess.[20] If you look hard enough, you can see conspiracy and the devil everywhere. Any idea that connects with some aspect of "New Age" thinking will immediately label the entire organization or person as part of the conspiracy. "Well, I heard the same thing from a known New Ager. He must be part of the conspiracy too."

Some have maintained that "getting your colors done" is a New Age concept. Now, it may very well be that there are a lot of New Agers who get their colors done because of some cosmic color scheme that supposedly puts them in tune with the spiritual forces of nature, but this does not make the practice evil and part of some New Age conspiracy. God created color. Arranging the colors of our wardrobe so the look is pleasing to the eye did not originate with New Age thinkers. Art in all its forms *"is God's gift."*[21] The Christian should not reject art, color-coordinated clothes, design forms, and beauty because some pagans distort and pervert their meaning. What do these people think about Joseph's coat of many colors? Were his brothers right in getting rid of him? Was he a secret New Ager?

---

20. Even under the Old Covenant, the devil had to ask God's permission to afflict Job (Job 1:6-22). Satan could do nothing without God's sanction (2:1-10). In the New and "better covenant" (Heb. 7:22; 8:6), we are led to believe that the devil has more power than he had under the Old Covenant. Supposedly he is in control of the world because he is described as the "god of this world [lit., *age*]" (2 Cor. 4:4). But this is not the proper conclusion to draw. First, the devil is chosen as a god by "those who are perishing," and he must blind them before they will follow him: "The god of this world *has blinded the minds of the unbelieving*, that they *might not see the light of the gospel* of the glory of Christ, who is the image of God" (2 Cor. 4:4). The point of the passage is that unbelievers are *fooled* into believing that Satan is a god. Like idols in general, the devil is "by nature" not a god (Gal. 4:8; cf. Deut. 32:17; Psalm 96:5; Isa. 44:9-20; 1 Cor. 8:4; 10:20). In Philippians 3:19, Paul tells us that those who are "enemies of the cross of Christ" worship "their appetite." Is the appetite a god?

21. Gene Edward Veith, Jr., *The Gift of Art: The Place of Arts in Scripture* (Downers Grove, IL: InterVarsity Press, 1983), p. 19.

A few years ago, Carol DeMar, wife of the co-author, was asked by Walk Thru the Bible, an Atlanta-based Christian ministry specializing in monthly devotional materials, to sew a quilted backdrop for their display booth. Part of the design was a rainbow. At the National Religious Broadcasters convention in 1986, co-author Gary DeMar had the opportunity to see the completed quilt displayed. I introduced myself to those manning the booth, telling them how my wife sewed the quilt. They told me that a few people chastised them for using the quilt because of the rainbow design. "Don't you know," the New Age critics said, "that the rainbow is the symbol of the New Age Movement?"

This is paranoia. The rainbow is *God's* covenant sign (Gen. 9:12-17). We should always be reminded of God's faithfulness, mercy, and grace every time we see the rainbow. If there are hidden dangers in the rainbow, then they are dangers to the humanists who refuse to recognize that God made the rainbow in order to remind Himself of His covenant with man (Gen. 9:16). There are Christians who believe with all their hearts that anything stolen by Satan's followers from Christianity is forever Satan's, and any attempt on the part of Christians to reclaim it in the name of Jesus Christ is an aspect of New Age theology. These Christians take the attitude that "what's Satan's is Satan's, and what's ours is negotiable." So, for that matter, does Satan.

In a statement prepared by Evangelical Ministries to New Religions (EMNR), a cautionary word was given: "New Age teachers often use a common terminology. . . . However, merely using a term popular among New Agers [such as consciousness, holistic, or global] no more indicates acceptance of New Age philosophy than the use of the term 'evangelism' indicates acceptance of Christianity."[22] Christian groups that adopt the rainbow, or use such terms as "holistic" (God heals the *whole* person) and "global" (our presentation of the gospel should be *global*) are not necessarily New Agers because they use similar terms.

---

22. "Experts on Nontraditional Religions Try to Pin Down the New Age Movement," *Christianity Today* (May 17, 1985), p. 68.

Networking

"Networking," we are told, is another one of those words that an orthodox Christian should not use if he does not want to be labeled a New Ager. Again, here's a theologically useful term being painted with the same brush—an anti-color brush, of course—used by some Christians to paint supposed New Agers.

John Naisbitt, author of *Megatrends* and *Re-inventing the Corporation*, would describe himself as a New Age thinker.[23] At least some of his statements and practices would put him in that category. He talks about setting out "to write a book about re-inventing the world we live in." This would include "business, the family, the workplace, the arts, politics, education, and on and on."[24] He and his co-author settled on re-inventing the corporation. They tell us that "there is no time like the present" to "change the world."[25] They go on to say that "there must be a confluence of both changing values and economic necessity. And that is precisely what we have now: new humanistic values and global economic imperatives."[26] These are tip-off words to those who see the New Age in everything and everybody: "humanistic values" and "global" anything.

Now, Naisbitt devotes an entire chapter to "Hierarchies and Networking" in *Megatrends*. What if Christian groups use the term "networking" to describe the tactic of organizing a large force? Are these Christian groups part of the "conspiracy"? Are they in

---

23. "Naisbitt's mission is to bring aspects of the New Age to the business world. He told *New Age Journal* that he was 'pro-New Age values.' Although he often avoids the term *New Age*, its message is manifested in his work. He meditates with his wife each day, believes in reincarnation, has been rolfed (New Age physical therapy) and goes to a spiritual advisor for 'life readings.' In an interview he reported that he 'recently had a life reading from a psychic in Washington who told me, among other things, that I'd become a builder of New Age communities.'" Douglas R. Groothuis, *The New Age Movement* (Downers Grove, IL: InterVarsity Press, 1986), p. 5.

24. John Naisbitt and Patricia Aburdene, *Re-inventing the Corporation* (New York: Warner Books, 1985), p. ix.

25. *Ibid.*, p. 1.

26. *Ibid.*, p. 2.

danger of being sucked into the vortex of New Age thinking? I don't think so. Networking grows out of man's limited abilities to do everything himself. By nature man is limited. This is Paul's point in 1 Corinthians 12-14. Christians in a sense "network" their gifts to create a unified body of effort for the advance of the kingdom. Just because some New Age groups have picked it up and demonized it does not mean that networking in and of itself is evil.

Pre-revolutionary America had a form of networking called the "Committees of Correspondence." The purpose of these Committees was to fight a larger enemy, the crown, the centralized British government. John Fiske writes:

> The system of committees of correspondence did indeed grow into a mighty tree; *for it was nothing less than the beginning of the American Union.* Adams himself by no means intended to confine his plan to Massachusetts, for in the following April he wrote to Richard Henry Lee of Virginia urging the establishment of similar committees in every colony. But Virginia had already acted in the matter. . . .[27]

Again, we find that the New Agers have stolen another Christian concept and used it for the advance of their demonic, man-centered, anti-Christian kingdom building. Jesus' words sum up the matter: "For the sons of this age are more shrewd in relation to their own kind than the sons of light" (Luke 16:8).

Immobilized for Jesus

Seeing a conspiracy under every rock, simply because there seems to be an abundance of evidence to support the thesis, leads to paranoia. Richard Hofstadter says that "what distinguishes the paranoid style is not, then, the absence of verifiable facts . . . but rather the curious leap in imagination that is always made at some

---

27. Quoted in *Christian History of the Constitution series: Self-Government With Union*, compiled by Verna M. Hall and edited by Joseph Allan Montgomery (San Francisco, CA: The American Christian Constitution Press, 1962), p. 478.

critical point in the recital of events."[28] From the supposed "verifiable facts" one then makes "the big leap from the undeniable to the unbelievable."[29] Doug Groothuis writes that "New Age influence in our culture is undeniable; its power as a comprehensive conspiracy is less certain."[30]

The little guy gets so overwhelmed by the immense task that looms before him that he is unable to mobilize himself and others to fight the enemy. But in God's eyes the size of the enemy is inconsequential. Too often we impute power to evil, making it seem more sinister than it really is (Numbers 13-14 compared with Joshua 2). In fact, it's an opportunity for God to show His strength. Didn't Paul tells us that "power is perfected in weakness"? (2 Cor. 12:9; cf. 1 Cor. 1:25; Heb. 11:32-34). Evil *never* has the upper hand because "we know that God causes all things to work together for good to those who love God, to those who are called according to His purpose" (Rom. 8:28; cf. Gen. 45:1-11; 50:20). There is often the *perception* of power and all too often the *imputation of power* to evil men by Christians. What does God think of the conspiracies of men?

Why are the nations in an uproar, and the peoples devising a vain thing? The kings of the earth take their stand, and the rulers take counsel together against the Lord and against His Anointed:

---

28. Richard Hofstadter, *The Paranoid Style in American Politics* (New York: Alfred A. Knopf, 1965), p. 37. G. K. Chesterton noted, in his inimitable style, that we cannot convince a paranoid person that there is no conspiracy by appealing to facts:

> If a man says . . . that men have a conspiracy against him, you cannot dispute it except by saying that all the men deny that they are conspirators; which is exactly what conspirators would do. His explanation covers the facts as much as yours. Or if a man says that he is the rightful King of England, it is no complete answer to say that the existing authorities call him mad; for if he were King of England that might be the wisest thing for the existing authorities to do. Or if a man says that he is Jesus Christ, it is no answer to tell him the world denies his divinity; for the world denied Christ's. *Orthodoxy*, in *The Collected Works of G. K. Chesterton*, 28 vols. (San Francisco: Ignatius, [1908] 1986), vol. 1, p. 222.

29. Hofstadter, *The Paranoid Style*, pp. 37-38.
30. Douglas R. Groothuis, *Unmasking the New Age* (Downers Grove, IL: InterVarsity Press, 1986), p. 34.

"Let us tear their fetters apart, and cast away their cords from us!" *He who sits in the heavens laughs, the Lord scoffs at them.* Then He will speak to them in His anger and terrify them in His fury: "But as for Me, I have installed My King upon Zion, My holy mountain" (Psalm 2:1-6. Emphasis added.).

This Psalm does not reflect the theology of pessimism. Dave Hunt's view of victory is "the martyrs going to their death, singing of their love for the Lord, and trusting in Him."[31] It is true that for the Christian there is victory even in death. The sting of death is removed. There will be no reason to fear it. But are we to believe that there is *no earthly victory for the people of God*? Are we to believe that the church will never succeed and be victorious in anything? Can we conclude that success or victory is really a delusion and a seduction? Was the church victorious in England in abolishing the slave trade? Or should William Wilberforce have preached to the slaves the song of "martyrs going to their death"?

The Last Days?

Second Timothy 3 is often quoted by those who see no earthly hope for the people of God. The first eight verses are a litany of pessimism, yet there is no mention of the end of the world—only *the end of humanism*—in this passage. While nearly everyone reads that "in the last days difficult times will come" (v. 1), few read this phrase in context and through to the end of the chapter.

The ungodly will manifest a variety of characteristics that show their opposition to God's purposes: "For men will be lovers of self, lovers of money, boastful, arrogant, evildoers, disobedient to parents, ungrateful, unholy, etc." (vv. 2-5). Timothy is told to "avoid such men as these" (v. 5). Questions remain, however. When are the last days? Will the ungodly dominate culture? When Christians see these characteristics surfacing, how should they respond?

First, let's keep in mind that Paul is writing to Timothy, a first-century pastor. The words have meaning for him. While applications of these principles can be made to other periods in history, it's to Timothy that the warning comes. Second, the phrase the

---

31. *Dominion: A Dangerous New Theology,* Tape #1 of *Dominion: The Word and New World Order,* distributed by the *Omega-Letter,* Ontario, Canada, 1987.

"last days" is contrasted with the days before Jesus came to earth: "God, after He spoke *long ago* to the fathers in the prophets in many portions and in many ways [in the former days], *in these last days* has spoken to us in His Son, whom He appointed heir of all things, through whom also He made the world" (Heb. 1:1-2). The writer to the Hebrew Christians made it clear that he and they, the Hebrew Christians, were living in the last days.

Peter sees Joel's prophecy as being applicable to the people who heard his message at the feast of Pentecost: " 'And it shall be in the last days,' God says, 'that I will pour forth of My Spirit upon all mankind' " (Acts 2:17). This was his answer to the Pentecost experience. It would have made no sense if the fulfillment were 2,000 years later. There is no hint of a "double fulfillment."

Finally, Paul makes this striking assertion: "Now these things happened to them [the Israelites who wandered in the wilderness] as an example, and they were written for our instruction, *upon whom the ends of the ages have come*" (1 Cor. 10:11). The early church, the church to whom Paul wrote his letters, was living in the last days; therefore, Paul's warning to Timothy was a message of encouragement as he describes the demise of the enemies of the gospel. Paul's intention was not to present the church with signs that will warn some future generation of when Jesus is about to return. As we've shown in chapter 3, this passage has been used by nearly every generation of Christians to "prove" that Jesus is about to rapture His church.

At first reading, 2 Timothy 3 seems to indicate that the ungodly will prevail and godly influence will decline. Further study, however, shows that the Apostle Paul describes a different scenario. Paul compares the progress of the ungodly in Timothy's day with that of Jannes and Jambres, the Egyptian sorcerer-priests who opposed Moses (Ex. 7:11): "But they will not make further progress; for their folly will be obvious to all, as also that of those two [Jannes and Jambres] came to be" (2 Tim. 3:9).

Paul tells us that the people in Timothy's day who exhibit the deeds of wickedness will suffer the fate of Jannes and Jambres. Paul backs up his assertion with reference to an incident from the Old Testament where it *seemed* that God's people were on the losing side of the battle:

> Then Pharaoh also called for the wise men and the sorcerers, and they also, the magicians of Egypt, did the same with their secret arts. For each one threw down his staff and they turned into serpents. *But Aaron's staff swallowed up their staffs* (Ex. 7:11-12).

While it is true there is an *attempt* by the ungodly to dominate culture, the fact is, "they will not make further progress"; their fling with ungodliness is only temporary (cf. Rom. 1:18-32). Christians can remain optimistic even if the actions of the ungodly increase. In time, if Christians remain faithful in influencing their world with the gospel, the actions of the ungodly will be eliminated.

Paul, however, does not allow the Christian to remain passive as the ungodly self-destruct. Timothy has followed Paul's "teaching, conduct, purpose, faith, patience, love, perseverance, persecutions, [and] sufferings" (2 Tim. 3:10-11), and he calls on us to do the same (vv. 16-17). While the ungodly expend their spiritual capital in present-oriented living, and therefore have nothing saved for the future, the Christian is to develop future-oriented spiritual capital to replace the bankrupt culture of humanism with a Christ-centered society. Notice that the characteristics of the ungodly are all self-directed and short-lived, summarized by this phrase: "lovers of pleasure rather than lovers of God" (v. 4). Sin has its pleasure for a short period of time: "He who loves pleasure will become a poor man; he who loves wine and oil will not become rich" (Prov. 21:17). The love of pleasure is no investment in the future.

The characteristics of the godly are future-directed, foregoing the lure of present pleasures for the benefit of future productivity. Teaching, conduct, purpose, faith, patience, love, and perseverance take time and energy from the present, but result in future reward. Moreover, persecutions and sufferings should not deter the future-oriented Christian because "out of them all the Lord" delivers us (2 Tim. 3:11).

If the Christian looks only at present happenings he loses his hope of becoming a cultural influence, since he perceives the statement, "evil men and impostors will proceed from bad to worse, deceiving and being deceived" (2 Tim. 3:13) as something permanent. But even this description should not disturb the faithful Christian. Everything the ungodly does is a deception that backfires. Their deception of other men returns to them so that even they are "being deceived." We also must remember the previous words of Paul: "But they will not make further progress; for their folly will be obvious to all" (v. 9). In the short-term, it appears that the ungodly will prevail. Christians, however, must begin to think long-term; while the ungodly burn themselves out, the godly steadily influence their world: "You, however, *continue* in the things you have learned and become convinced of" (v. 14). In time, the effects of perseverance will be seen: "And let us not lose heart in doing good, for in due time we shall reap if we do not grow weary" (Gal. 6:9).

In time and in history, God defeats His enemies through the empowerment of His Spirit and the faithfulness of His servants. Paul does not deny "persecutions" and "sufferings" (2 Tim. 3:11). But he does tell us that "out of them all the Lord delivered me!" (v. 11).

Was Peter escaping Dave Hunt's version of victory by not going to his death when the angel of the Lord opened the prison door for him to escape? (Acts 5:19-20). Was Paul missing out on true victory when some of the disciples lowered him in a basket so he could escape death at the hands of the "Jews who plotted together to do away with him"? (Acts 9:23-25). The Bible shows us that victory is described in numerous ways. In all circumstances, death and life, the Christian is victorious. Suffering for Jesus is victory (Acts 5:41) as is deliverance from suffering (2 Tim. 3:11).

Conclusion

Conspiracies exist. Psalm 2 points out that the kings of the earth counsel and conspire together against the Christ, and Pilate and Herod became friends as a result of their common opposition to Jesus. Though the Bible acknowledges that conspiracies exist, it also teaches that even the most powerful conspiracy is powerless before the Almighty King. However powerful and well-organized the New Age "movement" might appear, it is no match for our Lord. Though the battle be fierce, Christ's victory is assured. Christians must view the New Age Movement with the eyes of faith, and not be intimidated by its *apparent* power.

7

GUILT BY ASSOCIATION

Too often, a doctrine is judged because of its association with heretical groups that seem to hold the same doctrinal position. Instead of evaluating the doctrine on its own merits or demerits by using the testimony of Scripture as the "touchstone" of truth, the critic maintains that the position must be wrong because anti-Christian groups hold a similar position. This frequently happens in elections when a candidate holds to a controversial position, and it is learned that an extremist group holds a similar position. "John Jones supports work-fare. We've just learned that the Ku Klux Klan holds a similar position. That's typical of the KKK; they're racists anyway. Since John Jones advocates a position similar to that of the KKK, our organization is withdrawing its support from John Jones." The possible merits of work-fare are obscured by the association with the deserved negative press that follows the KKK. Work-fare should be evaluated on its own merits.

Millions of Americans have owned Volkswagens. Adolf Hitler pushed for the production of a "people's car," the Volkswagen;[1] therefore, anybody who drives a Volkswagen is a Nazi.

Dave Hunt has implied that those who hold to a "dominion theology" are being seduced by a New Age philosophy. For Dave Hunt, the idea of dominion "opens the door to a marriage with New Age beliefs."[2] If a New Ager talks about the threat of nuclear

---

1. William L. Shirer, *The Rise and Fall of the Third Reich* (New York: Simon and Schuster, 1960), p. 266.

2. *Dominion: A Dangerous New Theology*, Tape #1 of *Dominion: The Word and New World Order*, Ontario, Canada, 1987.

holocaust, the threat of ecological collapse, and a concern for the earth, and if those advocating dominion under the lordship of Jesus Christ also talk about these things, then there is something of a philosophical affinity between the two groups. Hunt *assumes* that there is an inevitable "joining together" of the various humanistic groups pushing these ideals with Christian groups with similar emphases. There are a number of non-Christian groups opposed to abortion. While Christian groups are fighting the same battle, we do not find them abandoning Jesus Christ in favor, for example, of the atheistic worldview of Dr. Bernard Nathanson, a staunch anti-abortionist.[3] An "open door" to seduction *always* exists. A preoccupation with the law can lead to legalism. A perverted view of grace can set the trap for lawlessness. We should be careful when we accuse people of being seduced when diametrically opposed groups hold to similar ideals.

Let's put the shoe on the other foot for a moment. Some of those who are fearful that many well-meaning Christians are being seduced by the New Age Movement are premillennial in their eschatological views. Did you know that Jehovah's Witnesses are also premillennial?[4] Does this mean that Christian premillennialists are being seduced by the Jehovah's Witnesses because their views on eschatology are similar? There are other premillennial groups as well:

3. Bernard Nathanson, *Aborting America* (New York: Doubleday, 1979).

4. "Probably the most vigorous propagandizing campaign ever launched in this country [by someone who held to premillennialism] was that begun by Charles T. Russell, more commonly known as Pastor Russell. That movement has been variously known as Russellism, Millennial Dawnism, Watch Tower, International Bible Students, and more lately as Jehovah's Witnesses. While it has many features that are opposed to the usual premillennial program, it also includes a very definite system of Premillennialism. Its superficial and literalistic method of handling Scripture, its doctrine that the world cannot be Christianized through the preaching of the Gospel, its denunciation of the established churches, its strong emphasis on a 1000 year earthly kingdom, and its indulgence in date-setting, are elements that it has in common with what we have designated as standard Premillennialism." Loraine Boettner, *The Millennium* (rev. ed.; Phillipsburg, NJ: Presbyterian and Reformed, [1957] 1984), p. 360.

For more on date setting by the Jehovah's Witnesses see, Edmond C. Gruss, *The Jehovah's Witnesses and Prophetic Speculation: An Examination and Refutation of the Witnesses' Position on the Second Coming of Christ, Armageddon, and the "End of the World"* (Nutley, NJ: Presbyterian and Reformed, 1972) and Robert A. Morey, *How to Answer a Jehovah's Witness* (Minneapolis, MN: Bethany Fellowship, 1980), pp. 27-90.

The notorious Children of God began as a premillennialist, fundamentalist sect. They believed that the end of the world was imminent and that their leader, David Berg, had had visions confirming it. Acting on their belief, they adopted an itinerant lifestyle and lived as a people waiting for the end. Many of their excesses can be understood in the light of the urgency their premillennialism created.[5]

Dave Hunt, David Wilkerson, Jimmy Swaggart, Hal Lindsey, and premillennialists in general are not being seduced by the Children of God because they share similar eschatological views. In the same way, those who hold to dominion theology should not be grouped with known New Agers who also aspire to have dominion. The differences between dominion theology advocates and New Age advocates are as great as they are between Dave Hunt and David Berg.

One could just as easily say that a pessimistic view of the future is humanistic because some humanists advocate the same view, and anyone holding a similar view is humanistic in his thinking. This is guilt by association.[6] There are dozens of hu-

---

5. Irving Hexham and Karla Poewe, *Understanding Cults and New Religions* (Grand Rapids, MI: Eerdmans, 1986), p. 91.

6. Guilt by association works both ways. Sometimes a doctrine is supported because an orthodox theologian holds a similar position or at least uses the same terminology. John Frame, professor of systematic theology and apologetics at Westminster Theological Seminary in Escondido, California, writes: "In this sort of evaluation, a theological idea may be commended because it is the same or similar to the idea of another theologian who is well-respected. Conversely, an idea may be condemned because it is the same as one found in the writings of a theological 'bad guy.' Such comparisons can be useful, but are never in themselves grounds for criticism. An idea might be identical to one in, say, Schleiermacher or Barth, even *derived* from one of these, and still be a good idea. This type of criticism is even worse when it is directed against a theologian's use of *terms*. I was told once never to use the term 'transcendent' because the Greeks used it to articulate a non-Christian world view. It is true that words must be used carefully to avoid misunderstanding; but if we were to avoid altogether the use of words with significant non-Christian histories, we could hardly speak at all! Such criticism should be avoided. If you find, e.g., in Berkouwer, a phrase similar to one in Barth, then take note of it; but then go on to determine whether or not that verbal similarity really indicates similarity of content, and then determine independently the value of that content by criteria." John Frame, *How to Study for My Courses* (rev. ed.; Escondido, CA: unpublished paper, 1985), p. 14.

manists and humanist organizations that paint a gloomy picture of our earthly future.[7] David Wilkerson is predicting a nuclear holocaust, and so did a prominent New Ager, author of the cult book *The Mayan Factor*:

> Mr. Arguelles from Boulder, Col., [is] an art historian by training but a "millennialist" by inclination, by divine direction, by the dictates of reincarnation. . . .
>
> Mr. Arguelles says the choice between a "new age" and all-out destruction is ours, and we had better decide within the next eight weeks. A new beginning can be assured only if enough people gather at sacred spots around the globe like Machu Picchu, Peru—on Aug. 16 and 17 [1987].[8]

Arguelles was counting the days until the New Age would dawn. He even drew on the biblical literature, asking his supporters—144,000 of them—"to go to places like the Pyramids, Machu Picchu and even Idaho."[9] And it was all to begin on August 16, 1987, a day when just about nothing noteworthy hap-

---

7. The original *Global 2000 Report to the President* was a frightening look into the future. It was the work of globalists and humanists. Two paragraphs summarize the "Major findings and Conclusions" of *Global 2000*:

> If present trends continue, the world in 2000 will be more crowded, more polluted, less stable ecologically, and more vulnerable to disruption than the world we live in now. Serious stress involving population, resources, and environment are clearly visible ahead. Despite greater material output, the world's people will be poorer in many ways than they are today.
>
> For hundreds of millions of the desperately poor, the outlook for food and other necessities of life will be more precarious in 2000 then it is now—unless the nations of the world act decisively to alter current trends (p. 1).

Global 2000 reads like Hal Lindsey's chapter, "Polishing the Crystal Ball," *The Late Great Planet Earth* (Grand Rapids, MI: Zondervan, [1970] 1973), pp. 180-86. Is Lindsey in with the Humanists and Globalists that put together the *Global 2000 Report to the President?* We don't think so.

8. Meg Sullivan, "New Age Will Dawn in August, Seers Say, And Malibu Is Ready," *The Wall Street Journal* (June 23, 1987), p. 1. This sounds very much like David Wilkerson when he writes: "America is going to be destroyed by fire! Sudden destruction is coming and few will escape. Unexpectedly, and in one hour, a hydrogen holocaust will engulf America—and this nation will be no more." *Set The Trumpet to Thy Mouth* (Lindale, TX: World Challenge, 1985), p. 1.

9. Sullivan, "New Age Will Dawn," p. 1.

pened. Since this all sounds like the end-of-the-world scenario presented in David Wilkerson's *Set The Trumpet to Thy Mouth*, should we then conclude that Wilkerson has been seduced by a highly intelligent group of Mayan aliens? We don't think so.

Finally, there are those who say that to use the writings of New Agers in defense of some aspect of dominion theology is tantamount to being a New Ager. If Jeremy Rifkin and John Naisbitt are quoted approvingly, then there must be some New Age connection. This is nonsense. Dave Hunt quotes John Calvin on pages 16, 176, 188, and 192-193 in *Beyond Seduction: A Return to Biblical Christianity.*[10] Calvin castigated the "chiliasts,[11] who limited the reign of Christ to a thousand years." Calvin went on to write:

> Now their fiction is too childish either to need or to be worth a refutation. And the Apocalypse [the Book of Revelation], from which they undoubtedly drew a pretext for their error, does not support them. For the number "one thousand" [Rev. 20:4] does not apply to the eternal blessedness of the church but only to the various disturbances that awaited the church, while still toiling on earth. On the contrary, all Scripture proclaims that there will be no end to the blessedness of the elect or the punishment of the wicked [Matt. 25:41, 46].[12]

So, we could argue like this: Dave Hunt quotes John Calvin; John Calvin does not hold to a premillennial interpretation of eschatology; therefore, Dave Hunt is anti-premillennial. This would be extremely unfair. What Mr. Hunt would want us to do is to look at everything he says and also to understand that while we might disagree with men on some issues, this does not mean that everything they say is wrong. Mr. Hunt even quotes the anti-Christian psychiatrist Thomas Szasz.[13] Does this make Dave

---

10. Eugene, Oregon: Harvest House, 1987.

11. The term "chiliasts" (millennialists) was applied to a number of ancient sects who held a belief in the one-thousand-year reign of Christ on earth.

12. *John Calvin: Institutes of the Christian Religion*, ed., John T. McNeill, trans. Ford Lewis Battles, 2 vols. (Philadelphia, PA: Westminster Press, 1969), vol. 2 (III.xxv.5), p. 995.

13. Hunt, *Beyond Seduction*, p. 110. See Thomas Szasz' negative comments about the Bible and Christianity in *The Myth of Mental Illness* (rev. ed.; New York: Harper & Row, 1974), pp. 165-75, and *The Manufacture of Madness* (New York: Harper & Row, 1970).

Hunt a follower of the humanistic psychology advocated by Dr. Szasz? Of course not.

Because they counterfeit the Christian faith, humanists often have some good things to say. In fact, humanism has made the major intellectual and scientific advances in recent decades because Christians have failed to understand that the Bible applies to every area of life. Humanists believe that their world view is comprehensive enough to include the world. They have been frantically working, with little opposition from Christians, to implement their crumbling world view in places where Christians have pulled up stakes and left culturally barren ground. Where do these anti-Christian thinkers and writers get their often valuable insights? They are *"stolen from the Bible* when they are correct. When men come to conclusions that are also the conclusions of the Bible, we should use their discoveries. These discoveries are our property, not theirs. God owns the world; the devil owns nothing. We are God's adopted children; they are God's disinherited children."[14]

Conclusion

It is true that "dominion theologians" use some of the same terms that New Agers use. In certain areas, the ideas may even be similar. The same can be said of premillennial, pretribulational dispensationalists. But these facts do not prove that "dominion theologians" have been seduced by the New Age Movement, nor does it mean that Jeremy Rifkin has seduced the faculty of schools

---

14. Gary North, *Moses and Pharaoh: Dominion Religion Versus Power Religion* (Tyler, TX: Institute for Christian Economics, 1985), p. x. Dr. North cautions us with these words: "The most important thing is how well I integrate such humanistic insights into my biblical reconstruction of economics [the topic of his book], without 1) losing the importance of these insights or 2) becoming a slave of the humanist presuppositions which officially undergird such insights. But this is the most important task in any field. Every Christian faces this problem. We buy and sell with pagans in many marketplaces, and one of these marketplaces is the marketplace for ideas. We must use their best ideas against them, and we must expose their worst ideas in order to undermine men's confidence in them. In short, in God's universe, it is a question of 'heads, we win; tails, they lose' " (p. xi).

where dispensational premillennialism is taught. Yet Dave Hunt has cautiously implied, and his less astute followers have repeatedly made, just this sort of erroneous, preposterous association. Such a conclusion is unfair to Christians who teach "dominion theology," and it ignores the possibility that New Agers may in fact be imitating dominion theology.

8

THE TIMING OF THE KINGDOM

One of the central issues in Hunt's critique of "dominion" or "kingdom" theology is the doctrine of the kingdom. What is the kingdom of God? When was it (or will it be) established? Do we have to wait for the millennium? Or do we have to wait until *after* the millennium? Does the kingdom affect the earth? Will it exist on earth during a future millennium? In this chapter and in the following one, we will try to answer these questions. We will first look at the question of the timing of the kingdom.

A Future Kingdom

Hunt believes that the kingdom is primarily a future reality. Though he does admit that the kingdom "begins in the hearts of all who obey Christ as King," he emphasizes that "the outward manifestation of this kingdom will not come in its fullness until God has destroyed this present universe and created a new one into which sin will never enter (2 Peter 3:10-13; Rev. 21:1; etc.)."[1] Thus, his emphasis is almost entirely on the *future* coming of the kingdom.

> Making temporary solutions to social problems the over-riding concern of Christians blunts the gospel and obscures God's eternal solution. The focus is turned from heaven to this earth, from a new universe that only God can create to a new world that

---

1. Dave Hunt and T. A. McMahon, *The Seduction of Christianity: Spiritual Discernment in the Last Days* (Eugene, OR: Harvest House, 1985), p. 224. We agree that the kingdom will be fully realized only after Christ's return.

we hope to fashion by our own efforts. It is just one more form of the selfism that plagues society and the church, another way of becoming little gods, of turning from Him to ourselves by assuming a responsibility to do what only He can do.[2]

The focus of the Christian's attention, Hunt says, is "heaven" and the "new universe" that God will create at the end of time.

Hunt claims that the kingdom is not even established during the millennium. He refers to 1 Corinthians 15:50 to prove that the kingdom is not a kingdom of flesh and blood people.

> Paul declared that "flesh and blood cannot inherit the kingdom of God" (1 Corinthians 15:50), so the kingdom cannot be the millennium, with its flesh-and-blood humans multiplying across the earth, much less the world of today taken over by Christians exercising dominion.[3]

Let us summarize the logic of Hunt's argument. Paul says that "flesh and blood cannot inherit the kingdom of God." Hunt appears to believe that "flesh and blood" refers to man's physical nature. Thus, the kingdom cannot come until men and women no longer have "flesh and blood." Because people in the millennium still have "flesh and blood," the millennium cannot be the kingdom. There is only one place where men and women cease to have "flesh and blood"—in heaven. Thus, Hunt concludes that heaven is the kingdom. Period.

It is difficult to figure out precisely what Hunt is trying to prove with this passage. After all, nearly every interpreter of 1 Corinthians 15 agrees that it refers to the final resurrection, the end of history, the time of Christ's Second Coming.[4] The "king-

---

2. Hunt, *Beyond Seduction: A Return to Biblical Christianity* (Eugene, OR: Harvest House, 1987), p. 255. Like Hunt, we do not believe that "temporary solutions to social problems" should be the "overriding concern of Christians."

3. Hunt and McMahon, *Seduction of Christianity*, p. 223.

4. See Gordon Clark, *I Corinthians: A Contemporary Commentary* (Nutley, NJ: Presbyterian and Reformed, 1975), p. 261: the context of this verse (15:20-29) talks about "the resurrection of believers at Christ's return." Frederic Louis Godet, *Commentary on First Corinthians* (Grand Rapids, MI: Kregel, 1977), pp. 771-868, assumes throughout his lengthy exposition that this passage refers to the

dom" in this passage is the *final* kingdom of the consummated new heavens and new earth, as we will discuss below. We admit that the biblical writers sometimes refer to our eternal state in the new heavens and new earth as "the kingdom." But that doesn't mean that "kingdom" can't refer to something else in other passages. Thus, this passage is only indirectly relevant to the question of whether or not the kingdom is present *now*. In other words, the kingdom could be *both* present *and* future. Just because this passage refers to a future kingdom does not mean that there can be no visible manifestation of the kingdom in the present. Even if Hunt is correct about the interpretation of this passage, he has yet to prove anything about the kingdom in history.

Moreover, the whole point of 1 Corinthians 15 is that we will be raised with *bodies*. Would Hunt deny this? We don't think so. What he seems to be saying is that these bodies will not be "flesh and blood" bodies. This is correct, but we must ask what "flesh and blood" means for Paul.

In trying to understand a phrase in Scripture, it is often helpful to study what it is contrasted with. Today, we use "flesh and blood" to denote man's physical nature, and contrast it to "mind" or "soul." Hunt appears to assume that Paul uses "flesh and blood" in the same sense that we do. This is not necessarily the connotation that Paul gives to this expression. It is true that "flesh and blood" in the New Testament refers in some passages to man's physical nature, as when the author of Hebrews tells us that Jesus partook of flesh and blood (Heb. 2:14). But it can also refer to human opponents in contrast to the demonic principalities and powers (Eph. 6:11-12). The New Testament writers, moreover, also use "flesh and blood" to refer to man in contrast to God, as a weak and dependent creature (Matt. 16:17; Gal. 1:15-17). In this

---

time of the Second Advent. Likewise R. C. H. Lenski, *The Interpretation of St. Paul's First and Second Epistles to the Corinthians* (Minneapolis, MN: Augsburg, [1937] 1967), p. 737; John Calvin, *The First Epistle of Paul the Apostle to the Corinthians*, trans. John W. Fraser (Grand Rapids, MI: Eerdmans, [1546] 1973), p. 312; Robert S. Candlish, *Life in a Risen Savior* (Minneapolis, MN: James and Klock, [1863] 1977), pp. 226-227.

sense, it has no suggestion of sin, but simply emphasizes that man is man and not God. He is weak and subject to decay.[5] As Ridderbos puts it, " 'flesh' has for [Paul] the significance of what is human in its weakness, dependence on God, and perishableness in itself." Man in his entirety is "flesh and blood."[6] C. S. Lewis's characterization of heavenly beings as "the Solid People" captured an important truth. In Lewis's dream, it is not heaven that is vaporous, but earth. The earth-bound "Ghosts" could not even walk on the grass of heaven because it was too solid.[7] Lewis was not making a theologically precise statement, but his description is a vivid reminder that we will be resurrected with bodies.

In order to understand what Paul meant by flesh and blood in 1 Corinthians 15:50 specifically, we should note that verse 50 is a summary statement of the previous discussion about different kinds of bodies. Thus, "flesh and blood" is equivalent to the "natural body" that Paul describes in verses 42-46. What characterizes this natural body, this flesh and blood existence? Corruption (v. 42), dishonor (v. 43), weakness (v. 43). These characteristics *define* what Paul means by "flesh and blood." "Flesh and blood" does not refer exclusively to man's physical nature. All of these things— corruption, dishonor, weakness—could just as easily describe man's soul or mind. Thus, Paul doesn't mean that men cannot inherit the kingdom of God as long as they have bones and sinews and muscles. He means that they cannot inherit the kingdom in

---

5. Even Hebrews 2:14 can be understood in this way: Christ took on *weak* human flesh. He did not take on the flesh of the uncorrupted Adam, but of the corruptible sons of Adam. After all, he took His flesh from the fallen nature of the Virgin Mary. This does not mean, of course, that Christ was morally corrupt.

6. Herman Ridderbos, *Paul: An Outline of His Theology* (Grand Rapids, MI: Eerdmans, 1975), p. 93. Thus, in Paul's terminology, even the souls and minds of men are "fleshly" (cf. Rom. 8:6-8; especially the phrase "mind set on the flesh"). Ridderbos notes, "Just as the Old Testament concept 'flesh' (e.g., Isa. 31:3; Jer. 32:27; Job 10:4), or 'flesh and blood,' it denotes in Paul especially the human as such and taken by itself, as distinguished from and in contrast to the divine. There is not yet here *per se* an indication of human sinfulness, but only of human limitation and weakness . . ." (p. 94).

7. C. S. Lewis, *The Great Divorce* (London: Geoffrey Bles, 1946).

the weakness and corruption of the fleshly existence.[8]

This interpretation is strengthened by the fact that the natural body is contrasted throughout this passage with the spiritual body (vv. 43, 46). For Paul, "spiritual" almost invariably refers to the Holy Spirit. Certainly it does in this passage. Thus, a "natural" or "flesh and blood" existence is the living death of men apart from the Holy Spirit. When Paul says that "flesh and blood" cannot inherit the kingdom, he is simply applying Jesus' statement in John 3:5-6 to the final kingdom. Jesus said, "unless one is born of water and the Spirit, he cannot enter into the kingdom of God. That which is born of the flesh is flesh, and that which is born of the Spirit is spirit." These words appear to be in the background of Paul's statement in 1 Corinthians 15:50.

It is also possible that Paul uses "flesh and blood" to refer to natural generation. Thus, he might be saying that men do not inherit the kingdom of God because they are born into the "right family." People do not inherit the kingdom because they are born as Jews, or because their parents are Christians. They inherit the kingdom only by Spiritual generation. John uses flesh and blood

---

8. A similar interpretation is adopted by Calvin, *Commentary on the First Epistle to the Corinthians*, p. 341: "we must understand *flesh and blood* to mean flesh and blood as they are at present constituted; for our flesh will share in the glory of God, but only after it has been renewed and restored to life by the Spirit of Christ." Though we do not agree with everything that he says, F. W. Grosheide, *Commentary on the First Epistle to the Corinthians* (Grand Rapids, MI: Eerdmans, 1952), p. 391, does note that "flesh and blood" should be taken figuratively. It designates man "as he is today in a world that has to bear the consequences of sin." The flesh and blood man is one "whose only connection is with this earth." Candlish, *Life in a Risen Savior*, p. 217, notes that "flesh and blood is identified with corruption. Corruption is its characteristic. Corruption is its distinguishing attribute; not, I again remind you, moral pollution; but if we may so speak, physical divisibility, liability to be broken into parts, dissolved or resolved into particles of dust. That is corruption; and that is flesh and blood." Gordon Fee understands "flesh and blood" in a broader sense: "Most likely it refers simply to the body in its present form, composed of flesh and blood, to be sure, but subject to weakness, decay, and death, and as such ill-suited for the life of the future." *The First Epistle to the Corinthians* (Grand Rapids, MI: Eerdmans, 1987), p. 799. All of these commentators agree that the emphasis of Paul's phrase is not merely on the physical nature of man, but on the corruption and weakness that characterize our present mode of life.

in this sense in John 1:12-13: "But as many as received Him, to them He gave the right to become children of God, even to those who believe in His name, who were born not of blood, nor of the will of the flesh, nor of the will of man, but of God."

Thus, Paul does not mean that believers will enter the kingdom as disembodied souls. They will enter the final kingdom with resurrected, spiritual *bodies*. Jesus ate with His disciples after His resurrection (Luke 24:40-43). His disciples were able to touch and see Him. He even called attention to His "flesh and bones" (Luke 24:39). Yet, He was raised with a spiritual body (1 Cor. 15:45-46). *A spiritual body is not a vapor or a mist. It is a body controlled by the Holy Spirit.* Those who enter the final kingdom will have bodies, but they will not be weak, corruptible, and depraved "fleshly" bodies. Men must be transformed to inherit the kingdom. They must be raised with spiritual bodies.[9]

What, then, does this passage actually teach about the timing of the kingdom? It does not teach that there is no kingdom in history. It teaches that men must be transformed to inherit the kingdom of God. This is true in the present, as well as in the future. If we are to be subjects of the kingdom of God now, we must be spiritual, not fleshly. In principle, we are already spiritual. We have been baptized into Christ, and therefore we are "freed from sin" (Rom. 6:1-7). In Romans 7:5, Paul says, "For while we *were* in the flesh, the sinful passions, which were aroused by the Law, were at work in the members of our body to bear fruit for death." Note that Paul tells Christians that they *were* in the flesh. In a sense, then, Christians are already spiritual, though we are not perfectly spiritual; we have already put off "flesh and blood," and now live in the "newness of the Spirit and not in oldness of the letter" (Rom. 7:6). Thus, what Paul says about the final kingdom in 1 Corinthians 15:50 is already true of Christians today. And, if

---

9. This resurrection has already taken place in principle because we already share in Christ's resurrection. Having been baptized into His death, we are raised in the likeness of His resurrection, to walk in newness of life (Rom. 6:1-11). See Norman Shepherd, "The Resurrections of Revelation 20," *Westminster Theological Journal* 37 (Fall 1974): 34-43.

Christians have already put off the flesh, then the kingdom has already come. When Christ returns, we shall be spiritual in the fullest sense, and the kingdom will come in fullness. But it is also true that we have already inherited the kingdom, because we are already spiritual.

Hunt uses a second argument to prove that the kingdom is not established in the millennium.

> We are told many times in the Bible that God's kingdom "is an everlasting kingdom." Of the coming Messiah, Isaiah prophesied that there would be no end both to His kingdom and to the peace it established (Isaiah 9:6,7). On this count also the kingdom cannot be the millennium, for that wonderful time of peace on earth as Christ reigns from Jerusalem not only ends, but with a great war (Revelation 20:7-9).[10]

Because the kingdom is eternal, it cannot be established during the limited period of the millennium. This argument again says nothing about whether the kingdom has *already* been established. It is clear from Scripture that the kingdom is eternal. But this fact does not tell us *when* the kingdom was (or will be) established. It merely tells us that, once the kingdom is established, it will never end. We will argue in this chapter that the kingdom is indeed everlasting, but that it has already begun, with the life, death, and resurrection of the Christ.

Hunt and Mainstream Dispensationalism

Hunt's position is not consistent with the traditional dispensationalist view, to which Hunt generally adheres. According to

---

10. Hunt and McMahon, *Seduction of Christianity*, p. 223-24. Hal Lindsey, though joined with Hunt in his opposition to dominion theology, does not agree with Hunt on the timing of the kingdom. Lindsey, working with the dispensationalist literal interpretation, writes that "if you interpret prophecy literally [Scripture] does teach that Christ will set up a literal kingdom in time which will last in history a thousand years and then go into an eternal form which will never be destroyed." *The Late Great Planet Earth* (Grand Rapids, MI: Zondervan, [1970] 1973), p. 176. Jimmy Swaggart also adopts a traditional dispensationalist interpretation of the millennium: "We believe that Christ's coming will usher in the visible Kingdom. We believe the Kingdom is eternal but will have a thousand-year visible manifestation on earth." "The Coming Kingdom," *The Evangelist* (September 1986), p. 8.

Charles Ryrie, a leading dispensationalist theologian, dispensationalism teaches that Christ offered the Davidic kingdom to Israel. Because Israel rejected the kingdom, its establishment was postponed. In the millennium, however, Christ will establish this Davidic kingdom.[11] In other words, Ryrie is saying that Christ will establish *the* kingdom during the millennium. Another leading dispensationalist theologian, John Walvoord, wrote a book in 1959 called *The Millennial Kingdom*.[12] Lewis Sperry Chafer, whose massive *Systematic Theology* has been a dispensationalist standard, claimed that the kingdom was postponed when the first-century Jews rejected the Messiah. It will, however, be realized when Christ returns and offers the kingdom again to the Jews.[13] Herman Hoyt of Grace Theological Seminary describes in glowing terms the "richness and greatness of the kingdom" during the millennium.[14] Postmillennial writer Loraine Boettner says that dispensationalism teaches that the rejected kingdom "is held in abeyance until the return of Christ, at which time it is to be established by overwhelming power."[15] Amillennialist Anthony Hoekema writes that, in the dispensational view, Christ's second coming establishes His "millennial reign," during which Christ "rules over a kingdom."[16] Thus, both dispensationalists and nondispensationalists agree that the teaching of mainstream dispensationalism is that Christ establishes His kingdom in the millen-

---

11. Charles C. Ryrie, *Dispensationalism Today* (Chicago, IL: Moody Press, 1965), pp. 170-173. Like Hunt, Ryrie admits that in a "spiritual" sense, Christ's kingdom is already established on earth. This kingdom refers to God's rule over the hearts of men. What was postponed, therefore, was the establishment of the external, earthly, Davidic kingdom.

12. Grand Rapids, MI: Zondervan, 1959.

13. Chafer's views are summarized in Clarence Bass, *Backgrounds to Dispensationalism: Its Historical Genesis and Ecclesiastical Implications* (Grand Rapids, MI: Baker, 1960), p. 31.

14. Hoyt, "Dispensational Premillennialism," in *The Meaning of the Millennium: Four Views* (Downers Grove, IL: InterVarsity, 1977), pp. 82-83.

15. Loraine Boettner, *The Millennium* (3rd rev. ed.; Phillipsburg, NJ: Presbyterian and Reformed, [1957] 1984), p. 284.

16. Hoekema, *The Bible and the Future* (Grand Rapids, MI: Eerdmans, 1979), p. 191.

nium. Hunt, as far as we can tell, disagrees.

It is important to stress this point. If our interpretation of Hunt's position is correct, he has abandoned the traditional dispensational system at this point. He has denied that the kingdom of God will ever be manifested on earth, even in the millennium. Hunt admits that during the millennium, the "whole earth will resemble the Garden of Eden before the fall."[17] But the Garden was where man first sinned. Similarly, the millennium will end in disaster:

> Converging from all over the world to war against Christ and the saints at Jerusalem, these rebels will finally have to be banished from God's presence forever (Revelation 20:7-10). The millennial reign of Christ upon earth, rather than being the kingdom of God, will in fact be the final proof of the incorrigible nature of the human heart.[18]

If this is the case, then all talk of the kingdom of God on earth is a delusion—a delusion of the Antichrist. This anti-historical bias was always implicit in dispensationalism, but Hunt has made it explicit. There is no hope for Christians in history, not even during the millennium. Christians will never exercise dominion, not even during Christ's personal reign from Jerusalem. The reason, Hunt says, is that it is impossible for God to set up an earthly kingdom. Apparently, Satan is too powerful.

> In fact, dominion—taking dominion and setting up the kingdom of Christ—is an *impossibility*, even for God. The millennial reign of Christ, far from being the kingdom, is actually the final proof of the incorrigible nature of the human heart, because Christ Himself can't do what these people say they are going to do. . . .[19]

We would like to believe that Hunt did not think through the implications of this statement very carefully. As it stands, Hunt is

---

17. *Beyond Seduction*, p. 250.
18. *Idem.*
19. *Dominion and the Cross*, Tape #2 of *Dominion: The Word And New World Order*, distributed by the *Omega-Letter*, Ontario, Canada, 1987.

simply denying the sovereignty of God. There seems to be no other way to interpret his statement. He does not say that God does not *want* to establish His kingdom. He says that God *can't* establish His kingdom. This statement reveals the rock bottom of Hunt's objections to dominion. The issue, it turns out, is not eschatology, but Hunt's doctrine of God. Hunt, perhaps unintentionally, says that God is unable to do what He wills to do. This, we think, is hardly an accurate description of the Almighty God of Scripture, the God who does as He pleases in heaven and on earth (Dan. 4:34-35). Such statements do not attribute to our God glory and strength, as Scripture exhorts us to do.

The Last Days

The main issue, of course, is not whether Hunt is an orthodox dispensationalist. The issue is whether the New Testament supports the belief that the kingdom is *primarily* or *exclusively* a future reality. We believe that it does not.

One source of confusion in this whole area is the biblical use of the terms "last days" and "latter days." Hunt and many other dispensationalists believe that this refers to the last days of history, that is, the very end of the world. Very often, however, this is obviously *not* the way that the Bible uses this phrase. At Pentecost, Peter defended the apostles from charges of drunken carousing by quoting from Joel 2:28-32: "And it shall be *in the last days* that I will pour forth of My Spirit upon all mankind" (Acts 2:17a). When was this "last days" prophecy fulfilled? Peter said that the events of Pentecost fulfilled Joel's prophecy (Acts 2:16).[20]

Similar language is used in the first verses of Hebrews 1: "In these last days [God] has spoken to us in His Son" (Heb. 1:2). Again, we might ask *when* God spoke to us in His Son. Clearly, the writer of Hebrews is referring to the *first* advent of Christ.

---

20. David Chilton notes: "Contrary to some modern expositions of this text, Peter did not say that the miracles of Pentecost were *like* what Joel prophesied, or that they were some sort of '*proto*-fulfillments' of Joel's prophecy; he said that this was *the* fulfillment." *Paradise Restored: A Biblical Theology of Dominion* (Ft. Worth, TX: Dominion Press, 1985), p. 117.

Later, the author of Hebrews said the "end of the ages" had come upon his readers (Heb. 9:26). Peter says that the Lamb "was foreknown before the foundation of the world, but has appeared *in these last times* for the sake of you" (1 Peter 2:20). *When* did the Lamb appear for us? Again, it is obvious that Peter is referring to the first coming of Christ.

Thus, when the biblical writers talk about the last days, we should not think immediately of the end of the world. Rather, we should think of the incarnation, life, death, and resurrection of Christ as the beginning of the last days. When Paul warned Timothy about the deception and heresy of "later times," he was not prophesying of the late 20th century (1 Tim. 4:1; 2 Tim. 3:1-9). Paul's warnings to Timothy were *urgent* because the things that he prophesied were *already* happening. After all, he told Timothy to "avoid such men as these" (2 Tim. 3:6). If Paul had been prophesying of the distant future, this warning would have been nonsensical to Timothy. There was no reason for Paul to warn Timothy to avoid people who wouldn't be born for twenty centuries. Paul warned Timothy about false teachers because Timothy was going to confront them in his ministry. These prophecies, in short, were fulfilled in the first century.[21]

It may seem odd that Scripture refers to this period as the last days. In fact, it seems odd to us only because we assume that these phrases refer to the end of the world. If we think about things biblically, and try to understand these passages as first-century Jews would have understood them, the coming of Christ *was* the end of the world.[22] With the death and resurrection of

---

21. Of course, we are not saying that the letters to Timothy are irrelevant to us in the 20th century. Rather, we are saying that the *primary* or *immediate* focus of Paul's concern was with his own century and the problems of the apostolic church.

22. Even the disciples, who were with Jesus for three years, could not separate the destruction of Jerusalem from the end of the world. When Jesus told them that the Temple would be destroyed, they immediately thought of the "end of the age" (Matt. 24:3).

We use the same kind of language rather frivolously, and no one thinks that we're talking about the end of the world. When Fred Astaire and Jackie Gleason died in the same week in 1987, the newsmen called it "the end of an era." How much more can we say that God's turning from Israel was the "end of the world!"

Christ, everything changed. In Christ the old things pass away
and all things are made new (2 Cor. 5:17). In order to understand
this, we must realize that the Bible views the nation of Israel as
the center of world history prior to the coming of Christ. When
Israel was rejected as the chosen race, the old world came to an
end. Christ came to found a new covenant, a new priesthood, a
new Israel, a new chosen people. Thus, when the New Testament
writers say that the world is coming to an end, or that the "last
days" have come, we should understand that the world *as it centered
on Israel* was ending.[23] In a very real sense, the world came to an
end with the life, death, and resurrection of Christ, Pentecost,
and the destruction of Jerusalem in A.D. 70. These events took
place in the last days of the old world.

The Establishment of the Kingdom

To keep a balanced perspective on the timing of the kingdom,
we must see it in three different time frames. First, it is *definitively*
established in the life, death, resurrection, and ascension of Jesus
Christ. Second, it increases and advances *progressively* from that
time to the end of the world. Finally, it is established *fully* at
Christ's second coming.

Definitive

Let us first examine the definitive aspect of the kingdom.

Even a superficial reading of the gospels shows that the king-
dom of God is the major theme of the ministries of both John the
Baptist and Jesus. In fact, this is what the gospels are all about:
The King is coming to establish His kingdom. John the Baptist

---

23. This is what Peter meant when he said that "the end of all things is *at hand*"
(1 Pet. 4:7). If Peter had meant that the physical earth would be literally destroyed
in the near future, he was simply wrong. Some people would take another view
of this verse and say that the "at hand" does not mean "in the near future." If that
is the case, there is little meaning in Peter's words at all. Peter deliberately put a
time indicator in his prophecy. Peter meant that the end was near. But he didn't
mean that the physical earth would disappear. He meant that all old things, all
the things of the Old Covenant, would pass away in the destruction of Jerusalem.

exhorted the people of Judea to repent because "the kingdom of heaven is *near*" (Matt. 3:2). From his very first sermon, Jesus preached a similar message: "Repent, for the kingdom of heaven is *near*" (Matt. 4:17). When Jesus sent out the seventy-two disciples, he told them to preach that "The kingdom of God is *near*" (Luke 10:9).[24] The "synoptic" gospels—Matthew, Mark, and Luke—all declare that the content of Jesus' entire teaching ministry can be summed up as the "good news of the kingdom" (Matt. 4:23; Mark 1:14-15; Luke 4:16-30; 4:43; 8:1).[25] These passages, and many others besides, prove that the establishment of the kingdom was imminent. It was "near" already in the time of Jesus.

There was, however, a very significant difference between the preaching of John and the preaching of Jesus. They often used the same words. But we find in Mark 1:15 that Jesus not only proclaims that the kingdom is near, but announces that "the time is fulfilled."[26] Thus, while John prophesied that it was almost time for the Lord to visit His people, Jesus "asserted that this visitation was in actual progress, that God was already visiting his people."[27] Moreover, in Luke 17:21, Jesus tells the Pharisees that

---

24. Note that the gospels say that both "the kingdom of heaven" and "the kingdom of God" are near. The phrase "kingdom of heaven" appears only in Matthew. There is, however, no sharp distinction between these two terms. Whatever distinctive shade of meaning Matthew might have given to "heaven," he uses the two phrases to refer to the same thing. See especially Matthew 19:23-24, where Jesus tells His disciples that it is hard for a rich man to enter the kingdom of heaven (v. 23), and that it is easier for a camel to go through the eye of a needle than for a rich man to enter the kingdom of God (v. 24). Clearly, the two phrases are parallel and, for most purposes, synonymous.

25. The passage in Luke 4 takes a somewhat different perspective from the other passages. Luke presents Jesus' first sermon as an announcement of the coming of the "acceptable year of the Lord," the cosmic Jubilee (cf. Lev. 25). The signs of the Jubilee year, however, are the same as those of the kingdom (cf. Isa. 61:2 with Isa. 11:1-5). These are just two ways of talking about the same reality.

26. Herman Ridderbos, *The Coming of the Kingdom* (Philadelphia: Presbyterian and Reformed, 1962), p. 48. Ridderbos notes that Jesus' words indicate that the coming of the kingdom is at "a more advanced point of time than that of John."

27. George Eldon Ladd, *Jesus and the Kingdom: The Eschatology of Biblical Realism* (2nd ed.; Waco, TX: Word, 1964), p. 107.

the "kingdom of God is within you." The Greek word for "within" can also mean "in the midst of." Whatever it means here, however, one thing is clear: Jesus was announcing that God's kingdom was *present*, not exclusively future.[28]

In short, a great change had begun to occur by virtue of Jesus' presence on earth. Jesus described this change in other terms as well. When the Pharisees complained that His disciples did not fast, He asked, "Can the children of the bridegroom mourn as long as the bridegroom is with them?" (Luke 5:33). The mere fact that Jesus was among them filled the disciples with joy, a sign of the kingdom (cf. Rom. 14:17). Ridderbos notes that "this person is not only the announcer, but he himself is the center and the cause of the joy, the bliss, which has started with his coming."[29]

Jesus also was establishing the kingdom by His works of healing. The clearest passages in this regard are Luke 4:21 and Matthew 11:2-6. In each case, Jesus quoted from the Old Testament prophecies of Isaiah about the kingdom of God (Isaiah 35:5; 61:2), and in each case Jesus applied the prophecy to His works of healing and His teaching. In other words, Jesus claimed to be fulfilling the prophecies of the Old Testament. When the Pharisees charged Jesus with casting out demons by the power of the devil, He denied it, and added, "But if it is by the Spirit of God that I cast out demons, *then the Kingdom of God has come upon you.*" The verb used for "come upon" implies that something is present, not merely close by.[30] Jesus was saying that the casting out of demons demonstrated that the kingdom of God had arrived.

Thus, Jesus was establishing His rule by defeating the enemy

---

28. For the arguments for different interpretations of "within," see Geerhardus Vos, *Biblical Theology: Old and New Testaments* (Grand Rapids, MI: Eerdmans, [1948] 1975), p. 382. Also, Vos, *The Kingdom of God and the Church* (Nutley, NJ: Presbyterian and Reformed, 1972), p. 33. This passage is especially relevant to the discussion of the timing of the kingdom, because of the question that the Pharisees posed. While Jesus sometimes refused to answer questions from the Pharisees, it seems that he did answer their question in this case. The question was, "*When* will the kingdom come?" (v. 20).

29. Ridderbos, *Coming of the Kingdom*, p. 51.

30. George Eldon Ladd, *A Theology of the New Testament* (Grand Rapids, MI: Eerdmans, 1974), pp. 65-66. See 2 Corinthians 10:14, where the same verb is used.

of the kingdom, Satan. He gained the *definitive* victory over Satan supremely in His death on the cross and in His resurrection (Col. 2:15; 1 Cor. 15). But even during his earthly ministry, He was winning early skirmishes. The casting out of demons, a sign of the presence of the kingdom, was also a victory over Satan. As one scholar has put it, "In each act of exorcism Jesus saw a defeat of Satan."[31] Or, as Geerhardus Vos states, "The underlying principle is that in the world of spirits there is no neutral territory; where the demons depart, the divine Spirit enters."[32] Jesus even gave His disciples the power to cast out demons. When they returned from their mission, Jesus told them that He had seen Satan fall as lightning from heaven (Luke 10:18).

In short, as George Eldon Ladd summarizes, "Jesus did not promise his hearers a better future or assure that they would soon enter the Kingdom. Rather he boldly announced that the Kingdom of God had come to them."[33] John Bright states, "It lies at the very heart of the gospel message to affirm that the Kingdom of God has in a real sense become a present fact, here and now."[34]

The definitive establishment of the kingdom takes place in several stages. Even in the initial establishment of the kingdom, a *principle of progress* is operating. The kingdom was dawning already when Christ was born. Throughout His life, He was routing enemy forces and extending His rule. His death was a triumph over Satan, and thus marked a further development in the founding of His kingdom. The Bible also says that Christ's kingdom is established by His resurrection. This was part of Peter's Pentecost message (Acts 2:32-36). Paul implies the same in 1 Corinthians 15:23-25 (NIV):

> But each in his own turn: Christ, the firstfruits; then, when he comes, those who belong to him. Then the end will come,

---

31. Quoted in *ibid.*, p. 67.

32. Vos, *Biblical Theology*, p. 382.

33. Ladd, *Jesus and the Kingdom*, p. 107.

34. John Bright, *The Kingdom of God: The Biblical Concept and Its Meaning for the Church* (New York: Abingdon-Cokesbury, 1953), p. 216.

when he hands over the kingdom to God the Father after he has destroyed all dominion, authority, and power. For he must reign until he has put all his enemies under his feet.

We could say a great deal about this passage. But we want to focus on several things. First, note that the passage is found within a chapter devoted to the reality of Christ's resurrection. Second, note that this passage speaks about Christ's reign. Finally, and this is the important point, note the time indicators that define the reign of Christ. The end will come *after* Christ has destroyed His enemies. He will reign *until* He has brought all things under His feet. In other words, the kingdom does not *begin* when Christ returns. Christ began reigning from the time of His resurrection. The kingdom *culminates* in His second coming.

Finally, Christ's ascension is described in Scripture as an enthronement (Eph. 1:20-23; Phil. 2:9-11). In Ephesians 1:21, Paul states that Christ has been placed "far above all rule and authority and power and dominion, and every name that is named, *not only in this age, but also in the one to come.*" This happened after God raised Jesus from the dead and "seated Him at His right hand in the heavenly places" (Eph. 1:20). As A. A. Hodge said, "In the strictest sense we must date the actual and formal assumption of [Christ's] kingly office, in the full and visible exercise thereof, from the moment of His ascension into heaven from this earth and His session at the right hand of the Father."[35]

The destruction of Jerusalem in A.D. 70 was also a central event in the establishment of the kingdom of Christ. In keeping with the language of the Old Testament prophets, Jesus uses "end of the world" language to describe the destruction of the temple (Matt. 24; Luke 21). Several details of these texts make it clear that He was referring to the destruction of Jerusalem, and not to the end of the world. He refers specifically to those who will be "in Judea" (Matt. 24:16), and warns that no one who is on the roof of his house should go into his house to retrieve his belongings

---

35. A. A. Hodge, *Evangelical Theology* (Edinburgh: Banner of Truth Trust, [1890] 1976), p. 227.

(Matt. 24:17). The reference to people on the roof shows that Jesus has first-century Palestine in mind; at that time, it was a common practice to use the flat roof of the house for gatherings. Moreover, Jesus refers to the Sabbath (Matt. 24:20), an institution that no longer exists. In Luke, He refers explicitly to armies surrounding Jerusalem (Luke 21:20, 24).

The real key to the interpretation of this passage, however, is the time reference. Jesus indicates the time of the fulfillment of His prophecy when He says "this generation will not pass away until all these things take place" (Matt. 24:34; Luke 21:32). In other words, these events would happen *during the lifetime of the disciples*. Some claim that the Greek word for "generation," *genea*, means "race." Thus, they argue, Jesus was not predicting that these things would happen within the disciples' lifetimes. Rather, He was saying that Israel as a nation would be preserved until these events are fulfilled. To determine what *genea* means, we need to examine the way Matthew uses the word in other places (cf. Matt. 1:17; 11:16; 12:38-45; 16:4; 23:36). Such an examination shows that there is no basis for understanding *genea* as "race." The fact that Jesus calls it *"this* generation" makes it even more unlikely that *genea* means "race."[36] Thus, if we are to take Jesus at His word, we must conclude that He was talking about a *local judgment on the first-century Jews*.[37]

For our purposes, the important thing to note is that this event was a demonstration of the power of the exalted King. The Son of Man came to Jerusalem "with great power and great glory" (Matt. 24:30). When the signs of the destruction of Jerusalem appeared, the disciples were to understand "that the kingdom of God is near"

---

36. See J. Marcellus Kik, *An Eschatology of Victory* (Phillipsburg, NJ: Presbyterian and Reformed, 1971), pp. 61-63.

37. There are many related issues that we cannot deal with in this book. The best defense of this position can be found in two books by David Chilton: *Paradise Restored* and *Days of Vengeance: An Exposition of the Book of Revelation* (Ft. Worth, TX: Dominion Press, 1987). See also Kik, *An Eschatology of Victory*; and R. T. France, *Jesus and the Old Testament: His Application of Old Testament Passages to Himself and His Mission* (Grand Rapids, MI: Baker, 1982), Appendix A.

(Luke 21:31). The judgment of Jerusalem is the final stage of the *definitive* establishment of His kingdom. Thus, the kingdom of God is definitively established in *several stages*: in Christ's earthly life and ministry, in His death and resurrection, His ascension, and the destruction of Jerusalem in A.D. 70.

What all this means is very simple, but revolutionary for our understanding of the kingdom and of eschatology. It means that *the most important events in the establishment of the kingdom have already taken place. The most important eschatological (end-time) events were the death, resurrection, and ascension of Christ.* As Roderick Campbell has written, "nothing more revolutionary will ever happen than the transformation which commenced with the advent and the other events which are recorded in the historical books of the New Testament."[38]

Premillennial dispensationalists are not the only ones who deny that the kingdom was established by Christ at His first advent. Many charismatic "dominion theologians" are also guilty of undercutting the present reign of Christ. Some of these are looking for a dramatic, apocalyptic event in the next few years. Earl Paulk has been quoted as saying, "I want to . . . see the Kingdom of God established NOW!" Bruce Larson says,

> I had and have now a growing belief that we are in the beginning of an exciting, new age . . . [a] new age which I believe is already imminent . . . [and will] change life for all people upon this globe.

Seattle pastor Casey Treat says, "In three years we're going to run this planet in the name of Jesus. If we're not running it, we'll be on the way to running it."[39]

These quotations show that a change in eschatology is indeed taking place. But so far the change is from pessimistic apocalypticism to optimistic apocalypticism. The psychology of these two

---

38. Roderick Campbell, *Israel and the New Covenant* (Tyler, TX: Geneva Divinity School Press, [1954] 1983), p. 105.

39. All quotations in this paragraph are from *Omega-Letter* 2 (April 1987), pp. 7, 8, 11.

positions is exactly the same. Both positions are based on a short-term mentality. It was precisely this kind of perspective that led to the revolutionary debacles in Munster and Muhlhausen during the sixteenth century.[40] We must therefore stress again that the decisive events of the "end times" are past, 2000 years past. The kingdom does not grow by revolution, but by grace, obedience, and faith. There may be dramatic changes in the coming years, but they will not usher in the kingdom. The kingdom has been ushered in. It is here. It has been here since Christ's day.

Progressive

What we are now engaged in is the long-term extension of the kingdom. And by long-term, we mean long-term: century after century of building, block by block. Dominion does not come overnight. There is no instant dominion. Dominion comes over a period of decades and centuries, through self-sacrificing service and obedience.

This *progressive* aspect of the kingdom is seen most clearly in Jesus' parables. In fact, one of the dominant notes of many parables is this progress of the kingdom. The kingdom of heaven is like a mustard seed that starts very small and grows into a huge tree, providing a resting place for the birds of the air (Matt. 13:31-32).[41] The kingdom is also like leaven placed in a loaf that eventually spreads throughout the loaf (Matt. 13:33).[42] The parable of the

---

40. See Norman Cohn, *The Pursuit of the Millennium*, (rev. and ex. ed.; New York: Oxford University Press, [1957] 1970); Igor Shafarevich, *The Socialist Phenomenon*, trans. William Tjalsma (New York: Harper and Row, [1975] 1980); Christopher Hill, *The World Turned Upside Down* (Middlesex, England: Penguin Books, 1975).

41. The very image of a "seed" to describe the kingdom implies that a process of growth will occur. The kingdom is not a pebble in the field. It's a seed. Seeds grow when they're planted.

42. Some have argued that "leaven" in this passage has evil connotations. To be sure, there are many places in Scripture where leaven is a symbol of invisible evil influence (see Matt. 16:6, 11; 1 Cor. 5:7-8; Gal. 5:9). But leaven is not always a symbol of evil. A cake made with leaven was brought with the fellowship offering in the Old Testament (Lev. 7:13), and the wave offering was made with leavened loaves of bread (Lev. 23:17). Thus, the context should determine what the leaven is to symbolize. In Matthew 13:33, Jesus equates the kingdom of heaven with leaven, and there is nothing in this context to suggest that the leaven has an evil connotation.

wheat and tares also implies a progressive development of the kingdom. This is again a central feature of the parable. The owner of the field knows there are weeds in his wheat field, but he delays the harvest. He lets the wheat and the weeds grow and mature before he sends his laborers to harvest them (Matt. 13:24-30, 36-43).

What, then, did Jesus say would happen to the kingdom after its establishment? The parables cited above teach that the kingdom would grow. It began as a seed in a field, or as leaven in a loaf. Gradually, almost imperceptibly, it has grown into a tree and has leavened the whole lump. This same principle of permeation and growth and extension is found in many of the Old Testament prophecies of the kingdom. Isaiah says that a *child* would be born a king, an obvious reference to the *first* advent of Christ. Once His kingdom is set up, there will be no end to the *increase* of His government and peace (9:2-7). It's not just that the *kingdom* is everlasting. Its *increase* is everlasting. In Daniel 2, Nebuchadnezzar has a dream in which "the God of heaven [sets] up a kingdom which will never be destroyed" (vv. 44-45). The kingdom is compared to a rock "cut without hands" that becomes "a great mountain" and fills "the whole earth" (vv. 31-34). In the New Testament, in addition to the parables of Christ, Paul says that the end will come *after* "He has put all His enemies under His feet" (1 Cor. 15:24), and that "the last enemy that will be abolished is death" (1 Cor. 15:26).

In other words, *Jesus will return to a world in which nearly all His enemies have been conquered.* The only enemy that will remain is death. This is *the* distinctive teaching that characterizes our view of the future. We believe that Christ's rule is a victorious and triumphant reign that will someday, in the present age, through His church, extend from sea to sea and from the mountains to the ends of the earth.[43]

---

43. Of course, sin will never be eradicated from the earth before Christ returns. There will always be sinners and unbelievers on earth, until the final coming of Christ. But where sin has abounded, grace will much more abound. Nor do we mean to imply that the kingdom will advance without hardship and

Final

The New Testament also teaches that we look for a future manifestation of the kingdom (Matt. 25; 1 Cor. 15:23-24; Rev. 21; etc.). In this sense, we agree with Hunt that the kingdom refers to heaven and the fullness of the new heavens and new earth. And we agree that our true and permanent home is in the heavenly mansion that Jesus is preparing for us, and that our life here is from one perspective a pilgrimage to that blessed land of rest. We look forward to heaven with joy and expection, knowing that we shall be forever with our Savior and King in His perfect Kingdom. The hope of heaven helps us endure the trials of the present life. We look forward to the day when all believers from all lands will gather to worship the Lamb that was slain from the beginning of the world, and when we will live in perfect peace and love, free from the last remnants of sin. Any Christian who does not eagerly await his heavenly reward is grievously confused. Any Christian whose *sole* hope is an earthly reward has not understood Christianity.

But this does not relieve us of responsibility on earth. On the last day, we will be judged according to our service on earth (Matthew 25). Thus, we cannot sit on our laurels and wait for Jesus to come. We must be seeking and, by His grace, extending Christ's kingdom throughout our lives. Moreover, we do not look for a *new* kingdom. The heavenly kingdom is not something that God will establish for the first time at the end of history. It's simply the full and final and glorious manifestation of the kingdom that was first established 2000 years ago. Since the coming of Christ, therefore, we can say that the kingdom is both *already* present in

---

battle. The kingdom follows the pattern of its King, who was exalted *after* enduring the Cross.

This is a good place to add that there are some differences among "reconstructionists." Many would agree with the view presented here, that the kingdom has already been established, and that it is growing over many centuries until the end of the world. Others, however, look forward to a "golden age" in which the kingdom will advance even more spectacularly than it has in the past. Despite these differences, however, there is one important common denominator: Christ and His people will be victorious on earth.

principle and *not yet* fully consummated.[44]

Conclusion

The Bible teaches that the kingdom of Christ is a present reality. It was established by Christ through the work He performed
in His first advent. It is advancing by His power as He works in
His people by His Spirit. His church will reach a glorious climax,
becoming the chief mountain among the mountains of the earth.
Then, Christ shall return in glory to judge all men and to bring in
the fullness of the new heavens and the new earth.

---

44. How are we to understand the relationship between the kingdom that is
already present and developing and the kingdom that is yet future? Are they
totally unrelated? It is best to think of the future kingdom as breaking into the
history of the world at the time of Christ. As the commercial used to say, the
future is *now*. We *now* enjoy the first-fruits of the new creation that will be fully
manifested when Christ returns and the dead are raised. Or, as Vos puts it, "our
Lord's conception was that of one kingdom coming in two successive stages."
"The Kingdom of God," in *Redemptive History and Biblical Interpretation: The Shorter
Writings of Geerhardus Vos*, ed., Richard B. Gaffin, Jr. (Phillipsburg, NJ: Presbyterian and Reformed, 1980), p. 309. In a sense, then, time flows backward. It flows
from the future to the present. It flows from the consummation into the present
kingdom.

9

DAVE HUNT'S HEAVENLY KINGDOM

As we have seen, Hunt believes that the kingdom is predominantly a future reality. His view of the timing of the kingdom is very closely linked with his view of what the kingdom is. In other words, the *when* of the kingdom determines and is determined by the *what* of the kingdom. In this chapter, we will examine Hunt's understanding of the nature of the kingdom of God by looking closely at the passages that he quotes in defense of his position.

As with the timing of the kingdom, Hal Lindsey is not to be classified with Hunt on this particular issue. Lindsey writes:

> God's [millennial] kingdom will be characterized by peace and equity, and by universal spirituality and knowledge of the Lord. Even the animals and reptiles will lose their ferocity and no longer be carnivorous. All men will have plenty and be secure. There will be a chicken in every pot and no one will steal it! The Great Society which human rulers throughout the centuries have promised, but never produced, will at last be realized under Christ's rule. The meek and not the arrogant will inherit the earth (Isaiah 11).[1]

In this respect, Lindsey is much closer to the standard dispensationalist view of the kingdom than are Dave Hunt and others.

Actually, Hunt's view of the kingdom is hard to come by. So, we have been forced to examine the statements of some of Hunt's allies in an attempt to discern what Hunt might believe about the kingdom. Their views are no easier to obtain. An indication of

---

1. *The Late Great Planet Earth* (Grand Rapids, MI: Zondervan, [1970] 1973), p. 177.

our difficulty is found in the April 1987 issue of Peter Lalonde's *Omega-Letter.* Under a subheading entitled "Our View of the Kingdom," we find the following:

> What is our view of the Kingdom of God? Are we really to believe that God's Kingdom is of this world when He has said "My kingdom is not of this world"?
>
> Is the "Kingdom of God" just an eschatological point to be debated among prophetic scholars? It is not.
>
> As Alva J. McClain has written in his book "The Greatness of the Kingdom":
>
> *"In the Biblical doctrine of the Kingdom of God we have the Christian philosophy of history* . . . No adequate system of Biblical eschatology can possibly be constructed apart from the history and meaning of the concept of the Kingdom of God. Furthermore, it has been rightly noted that any failure to understand the kingdom as set forth in Biblical revelation, with its rich variety and magnificence of design, may actually blur the vision of good men to other matters of high theological importance to Christian faith."
>
> You see, this is why a clear understanding of prophecy is so important. A wrong view of prophecy can lead to a misunderstanding of central elements of the Christian faith just as easily as a wrong view of central elements of the Christian faith can lead to a wrong view of prophecy.[2]

This is the entire section. Yet, nowhere are we told exactly what is meant by the kingdom of God. All that we find is an emphasis on the *importance* of the kingdom, a point that is not disputed by any serious student of Scripture. The only substantive statement is that the kingdom is the key to a Christian philosophy of history. We would not dispute this, either. In fact, we affirm very strongly that the kingdom and people of God are at center stage in the history of the world. As we shall see, however, Hunt's kingdom has little to do with history. At any rate, because neither Hunt nor Lalonde has provided a detailed statement of the doctrine of the kingdom, we have had to gather snippets from various places in Hunt's writings.

---

2. *Omega-Letter* 2 (April 1987), p. 15.

Not of This World

Hunt refers to John 18:36 ("My kingdom is not of this world") to establish that the kingdom is essentially (exclusively?) a heavenly and inner reality.[3] David Wilkerson quotes this passage and adds, "That settles it for me, as it should for all believers who tremble at His Word."[4] We must, as Wilkerson says, take Christ's words with the utmost seriousness. The question is, *what* does Christ's statement mean? It settles *what*? Does it mean that Christ's kingdom is like the invisible ether that scientists a century ago believed to pervade outer space? Does it mean that Christ's kingdom has no effect on the course of history? Quoting the verse without explanation only creates confusion. It doesn't settle anything at all.

Several important issues need to be discussed in order to arrive at a proper interpretation of John 18:36. Perhaps the most important question to answer is what the "of" (Greek, *ek*) means.[5] Essentially, it means "out of," and it can have several shades of meaning : separation, the direction from which something comes, source or origin, as well as a host of minor meanings.[6] Many commentators agree that here *ek* has the sense of "source"; thus, Jesus' statement has to do with the *source* of the kingdom. In the last century, Charles John Ellicott noted that

> By 'not of this world' we are to understand that the nature and origin of His kingdom are not of this world, not that His king-

---

3. Dave Hunt and T. A. McMahon, *The Seduction of Christianity: Spiritual Discernment in the Last Days* (Eugene, OR: Harvest House, 1985), p. 224.

4. David Wilkerson, "The Laodicean Lie!," fourth page. Published by World Challenge, P.O. Box 260, Lindale, Texas, 75771.

5. This may seem obvious, but it is not. Just think of how many different ways we use "of" in English: John of Gaunt (tells us John's hometown), puddle of water (tells what kind of puddle), box of nails (tells the contents of the box), etc. Greek has the same kind of variety.

6. William F. Arndt and F. Wilbur Gingrich, *A Greek-English Lexicon of the New Testament and Other Early Christian Literature* (Chicago: University of Chicago Press, 1957), pp. 233-36. This lexicon, the standard dictionary of New Testament Greek, has a two-and-one-half page discussion, in small print, of the various meanings of the two-letter preposition, *ek*.

dom will not extend in this world. In the world's sense of king and kingdom, in the sense in which the Roman empire claimed to rule the world, He had no kingdom.[7]

The French commentator Godet wrote, "The expression *ek tou kosmou, of this world* is not synonymous with *en to kosmo, in this world*. For the kingdom of Jesus is certainly realized and developed here on earth; but it does not have its *origin* from earth, from the human will and earthly force."[8]

More recently, the Lutheran commentator R. C. H. Lenski has written, "The origin of Jesus' kingdom explains its unique character: it is 'not of this world.'. . . [All other kingdoms] sprang out of [*ek*] this world and had kings that corresponded to such an origin."[9] B. F. Westcott agrees that Jesus meant that His kingdom "does not derive its origin or its support from earthly forces. . . . At the same time Christ's kingdom is 'in the world,' even as His disciples are (xvii.11)."[10] Charles Ryrie's study Bible explains that Jesus meant that His kingdom is "not of human origin."[11] Robert Culver comments in *Toward a Biblical View of Civil Government*,

> The words "of this world" translate *ek tou kosmou toutou*, that is, out of this world. Source rather than realm is the sense. . . . The future consummation of the kingdom of Christ cannot rightly be said to be beyond history. No indeed! It will occur in history and is history's goal. . . . So Jesus very clearly is making no comment on either the nature of his kingdom or His realm, rather on the power and source of its establishment.[12]

---

7. Charles John Ellicott, ed., *A New Testament Commentary for English Readers*, (London: Cassell and Company, 1897), vol. 1, p. 532.

8. F. Godet, *Commentary on the Gospel of John*, trans. Timothy Dwight, 2 vols. (New York: Funk and Wagnalls, 1886), vol. 2, p. 369.

9. R. C. H. Lenski, *The Interpretation of St. John's Gospel* (Minneapolis, MN: Augsburg, [1943] 1961), p. 1229.

10. B. F. Westcott, *The Gospel According to St. John* (Grand Rapids, MI: Eerdmans [1881] 1973), p. 260.

11. Quoted by John Lofton, "Our Man in Washington," Number 18, December 1986. Available from Chalcedon Foundation, P.O. Box 158, Vallecito, California, 95251.

12. Robert Duncan Culver, *Toward a Biblical View of Civil Government* (Chicago, IL: Moody, 1974), p. 195.

Thus, when Jesus said that His kingdom is not "of" this world, He meant that it does not *spring from* the world. As he added, His kingdom is from another place. This verse refers to the *origin* of the kingdom, not to its *location* in the universe. Jesus was not saying that His kingdom floats in the air, without touching the world. He did not mean that He rules heaven, but has left earth to be ruled by Satan. Rather, He meant that His rule has its *origin* in heaven, not in earth. It doesn't mean that the kingdom is *solely* in heaven.

Hunt also quotes several other passages from John's gospel to prove that the kingdom is an other-worldly kingdom.

> If you were of (*ek*) the world, the world would love its own; but because you are not of (*ek*) the world, but I chose you out of (*ek*) the world, the world hates you (John 15:19);
> I manifested Thy name to the men whom thou gavest Me out of (*ek*) the world (John 17:6);
> I do not ask on behalf of the world, but of those whom thou hast given me (John 17:9);
> They are not of (*ek*) the world, even as I am not of (*ek*) the world (John 17:16). [13]

Again, we must be careful not to assume that we know what Jesus is talking about in these verses without studying the context. We must carefully examine what He says and seek to understand it in the light of Scripture. Several observations are in order. First, we find nearly the same phrase, "out of the world," in John 15:19 that we found in John 18:36. We have already seen that "of" or "out of" refers to the *source* of Christ's kingdom, not its geographic position. When Jesus says the same thing about His disciples ("They are not *of* the world"), we are justified in suspecting that it means the same thing. Though the disciples are *on* earth, they do not derive their power and authority *from* earth.

As for the other passages, to be *chosen* "out of the world" does

---

13. Hunt, *Beyond Seduction: A Return to Biblical Christianity* (Eugene, OR: Harvest House, 1987), p. 245. It seems a little deceptive of Hunt to leave out John 17:15: "I do not ask Thee to take them out of the world, but to keep them from the evil one." But, we'll give him the benefit of the doubt and look only at the verses that he *does* quote.

not mean "to be relieved of all responsibility in the world" or the like. The *ek* here quite obviously implies separation. It could mean separation from several things. It could mean simply that the disciples have been chosen out of the whole mass of humanity to be Christ's own people. Probably it means that the disciples have been separated from the world-system that dominates the unbeliever. Particularly in the book of John, "world" (Greek, *kosmos*) often refers to a system and world order under the control of Satanic forces. It refers to the "world below" in contrast to the "world above."[14] The word has ethical significance. It does not refer simply to the planet earth or to mankind. It refers to the *king-dom of darkness*. Thus, to be chosen "out of the world" means to be separated by the sovereign choice of Christ from the world-system that is headed for destruction. It means that the disciples have been liberated from bondage to Satan.

Finally, the strongest point undergirding our interpretation is the parallel that Jesus draws between His relation to the world and the relation of His disciples to the world. Jesus says that the disciples are not of the world, "just as" He is not of the world. Now, in what sense was Jesus, during His earthly ministry, not "of the world"? What does it mean when we say that Jesus is not "of this world"? Does it mean that He didn't have any impact on his-tory? Does it mean that He didn't have a physical body? No. Hunt would certainly not say these things. But if we apply what Hunt is saying about the kingdom to Jesus, we would have to con-clude that *Jesus never left heaven to take human flesh*. If "not of the world" refers to a location, a "geographic position," then these verses imply that Jesus was never really incarnate on earth.[15]

Jesus was not of the world in the sense that He did not derive

---

14. George Eldon Ladd, *A Theology of the New Testament* (Grand Rapids, MI: Eerdmans, 1974), p. 225. Ladd shows that while John often uses *kosmos* in more general senses, he also uses it to refer to "fallen humanity," which is "enslaved" to an "evil power."

15. We wish to emphasize that this is *not* what Hunt is saying. We are trying to show inconsistencies in his interpretation of this text by pressing him to the logical conclusion.

His authority, His power, His standards of conduct from the world. In the same sense, Christians are not of the world. In the same sense, the kingdom of God is not of the world.

Thus, in one sense, Christians are to be separated from the world. We are not to live by its standards or seek its acclaim or seek power from below. In another sense, however, we are not to go "out of the world" (1 Cor. 5:9-10). Instead, we are to transform it as we bring the redeeming message of the gospel to all nations and as we obediently implement Christ's dominion over the earth. Just as Christ came from heaven to earth, so also the kingdom flows from heaven to earth. As we pray, "Thy will be done on earth as it is in heaven."

"Both/and," not "Either/or"

One of the most prevalent criticisms of dominion theology is that its proponents stress man and his relationships on the earth. Hunt, for example, wants Christians "to make a choice between earth and heaven."[16] Now, it is true that where the gospel is concerned the choice is abundantly clear: either Jesus or self, heaven or earth, forgiveness or judgment, good or evil, life or death. As far as we can tell, those who hold to a dominion theology agree wholeheartedly with Hunt's assertion that "every solution to earth's problems which is not founded upon the lordship of Jesus Christ and the forgiveness of sins we have in Him is temporary at best and ultimately doomed to fail."[17]

Yet, Hunt has obscured the argument by forcing the Christian into a false dilemma. While he has a token interest in the earth, the force of his arguments leads Christians to believe that *any* interest in the things of this world is mistaken:

> Now . . . when . . . your focus turns from heaven to this earth, you have pretty much aligned yourself with the goals of the humanists, the New Agers, of various religions, and, of course, as you mentioned [speaking to Peter Lalonde], each participant

16. *Beyond Seduction*, pp. 254-55.
17. *Ibid.*, p. 254.

or each group participating feels their beliefs will eventually come out on top. And the Christians may, in the back of their minds, have the goal that "Well, eventually we'll convert the whole world." But in the meantime, they are laying the foundation for the anti-christ's one-world religion.[18]

Dave Hunt and others want to give Christians one of only two options: choose either heaven or earth. If you choose heaven, then you are an orthodox Christian. On the other hand, if you choose the earth, then you "are being deceived by a new world view more subtle and more seductive than anything the world has ever experienced."[19] This is a false dichotomy. Hunt has committed the *bifurcation* fallacy.[20] S. Morris Engel, in his classic work on informal fallacies, writes that "this fallacy presents *contraries* as if they were *contradictories*."[21] There is nothing contradictory in saying that both heaven and earth are domains where the Christian shows his faithfulness to His Lord.

The Great Commission

Hunt contends that the mission of the church involves only personal discipleship and salvation. The Great Commission, in the eyes of Hunt and many others, is fulfilled by preaching and tract passing and saving individual souls. The mission of the church is to "prepare people for heaven."[22]

This is certainly part of the church's mission in the world. But it is not all that Jesus commanded His disciples to do. He commanded them to "make disciples of all the nations" (Matt. 28:19). It is important to observe several things about this commission. First, the task is not to "save souls" or to "prepare people for heaven." The task is to "make disciples." William Hendriksen writes:

---

18. *Dominion: A Dangerous New Theology*, Tape #1 of *Dominion: The Word and New World Order*, distributed by *Omega-Letter*, Ontario, Canada, 1987.

19. Back cover copy of *The Seduction of Christianity*.

20. The other names for this fallacy are: either/or fallacy; black-and-white fallacy; false dilemma.

21. S. Morris Engel, *With Good Reason: An Introduction to Informal Fallacies* (3rd ed.; New York: St. Martin's, 1986), p. 137.

22. Peter Waldron, Interview with Dave Hunt, "Contact America," August 12, 1987.

> But just what is meant by "make disciples"? It is not exactly the same as "make converts," though the latter is surely implied. . . . The term "make disciples" places somewhat more stress on the fact that the mind, as well as the heart and the will, must be won for God.[23]

A disciple is one who is wholly committed and obedient to his master, in thought, word, and deed. When, by God's grace, men confess Christ as Lord, they begin their discipleship. But discipleship is life-long and life-wide. Part of Jesus' instructions to His disciples was to be salt and light in the world (Matt. 5:13-14; cf. 5:1). Thus, the commission of the church is not only to bring men to confess Christ with their mouths, but to teach men to observe the commandments of Christ in every area of life and to act in society to preserve righteousness.

Second, the *nations* are to be discipled. Hunt claims that Jesus meant that individuals in the nations are to be discipled. He paraphrases Jesus' command by saying that Jesus called us to make disciples "from all nations."[24] Albert Dager makes the same claim:

> To "disciple all the nations," or, "make disciples of [out of] all the nations," does not mean that every nation as a whole is one day going to sit at the feet of the Reconstructionist gurus and learn the ways of Truth. The Great Commission requires us to go into all the nations and disciple "whosoever will" be saved.[25]

Aside from the patently false implication that "reconstructionists" claim to be the source of truth or recipients of special, extrabiblical revelation, Dager has read into Matthew 28:19 something that is not there. In the Greek, "nations" or "peoples" (Greek, *ethnos*) is the *object* of the verb, "make disciples." In other words, the target of our activity is not "individuals from all nations," but precisely the nations themselves. Matthew 28:19 does not contain

---

23. William Hendriksen, *New Testament Commentary: Exposition of the Gospel according to Matthew* (Grand Rapids, MI: Baker, 1973), p. 999.

24. Waldron interview.

25. Albert James Dager, "Kingdom Theology: Part III," *Media Spotlight* (January-June 1987), p. 11.

the word *ek*, "out of." To insert the words "out of" into Jesus' commission is deceiving, particularly if the reader is not equipped to check Dager's interpretation against the Greek. This reading of the commission also seriously distorts the scope of Jesus' words.

It is possible, of course, that Dager has made an honest mistake, or that he has simply not done his homework. But when a writer *adds* words to a text, it is hard to avoid the conclusion that he has done so deliberately. Perhaps Dager has inserted these words to make this passage fit his own preconception of the Great Commission. Regardless of his intent or motivation, Dager is attacking "kingdom theology" on the basis of a misreading of Scripture.

Many years ago, Matthew Henry paraphrased the commission: "the principal intention of this commission [is] to *disciple* all nations. '*Admit them disciples*'; do your utmost to make the nations Christian nations.' "[26] Individuals are, of course, included in the commission. But the commission includes men in their social and political associations as well. Not only are men and women to be instructed in the commandments of Christ, but, through the preaching of the gospel, nations are to be brought under the discipline of Christ's Word. Thus, Hunt's (and Dager's) view that the church fulfills its purpose by simply saving souls is a much narrower perspective than that of our Lord. Here is a clear example of the reduction of Christianity, supported with questionable exegesis (biblical interpretation).[27]

Dager also complains about "reconstructionist" writer David Chilton's exegetical rule that "literalism is secondary to consistent biblical imagery." Dager notes that Chilton "goes against his own

---

26. Matthew Henry, *Matthew Henry's Commentary on the Whole Bible*, 6 vols. (New York: Fleming H. Revell, [1721] n.d.), vol. 5, p. 446.

27. The account of Jesus' commission in Mark 16:15 is also instructive. Some would argue that this is part of a passage that was added to the gospel of Mark at a later date. We will not address that question here. If these are not Jesus' words, they are at least the words of early Christians, and therefore show the early church's understanding of its role. In Mark, the commission is even wider than the "all nations" of Matthew 28:19. Here the disciples are instructed to proclaim the gospel to "every creature." The comprehensive scope of the command supports our interpretation of the passage in Matthew.

rule" when he interprets Matthew 28:19 literally as a command to disciple *all* nations. Dager comments,

> If Chilton's reasoning is good for Matthew 28:19-20, it must be good for Matthew 24:9: ". . . ye shall be hated of all nations for my name's sake." Therefore, everyone in every nation will hate all Christians. Ergo, no one will ever be converted.[28]

It is not our intention to defend Chilton's method of interpretation here. But, Dager's argument clearly doesn't come close to answering Chilton's exegesis of Matthew 28:19-20. Dager's argument assumes that "all" always means the same thing. Obviously it does not. How do we decide what "all" means in a particular passage? The only way to do so is to attempt to determine whether the *context* of the passage limits the word in any way. For example, suppose that someone told you that a church had a picnic, and that "everyone was there." Only a lunatic would infer that "everyone" meant "every individual in the entire world." In this conversation "everyone" would obviously mean everyone in the church or, at least, most of the church.

The same is true in the Bible, in Matthew's gospel in particular. When Herod heard from the wise men about the birth of Jesus, "all Jerusalem" was troubled (Matt. 2:3). When John the Baptist began to preach "all Judea" went out to hear him (Matt. 3:5). The chief priests hesitated to answer Jesus' questions about John the Baptist because "all" the people held that John was a prophet (Matt. 21:26). When Pilate asked what he should do with Jesus, "all" the people said, "Let Him be crucified" (Matt. 27:22). It is clear in all of these passages that "all" does not have an absolutely comprehensive scope.

Yet, this is precisely the kind of argument that Dager presents against Chilton. He argues that if Chilton claims that "all nations" has a comprehensive meaning in Matthew 28:19, he "must" claim that it has a comprehensive meaning in Matthew 24:9. But even a brief look at the contexts of the passages clearly shows that this is not the case. In the last chapter, we defended the interpretation

---

28. Dager, "Kingdom Theology, Part III," p. 11.

that in Matthew 24 Jesus is talking about a "local judgment on the first-century Jews." If this interpretation is correct, then Jesus' warnings were directed specifically to the disciples. Thus, the hatred of "all nations" in Matthew 24:9 is the hatred of the nations toward *first-century* Christians. It does not refer to a general condition of the church throughout the centuries.

The commission of Matthew 28:19-20, by contrast, has the most comprehensive scope. The fact that this passage closes Matthew's gospel surely indicates something of its importance and scope. It is also significant that "all" occurs three times in the space of three verses. Thus, the literary structure and position of this commission in Matthew suggest that the Great Commission is a comprehensive mandate for the disciples. Moreover, Jesus introduces the commission with the declaration that He possesses "all authority in heaven and on earth" (Matt. 28:18). It is clear from the rest of the New Testament that this "all" is absolutely universal. Christ is above all authority and power and dominion (Eph. 1:19-23), and He is given a name exalted above every other name (Phil. 2:9). Moreover, Jesus instructs His disciples to teach the nations "all that I commanded you" (Matt. 28:20). Finally, Jesus promises to be with the disciples "always, even to the end of the age" (Matt. 28:20). On the basis of this declaration of comprehensive authority, Jesus gives His disciples their commission.[29]

Thus, the gospel commission of the church is much broader than Hunt and Dager teach. The mission of the church is nothing

---

29. There is a clear progression in these three uses of "all." First, Jesus provides the theological basis for the commission in the fact that *"all* authority" has been given Him. On the basis of His comprehensive dominion, He gives the disciples a comprehensive commission, to disciple *"all"* nations. The method of comprehensive discipleship includes teaching of *"all* that I commanded you." And the disciples are supported with the promise of Christ's enduring and universal presence, the promise that He would be with them through *all* time.

"In the context of Matthew's gospel, which is particularly addressed to Jewish readers, it is also important to note that Jesus' commission went beyond the Jewish nation. Thus, in contrast to the earlier preaching of the disciples to the Jews, they are now instructed to preach to all nations." Herman Ridderbos, *Matthew*, trans. Ray Togtman, Bible Student's Commentary (Grand Rapids, MI: Zondervan/Regency Reference Library, 1987), pp. 554-55.

less than discipling all the nations of the earth. The mission is to bring the world under the dominion of Christ, in the power of His Spirit, and through the ministries of teaching and baptizing.

How Big Is the Gospel?

Other passages make it clear that the message of the gospel itself includes more than a message of individual preparation for heaven. In Acts 20:18-35, we find Paul's farewell message to the Ephesian elders. Paul repeatedly declares that he has fulfilled completely his apostolic mission in the Ephesian church. It is interesting to note the various ways that he describes that mission. He declared everything profitable (v. 20). He testified of "repentance toward God and faith in our Lord Jesus Christ" (v. 21). The mission he had received from Christ was to witness to "the gospel of the grace of God" (v. 24). Among the Ephesian Christians, he "preached the kingdom" (v. 25) and declared "the whole purpose of God" (v. 27).

A careful reading of this passage will show that these phrases are parallel to one another and are closely interconnected. They are all different ways of describing what Paul had taught and preached among the Ephesians. For our purposes, it is important to note that preaching the "gospel of grace" is simply another way of declaring "the whole purpose of God." Paul knew nothing of a narrow gospel; to preach the gospel was to preach the whole counsel of God. The gospel affects man in his totality. It speaks to every area of life. This does not mean that Paul was unable to make distinctions between central and peripheral elements of the gospel. The point is that, for Paul, all elements of the gospel were important, and the gospel was the whole counsel of God.[30]

Thus, practically, when an individual becomes a Christian, there is more that the Lord wants him to do. He is to live out the implications of his confession in his whole life. He is to live in obe-

---

30. For these comments, we are indebted to lectures on Pauline theology by Richard B. Gaffin, Jr., Westminster Theological Seminary, Philadelphia, Spring 1986.

dience to the gospel, and he is to contribute to the church's mission of bringing others into the kingdom of Christ.

R. J. Rushdoony, who could be described as the father of modern-day dominion theology, clearly spells this out in *The Philosophy of the Christian School Curriculum*:

> All too many pastors and teachers assume that the goal of their work is to save souls for Jesus Christ. This is not the goal: it is the starting point of their calling. The goal is to train up those under our authority in God's word so that they are well-fitted and thoroughly equipped for all good work, to go forth and to exercise dominion in the name of the Lord and for His kingdom (Gen. 1:26-28; Joshua 1:1-9; Matt. 28:18-20). We are not saved just to be saved, but to serve the Lord. We are not the focus of salvation: the Lord's calling and kingdom are.[31]

In an interview with Hunt, Peter Lalonde, publisher of *The Omega-Letter*,[32] took a narrow view of the gospel when he responded to a statement made by Dr. Gary North about David Wilkerson's brand of theology. Gary North wrote of David Wilkerson:

> He is clinging to a worn-out view of what the gospel is all about, a view which did not become widespread in American Protestant circles until the turn of this century. By shortening their view of the time Jesus supposedly has given to His people to accomplish their comprehensive assignment, fundamentalists after 1900 chose to focus their concerns on preaching and tract-passing. These are necessary minimal activities, but they are only the beginning in God's program of comprehensive redemption. The dominion covenant requires men to subdue the earth to the glory of God (Gen. 1:28; 9:1-17). His people still must accomplish this task before He comes again to judge their success. They have been given *sufficient time*; they must redeem it.[33]

---

31. Rousas John Rushdoony, *The Philosophy of the Christian School Curriculum* (Vallecito, CA: Ross House Books, 1981), p. 148.

32. *Dominion: A Dangerous New Theology*, 1987.

33. North, "The Attack on the 'New' Pentecostals," *Christian Reconstruction*, Vol. X, No. 1 (Jan./Feb. 1986), p. 2.

Lalonde says that North believes that "preaching and tract-passing" is a "worn-out" belief. This is not at all what North writes. Hunt, Wilkerson, Lalonde, and others do not believe that the gospel is comprehensive, embracing the whole counsel of God. This is the view that is "worn out."

Heavenly Citizenship

Hunt believes that only heaven is the kingdom. The Christian is a citizen of heaven, not of an earthly kingdom.[34] This is not entirely true. There is no indication in Scripture that we can't be citizens of both heaven and an earthly nation. The apostle Paul saw no contradiction in claiming his Roman citizenship (Acts 16:37-39; 22:22-29) and maintaining that he was also a citizen of heaven (Phil. 3:20). The apostle did not cry out: "Persecute me all you want. I'm a citizen of heaven!" Instead, he called on the privileges granted to him as a Roman citizen. In fact, he appealed, not to heaven, but to "Caesar" (Acts 25:11). Of course, he was using the appeal to Caesar as a means to advance the gospel. The point is that Paul did not believe that his heavenly citizenship cancelled his rights as a citizen of Rome. Paul was prepared to use his earthly citizenship to advance the gospel of the heavenly kingdom.

Moreover, the church is spoken of as a citizenship: "So then you are no longer strangers and aliens, but you are fellow-citizens with the saints, and are of God's household" (Eph. 2:19). We might say that membership in the church and heavenly citizenship are two aspects of the same thing. The Christian's heavenly citizenship places him in an ecclesiastical body where a law order should operate (Matt. 16:13-19; 18:15-20; 1 Cor. 6:1-11). To be joined with Christ's body is to be a citizen of heaven. The point here, though, is that heavenly citizenship doesn't cancel out our earthly responsibilities in the church.

The Christian's heavenly citizenship makes him an alien, stranger, and exile on earth (Heb. 11:13; 1 Peter 2:11). But the

---

34. *Beyond Seduction*, p. 252.

Christian does not repudiate his earthly citizenships. Rather, this means that our earthly citizenships are not primary. Earthly citizenships are temporary and have meaning only within the context of the kingdom of God that encompasses all citizenships: "Seek first His kingdom and His righteousness" (Matt. 6:33).

But, let's grant Hunt's major point, which is that our *primary* citizenship is in heaven. This statement is entirely biblical. In Philippians 3:20, Paul tells us: "For our citizenship is in heaven, from which also we eagerly await for a Savior, the Lord Jesus Christ." This idea corresponds to Jesus' informing Nicodemus that he must be "born again" [lit., *born from above*] (John 3:5; cf. John 14:1-3). In effect, one must become a citizen of heaven to enjoy the benefits of heaven.

As far as we can tell, in all the reading we've done and conversations we've had with "reconstructionists," heaven has not been abandoned for the earth. Heaven *is* the focal point, the reference point by which the Christian gets his bearing for living. He knows that even in death Jesus is with him. In fact, Jesus has gone to prepare a place for us (John 14:1-6). But the earth, and Christ's cause in every area of life on the earth, are also important. Paul made this abundantly clear when he wrote to the Philippian Christians: "For me, to live is Christ, and to die is gain" (Phil 1:21). We often forget what Paul said first: "For me, *to live is Christ.*" Why? Living allowed him to serve the body of Christ: "To remain on in the flesh is more necessary for your sake" (v. 24). Did Paul turn his focus from heaven because he showed an interest in the things of this life? Certainly not. Paul saw no either/or dichotomy. Heaven *and* earth are important. Heaven happens to be *more* important. This is why Paul describes it as "gain."

The Christian has an obligation to follow the law of God as it applies to all locales. God's law is the standard whereby all citizenships must operate. Our heavenly citizenship involves comprehensive law-keeping. Jesus said, "If you love Me, you will keep My commandments" (John 14:15). Jesus did not restrict the locale of law keeping; therefore, we can conclude that the keeping of His commandments includes every citizenship without exception.

When Scripture speaks about obeying the civil magistrate (Rom. 13:1-7; 1 Peter 2:13-17), citizens must obey. When State laws conflict with the laws of heaven, the Christian's first obligation is to his heavenly citizenship (Acts 5:29). While the Christian lives on earth, he remains responsible to various governments; but he also looks for the day when his heavenly citizenship will be fully realized: "All these [Old Testament believers] died in faith, without receiving the promises, but having seen them and having welcomed them from a distance, and having confessed that they were strangers and exiles on the earth. . . . But as it is, they desire a better country, that is a heavenly one" (Heb. 11:13, 16; cf. 1 Peter 2:11).

Ultimately the issue is, what does it *mean* to be a citizen of heaven? Does it mean that we abandon the earthly battles that surround us? Does it mean we leave the earth to the devil? Does it mean we don't polish brass on the sinking ship? Does it mean that we don't have any dominion on earth?

In fact, the Bible teaches that heavenly citizenship means precisely the opposite. We are citizens of heaven in order to exercise effective dominion on the earth. We find this particularly in Ephesians 1 and 2. In Ephesians 1:20-23, we're told that Christ has been raised and exalted above all rule and authority and power and every name that is named. He is "in the heavenlies" to *rule* over all things. This is what it means for all things to be under His feet. Why was Christ raised to heaven and seated at the right hand of the Father? To exercise *dominion*. He is "seated in the heavenly places" as a King, to exercise His authority over heaven and earth.

This is a spectacular thought. But Paul says something equally spectacular in Ephesians 2:6-7. After discussing the believer's resurrection from death in sin into life in union with Christ, he adds that God has "raised and seated (us) in the heavenlies in Christ Jesus, so that in the coming ages he might show the incomparable riches of his grace." We are seated in the heavenlies with Christ! Paul does not use a future tense of the verb. He's not saying we *will* be raised to the heavenlies. He says we *have been* raised, and we are seated with Christ in the heavenly places.[35] Now, what do you suppose we're doing up in heaven with Christ? As Christ's people, we are doing what Christ is doing: ruling the earth (cf. Rev. 1:6; 4:4). In other words, Paul implies that we are citizens of heaven *so that* we can exercise dominion on earth. To be "seated in the heavenlies" means to be in a position of authority and privilege.

Thus, *heavenly citizenship is not a retreat from earthly dominion. Heaven is the source of dominion, the place from which we begin to exercise dominion.* Before we can rule obediently as God's representatives on earth, we must have access to the blessings and privileges of heaven. It is precisely because our *citizenship is in heaven* that we are able to *rule the earth* obediently and effectively. The first step of dominion is prayer, by which we offer petitions before the heavenly King. Individually and in the corporate worship of the Church, we ask Him to bless and prosper our labors. In Christ, our Advocate, we have access to the Ruler of all creation.

We derive our earthly standards of conduct and judgment from heaven. We receive the power to live in obedience by feeding on the heavenly bread. We can take financial risks because we know that our treasures are secure in heaven.[36] We can live joyfully and productively in less than ideal conditions because we know that a heavenly mansion awaits us. We can stand boldly against evil in our society, risking persecution and even martyrdom, because our lives are hidden with Christ in God.

Hunt's concern with heaven is entirely proper. But he has not understood heavenly citizenship. Hunt quotes Herbert Schlossberg

---

35. We may also view our ascension with Christ in three time frames. We have been *definitively* raised with Christ when we are baptized into Him. We are *repeatedly* raised in the weekly worship of the Church. And we will be *finally* raised when Jesus returns at the end of history. See Chilton, *The Days of Vengeance* (Ft. Worth, TX: Dominion Press, 1987), p. 149. Ultimately, we are in heaven so that God can display His grace through us to the entire world.

36. Of course, we are not to use our resources foolishly. We are stewards of all that we have; we don't own anything outright, because God owns all things. Thus, we must use our resources in obedience to His Word. Part of this obedience, however, is *using* our resources and not simply hiding them in the ground (see Matt. 25:14-30). Using resources necessarily involves risk.

as saying that only those who find their ultimate value in the next world are much good in this world.[37] This is precisely our point. Those who are citizens of heaven are alone fit instruments for extending the kingdom in this world.

Peace and Liberty

Hunt claims that the gospel has to do with "peace with God," established between God and the individual sinner. Peace is established only through "transformation of the human heart through Christ." He castigates those who say that "the world [is] seemingly able to solve all its problems without embracing the true gospel of our Lord Jesus Christ."[38]

Who says this? Who says that the world is able to solve *any* problem apart from embracing the gospel of Christ? Certainly "reconstructionists" are not saying this. The whole point, reiterated again and again, is that *evangelism is the starting point of social transformation.* The whole point has been that the world *can't* solve any of its problems without embracing the true gospel of Christ. As far back as 1973, R.J. Rushdoony wrote that "the only true order is founded on Biblical law." He added,

> But the key to remedying the [modern] situation is *not* revolution, nor any kind of resistance that works to subvert law and order. The New Testament abounds in warnings against disobedience and in summons to peace. The key is regeneration [being born again], propagation of the gospel, and the conversion of men and nations to God's law-word.[39]

In a 1981 article, Rushdoony again emphasized the centrality of evangelism and regeneration when he wrote that evangelism "places men under the dominion of the Lord and then orders them to exercise dominion in and under Him. Having been made a

---

37. *Beyond Seduction*, p. 255.
38. *Ibid.*, pp. 248-9.
39. Rushdoony, *The Institutes of Biblical Law* (Phillipsburg, NJ: Presbyterian and Reformed, 1973), p. 113. See also p. 449: "Clearly, there is no hope for man except in regeneration." Also, p. 627: ". . . true reform begins with regeneration and then the submission of the believer to the whole law-word of God."

new creation, they are in faith and obedience to their Savior-King to make of their sphere and the whole world a new creation."[40] A book published by American Vision Press stresses that the basic form of government is self-government. "A self-governed individual is one who has been born again, where the heart of stone has been removed and replaced with a heart of flesh."[41]

These quotations indicate two things. First, "reconstructionists" teach that being born again is a prerequisite to exercising godly dominion. And, of course, evangelism is a prerequisite to being born again. Second, they show that their idea of evangelism is much broader than that of many other evangelical Christians. The point is that we evangelize to increase and serve the kingdom of God, not merely to save men from hell.

We agree with Hunt that the fundamental peace established by the gospel is *peace with God*. This is basic. It is the foundation of everything else. But peace in Scripture is not confined to internal and spiritual peace. Biblical peace, which is extended as the kingdom spreads throughout the earth, is much fuller. It refers to a comprehensive prosperity, healthfulness, and harmony. This peace flows from heaven to earth. The peace established by Christ between the Holy God and sinful men emanates into man's entire social life. The peace of Christ has produced and should produce peace among men. As men are reconciled to God, they should be

---

40. Rushdoony, "Evangelism and Dominion," *Journal of Christian Reconstruction* vol. 7, no. 2 (Winter 1981), pp. 11. Later in the same article, he wrote, "We are not converted merely to die and go to heaven but to serve the Lord with all our heart, mind, and being. We are born again to be God's people, to do His will, to serve His Kingdom, and to glorify Him in every area of life and thought" (p. 18).

41. Gary DeMar, *God and Government: A Biblical and Historical Study* (Atlanta, GA: American Vision Press, 1982), p. 13. In another American Vision publication, we find this statement: "*self-government* supports all other forms of government. Christian *self-government* requires God's grace in regeneration. The far reaches of civil government will not be changed until rebels against God are turned into faithful subjects. . . . God changes the heart, a new spirit is put inside the once-dead rebel, a teachable heart is implanted, *then* we will walk in His statutes, and *then* we will observe all His ordinances." In Gary DeMar, *Ruler of the Nations: Biblical Principles for Government* (Ft. Worth, TX: Dominion Press, 1987), pp. 164-65.

reconciled to one another. Is it really plausible to think that Christ can "reconcile the world to Himself" (2 Cor. 5:18-19) without reconciling the world to itself? "Peace on *earth*," the angels sang at Christ's birth. This means that the coming of the Christ, who is our Peace, is the coming to earth of the kingdom of peace prophesied in the law and the prophets.

Hunt says that "the gospel was not designed to liberate men from the corrupt Roman Empire but from the far worse bondage of sin and its eternal penalty."[42] It is absolutely true that the gospel liberates men from sin. As a result of this liberation, however, men are progressively liberated from the oppressive institutions and systems that are the result of sin. The gospel was not *designed* to liberate men from the Roman Empire. But in fact it *did* liberate men from the Roman Empire!

Hunt goes on: "It is no less erroneous to imagine that one's Christian mission is to set up God's kingdom by taking over the world for Christ, when in fact we are to call disciples (out of a world that is doomed by God's judgment) to become citizens of heaven."[43] But, as we have already seen, we are citizens of heaven precisely so that we can rule for Christ, or, more precisely, so that we can share in Christ's own dominion (Eph. 2:6). Even Hunt admits that men who are citizens of heaven are the most productive men on earth. Thus, we must distinguish between the primary and secondary effects of the gospel. Our entrance into the kingdom of Christ liberates us from sin. As more and more men are *liberated from sin*, and as we are progressively sanctified by the Spirit and the Word, *political and social liberties follow.*

Utopia?

Hunt implies that anyone who predicts an historical victory of Christianity on earth is utopian. Utopia literally means "nowhere." It describes perfected earthly conditions. A utopian belief is one that will never come to pass in reality.

---

42. *Beyond Seduction*, p. 249.
43. *Idem.*

Hunt points out again that the millennium itself will not even usher in a utopia. "A perfect Edenic environment where all ecological, economic, sociological, and political problems are solved fails to perfect mankind. So much for the theories of psychology and sociology and utopian dreams."[44] In fact, no one is talking about utopia. Utopian theories are always based on an environmentalist view of man. Change the environment and you'll change men, says the utopian. Hunt disagrees with this outlook, and so do we. Change must begin in the hearts of men. After that, men must be disciplined by the Word of God. As they grow and mature in God's grace, they will restore the environment around them. The environment does not change men. Redeemed men change the environment.[45]

In another place, Hunt writes,

> How could the church be expected to establish the kingdom by taking over the world when even God cannot accomplish that without violating man's freedom of choice? During His thousand-year reign, Christ will visibly rule the world in perfect righteousness from Jerusalem and will impose peace upon all nations. Satan will be locked up, robbed of the power to tempt. Justice will be meted out swiftly.[46]

This is an interesting statement in several ways. First, we do not believe that the church "establishes the kingdom." The kingdom has already been established. The New Testament clearly teaches that *Christ* established the kingdom in His life, death, and resurrection. In one sense, both Christians and non-Christians

---

44. *Ibid.*, p. 251.

45. We must be careful, of course, not to go to an opposite extreme and conclude that the environment has nothing to do with our behavior. In fact, Scripture teaches that there is a created, built-in relationship between man and the world. Man is made from dust, so he has affinities with the earth. The many analogies that the Bible draws between men and plants and animals are all based on the fact that God has built analogies into His creation. Thus, as every parent knows, a good environment is important to healthy and sane behavior. But we are not environmental*ists* who claim that sin can be eradicated by changing the environment.

46. *Beyond Seduction*, p. 250.

alike are now living in God's kingdom: Christians as sons and daughters of the King, non-Christians as rebels. Critics of dominion theology have chosen to believe that efforts to bring about long-term reconstruction in society are foolhardy and even satanic. They opt to live in Satan's kingdom when the Bible clearly states that the kingdom of God has come upon us.

Second, where in the Bible does it say that God's actions are dependent on man's will? Is Hunt saying that God can't act unless man acts first? This is the essence of New Age humanism. The basis of the "human potential movement" is that man makes his own god-like decisions. Again, we find that Hunt's doctrine of God affects his perspective on the future.

Third, how is it that God can "impose peace upon all nations" during the millennium, yet He cannot do it before? What if some men do not want peace during the millennium? Will God violate "man's freedom of choice" to "impose" it upon them?

In addition to criticizing "dominion theology" as utopian, many believe that this perspective undermines the suffering that is part of the Christian life. Peter Lalonde stated in a taped interview with Dave Hunt that "everybody seems to want to join in the power of His resurrection, but nobody wants to get into the fellowship of His suffering."[47] They are correct that suffering has not been an emphasis among reconstructionists,[48] and it may be that the necessity of suffering has been denied outright by some. Still, we should strive to maintain a balance among the various teachings of Scripture. As we have seen in dealing with other statements, Lalonde forces us into an illegitimate "either/or" situation. The biblical picture is that we share *both* in Christ's sufferings (cf. 2 Cor. 12:10) *and* in the surpassing power of His resurrection (Eph. 1:19-23). It is through suffering that the church shares in

---

47. From *Dominion: A Dangerous New Theology*, 1987.

48. On the other hand, see Peter J. Leithart, "The Iron Philosophy: Stoic Elements in Calvin's Doctrine of Mortification" (Th.M. Thesis, Westminster Theological Seminary, 1987). One of the main emphases of this thesis is that the Christian life is inescapably one of suffering and self-denial.

Christ's rule. Like Jacob, the Church limps; but like Jacob, the Church wrestles with God and man and prevails (Gen. 32:22-32).[49]

Conclusion

Hunt believes that Christ's kingdom is other-worldly, "spiritual," heavenly. In a certain sense, all of these things are true. The problem with his position is that he understands these terms in an unbiblical way and draws unbiblical conclusions from these truths. We have tried to show that many of the passages that he uses to support his position do not in fact do so. Thus, though Hunt's view of the kingdom has some biblical support, it is one-sided and therefore distorts what the Scriptures teach about the kingdom of God.

---

49. See James B. Jordan, "The Church: An Overview," in Jordan, ed., *The Reconstruction of the Church*. Christianity and Civilization, No. 4 (Tyler, TX: Geneva Ministries, 1985).

10

MYTHS OF MILITANCY

One of the major distortions of postmillennial and "reconstructionst" teaching is that this position leads to revolutionary militancy. It is true that the rhetoric of some Christian "reconstructionist" writers is confrontational and militant, in some cases overly so. But it is misleading to equate militant language with advocating revolution. Jesus used militant language in condemning the Pharisees, but He was certainly no advocate of revolution.

Our position is that Christians should follow the examples of biblical characters such as Joseph, Daniel, and Jesus Christ Himself. Joseph and Daniel both exercised enormous influence within the world's greatest empires. But they attained their positions by hard work, perseverence in persecution and suffering, and faithful obedience. Jesus Christ attained to His throne only by enduring the suffering of the cross. Christians are no different. We are not to attain positions of leadership by revolution or rebellion. Instead, we are to work at our callings and wait on the Lord to place us in positions of influence, *in His time*.[1]

Bringing Persecution on Ourselves

Dave Hunt and Peter Lalonde perpetuate the myth that postmillennialism is militant. In the *Omega-Letter*'s taped interview with Dave Hunt, Peter Lalonde responds to an advertisement for

---

1. See David Chilton, *The Days of Vengeance* (Ft. Worth, TX: Dominion Press, 1987), pp. 511-12; James B. Jordan, "Rebellion, Tyranny, and Dominion in the Book of Genesis," in Gary North, ed., *Tactics of Christian Resistance*, Christianity and Civilization No. 3 (Tyler, TX: Geneva Ministries, 1983), pp. 38-80.

a book series called "The Biblical Blueprints Series," published by Dominion Press. The advertisement copy reads in part:

> For the first time in over 300 years, a growing number of Christians are starting to view themselves as an army on the move. This army will grow. This series is designed to help it grow and grow tougher.

Lalonde responds by saying that "They're very militant about this. They're really giving cause to the . . . People for the American Way." Hunt replies: "Right, right, they literally are, because they're saying, 'Well, these Christians want to take over the world.' Well, indeed they do."[2]

Several comments on these views are in order. First, Lalonde describes this view as "very militant." The word "militant" conjures up images of armed conflict or "Islamic fundamentalism." Yet, though not pacifistic in matters of national defense, "reconstructionists" regularly condemn revolutionary armed conflict or direct civil disobedience as the way to extend the kingdom.[3] R. J.

---

2. *Dominion: A Dangerous New Theology*, Tape #1 of *Dominion: The Word and New World Order*, distributed by *Omega-Letter*, Ontario, Canada, 1987.

3. A word must be said about the legitimacy of certain acts of civil disobedience. Scripture gives us clear examples, such as Daniel (Dan. 6) and the apostles (Acts 4:19-20), of men who refused to obey laws that directly conflicted with God's Law. Thus, we may disobey the State when obedience to the State would mean disobedience to God.

The question of legitimate resistance is much more complex, too complex to be treated fully here. Suffice it to say that we believe, with Calvin and many English, Dutch, and Scottish Calvinists (see Calvin's *Institutes*, 4.20.31), that a subordinate government, such as a state or a colony, may legitimately resist against an oppressive master. In saying this, we are not advocating anarchy. The resistance must be led by a legitimate government, as it was for example in the American Revolution. Moreover, every legal means of relief must be exhausted before an oppressed people rebels. Having said all this, we think that rebellions of this kind are successful only in very rare instances, and we think it is far more important that Christians resist the humanistic culture through other means.

For reconstructionist opinions on the American Revolution, see *Journal of Christian Reconstruction* vol. 3, no. 1 (Summer 1976), a symposium on "Christianity and the American Revolution." For a traditional Calvinist view of civil disobedience and legitimate rebellion, see Samuel Rutherford, *Lex, Rex* (Harrison, VA: Sprinkle, [1644] 1982).

Rushdoony, for example, wrote a 1975 article on "Jesus and the Tax Revolt," in which he contended that "our Lord ruled out . . . the tax *revolt*, revolution as the way, rather than regeneration." The Christian response to unjust taxation is not revolt but rendering to God the things that are God's.

> We render ourselves, our homes, our schools, churches, states, vocations, *all* things to God. We make Biblical law our standard, and we recognize in all things the primacy of regeneration.[4]

Similarly, Gary North calls advocates of kingdom by revolution "romantic revolutionaries."[5] This is not a recent emphasis in North's writings. His first major book was *Marx's Religion of Revolution*, in which he insisted that "faithful men will remain orderly in all the aspects of their lives; they are not to create chaos in order to escape from law (Rom. 13; I Cor. 14:40). It is reserved for God alone to bring His total judgment to the world." In the biblical world view, "it is God, and only God, who initiates the change."[6] North has pointed out repeatedly that the kingdom of God advances *ethically* as the people of God work out their salvation with fear and trembling. In fact, one of Dr. North's books, *Moses and Pharaoh*, is subtitled *Dominion Religion Versus Power Religion*. Power Religion

> is a religious viewpoint which affirms that the most important goal for a man, group, or species, is the capture and maintenance of power. Power is seen as the chief attribute of God, or if the religion is officially atheistic, then the chief attribute of man. This perspective is a satanic perversion of God's command to man to exercise dominion over all the creation (Gen. 1:26-28). It is the attempt to exercise dominion apart from covenantal subordination to the true Creator God.

---

4. Rushdoony, "Jesus and the Tax Revolt," *Journal of Christian Reconstruction* vol. 2, no. 2 (Winter 1975-76), p. 140.

5. Gary North, "Editor's Introduction," *Tactics of Christian Resistance*, pp. xxxii-xxxvii.

6. North, *Marx's Religion of Revolution* (Nutley, NJ: Craig Press, 1968), p. 99.

What distinguishes biblical dominion religion from satanic power religion is *ethics*.[7]

Biblical Militancy

On the other hand, the Bible itself uses military metaphors to show that the Christian is engaged in relentless battle with the enemy. Of course, the Bible calls us to fight our *ethical* battles with *spiritual* weapons, but the People for the American Way folks don't understand that. The church has sung the hymn, "Onward, Christian Soldiers," for decades. Consider the militant words and how unbelievers would respond to the militaristic tone:

> Onward Christian soldiers, marching as to war,
> With the cross of Jesus going on before
> Christ the royal Master leads against the foe;
> Forward into battle, see His banners go.

The Apostle Paul tells Christians to "put on the full armor of God" (Eph. 6:11). Of course, Paul is talking about a spiritual battle, but those outside the church community may not perceive it in those terms, just as Norman Lear and People for the American Way (PAW) misconstrue our intentions. What if a pastor quoted Paul's words in Ephesians 6:11 to his congregation and a representative from PAW was there? Imagine the headlines: "Minister advocates taking up arms. Every man is to be armed with weapons to defeat the enemy." The word would go out warning Americans that Christians are advocating armed conflict.

At first, even Pilate considered Jesus' kingdom to be militaristic and political (John 18:28-40). In Acts, the Christians were described as a sect preaching "another king, Jesus" (Acts 17:7). Their persecutors were the forerunners of People for the American

---

7. (Tyler, TX: Institute for Christian Economics, 1985), p. 2. Dr. North distinguishes between "Power Religion," "Escapist Religion," and "Dominion Religion" (pp. 2-5). He makes it very clear that "Power Religion" is the militant religion.

Way. They said of the first-century Christians, "These men who have upset the world have come here also; and Jason has welcomed them, and they all act contrary to the decrees of Caesar, saying there is another king, Jesus" (vv. 6, 7). There was another King, but those outside of Christ put a political and revolutionary slant on Christ's kingship. So then, it is perfectly natural for anti-Christian groups like Norman Lear's People for the American Way to misrepresent Christians who believe that there is a dominion feature to the gospel. The first-century Christians were accused in a similar way.

The anti-dominionists don't want to stir up the enemies of Christ with a victory-oriented gospel. Lalonde suggests that people who believe that the Bible applies to every area of life, including politics, are "bringing persecution on themselves."[8] The first-century humanists understood the implications of the gospel better than Hunt and Lalonde. They saw that if the gospel message is true, their total allegiance would have to change from Caesar to Christ. Caesar's worldview then dominated every facet of society; this new Lord Jesus would make a similar demand. In time, the Christian world view came to dominate society. Kenneth Scott Latourette wrote:

> One of the most amazing and significant facts of history is that within five centuries of its birth Christianity won the professed allegiance of the overwhelming majority of the population of the Roman Empire and even the support of the Roman State.[9]

---

8. *Dominion: A Dangerous New Theology*, 1987. Hunt interprets Lalonde's statement about militancy this way: "Well, these Christians want to take over the world." He leaves the impression that to "take over the world" means some sort of top-down imposition of Christianity on the citizenry rather than a progressive leavening of society by Christians who apply the Word of God to every area of life.

9. *A History of Christianity* (London: Eyre and Spottiswoode, n.d.), p. 65. Quoted in John Jefferson Davis, *Christ's Victorious Kingdom: Postmillennialism Reconsidered* (Grand Rapids, MI: Baker, 1987), p. 66. Davis notes that Constantine's "endorsement of the Christian religion gave further impetus to trends already under way. It meant as well, however, that many half-converted people were now entering the church, with a consequent slackening of spiritual fervor and discipline" (p. 69). A valuable comparison could be made of this "slackening

Who's the Revolutionary?

Other premillennial writers have also attempted to paint post-millennialism in blood-red colors. Norman Geisler writes:

> Many evangelicals are calling for civil disobedience, even revolution, against a government. Francis Schaeffer, for example, insisted that Christians should disobey government when "any office commands that which is contrary to the word of God." He even urges a blood revolution, if necessary, against any government that makes such laws. He explains that "in a fallen world, force in some form will always be necessary."[10]

What makes this comment particularly interesting is the fact that Schaeffer was a *pre*millennialist, not a postmillennialist. Geisler admits that this is true, but adds that "it appears that in actual practice at this point his views were postmillennial." This is certainly a strange, and we must add, a very deceptive argument. Geisler cites Francis Schaeffer, a *pre*millennialist, to try to show that the *post*millennial position encourages revolution. And Schaeffer is the *only* writer that Geisler cites. Geisler does not cite a single postmillennial writer who advocates revolution, so it is sheer bias on his part to conclude that Schaeffer is operating as a postmillennialist. In fact, he has not even proven that Schaeffer was a revolutionary. Schaeffer, with Calvin and many other Calvinists, simply claims that resistance against tyranny is legitimate in some cases. Not only has Geisler failed to *prove* his point, but he offers absolutely no evidence that would contribute to such a proof.

In fact, the evidence Geisler does cite proves precisely the opposite of what he concludes. The fact that Francis Schaeffer "advocated revolution" would be evidence that *pre*millennialism encourages violent civil disobedience. We are not saying that premillen-

---

of spiritual fervor and discipline" with our age and what David Wilkerson describes as "pillow prophets" and a "Laodicean church." It wasn't the end of the world after Constantine, and it may not be the end in our day.

10. Norman Geisler, "A Premillennial View of Law and Government," *The Best in Theology*, gen. ed., J. I. Packer (Carol Stream, IL: Christianity Today/ Word, 1986), p. 261-262.

nialism is revolutionary. We are simply pointing out that Geisler's evidence does not prove what he says it proves.

In fact, revolutionary forms of Christianity can be associated with either pre- or postmillennial eschatologies. The issue is not one's millennial view, but one's time frame. Some postmillennialists in the history of the church have believed that Christ was going to return soon. Think about it. If you believe that the world will be Christianized, as postmillennialists do, and also believe that you have only a few years or months to do it, then there is no alternative but to impose Christianity by force on the nations. The quickest means to leadership is political and military take-over. These short-term postmillennialists are revolutionaries because they cannot see any other way for Christians to take dominion.

By contrast, modern postmillennial "reconstructionists" are not revolutionary because they have a more consistently biblical view of the future. "Reconstructionists" generally believe they have time, lots of time, to accomplish their ends.[11] Moreover, they are not revolutionary because they believe that Christians achieve leadership by living righteously. Dominion is by ethical service and work, not by revolution. Thus, there is no theological reason for a postmillennialist to take up arms at the drop of a hat. Biblical postmillennialists can afford to wait for God to judge ungodly regimes, to bide their time, and to prepare to rebuild upon the ruins. Biblical postmillennialists are not pacifists, but neither are they revolutionaries.

Many premillennial theologians, however, believe that Christ is coming in the very near future. Those premillennialists who believe that Christ wants them to be culturally influential, as Francis Schaeffer did, thus imply that Christians have to gain leadership

---

11. David Wilkerson has written that the Puritans believed that the denial of the imminent return of Christ would be the final deception. *Omega-Letter* 2 (April 1987), p. 1. Unfortunately, Wilkerson does not cite any Puritans who believed this, and it is worth noting that this view was not embodied in any of the confessions that the Puritans subscribed to. Wilkerson's comment is another example of someone judging orthodoxy by a subjective, non-creedal standard.

now. This is also the problem with many charismatic "Kingdom Now" writers. They believe that Christians are meant to lead, but they don't believe that Christians have the time to gain positions of leadership through service and faithfulness. Their position is potentially dangerous not because it is optimistic, but because it lacks a long-term time frame.

Revolution and the Timing of the Kingdom

Historically, the Christians who have advocated violent revolution have believed that the end of the world was at hand. For example, Christopher Hill writes that the Fifth Monarchists, a sect that appeared during the Puritan Revolution, "believed that the reign of Christ upon earth was shortly to begin." They believed that this reign was imminent, and inspired by prophecy, led uprisings against the government in 1657 and 1661.[12] The Fifth Monarchists were not the only ones in 17th-century England who were expecting some kind of cataclysmic change. In another book, Hill writes,

> To many men the execution of Charles I in 1649 seemed to make sense only as clearing the way for King Jesus, as the prelude to greater international events. . . . A Bristol Baptist in 1654, hearing that two Frenchmen had been imprisoned for foretelling the end of the world in 1656, was worried because he was not prepared for that event. Between 1648 and 1657 Ralph Josselin was reading millennarian tracts, one of which suggested that Oliver Cromwell would conquer the Turk and the Pope. He was continually thinking and dreaming about the millennium. He noted in his Diary that men expected the world to end in 1655 or 1656, though he did not share the belief. "This generation shall not pass," declared John Tillinghast in 1654, until the millennium has arrived. John Bunyan announced in 1658 that "the judgment day is at hand."[13]

12. *The Century of Revolution, 1603-1714* (New York: W. W. Norton, 1961), pp. 168-70.

13. Hill, *The World Turned Upside Down* (Middlesex, England: Penguin Books, 1975), pp. 96-97.

These ideas were in the air from the beginning of the Puritan Revolution and doubtless contributed to the revolutionary fervor. It is not clear whether these men were pre- or postmillennial, but their tendency toward revolution was obviously fed by a sense that some dramatic eschatological event was just around the corner. This frantic sense of imminence, combined with the Puritan emphasis on reform, was, we believe, a major flaw in the Puritan outlook at that time, and the Puritans might have avoided some mistakes if they had not had such a truncated historical perspective.

This short-term view of the future was a motivating force for the "People's Crusades" of the eleventh and twelfth centuries. The people who participated in the Crusade to the Holy Land

> saw themselves as actors in the prodigious consummation towards which all things had been working since the beginning of time. On all sides they beheld the "signs" which were to mark the beginning of the Last Days, and heard how "the Last Trump proclaimed the coming of the righteous Judge."[14]

They believed that the biblical prophecies of the end of the world were just beginning to be fulfilled and that

> Antichrist is already born—at any moment Antichrist may set up his throne in the Temple at Jerusalem: even amongst the higher clergy there were some who spoke like this. And little as the phantasies had to do with the calculations of Pope Urban, they were attributed to him by chroniclers struggling to describe the atmosphere in which the First Crusade was launched. It is the will of God—Urban is made to announce at Clermont—that through the labours of the crusaders Christianity shall flourish again at Jerusalem in these last times, so that when Antichrist begins his reign here—as shortly he must—he will find enough Christians to fight.[15]

Similar sentiments were expressed by the Anabaptists who seized Munster in 1534-1535: "The rest of the earth, it was announced, was doomed to be destroyed before Easter; but Munster

---

14. Norman Cohn, *The Pursuit of the Millennium* (rev. ed.; New York: Oxford University Press, [1957] 1970), p. 71.

15. *Ibid.*, p. 75.

would be saved and would become the New Jerusalem."[16] One of the leaders of the German Peasant Revolt, Thomas Muntzer, saw himself as the Lord's instrument of judgment to prepare for the return of Christ. He exhorted his followers to put on their swords "to exterminate" the ungodly, "for the ungodly have no right to live, save what the Elect choose to allow them."[17]

This brief glance at Christian revolutionary movements suggests that the unifying thread through the eschatologies of all such movements is not postmillennialism, but an obsession with the imminent return of Christ. Faced with the prospect of almost immediate final judgment, a few Christians have turned to violence.

Kingdom Weapons

Mr. Hunt himself admits that Christians are engaged in some kind of warfare. The issue is, what are the weapons of kingdom warfare? Hunt says that the Christian's weapons are obedience, prayer, holy living, self-sacrifice, love, preaching, and applying God's Word. Our weapon is not "political/social action."[18] We agree that our weapons are prayer, the Word, righteousness, the sacraments, etc. Our warfare is not with flesh and blood, but with the hidden forces of satanic darkness (Eph. 6) We do not wage war as the world does (2 Cor. 10:1-6). We are to disciple the nations by teaching the commands of Christ and baptizing them into the Triune name (Matt. 28:18-20).

But our spiritual fighting has an effect on the world. It has an effect on the progress of history. Paul implies this in the very passage where he says we do not fight as the world does. We are *in* the world, but we do not fight as the world does. Moreover, we fight *so that* we can take every thought captive to Christ (2 Cor. 10:4-5). Whose thoughts are to be taken captive? Obviously, the thoughts of real men and women are taken captive. If the thoughts of men and women are to be taken captive to Christ, is it plausible to sug-

---

16. *Ibid.*, p. 262.
17. *Ibid.*, p. 239.
18. Dave Hunt, *Beyond Seduction: A Return to Biblical Christianity* (Eugene, OR: Harvest House, 1987), pp. 246-47.

gest that there will be no visible effects on society and politics? Ideas have consequences.

Moreover, we might ask what Hunt means by "obedience"? Might it involve picketing an abortion clinic or lobbying a congressman? Might it involve ministering to the homeless, the unwed mother, the alcoholic (all of which is, after all, "social action")? Isn't the heart of obedience to seek justice, to love mercy, and to walk humbly with our God (Micah 6:8)? Might not "seeking justice" possibly involve political action of some sort? What does Hunt disagree with here? Does he think Christians who fight abortion politically are being *dis*obedient? Hunt would not say this, we're quite certain. All that "reconstructionists" are saying is that civil governments must be obedient to Christ, and that obedience will bring God's blessing and restoration.

Conclusion

Biblical postmillennialism provides the Christian with a *long-term* hope. Because of his long time-frame, the postmillennialist can exercise that chief element of true biblical faith: patience. Because he is confident that the Lord has given him time to accomplish the Lord's purposes, the postmillennialist need not take things into his own, sinful hands. The Lord will exalt us when He is ready, and when He knows that we are ready. Our calling is to wait patiently, praying and preparing ourselves for that responsibility, and working all the while to advance His kingdom. Historically, some Christians who lack this long-term hope have taken things into their own hands, inevitably with disastrous consequences. Far from advocating militancy, biblical postmillennialism protects against a short-term revolutionary mentality.

11

THE KINGDOM IS NOW!

In the last several chapters, we have examined Dave Hunt's view of the kingdom of God. Hunt teaches that the kingdom is an internal and "spiritual" reality. The present kingdom of God is not "of the world." Instead, the kingdom is heaven. We will enter the kingdom only when we die, though Hunt admits that the kingdom is already in our hearts in some way. We have already anticipated much of what we will say in this chapter. Still, we need to present our position systematically and defend it more positively than we have done in earlier chapters.

The kingdom is one of the most complex concepts in all of Scripture. One of the reasons for this is that Jesus used it as the comprehensive "umbrella" doctrine that explained His entire work of redemption. *Every teaching of the New Testament relates in a more or less direct way to the kingdom.* Another reason is that much of Old Testament prophecy was concerned with the coming of the Messianic kingdom. Because of the complexity of this doctrine, we have not attempted to be comprehensive. Rather, we have tried to highlight some of the main features of the biblical doctrine of the kingdom of God, focussing mainly on the New Testament.

In order to clarify what we will say below, we will first summarize our view. *The kingdom is the rule of God through the God-man, Jesus Christ.* It was established when Jesus came to conquer His enemies, and to bring order out of the chaos of sin. After conquering His enemies, the King was seated on His throne to rule over all things. *In principle, Christ's rule is already universal; He graciously rules over everything and He rules everywhere. He rules all men and all human associations.* Those who submit to Him enter into the blessedness of the kingdom, enjoying the power and privileges of being His subjects, and committing themselves to righteous living. Christ advances the kingdom through the proclamation of the gospel and the working of His Spirit, extending His mercy and bringing more and more men and nations under the protection and blessing of His rule. He also advances His rule by ordering the events of history for the benefit of His church, including the conversion or destruction of His enemies. Christ's ultimate purpose is to glorify, exalt, and vindicate the Father. His more immediate purpose is to save His people and to establish justice and peace throughout the earth.

Our view of the kingdom, oddly enough, has been well summarized by the dispensationalist theologian Herman Hoyt of Grace Theological Seminary. He claims that the kingdom is spiritual in the sense that it is "governed by the Spirit of God." The Spirit's control of individuals will be manifested in individual ethical conduct, the healing of social relations, political transformation, physical and ecological improvement, and religious purity.[1] The major differences between Hoyt's position and ours are 1) the question of timing, and 2) whether or not Christ will be physically present during the millennium. We believe that these things will develop gradually throughout the present age, while Hoyt believes that they will occur only after Christ returns and establishes His throne in Jerusalem.

The Conquering King

The Greek word for kingdom, *basileia*, has a different primary meaning from the English word "kingdom." The Greek word

---

1. Herman Hoyt, "Dispensational Premillennialism," in *The Meaning of the Millennium: Four Views*, ed., Robert G. Clouse (Downers Grove, IL: InterVarsity Press, 1977), pp. 82-83.

basically means dominion, rule, or kingship, while our English word refers to a realm. The Greek refers to the authority of a king, not the land or subjects that a king rules.[2] But God is not a figurehead King, who retains His royal title without actually ruling. In Christ, God actually exercises His royal authority and power. In fact, Paul says that the kingdom *consists* in power (1 Cor. 4:20). Moreover, throughout the gospels, Jesus talks about "entering the kingdom" (Matt. 7:21; John 3:5; etc.) and feasting in the kingdom (Matt. 8:11; Luke 13:29), and promises that He will someday sit at His table with His disciples in the kingdom (Matt. 26:29; Mark 14:25; Luke 22:16-18). This usage suggests the idea of "realm" or "sphere of power or authority." Thus, while the basic meaning of the word is "rule," the full doctrine of the kingdom has a wider reference. God's rule implies that there are people and a realm to be ruled.

If the kingdom is God's reign, how can we talk about the kingdom's "coming"? How can we talk about the "establishment" of God's rule? How can we talk of its growth? Hasn't God always ruled everything? Of course, the Bible teaches that God has eternal and comprehensive dominion (Dan. 4:34). But Scripture also speaks about the kingdom's "coming" and "growing" and "increasing." So, we must distinguish between the eternal rule of God and the rule of Jesus Christ, the Incarnate Word.[3]

Let us return to a parallel argument that we have used before. When a Christian is saved, he receives eternal life. "He who believes in the Son has everlasting life" (John 3:36a). Yet, he also says that he is prepared to die. But if he is going to die, how can he say that he has received eternal life? The answer is simple: *we*

---

2. Herman Ridderbos, *The Coming of the Kingdom* (Philadelphia, PA: Presbyterian and Reformed, 1962), pp. 24-26.

3. Theologians use the phrase "mediatorial reign" to refer to Christ's rule over all things as the God-man. This is distinguished from His rule as the second Person of the Trinity. As God, "the eternal Son of God was exercising his sovereign dominion over the entire universe" even before the incarnation. As the divine-human mediator, Christ is given the authority to rule as a reward of His obedience unto death. See A. A. Hodge, *Evangelical Theology* (Edinburgh: Banner of Truth Trust, [1890] 1976), pp. 224-25.

are not talking about an either/or condition. Salvation is a *both/and* condition: present and future. Christians have received eternal life in
principle; they keep it throughout their lives; and then they receive it at the resurrection of the dead. All three statements are
true. Therefore, our salvation has three stages: *definitive, progressive, and final.* So does the kingdom of God in its earthly manifestations.

Sin and Deliverance

In order to understand how Christ can be said to be "establishing" God's rule, we must look back to the first chapters of Genesis.
Man was created to be God's servant, to rule over the earth and to
glorify his Lord in doing so. Man was not to be God's equal, but
to be God's representative ruler over the earth. Adam was not to
be the King, but the King's representative. In succumbing to the
temptation of the serpent, however, Adam attempted to be his
own God, and instead came under the dominion of Satan.

After the fall of Adam and Eve, God promised to send a
Deliverer to defeat Satan and to destroy his rule over men (Gen.
3:15). Throughout the Old Testament, God raised up deliverers to
save His people and to secure the blessings of life under God's
rule. All of these, however, failed to bring lasting peace and order.
In the incarnation of the Son, the King Himself comes into the
world to conquer the enemy once and for all. Jesus came as the
Greater Joshua, who makes war against God's enemies, and as
the Greater Son of David who rules the world in righteousness.

It is important to note the God-centeredness of Jesus' mission.
He didn't come merely to save men from eternal death and punishment, as important as that is. He came to establish the kingdom of *God,* or the kingdom of *heaven.* He came to reassert *God's*
rule. The kingdom *belongs* to the Father: "Thine is the kingdom"
(Matt. 6:13; cf. Matt. 13:43). As Ridderbos puts it, "In the coming of the kingdom God first and foremost reveals *himself* as the
creator and king who does not abandon the world to perdition but

is his people's saviour and promiser."⁴ Hence, the ultimate goal of Christ's rule is God's glory and good pleasure. The failure of the Old Testament kings had led Israel to doubt whether God truly ruled. The nations had seen Israel's sinfulness and oppression, and they blasphemed God (Isa. 52:5; Rom. 2:24). How could God really be King if His people were constantly oppressed and enslaved? Christ delivered His people so that God's honor would be vindicated and His name glorified, so that the ends of the earth would know that the Lord is God indeed.

Of course, Christ's deliverance and His rule were different from what many Israelites had expected. Rather than throwing off the chains of Rome, Christ broke the chains of sin and death. He conquered the Enemy behind the enemy. In contrast to the conquests of the Old Testament judges and kings, Jesus' conquest was not over external enemies, but over the invisible accuser and oppressor of men. In extending His kingdom, He does not conquer enemies by the sword of iron, but by the sword that comes out of His mouth (Rev. 19). Also, Christ did not deliver Israel only. In fact, He spent a lot of time telling Israel that the Old Covenant people would be judged, and He delivered men and women from every nation and tribe and tongue. Finally, Christ became King through His self-sacrifice on the Cross. He performed His visible redemptive work not as the majestic Son of David, but as the Suffering Servant. Likewise, His kingdom grows not by an exercise of brute force, but by the selfless service of His people.

Christ's Conquest of Satan

Christ's miracles were, among other things, signs of His conquest of Satan and His establishment of the rule of God. Jesus drove out demons by the Spirit of God as a sign that "the kingdom of God has come upon you" (Matt. 12:28-29). Even the demons recognized why Jesus had come: "What do we have to do with You, Jesus of Nazareth? Have You come to destroy us? I know who You are—the Holy One of God" (Mark 1:24). Jesus bound

---

4. Ridderbos, *The Coming of the Kingdom*, p. 22.

the strong man so that He could plunder His house (Mark 3:27). Through the cross, Christ disarmed the demonic powers, and publicly triumphed over them in His resurrection (Col. 2:15).[5]

One aspect of Christ's triumph over Satan can be discovered by examining the book of Job in the light of the New Testament. In the first two chapters of Job, we find Satan, the accuser, in the heavenly courtroom of God (cf. Zech. 3:1-2). He is among the angels who report to the King. He has a position of power and authority. In fact, one of Job's complaints throughout the book is that he has no "Advocate," no one to argue his case before the Judge. When Christ came, however, He cast Satan from heaven (Luke 10:18; Rev. 12:7). Thus, instead of having the accusing Satan in heaven, we now have an Advocate, Jesus Christ the Righteous One, who argues our case before the Father (1 John 2:1). Satan no longer has authority to accuse us before God.

The Reigning King

Having completed His *definitive* conquest of Satan, Christ was exalted to the right hand of the Father, and given the nations as His inheritance. This exaltation fulfills the prophecy of Psalm 2: "Ask of Me, and I will surely give you the nations as Thine inheritance and the very ends of the earth as Thy possession" (v. 8). Daniel also prophesied that when the Son of Man ascended to the Ancient of Days, He would be given dominion, glory, and rule over all nations (Dan. 7:13-14). The New Testament everywhere teaches the same truth. As a result of His suffering and death, He is "crowned with glory and honor" (Heb. 2:9). After Jesus humbled

---

5. The picture of Jesus in the gospels is not of a meek teacher of non-violence. Jesus is not a Gandhi-Christ. To be sure, Jesus is supremely kind and gentle. But the Jesus pictured in the gospels is much more a warrior than a benign guru. William Kirk Kilpatrick describes the same things in different terms: "The Gospels . . . give us a picture of a man of powerful passions who wept openly and threw people around bodily. It is difficult in places to avoid the impression of an impassioned lover: the kind of man willing to take rash action to win over his beloved, willing to make public scenes; willing to do almost anything short of tying her up and dragging her off." *Psychological Seduction* (Nashville, TN: Thomas Nelson, 1983), p. 215.

Himself unto death, the Father exalted Him and gave Him a name above every name (Phil. 2:8-9).

In Ephesians 1:22, Paul states that God "has placed all things under his feet." Every part of this phrase deserves emphasis. First, Paul is writing in the past tense. He does not say that God *will* place all things under Christ's feet. God *has* placed all things under Christ's feet. When did this happen? The text tells us that it happened when God "seated [Christ] at His right hand in the heavenly realms," that is, at His ascension.

Second, note that *all things* have been placed under the feet of the ascended Christ. There is nothing in the text to restrict the scope of this word. It means, very literally, *all* things: all men, all the forces of creation, all nations and societies. *All* authority in heaven and on earth is given to the Risen Christ (Matt. 28:18-20). Christ is Lord of *all* (Acts 10:36), the head of *all* authorities and powers (Col. 2:10). Late in the last century, Princeton theologian A. A. Hodge wrote, "The present mediatorial kingdom of the God-man is absolutely universal, embracing the whole universe and every department of it."[6]

Abraham Kuyper, Jr., the son and namesake of the great Dutch theologian and statesman, wrote, "From that moment on that Christ has been seated in heaven at the right hand of the Father and has poured out the Holy Spirit, the Kingdom of Heaven has been founded upon earth."[7] Christ rules everywhere over everything. And He rules *now*.

Christ rules over all things in order to gather the nations into His one church. Paul wrote to the Ephesians that Christ rules all things "for the church" (Eph. 1:22). As the Scottish theologian of the last century, William Symington, wrote,

> . . . the possession of universal power must, on a moment's reflection, appear to be intimately connected with the interests of the church. Power beyond the church, is essential to the existence, increase, and welfare of the church itself. That the mem-

---

6. Hodge, *Evangelical Theology*, p. 228.

7. Quoted in Raymond O. Zorn, *Church and Kingdom* (Philadelphia, PA: Presbyterian and Reformed, 1962), p. 43.

bers of his mystical body may be complete in him, he must have dominion over all principalities and powers. The overthrow of the church's foes, the fulfillment of the church's prospects, and the final victory of every member over death and the grave, suppose him to rule with uncontrollable sway in the midst of his enemies.[8]

It is Christ who opens the doors for the gospel in remote regions of the world (Acts 16:6-10; Rev. 3:8). It is Christ, operating by His Spirit, who ensures that the preaching of the gospel will be effective. It is Christ who raises and destroys nations, all for the benefit of His people. It is Christ the King who, having inherited the nations, now causes His reign to be acknowledged from one end of the earth to the other.

A clear example of Christ's rule over the nations for His church was the destruction of the Jewish state that persecuted the early church (Matt. 24; Luke 21; cf. Acts 6:8-15). In destroying Israel, Christ transferred the blessings of the kingdom from Israel to a new people, the church. This is an important theme in the gospels. After healing the centurion's servant, for example, Jesus noted that the centurion's faith was greater than any he had found in Israel. He added that the "sons of the kingdom" would be cast out to make room for Gentiles to eat with Abraham, Isaac, and Jacob in the kingdom (Matt. 8:10-12). The parable of the vineyard makes the same point; Jesus concludes by telling the chief priests and elders that "the kingdom will be taken from you, and be given to a nation producing the fruit of it" (Matt. 21:43). In the very next chapter, Jesus tells the parable of the wedding feast. In the context, the first group invited to the kingdom refers to the Jews. When they refuse to come to the feast, the king sends his slaves into the highways and byways, inviting the rejected Gentiles to feast with him (Matt. 22:1-14).[9]

---

8. William Symington, *Messiah the Prince: or, The Mediatorial Dominion of Jesus Christ* (Philadelphia, PA: The Christian Statesman Publishing Company, [1839] 1884), p. 72.

9. This parable ends with the oft-quoted verse: "Many are called but few are chosen" (Matt. 22:14). This verse is usually quoted to prove that the number of those who are eternally saved is very small, compared with the huge number of

Christ's universal dominion over all things was *definitively* established when Jesus entered heaven and received His inheritance (Psalm 2:6; Phil. 2:9-11). But it must also be *progressively* acknowledged and manifested. Peter quoted Psalm 110:1 ("The Lord said unto my Lord, 'Sit at my right hand until I make your enemies a footstool for your feet.'") during his Pentecost sermon, and applied it to Jesus (Acts 2:34). This verse implies that Christ's enemies have not yet been fully conquered. Christ will reign *until* His enemies have been conquered. Paul implies the same thing in 1 Corinthians 15:25: "For He must reign until He has put all His enemies under His feet." Again, we find here the idea that Christ's reign advances and increases (cf. Is. 9:7).

How do we reconcile these passages with Ephesians 1, which teaches that Christ already reigns over everything? We should not ignore either emphasis, because both are found in Scripture. Instead, we should emphasize both equally. Christ is *already* reigning over all things, but His reign is *not yet* fully acknowledged. A helpful parallel is found in the doctrine of sanctification. Paul says that we have died to sin at baptism (Rom. 6:1-8). But we still have to struggle against sin (Rom. 7). The flesh has been crucified, but we must daily crucify the flesh. This is not a contradiction. Rather, each of these truths sets the proper context for the other. We fight against sin daily in the knowledge that sin has been crucified (Rom. 6:11-12). We are able to fight against sin with confidence *because* sin has been crucified. Similarly, Christ extends His rule throughout the earth *because* He already reigns from heaven.

Christ's definitive, progressive, and final reign parallels that of the Father. The Father has ruled, with the Son and Spirit, from all eternity. The Father "does as he pleases with the armies of

---

those who are damned. Non-Christians use this verse to defend their unbelief by saying, "I won't worship a God who sends more than half the world to hell."

In context, the verse does not teach that there will be more people in hell than there will be in heaven. Jesus' parable is about the *Jews* rejecting their Messiah. The few that are chosen are the first-century *Jews*, the first group of people invited to the feast. But the wedding hall is still full (vs. 10). Heaven will be full. It will be filled with people from the east and west and from the ends of the earth (Matt. 8:11-12).

heaven and with the peoples of the earth" (Dan. 4:34-35). He "forms light and creates darkness." He "brings prosperity and creates disaster" (Is. 45:5-7). Yet, it is clear that Satan continues to operate on earth (Job 1-2). Thus, though the Father has ruled since creation, He also progressively vanquishes the forces of darkness. On the last day, the Son will deliver the kingdom to the Father, so that He may be all in all (1 Cor. 15:28).

From Heaven to Earth

It may be helpful at this point to discuss the relationship of the "kingdom" to heaven. It is true that Jesus and the New Testament writers sometimes use the word "kingdom" to refer to the eternal state in heaven. This is especially apparent in those passages where Jesus talks about the kingdom as an inheritance (Matt. 25:34) or a reward (Matt. 20:1-16). In many passages, Paul warns that the wicked will not inherit the kingdom, implying that it is a future reality (1 Cor. 6:9-10; Gal. 5:21; Eph. 5:5). In 2 Timothy 4:18, Paul refers to Christ's "heavenly kingdom." Matthew uses the phrase "kingdom of heaven" in the same way that the other evangelists use the phrase "kingdom of God."

Nevertheless, this usage of "kingdom" should not lead us to the conclusion that the kingdom is *exclusively* in heaven, or that the kingdom has no impact on the history of the earth. Just as the King becomes incarnate on earth and enters history, so also His kingdom enters the world of human affairs. In Christ and by His work, *heaven comes to earth*. As Vos says, "the Kingdom of God becomes incarnate."[10] John Bright agrees: "In the person and work of Jesus the Kingdom of God has intruded into the world."[11]

This does not mean that Christ's rule is "earthly" or "fleshly," like the kingdoms of the world. It's realm is not limited to earth,

---

10. Geerhardus Vos, *Biblical Theology: Old and New Testaments* (Grand Rapids, MI: Eerdmans, [1948] 1975), p. 376.

11. John Bright, *The Kingdom of God* (New York: Abingdon-Cokesbury, 1953), p. 216. Neither Vos nor Bright, however, would agree with all of the implications that we draw from this fact. We quote them simply to show that we are not alone in insisting that the kingdom is a reality on earth.

but includes heaven as well. It is everlasting. It is ruled on different principles and is established by different methods than earthly kingdoms. It is Spiritual in the full biblical sense, namely, that Christ rules through the Holy Spirit. Nor does it mean that earth will ever *perfectly* reflect the reality of heaven. But the kingdom operates *on* earth, just as Christ lived on earth and still works by His Spirit. And we are to strive and pray to make earth reflect and image heaven.

The very nature of Christianity implies that the rule of Christ affects earthly history. Biblical Christianity has always been *historical*. The early creeds of the Church are simply recitals of the history of Christ's birth, death, and resurrection. These all occurred on earth, in history. It would be more than strange if the King had come to earth, died on earth, and risen again in a spiritual body so that He could establish a kingdom that has nothing to do with earth. Why did Christ do this on earth? Why did He become incarnate and enter human history? The answer of Scripture is that He came to redeem what was fallen. He came into the world to redeem the world. He came into the world to establish His redemptive reign among men on earth.

Moreover, several passages explicitly claim that Christ exercises dominion on earth. Christ claimed that He had been given all authority in heaven *and* on earth (Matt. 28:18-20).[12] Paul wrote to the Colossians that Christ, the Creator of all things, had come to earth to restore all things (Col. 1:16).[13] Christ's rule is as extensive as creation itself. People, real historical people, enter the kingdom (Col. 1:13). When Jesus gave Peter the keys of the king-

---

12. Some dispensationalists say that Christ was given this authority at His resurrection and ascension, but hasn't yet entered into the exercise of that authority. But this does great violence to the text. Jesus does not make this statement in a vacuum. He is saying this to His disciples to encourage them in their work of discipling the nations. It would have been a cruel joke indeed if Jesus had encouraged His disciples to take up the task of discipling the nations, sending them out confidently to Judea, Samaria, and the uttermost parts of the earth, if He were not actually reigning after all.

13. See Appendix D.

dom, He told him that they were for the binding and loosing of things both in heaven and *on earth* (Matt. 16:19). The signs of the coming of the kingdom in Jesus' ministry—healing and exorcism —had real effects on real people. Christ exhorted His followers to pursue the righteousness of the kingdom (Matt. 6:33), a righteousness manifested visibly and historically in acts of charity and justice. Though the operation of the kingdom is Spiritual, and though our King sits on a heavenly throne, His rule nevertheless has visible and historical effects.

Kingdom Blessing and Kingdom Righteousness

As we have seen, Christ rules over all things in heaven and on earth. The kingdom of the world has already become the kingdom of our Lord and of His Christ, and He now reigns and will reign eternally. But the Bible usually uses the word "kingdom" in a more restricted sense, to connote the blessings, privileges, and responsibilities that come to those who submit willingly to the rule of Christ.

Because Jesus has conquered the enemies of His people, the present, New Testament period of history is an age of salvation. The world has been delivered from its enslavement to Satan and to sin. Those who submit to the King in faith and obedience enjoy the blessings of the kingdom. The *chief blessing* of the kingdom is *forgiveness of sins* (Matt. 18:23). We are cleansed by the blood of Christ, which is effective for cleansing the conscience. Thus, we can draw near to God, know Him, and enjoy continual fellowship with Him in a way that Old Testament believers could not. One of the central symbols of fellowship with God throughout Scripture is the feast. In keeping with this, Jesus describes the blessings of the kingdom as sitting at His table (Matt. 8:11; Luke 13:29). The Lord's Supper is a foretaste of the joy and fellowship of the final wedding feast that Christ's people will enjoy at the end of the age (Matt. 26:29; Mark 14:25; Luke 22:16-18).

Those who enter the kingdom participate in the power of the resurrected Christ (Eph. 1:18-19). Power is one of the main emphases in the New Testament's teaching about the kingdom.[14] This power is brought to us by the Spirit of the Risen Christ. When He entered heaven, Christ received the Spirit, and poured it out on His people (Acts 2:33). The Spirit brings to the church the power and blessing of the kingdom.[15] Rev. Raymond Zorn has written,

> Christ had ascended to heaven to be from henceforth seated at the right hand of the Father until His reign was consummated in the fulfillment of every purpose of His rule, but His work on earth would be continued by the Spirit, coming to expression in the Church and going progressively forward until the very atmosphere of the eternal state would be created, maintained, and pervaded by the supernatural power of the Spirit. The power of God's Kingdom therefore continues to be active in the world, centered in the exalted reign of Christ, but furthered by His Spirit Who makes the Church the locus of His operation.[16]

Equipped with this Spiritual kingdom power, we are able to obey the commands of the King. In Christ, we have the power to resist the devil and his temptations. The law is written on our hearts (Heb. 8:8-13), and we are no longer slaves to sin, but slaves to Christ (Rom. 6:15-23).

Thus, the subjects of Christ's kingdom have certain responsibilities. His kingdom is a kingdom of righteousness.[17] Ultimately,

---

14. See Vos, *Biblical Theology*, pp. 386-87.

15. The connection of the Holy Spirit with the kingdom is implied by the first verses of the book of Acts. After His resurrection, Jesus taught His disciples about the kingdom. One of them, still confused by the Jewish nationalistic view of the kingdom, asked when Jesus would restore the kingdom to Israel. Jesus told him that the disciples did not need to know the times that the Father fixed, and added that the disciples would "receive power when the Holy Spirit has come upon you" (Acts 1:6-8). It is also significant that many of the gifts of the Spirit are kingdom gifts: joy (Rom. 14:17), healing (1 Cor. 12:9; cf. Acts 3:1-10 and note the context), miracles, prophecy (1 Cor. 12:10), peace (Gal. 5:22), etc. The Spirit brought the power of the kingdom to the disciples, and the Spirit continually brings to us the power of the kingdom as well. When we are born again by water and the Spirit, we enter into the kingdom and begin to enjoy its power and life (John 3:5).

16. Zorn, *Church and Kingdom*, pp. 45-46.

17. Vos, *Biblical Theology*, p. 392.

God alone can make us willing and righteous subjects of His kingdom: As Jesus told Nicodemus, we cannot enter the kingdom unless we have been born from above (John 3:5). But there are other requirements for those who would persevere in the kingdom. Both John and Jesus required repentance of those who would enter the kingdom. The kingdom should be our highest priority and our greatest joy (Matt. 6:33). The King requires total surrender (Luke 9:60-62; 18:29). Jesus said that our status in His kingdom depends on our attention to the details of His law (Matt. 5:19). In fact, in some passages, Jesus goes further and says that righteousness is a condition of entrance into the kingdom (Matt. 5:20; 7:21).[18] A major part of the righteousness that the King requires is humility (Matt. 5:3, 10; Luke 6:20). We must humble ourselves as little children to be fit for the kingdom (Matt. 18:1-4; 19:14; Mark 10:13-16). This humility is shown in our willingness to forego our own rights and to serve others.

The whole world benefits in many ways from the rule of Christ. But the rule of Christ also means condemnation for those who despise His offer of blessing and salvation. Ridderbos notes that the kingdom "means judgment because God maintains his royal will in opposition to all who resist his will."[19] Thus, Christ's universal rule over all things is manifested either in blessing or cursing. The Psalmist warned that the enthroned King would rule the nations with a rod of iron and shatter the disobedient like pottery (Psalm 2:9). The punishment of the wicked is more severe than under the Mosaic system, "for if the word spoken through angels proved unalterable, and every transgression and disobedience received a just recompense, how shall we escape if we neglect so great a salvation?" (Heb. 2:2-3). Throughout the book of Acts, the apostles warned people to repent because Christ had been raised and exalted to judge all nations (Acts 2:32-36; 10:40-42; 17:31). Thus, the age of the kingdom is an age of crisis. When the

---

18. We do not mean that there is any merit in our righteousness. Rather, righteousness, or obedience to God's Word, is a necessary mark of the Christian who has been redeemed apart from the law.

19. Ridderbos, *The Coming of the Kingdom*, p. 20.

apostles preached that *now* is the time of salvation, they were referring to the *present* age of history, the time between Christ's first and second advents.[20]

The Reign of the Saints

As we have seen, Christ rules the world for the good of the church. But the reverse is also true: Christ rules His church for the good of the world. The church has been given the ministry of the Word of life, which calls men to repentance and faith (Rom. 10:14-17). In the Lord's Supper, the church distributes the bread of life, which has been given for the life of the world (John 6:32-33).[21] The law and gospel flow from the mountain of the Lord, the church, and bring the nations to the church for justice (Isaiah 2:2-4). Christ rules from His heavenly throne, through His Spirit, to make these instruments effective for the conversion of the nations. Thus, it is through the Spirit-filled church, proclaiming the gospel, that the kingdom of Christ extends throughout the world. The church is Christ's instrument of rule.

More than that, the church actually participates in Christ's rule over the nations. The ascension of Christ thus marks a transition in *our* relationship to God's dominion over the world. Man was created to rule the earth, as a subject of the heavenly King (Gen. 1:28). When Adam sinned, he lost dominion. Hunt criticizes "dominion theologians" for talking about the *restoration* of man's dominion.

> It is the task of Christians, so we are told, to take *dominion* back from Satan (as the rightful gods of this world, according to

---

20. We may go a step further and say that the crisis that begins with the work of Christ is actually a preliminary manifestation of the final kingdom, with eternal blessedness for the elect and eternal punishment for the reprobate. We are already new creatures in Christ (2 Cor. 5:17), having been united with the One who is the first-fruits of the new creation. Similarly, the judgments that occur in this age are preliminary manifestations of the final judgment at the end of history. Thus, the final, eschatological kingdom is present already in the present age.

21. See Alexander Schmemann, *For the Life of the World* (Crestwood, NY: St. Vladimir's Seminary Press, [1963] 1973).

some) to restore planet Earth to the beautiful paradise that it once was before Adam and Eve sinned. However, man has not lost the dominion that God gave him "over the fish of the sea, and over the fowl of the air, and over every living thing that moveth upon the earth" (Genesis 1:26, 28; Psalm 8:6). To speak of *restoring* man's dominion is therefore meaningless. The problem is not man's *loss* of dominion but his *abuse* of it. Nor was dominion intended to be exercised by some men over other men, but only by man over creatures under him.[22]

He concludes by quoting Matthew 20:25-26, where Jesus warns against lording it over others.

In some ways, Hunt is simply playing a semantic game with "abuse" and "loss." Of course, what we are talking about is a loss of true and godly dominion. On the other hand, the Bible also says that we have become slaves of sin and of Satan. Doesn't this imply a loss of dominion? Moreover, is it really true that we have dominion over the animals and the earth? Have we really tapped the potentials of the earth's resources? Have we domesticated bears and lions? While we do continue to exercise some dominion over the earth, the curse of Genesis 3 implies that the earth is recalcitrant. The curse on the ground has made dominion more difficult. In principle, the curse has been removed by the resurrection of Christ, but we still have the progressive task of restoring the creation to godly use.

Hunt's quotation of Matthew 20:25-28 is a good reminder of the biblical teaching on leadership. But, several things should be noted. First, leadership is a form of dominion. The Christian leads by service, not by domination. This is accurate and needs to be said. But Jesus is talking about *leadership*. That's one of the things that we mean by "dominion." We don't mean domination. Christians are meant to rule, to be leaders. But we are to *lead by service*, not by domination.

Second, the implication is that "dominion theologians" teach

---

22. Dave Hunt, *Beyond Seduction: A Return to Biblical Christianity* (Eugene, OR: Harvest House, 1987), pp. 244-45.

that some men should dominate others. In one sense, nothing could be further from the truth. We are adamantly opposed to totalitarianism. We do not believe that the State is our Lord and Savior.

On the other hand, we recognize that God providentially establishes some people in places of authority and others in places of submission. When Christians are in places of authority, they should apply the Word of God, even if those under them dislike it. For example, the Christian parent should apply the Bible in disciplining his children. Is it "domination" to require a child to be obedient? We don't think so. We think that disciplining children according to biblical principles is what God requires. And we hope that Hunt would agree.

What about the church? Should elders seek to apply the Bible to the worship and activity of the church? What if they discover that something in their practice is unbiblical? Should they change it? What if the congregation objects? We're not counseling church leaders to "lord" it over their congregations. We are not saying that church leaders must make changes rapidly without any consideration of the congregation's feelings and interests. But the Bible talks about elders "ruling" in the church (1 Tim. 5:17). This implies, we think, that it is sometimes necessary, for the good of the church, to implement even unpopular changes. We consider this to be part of proper leadership.

So, whether we talk about "abuse" or "loss," sin disturbed God's plan for Adam. But Christ, the God-*Man*, has now been given all authority and power and dominion. When we are united with this Man by faith, we are restored to dominion and kingship over the earth. We are united with the Christ who reigns over all things. We are made kings and priests with Him (Heb. 2:5-9; Rev. 1:6; 4:10).[23] We are co-heirs with Christ, sharing both in His

---

23. Hebrews 2:5-9 includes a quotation of Psalm 8:4-6. It is interesting to note some of the differences between these two passages. In the Psalm, man has dominion specifically over animals, birds, and fish (corresponding to the three environments of the first creation: land, sky, water). Spiritual powers and beings

suffering and His kingly glory (Rom. 8:17). By enduring suffering, we also share in His reign (2 Tim. 2:12). God's people, His church, is the instrument by which the blessing of His reign is extended throughout the earth. As A. A. Hodge put it,

> The special agency for the building up of this kingdom is the organized Christian Church, with its regular ministry, providing for the preaching of the gospel and the administration of the sacraments. The special work of the Holy Ghost in building up this kingdom is performed in the regeneration and sanctification of individuals through the ministry of the Church.[24]

This is part of what Jesus meant when He told His disciples, who constituted the foundation of the church (Eph. 2:20), that the kingdom would be given to them. As the Father had conferred the kingdom on Christ, so also Christ conferred the kingdom on the disciples, and by extension, on His church. In particular, the church is given the authority to judge (rule) the twelve tribes of Israel, and the related privilege of sitting at the King's table (Luke 22:29-30).[25] Moreover, the keys of the *kingdom* were given to the church. The church is the gateway to the kingdom of heavenly blessing, authority, and privilege (Matt. 16:19).

Taken together, these verses suggest that there is a very close connection between the kingdom of Christ and the church. The church, the people of God, possesses the power, blessing, and

---

are not explicitly mentioned. Man has dominion over the *visible* creation. In Hebrews 8, however, the quotation does not include the references to the *visible* creation, and the comprehensive nature of Christ's dominion is emphasized. Thus, Christ was not merely exalted to the same status of Adam, but given a *more* comprehensive dominion. In Christ, we also are exalted, not only above the visible creation, but above invisible powers and authorities (cf. Eph. 1:19-23; 2:6). This is of the greatest importance, because it is only in this way that we are able to battle our most dangerous enemies.

24. Hodge, *Evangelical Theology*, p. 256.

25. In this passage, we find that sharing in Christ's reign is preceded by standing by Him in His sufferings (Luke 22:28). We also discover that service is the means to ruling in a Christ-like way (vv. 24-28). The same pattern is reflected in the letters to the seven churches at the beginning of the Revelation. Authority and dominion are promised to those who "overcome," those who persevere through persecution (Rev. 2:26).

privileges of the kingdom because the King is present among them and in them by His Spirit. Thus, the church and the kingdom refer to the same thing from different angles. The kingdom, with its authority and benefits, is what the church possesses; the church is the covenantal people that possesses the kingdom (cf. Matt. 21:43). We must always, however, maintain the distinction between the church and the kingdom, because the church never rules in perfect righteousness while on earth.

Roderick Campbell summarizes the various ways in which believers reign with Christ.

(1) As "heirs of God and joint-heirs with Christ," they possess "all things" necessary for their highest well being (cf. Rom. 8:17; 1 Cor. 3:21-22; James 2:5).

(2) They reign, or rule, in the sense that all things in nature and in history are working together for their good (cf. Rom. 5:17; 8:28; 1 Peter 3:13).

(3) They rule in the sense that Christ has no other earthly instrumentality, or agency, for the propagation of His gospel and law — the only method by which true victory and lasting peace can be achieved on earth (cf. Mat. 28:19; 2 Cor. 6:1).

(4) By faith in the unlimited resources and powers of Christ, they triumph over the world, the flesh and the devil. They become "more than conquerors" over all their deadly foes (Rom. 8:37; cf. James 4:7; 1 Peter 5:9; 1 John 2:13-14; 3:8).

(5) They rule, or will rule, in the sense (which is everywhere implied in Scripture) that there can be no stable, peaceful, and righteous civil government except as it is administered by Christian men, or by rulers elected to office by Christian people. As, and when, these conditions are fulfilled, the saints will reign on earth in the most literal sense.

(6) In position and dignity, in the truest sense, and in the sight of God, they are higher than the kings and potentates of earth. All have freedom of access at all times to the presence of the King of kings and Lord of lords (cf. Eph. 2:6; Heb. 10:19-22; 1 Peter 2:5, 9).

(7) As intercessors they plead with God on behalf of men. By their prayers they move the arm that controls the winds, the rain, all the potent forces of the physical world, and even the powers of

wicked nations and men (cf. Jer. 1:10, 18; Mat. 7:7-8; 18:19; Acts 12:5; James 5:14-18).[26]

In sum, while we are in one sense in submission to the rule of Christ, in another sense we are kings who reign with Him. The rule of Christ is extended through the gospel witness of His Spirit-filled people. Blessed with the power and righteousness that are central to the kingdom, we submit to Him and apply His Word to our lives. By service, suffering, witness, and obedience, we participate in the progressive advance of His rule over all people and nations.

The Growth of the Kingdom

In trying to understand the growth of the kingdom of God, it is important that we keep in mind Jesus' warning that the kingdom does not come perceptibly. It is advanced by the invisible power of the Holy Spirit. Thus, as A. A. Hodge said, "The process by which this kingdom grows through its successive stages toward its ultimate completion can of course be very inadequately understood by us."[27] Still, we shall attempt to explain, as best we are able, how the kingdom of God grows practically and concretely through time.

As we have seen, the kingdom of Christ is comprehensive. He rules over all things in every way. This is already true. Yet, the kingdom also *grows*. We must here recall the distinction that we made between the universal rule of Christ, and the blessings that come to those who submit to Him. Christ already rules over all men and nations, but not all men and nations acknowledge Him. There are still rebels. The kingdom grows when rebels submit to the King's rule. Let us look at several examples of how this operates concretely.

Christ already rules over our hearts and minds. This is implied by the fact that Christ rules *all* things. If He rules every-

---

26. Roderick Campbell, *Israel and the New Covenant* (Tyler, TX: Geneva Divinity School Press, [1954] 1983), pp. 134-35.

27. Hodge, *Evangelical Theology*, p. 256.

thing, He must also rule our hearts and minds. What does it mean for Christ to be King of our hearts? In an "objective" sense, it means that Christ blesses obedient and faithful thoughts and casts down vain imaginations. By His Word, the Incarnate Word tests the thoughts and motives of our hearts (Heb. 4:12-13). This is true of everyone, whether or not he or she recognizes it. Even those whose mind is set on the flesh are under Christ's authority; unless they repent, they will receive the punishment due their sins (Rom. 8:6).

Christ's rule advances when rebels submit their minds and hearts to Him. Actually, sinners cannot do this of themselves. Only the Spirit can give a man a Spiritual mind (cf. Rom. 8:1-5). When the Spirit unites us to Christ, we receive new life, the life of the resurrected Christ. We are given a new heart (Ezekiel 36:26). This enables us to acknowledge willingly and openly that Christ is Lord (1 Cor. 12:3). When we do this, we are removed from the curses of Christ's rule and enter into its blessings: peace, joy, contentment.

Paul exhorts us to submit our minds and hearts to Christ's rule (Rom. 12:1-2; 2 Cor. 10:4-5). This occurs *definitively* when we are converted, but there is also a *progressive* aspect. Each of us individually must become more and more obedient to His rule as we submit ourselves to His commands and, in the power of the Spirit, put our flesh to death (Rom. 8:13; Col. 3:5). When Christ returns and we are transformed fully into His image, our minds will be *finally* purified and made submissive to Him. This personal submission to Christ's rule is basic. To that extent, Hunt is correct: the rule of Christ is inner and "spiritual."

We are also called to preach the good news of the kingdom to those around us. The Spirit uses our witness and service to bring others under the rule of Christ. Thus, the kingdom increases both *intensively* and *extensively*. That is, the subjects of the King become more and more submissive and responsive to Him, and more and more people submit to the King and His commands.

But we cannot stop with individual submission to Christ. We must also submit our families to His rule; we must acknowledge that Christ rules our homes and we must obey Him in our family relationships. All families are already under Christ's rule. Families that rebel against Him will be judged unto the third and fourth generations. When a family comes under Christ's gracious rule, they receive His blessing, and commit themselves to live by His standards for family life. Wives must submit themselves to their husbands, and children must be obedient to their parents (Eph. 5:22-6:4). Over time, our families should become more faithful to Christ and more obedient to His commands. In this way, Christ's rule is acknowledged and progressively manifested in our homes. Moreover, as the gospel is preached to all creatures, more and more families will enjoy the blessings of Christ's rule.

Christ is still our King when we enter the workplace. He owns all things and has given us whatever we have. We are His stewards. We must use His resources as He directs. Thus, for example, we must avoid debt (Rom. 13:8). As employees and employers, we must acknowledge His rule and submit to His commands. Employers are to treat their employees fairly (Eph. 6:9), and employees are to render good service as to Christ (Eph. 6:5-8; 2 Thess. 3:6-12). Christ blesses any business or organization that functions in this way.

Christ is King over all civil officials and civil governments, the King of kings and the Lord of lords (1 Tim. 6:15; Rev. 11:15; 19:16). Civil officials must acknowledge the lordship of Christ, and obey His rules for civil governments (Psalm 2:10-12; Rom. 13:1ff.). The blessings of the kingdom—peace, stability, and justice—will come to all nations that acknowledge the King and enforce His laws.

Richard B. Gaffin, Jr., in writing of the filling of the Spirit, makes a comment that captures well the implications of what we mean by "submitting to the rule of Christ."

> Being filled with the Spirit means marriages that work and are not poisoned by suspicion and bitterness; homes where parents, children, brothers and sisters really enjoy being with each other, free from jealousy and resentment; and job situations that are not oppressive and depersonalizing, but meaningful and truly rewarding.[28]

---

28. Richard B. Gaffin, Jr., *Perspectives on Pentecost: New Testament Teaching on the Gifts of the Holy Spirit* (Phillipsburg, NJ: Presbyterian and Reformed, 1979), p. 33.

We would simply add that an orderly and just political order is a further manifestation of the kingdom of Christ and the working of His Spirit. It is important to note that none of these institutions is *equivalent* to the kingdom. Rather, when we speak of the kingdom, our attention is focussed on the heavenly throne of the Lamb. The blessings described in this section are the fruit and effect of Christ's gracious rule over His people.

Conclusion

As we have seen, the "kingdom" refers to Christ's righteous and merciful rule over all things. This includes all men in all their associations — families, churches, businesses, and civil governments. Those who willingly submit to His rule by faith receive the blessings of the kingdom, but those who refuse to acknowledge the King are shattered. Thus, the rule of Christ is gradually acknowledged, and its fruit is made visible in the world. By the grace of God it will triumph over all opposition.

12

FROM THE CHURCH FATHERS
TO THE REFORMATION:
THE THEOLOGY OF THE KINGDOM

The view of the kingdom of God outlined in the previous chapter was not developed in the last few decades. It was not invented by "kingdom theologians" or "Christian reconstructionists." Some individuals in these groups do hold some distinctive beliefs about the kingdom and its advancement in history, but the basic outlines of the doctrine have been taught within the church since its inception.

We believe that the kingdom of God will triumph in history and on earth. This is what makes our view of the kingdom different from other positions. There are many other issues that deserve attention, but in the interests of space we can make only passing references to them. This also appears to be the main point of issue between Mr. Hunt and ourselves. The purpose of this chapter is to note some major figures from church history who taught an optimistic view of the kingdom's future on earth. We do not claim that this was the only, or even the dominant view. But it has always been accepted as being within the bounds of orthodoxy. And, this brief survey will prove that "dominion theologians" are not necessarily being seduced by the New Age.

Church Fathers

On one point, all early Christian writers were agreed: Christ will be victorious. Justin (*c.* 110-165), one of the early Christian apologists (defenders of the faith), wrote that the Old Testament had predicted the life and death of Christ and that the Father "has declared that He will subdue all His enemies under Him [Christ]."[1] Justin believed that even dreadful persecutions — beheadings, crucifixions, wild beasts, chains, fire — could not stand in the way of the victory of Christ's people. On the contrary, "the more such things happen, the more do others and in larger numbers become faithful, and worshippers of God through the name of Jesus."[2] Justin recognized the change that had taken place in those who became Christians as a fulfillment of prophecy:

> . . . we who were filled with war, and mutual slaughter, and every wickedness, have each through the whole earth changed our warlike weapons, — our swords into ploughshares, and our spears into implements of tillage, — and we cultivate piety, right-eousness, philanthropy, faith, and hope, which we have from the Father Himself through Him who was crucified.[3]

Irenaeus (*c.* 120-202), one of the major early theologians from Asia Minor, taught that Adam himself had been redeemed by Christ. Though "Adam had been conquered, all life having been taken away from him," still "when the foe was conquered in his turn, Adam received new life."[4] Christ, by rising from the dead, had "conquered the foe."

Christian writers differed on the timing of the kingdom.[5] Ac-

---

1. Justin, "First Apology," chapter XL. In *Ante-Nicene Fathers*, 10 vols. eds., Alexander Roberts and James Donaldson (Grand Rapids, MI: Eerdmans, [1885] 1985), vol. 1, p. 176.
2. Justin, "Dialogue with Trypho," chapter CX. In *Ante-Nicene Fathers*, vol. 1, p. 254.
3. *Idem.*
4. Irenaeus, "Against Heresies," III.XXIII.7. In *Ante-Nicene Fathers*, vol. 1, p. 457.
5. The different views of *when* the kingdom was established were linked to different views of *what* the kingdom was. Despite the optimistic statements quoted above, Justin virtually equated the kingdom with heaven. Thus, he taught that the kingdom would be established at Christ's Second Coming. He said that the kingdom that we look for is not a "human kingdom." Thus, "since our thoughts are not fixed on the present, we are not concerned when men cut us off." In "First Apology," chapter XI, in *Ante-Nicene Fathers*, vol. 1, p. 166. Justin was confident that God would someday "raise all men from the dead, and appoint some to be incorruptible, immortal, and free from sorrow in the everlasting and imperishable kingdom." Still, even Justin said that the prophecies of the Old Tes-

cording to the British historian J. N. D. Kelly, however, the emphasis of the apostolic church was that a decisive victory had already been won by Christ's death and resurrection. Thus, "history had reached its climax and the reign of God [i.e., the kingdom of God], as so many of our Lord's parables imply, had been effectively inaugurated." The hope of the early church "was a twofold consciousness of blessedness here and now in this time of waiting, and blessedness yet to come."[6] Kelly notes that this "assurance of living in the Messianic age" gradually weakened in the second generation of the church, and a view arose that the kingdom was an exclusively future reality. In spite of this decline in the apostolic view of the kingdom, "wherever religion was alive and healthy, the primitive conviction of enjoying already the benefits of the age to come was kept vividly before the believer's consciousness."[7]

Athanasius

This view continued into the following centuries. Athanasius (*c.* 305-373), called "the Father of orthodoxy" and the major orthodox theologian during the Nicene controversy, placed central emphasis on the significance of Christ's first advent. In fact, one of the main points of his classic work, *On the Incarnation of the Word*, was that the incarnation, life, death, and resurrection of Christ had changed the course of human history.

---

tament were partly fulfilled in the first advent of Christ, and will be partly fulfilled in His Second Coming. "Dialogue with Trypho," chapter CXVII, in *Ante-Nicene Fathers*, vol. 1, p. 257. Thus, while Justin's emphasis is on the future kingdom, he seems also to claim that the kingdom is present already as well.

6. J. N. D. Kelly, *Early Christian Doctrines*, (rev. ed.; San Francisco, CA: Harper and Row, 1978), pp. 459-60.

7. *Ibid.*, pp. 460-61. Kelly points out that this view of the present reality of the kingdom is especially seen in the sacramental theology of the early church. The sacraments provided Christians with "a foretaste of the blessedness in store for them" (p. 461). Russian Orthodox theologian Alexander Schmemann agrees with Kelly's description of the apostolic view of the kingdom: "In one Man the kingdom of God—of love, goodness, and eternal life—has penetrated the realm of sin and death. Christ did not win this victory for Himself, but for all men—to save them all and lead them into that kingdom which He brought into being." *The Historical Road of Eastern Orthodoxy* (Crestwood, NY: St. Vladimir's Seminary Press, 1977), p. 6.

> Now if by the sign of the Cross, and by faith in Christ, death
> is trampled down, it must be evident before the tribunal of truth
> that it is none other than Christ Himself that displayed trophies
> and triumphs over death, and made him lose all his strength. . . .
> Death has been brought to nought and conquered by the very
> Christ that ascended the Cross.[8]

Christ not only conquered death; He dealt a death blow to Satan.
As a result, "idols and spirits are proved to be dead."[9] The purpose of Christ's death and resurrection, moreover, was not simply
to deliver believers from death and the devil, but positively to
"create anew the likeness of God's image for them," the image that
they had lost when Adam sinned.[10]

Just as there were different views about the beginning of the
kingdom, there were different views about its future course.[11]
Athanasius taught that the victory of Christ on Calvary had
effects on world history, effects that were already visible in his day.
He quoted Isaiah's prophecy that the nations "will beat their
swords into ploughshares," and concluded that this prophecy was
being fulfilled already.

---

8. Athanasius, "On the Incarnation of the Word," 29. In *The Nicene and Post-
Nicene Fathers*, 14 vols. Second Series, eds., Philip Schaff and Henry Wace (Grand
Rapids, MI: Eerdmans, [1891] 1980), vol. 4, p. 51.

9. *Ibid.*, 31, p. 53.

10. *Ibid.*, 20, p. 47.

11. For example, Irenaeus taught a kind of millenarianism. He believed that
Christ would return bodily to establish His kingdom on earth for a thousand
years. This millennial reign would be the fulfillment of the Old Testament prophecies about peace and prosperity.

> . . . when this Antichrist shall have devastated all things in this world,
> he will reign for three years and six months, and sit in the temple at Jeru-
> salem; and then the Lord will come from heaven in the clouds, in the
> glory of the Father, sending this man and those who follow him into the
> lake of fire; but bringing in for the righteous the times of the kingdom,
> that is, the rest, the hallowed seventh day. "Against Heresies," V.XXX.4,
> p. 560.

Justin apparently held to a similar view (see "Dialogue with Trypho," chapters
LXXX-LXXXI, pp. 239-40), though he admitted that other Christians held
other opinions.

. . . even now those barbarians who have an innate savagery of manners, while they still sacrifice to the idols of their country, are mad against one another, and cannot endure to be a single hour without weapons: but when they hear the teaching of Christ, straightway instead of fighting they turn to husbandry, and instead of arming their hands they raise them in prayer, and in a word, in place of fighting among themselves, henceforth they arm against the devil and against evil spirits, subduing these by self-restraint and virtue of soul.[12]

Athanasius believed that Christ would someday return,[13] but before that occurred, Christ was already triumphing over His enemies.

And to sum up the matter: behold how the Saviour's doctrine is everywhere increasing, while all idolatry and everything opposed to the faith of Christ is daily dwindling, and losing power, and falling. . . . For as, when the sun is come, darkness no longer prevails, but if any be still left anywhere it is driven away; so, now that the divine Appearing of the Word of God is come, the darkness of idols prevails no more, and all parts of the world in every direction are illumined by His teaching.[14]

Tertullian and Eusebius

Some of the Fathers described the future progress of the world in less biblical and theological terms. Tertullian (*c.* 150-220), the "father of Latin theology" and the first Christian theologian to write in Latin, wrote,

If you look at the world as a whole, you cannot doubt that it has grown progressively more cultivated and populated. Every territory is now accessible, every territory explored, every territory opened to commerce. The most delightful farmsteads have obliterated areas formerly waste, plough-land has subdued the woods, domestic cattle have put to flight the wild beast, barren

---

12. "On the Incarnation," 52, p. 64.
13. *Ibid.*, 56, p. 66.
14. *Ibid.*, 55, p. 66.

sands have become fertile, rocks are reduced to soil, swamps are drained, the number of cities today exceeds the number of isolated huts in former times, islands no longer inspire fear nor crags terror: everywhere people, everywhere organized communities, everywhere human life. . . .[15]

The early church historian Eusebius of Caesarea (*c.* 260-*c.* 339), according to one scholar, viewed Constantine as a fulfillment of the Lord's promise to Abraham. Thus, "the Roman Empire of which Constantine is head becomes [for Eusebius] the definitive force of providence in history, and promises to the Christian the prospect of an ever triumphant and ever improving society."[16]

Augustine

Augustine (354-430), bishop of Hippo, was without question the most influential of the early fathers and is arguably the most influential thinker and writer in Western history. According to one scholar, it was Christianity's philosophy of history, developed largely by Athanasius and Augustine, that "marked the crux of the issue" between Roman Classicism and Christianity. In contrast to the pagan idea of cyclical time, Augustine taught that time is linear, moving toward a definite goal.[17] Augustine's eschatology is complex, but the note of optimism and progress is not absent. There is progress, for example, in the "education of the human race" which "has advanced, like that of an individual, through certain epochs or, as it were, ages, so that it might gradually rise from earthly to heavenly things, and from the visible to the invisi-

---

15. Quoted in Robert Nisbet, *The History of the Idea of Progress* (New York: Basic Books, 1980), p. 52. Nisbet also notes that "Nothing of what I have just cited from Tertullian can take away from the centrality of the divine, the spiritual, and the eternal in his writings and teachings" (p. 53). Thus, to say that Tertullian does not use theological terms to describe this progress does not mean that he believed that it occurred "naturally," apart from God's grace.

16. Robert Hanning, *The Vision of History in Early Britain.* Quoted in Nisbet, *History of the Idea of Progress*, p. 53.

17. Charles Norris Cochrane, *Christianity and Classical Culture* (London: Oxford University Press, [1940] 1980), p. 456.

ble."[18] It appears that Augustine believed that this progress in the knowledge of God would eventually lead to an earthly golden age. After outlining the six ages of history, Augustine described the seventh and eighth ages,

> . . . the seventh [age] shall be our Sabbath, which shall be brought to a close, not by an evening, but by the Lord's day, as an eighth and eternal day, consecrated by the resurrection of Christ and prefiguring the eternal repose not only of the spirit but also of the body.[19]

Some scholars deny that Augustine believed in a future golden age within history. Certainly, there are passages in Augustine that are difficult to reconcile with a "postmillennial" view, and Augustine believed that the future included a continuing conflict between the city of God and the city of man. Still, Nisbet concludes that "there are grounds for belief that Augustine foresaw a progressive, fulfilling, and blissful period ahead, *on earth*, for humanity — prior to entry of the blessed into heaven."[20]

Thus, the early church does not present a unified view of the kingdom of God, its coming, its nature, and its future. There is, to be sure, a properly sober thread of teaching in the Church Fathers, naturally flowing from their Christian sense of sin. But

---

18. Quoted in Nisbet, *History of the Idea of Progress*, p. 61. As Nisbet notes, Augustine's vision of future history is significant because it embraces all mankind, not merely a city state or an empire.

19. Quoted in *ibid.*, p. 66.

20. *Ibid.*, p. 67. Nisbet's argument for this conclusion is worth repeating.

It may not be altogether clear and certain just what St. Augustine had in mind in his fleeting reference to a seventh, penultimate [next-to-last] epoch ahead. I myself am disposed to the belief that he meant it as a prophecy of a future millennium, a kind of golden age, on earth. After all, he refers to this seventh stage as 'our Sabbath which shall be brought to a close, not by an evening but by the Lord's day . . .' Clearly it is not the epoch of mankind's final destination, for that is described by Augustine as the *eighth* epoch, that which shall be eternal and begin only after this world has been brought to end. What else could the seventh epoch be but the kind of earthly millennium . . . that the Puritans of the seventeenth century, in England and America, were so obsessed by? (*Ibid.*, p. 66).

we find in this period the development of "a confidence in the future that would become steadily greater and also more *this*-worldly in orientation as compared with *next*-worldly." There was an "emphasis upon the gradual, cumulative, *spiritual* perfection of mankind, an immanent process that would in time culminate in a golden age of happiness on earth, a millennium with the returned Christ as ruler."[21]

The Reformation[22]

As in the early church, the Reformers did not present a unified eschatology. Martin Luther (1483-1546), for example, did not believe that the kingdom would triumph on earth and in history. In fact, he expected the world to end soon. His anti-millennial opinions were formalized in the Augsburg Confession (1530), which rejected "certain Jewish opinions which are even now making an appearance and which teach that, before the resurrection of the dead, saints and godly men will possess a worldly kingdom and annihilate all the godless."[23]

By contrast, the Reformed (Calvinistic) churches have generally taught a more optimistic view of the future of Christ's kingdom on earth. John Calvin (1509-1564) taught that the kingdom is already present as a result of the work of Christ. Calvin did not

---

21. *Ibid.*, p. 47.

22. We skip from the early church to the Reformation, not because we believe there is nothing important or helpful about the Medieval Church, but in the interests of space. The interested reader should consult *ibid.*, chaps. 3-4.

Also, it should be noted that hereafter we do not attempt to describe the views of different segments of the church, lest this chapter should become a book in its own right. Instead, we have concentrated on the history of the Reformed or Calvinistic churches. In fact, our focus is even narrower than that, focussing on English and American Calvinism. This is not an inappropriate emphasis, however, because this branch of the church embraced the optimistic vision of the church's earthly future more consistently than most other branches.

23. Article XVII. In *The Book of Concord: The Confessions of the Evangelical Lutheran Church*, trans. and ed. Theodore G. Tappert (Philadelphia, PA: Fortress, [1959] 1983), pp. 38-39. This article of the confession was specifically directed against radical Anabaptists, but it is used by Lutheran theologians to cover less militant forms of millennial doctrine as well. See John Theodore Mueller, *Christian Dogmatics* (St. Louis, MO: Concordia, 1955), p. 621.

interpret the millennium as a literal thousand-year period in which Christ would physically reign from Jerusalem. Rather, the millennium was the time during which the church continued "toiling on earth."[24]

What would happen during this period? In contrast to Luther, Calvin believed that the kingdom would "have a yet greater triumph in history prior to the consummation [the Second Coming]."[25] While Calvin wrote a great deal about the suffering and tribulation of the church and its members, he also says a surprising amount about the triumph and growth of the church. As a result, his view of the kingdom is remarkably balanced. Commenting on 2 Thessalonians 2:8, Calvin writes,

> Paul . . . intimates that Christ will in the meantime, by the rays which he will emit *previously to his advent*, put to flight the darkness in which antichrist will reign, just as the sun, before he is seen by us, chases away the darkness of the night by the pouring forth of his rays. *This victory of the word, therefore, will show itself in this world*. . . . He also furnished Christ with these very arms, that he may *rout his enemies*. This is a signal commendation of true and sound doctrine—that it is represented as sufficient for putting an end to all impiety, and as destined to be *invariably victorious, in opposition to all the machinations of Satan*.[26]

Calvin thus believed that the kingdom was already present, and that it was triumphantly advancing to a great climax.

This, he said, is what we ask for when we pray, "Thy Kingdom come": "As the *kingdom* of God is continually growing and advancing to the end of the world, we must pray every day that it *may come*: for to whatever extent iniquity abounds in the world, to

---

24. John Calvin, *Institutes of the Christian Religion*, ed., John T. McNeill, trans., Ford Lewis Battles, 2 vols. (Philadelphia, PA: Westminster, 1976), vol. 2 (III.xxv.5), p. 995.

25. Iain Murray, *The Puritan Hope* (London: Banner of Truth Trust, 1971), p. 40.

26. Quoted in Greg Bahnsen, "The *Prima Facie* Acceptability of Postmillennialism," *Journal of Christian Reconstruction*, vol. 3, no. 2 (Winter 1976-1977), p. 70. Emphasis was added by Dr. Bahnsen.

such an extent *the kingdom of God*, which brings with it perfect righteousness, is not yet *come*."[27] Ultimately, "the kingdom of God . . . [will] be extended to the utmost boundaries of the earth . . . so as to occupy the whole world from one end to the other."[28] Thus, "the worship of God will flourish everywhere" and "his law [will] be known to all nations, so that his will might be known everywhere."[29]

Other reformers held similar views about the future of the kingdom of God. The Reformer of Strassburg, Martin Bucer (1491-1552), taught, according to one scholar, an "eschatology [that] was less quietistic and more dynamic, leaving more room for the renewal of this world and for the realization of the will of God in history, than that of Luther."[30]

English Puritanism

As heirs of the Calvinistic Reformation, the early English Puritans almost invariably held to an optimistic view of the future of the church. As Nisbet writes, the Puritans "had a philosophy of human progress that united past, present, and future into one seamless web that pointed to a golden future on earth, one of a thousand, or perhaps many thousands of years."[31] Puritan theologians taught that the kingdom of God would triumph on earth before the return of Christ. This view of the future of the kingdom was held by English Calvinists from the 16th through the early 18th centuries. In his commentary on Revelation, first published in Latin in 1609, Thomas Brightman wrote that after the conversion of the Jews

> shall the end of all prophets come, both when all the enemies shall
> be utterly and at once abolished, and when there shall be one

---

27. Quoted in *ibid.*, pp. 71-72.

28. Quoted in *ibid.*, p. 73.

29. Quoted in *ibid.*, p. 74.

30. Johannes Van Den Berg, *Constrained By Jesus' Love* (Kampen: J. H. Kok, 1956), p. 10. Quoted in James R. Payton, Jr., "The Emergence of Postmillennialism in English Puritanism," *Journal of Christian Reconstruction*, vol. 6, no. 1 (Summer 1979), p. 90.

31. Nisbet, *History of the Idea of Progress*, p. 115.

sheepfold made upon earth, of all the Elect both Jewes and Gentiles under one shepheard Jesus Christ. It is certain, that this Kingdom of Christ that is thus begun, shall be eternall, and shall never be broken off againe, and discontinued, and that it shall be translated at length from earth into heaven; But I find no mention in this Booke of the time, into which this translation shall fall, that shall be finished perfectly in Christs second coming.[32]

Later in the 17th century, the great John Owen (1616-1683) summarized the triumph of the kingdom of God as follows:

1st. Fulness of peace unto the gospel and professors thereof . . .

2dly. Purity and beauty of ordinances and gospel worship . . .

3dly. Multitudes of converts, many persons, yea nations . . .

4thly. The full casting out and rejecting of all will-worship, and their attendant abominations. . . .

5thly. Professed subjection of the nations throughout the whole world unto the Lord Christ. . . .

6thly. A most glorious and dreadful breaking of all that rise in opposition to him. . . .[33]

This victorious outlook was embodied in the 1648 Westminster Larger Catechism.[34] The answer to question 191 states:

In the second petition, (which is, *Thy kingdom come,*) acknowledging ourselves and all mankind to be by nature under the

---

32. Quoted in J. A. De Jong, *As the Waters Cover the Sea: Millennial Expectations in the Rise of Anglo-American Missions, 1640-1810* (Kampen: J. H. Kok, 1970), p. 19.

33. Quoted in *ibid.*, p. 39.

34. A catechism is a series of questions and answers used to instruct children and new Christians in the basic doctrines of Christianity. This catechism was produced by the Westminster Assembly, which was called by the Parliament in the early 1640s to set up a suitable government for the church. Scottish and English Presbyterians and English Puritan Congregationalists dominated the Assembly. The Assembly also produced a Confession of Faith, which summarized the teaching of the English churches of that era. Although the Confession was primarily a statement of Presbyterian doctrine and church government, historian John Leith has written that the Confession and catechisms of the Westminster Assembly also influenced Baptists and Congregationalists. John Leith, *Assembly at Westminster* (Atlanta, GA: John Knox, 1973), p. 11.

dominion of sin and Satan, we pray, that the kingdom of sin and Satan may be destroyed, the gospel propagated throughout the world, the Jews called, the fulness of the Gentiles brought in; the church furnished with all gospel-officers and ordinances, purged from corruption, countenanced and maintained by the civil magistrate: that the ordinances of Christ may be purely dispensed, and made effectual to the converting of those that are yet in their sins, and the confirming, comforting, and building up of those that are already converted: that Christ would rule in our hearts here, and hasten the time of his second coming, and our reigning with him for ever: and that he would be pleased so to exercise the kingdom of his power in all the world, as may best conduce to these ends.

The fact that this statement was produced by a church assembly shows that a victorious view of the kingdom was widespread among English Christians in the seventeenth century.

These expectations, especially the expectation of the conversion of the Jews, motivated the English to missions. One of the leaders of the missions movement was John Eliot, who had a mission to the Indians in Massachusetts. Eliot believed that the kingdom of God was imminent, but he had a different view of the kingdom from what we now call "premillennialists." Eliot defined the kingdom of Christ "not as a personal, physical reign of Christ on earth but as the condition which prevails 'when all things among men, are done by the direction of the word of his mouth; his Kingdom is then come amongst us, when his will is done on earth, as it is done in heaven.' Broadly speaking, it has several dimensions: rule over individual Christians, over the church, over civil governments, and over his eternal kingdom in heaven."[35] Eliot believed that

the Gospel shall spread over all the Earth, even to all the ends of the Earth; and from the riseing to the setting Sun; all Nations shal become the Nations and Kingdoms of the Lord and of his Christ.[36]

---

35. De Jong, *As the Waters Cover the Sea*, p. 74.
36. Quoted in *ibid.*, p. 75.

This confidence led Eliot to support a broad range of mission activities among the American Indians, including education, translation of the Scriptures, legal reform, church planting, and training of native pastors and evangelists.[37]

The influence of optimistic eschatology did not stop with the theologians and missionaries, however. The Puritans' view of an earthly and victorious kingdom was rooted in the church fathers, especially Augustine, and medieval sources. But they accomplished something new. Earlier, Christians had viewed progress as exclusively *spiritual* progress, rather than advancement in scientific and artistic knowledge. The Puritans, however, united these two lines of thinking. They did not deny the spiritual advancement of the kingdom, but they believed that progress in the arts and sciences was both a *sign* of the coming of the golden age and a *means* of bringing the golden age to fruition.[38]

Thus, the optimism of the theologians appears also in the writings and speeches of a wide spectrum of 17th-century English figures. One scholar claims that Isaac Newton's work in physics and optics was motivated in part by the belief "very much alive in Newton's England, that the millennium would be preceded by a flourishing of the arts and sciences that would bring men nearest to the condition of prelapsarian [before the fall] Adam."[39] Politicians echoed the same optimism. Oliver Cromwell speculated that the Puritan Revolution might be "the door to usher-in the Things that God has promised."[40]

---

37. *Ibid.*, p. 76. One rather quaint sidelight on Eliot's eschatology is his conviction that the Indians were in fact descendants of Shem. He thought he was fulfilling biblical prophecy in a very direct way when he set about to disciple the Indians.

38. Nisbet, *History of the Idea of Progress*, p. 127.

39. Quoted in *ibid.*, p. 128.

40. Quoted in *ibid.*, p. 137. The details of Cromwell's views are not exactly ours. He believed that the kingdom would be set up in the near future, perhaps through the triumph of the saints in the English Revolution. As noted in an earlier chapter, we believe that the kingdom was established by Jesus Christ, though, of course, there are periods of church history when the kingdom advances dramatically. Moreover, we see in Cromwell's views some of the same short-term, revolutionary psychology that came to expression in the Fifth Monarchy movement. What we wish to illustrate by this quotation is simply that Cromwell was optimistic about the *earthly* advancement of Christ's kingdom.

In 1641, shortly before the outbreak of the English civil war, one member of Parliament expressed the hope the Parliament might "lay the cornerstone to the world's happiness." Another contemporary expressed his belief that Parliament was "able if need require to build a new world."[41]

By the 1660s, however, this optimism was waning in England. De Jong concludes that the restoration of the pro-Catholic Stuart monarchy to the English throne threw a damper on the expectations of many Puritans.[42] Yet, the early 18th-century commentator Matthew Henry retained optimism about the future of Christ's kingdom. He had this to say about Daniel 2:44-45, where Daniel interprets the "stone made without hands" that grows into a mountain:

> It is a kingdom that shall be victorious over all opposition. . . . The kingdom of Christ shall *wear out* all other kingdoms, shall outlive them, and flourish when they are sunk with their own weight, and so wasted that their place *knows them no more*. All the kingdoms that appear against the kingdom of Christ shall be broken with a *rod of iron*, as a *potter's vessel*, Ps. ii. 9. And in the kingdoms that submit to the kingdom of Christ tyranny, and idolatry, and every thing that is their reproach, shall, as far as the gospel of Christ gets ground, be broken. The day is coming when Jesus Christ shall have *put down all rule, principality, and power*, and have made *all his enemies his footstool*; and then this prophecy will have its full accomplishment, and not until then, 1 Cor. xv. 24, 25.[43]

---

41. Quoted in Lawrence Stone, *The Causes of the English Revolution* (New York: Harper and Row, 1972), p. 52. We have the same objections to these sentiments that we have to Cromwell's views. See footnote 40, above. These statements, moreover, place hope in political change as the instrument for realizing the kingdom. This, we have emphasized earlier, is an idolatrous view of politics, and we repudiate such messianic dreams. Again, our main objective is to document that the English Puritans believed 1) that the kingdom affects the earth, and 2) that the future of the kingdom will be triumphant. Though they had flaws in their thinking, these flaws are not at all logically necessary to these two teachings about the kingdom.

42. De Jong, *As the Waters Cover the Sea*, p. 78.

43. Matthew Henry, *Commentary on the Whole Bible: Isaiah to Malachi*, 6 vols. (Old Tappan, NJ: Fleming H. Revell, [1712] n. d.), vol. 4, p. 1032.

In commenting on Isaiah 9:1-7, Henry says that Christ's kingdom

> shall be an increasing government. It shall be multiplied; the bounds of his kingdom shall be more and more enlarged, and many shall be added to it daily. The lustre of it shall increase, and it shall shine more and more brightly in the world. The monarchies of the earth were each less illustrious than the other, so that what began in gold ended in iron and clay, and every monarchy dwindled by degrees; but the kingdom of Christ is a growing kingdom, and will come to perfection at last.[44]

Thus, though De Jong is right that this optimistic view of the future was less widespread after 1660, it certainly did not die out entirely in England. And, it was renewed during the revivals of the early 18th century.[45]

Conclusion

From the earliest centuries to the 18th century, the doctrine that the kingdom of God would triumph on earth has been taught by many Christians. While this emphasis varies from writer to writer and from century to century, a strain of this teaching has always existed within the Western church. It was very strong in Reformed churches during the 16th and 17th centuries. In the next chapter, we will continue this historical survey by examining the history of American Christianity.

---

44. *Ibid.*, p. 60.
45. See Murray, *The Puritan Hope*, chapter 6.

13

FROM THE AMERICAN PURITANS TO THE REVOLUTION: THE THEOLOGY OF THE KINGDOM

Christianity is a religion of hope. Every Christian agrees with this. The issue is, what is the nature of the church's hope? As we showed in the last chapter, there have been many orthodox Christian leaders throughout the centuries who believed that the hope of the church included earthly and historical victory. This hope was always combined with the hope for the resurrection and eternal life, as well it should be. The hope of the church has never been *exclusively* or *primarily* earthly. But in many cases Christians have expected social renewal, peace, justice, and holiness as the gospel advances powerfully throughout the earth.

This part of the hope of Christianity has nowhere been stronger than among American Christians. In this chapter, we will show that some important early American theologians, political leaders, and teachers perpetuated the belief that the kingdom of God would be victorious on earth.

The Puritans and the End of the World

To a large extent, America was first settled by English Puritans. Though, strictly speaking, Puritanism was confined to the New England colonies, the English settlers of Virginia and the Dutch settlers of New Amsterdam shared a "puritan" outlook in a general sense. Moreover, by the time of the revolution, a large contingent of Scotch Presbyters could be found in nearly every colony. The late Yale church historian Sidney Ahlstrom wrote that

"Puritanism provided the moral and religious background of fully 75 percent of the people who declared independence in 1776."[1] Nonetheless, we will confine our survey in this section to the Puritans and Pilgrims of New England. We should expect that early American Christians held views of the future of the church similar to those of the English Puritans.

Our survey is especially important because of the distortions of Puritanism in some circles. In the April 1987 issue of the *Omega-Letter*, for example, David Wilkerson states that

> There is a deadly doctrine sweeping through Charismatic circles called THE KINGDOM MESSAGE. It is infiltrating even Baptist and Assembly of God churches. Jimmy Swaggart is boldly taking a stand against it—and so am I. This is not an attack on any individual—but rather, a Scriptural expose of a doctrine that denies the soon return of Jesus Christ. *The Puritans, way back in the seventeenth century, prophesied this doctrine would be THE FINAL DECEPTION.*[2]

It is true that after 1660 some colonial Puritan leaders spoke of the imminent return of Christ. And, many emphasized that the primary hope of the Christian was eternal heavenly life.[3] But in general the Puritans were not preoccupied with the end of the world, and their heavenly focus did not divert them from cultural effort. As historian Harry S. Stout has written,

---

1. Sydney E. Ahlstrom, *A Religious History of the American People* (New Haven, CT: Yale University Press, 1972), p. 124. Ahlstrom adds in a footnote that the percentage of Americans who were affected in some way by the Calvinist Reformation may have been as high as 85 or 90 percent. During the seventeenth century, in certain colonies, virtually *everyone* was a Puritan.

2. *Omega-Letter*, (April 1987), p. 1. Wilkerson provides no documentation of this claim. While it may be true that some Puritans said this, it is, at best, an oversimplification to say that the Puritans in general taught this, or that it was somehow a dominant view among them. One of the problems is the vagueness of the term, "Puritan." There were Puritans who believed that the individual struggle with sin was the only struggle that the Christian had to face. Yet, Oliver Cromwell and many members of Parliament were also Puritans.

3. See Harry S. Stout, *The New England Soul: Preaching and Religious Culture in Colonial New England* (New York: Oxford University Press, 1986), pp. 46-47.

Throughout the colonial period, ministers rarely preached specifically on millennial prophecies pointing to the end of time, and when they did it was generally in the most undogmatic and speculative of terms. For the most part, they did not base their preaching on the assumption that history would stop tomorrow, and in this respect they differed radically from popular millenarian movements in Europe and post-Revolutionary America whose plans of action were governed exclusively by apocalyptic considerations. The past was the tried-and-true key invariably invoked by [Puritan] ministers to interpret the present.[4]

In many cases, they were optimistic about the future even in the face of seemingly inconquerable odds. One scholar notes:

. . . from the very beginning, the bent of the colonists in Massachusetts Bay—unlike their brethren in Plymouth—was not to withdraw from the world but to reform it, to work within the institutional continuities of history rather than to deny them. . . . Somehow this world's institutions had to be refashioned to conform to Christ's spiritual Kingdom.[5]

The vision of our Puritan forefathers, given expression by John Winthrop in his "Model of Christian Charity" in 1630 aboard the *Arabella*, was that there was an earthly future for the faithful people of God.

. . . the Lord will be our God and delight to dwell among us, as His own people, and will command a blessing upon us in all our ways, so that we shall see much more of His wisdom, power, goodness, and truth than formerly we have been acquainted with. We shall find that the God of Israel is among us, and ten of us shall be able to resist a thousand of our enemies, when He shall make us a praise and glory, that men shall say of succeeding plantations: "The Lord make it like that of New England." For we

---

4. *Ibid.*, p. 8.

5. Quoted by Gary North, "Editor's Introduction," *Journal of Christian Reconstruction*, vol. 6, no. 1 (Summer 1979), p. 7. This thesis is developed at greater length in Aletha Joy Gilsdorf, "Purity and Progress: New England's First Generation," *Journal of Christian Reconstruction*, vol. 6, no. 1 (Summer 1979), pp. 107-135.

must consider that we shall be like a city upon a hill; the eyes of
all people are upon us.[6]

Times were tough for the Puritans, but they did not conclude
that the end of the world was just around the corner. They set out
to carve a paradise out of a wilderness. They did not allow death,
persecution, and tyranny to sway them from a dominion task. We
are living off their spiritual capital.[7]

Education: Colleges and Publishing

One of the evidences that the Puritans had a long-term vision
of the future is the establishment of colleges. Harvard College
(founded in 1636, six years after the arrival of the Arabella) stated
its purpose clearly: "Let every student be plainly instructed, and
Earnestly pressed to consider well, the maine end of his life and
studies is, to know God and Jesus Christ which is eternal life, Joh.
17:3. and therefore lay Christ in the bottome, as the only foundation of all sound knowledge and Learning."[8] The initiators of
Harvard wanted the Puritan legacy to continue: "One of the next
things we longed for, and looked after was to advance *Learning* and
perpetuate it to Posterity; dreading to leave an illiterate Ministery
to the Churches, when our present Ministers shall lie in the
Dust."[9] Obviously, the founders of Harvard assumed that there

---

6. John Winthrop, "A Model of Christian Charity," in *The American Puritans: Their Prose and Poetry*, ed., Perry Miller (Garden City, NY: Doubleday, 1956), p. 83.

7. Unfortunately, we are investing very little spiritual capital to make up what we've withdrawn. What will our children and grandchildren be left with if Jesus does not come back for a thousand years? Nothing is lost if Jesus returns tomorrow, but a genuine Dark Age awaits us if we postpone our dominion task. The new book by Jack Van Impe, *11:59 and Counting*, suggests that it is impossible to change anything, no matter how sincere the effort. How can you expect to change the world if there are only a few ticks left on the clock?

8. Quoted in *Christian Liberal Arts Education*, Report of the Calvin College Curriculum Committee (Grand Rapids, MI: Calvin College/Eerdmans, 1970), p. 17.

9. Anonymous, "New England's First Fruits," in *American Higher Education: A Documentary History*, eds., Richard Hofstadter and Wilson Smith (Chicago, IL: University of Chicago Press, 1961), vol. 1, p. 6.

would be a posterity to be educated. These quotations also show that the Puritan founders were interested in a specifically Christian education.[10]

To counter the theological drift of Harvard, Yale College was established in 1701. The founders of Yale yearned to return to the Christian foundation first laid at Harvard: "Yale in the early 1700s stated as its primary goal that 'every student shall consider the main end of his study to wit to know God in Jesus Christ and answerably to lead a Godly, sober life.'"[11]

The colonists understood the relationship between a sound education based upon biblical absolutes and the future of the nation. Yale College demanded the same rigorous education as Harvard: "All Scholars Shall Live Religious, Godly, and Blameless Lives according to the Rules of God's Word, diligently Reading the holy Scriptures the Fountain of Light and Truth; and constantly attend upon all the Duties of Religion both in Publick and Secret."[12]

The influence of these early colleges should not go unnoticed. Not only were church leaders educated in their classrooms, but civil rulers gained an understanding of the application of biblical law to civil affairs.

Puritans also rapidly began publishing concerns to educate their children for the future. "The first printing press in the American colonies was set up at Cambridge in 1639, and from it in 1640

---

10. A curious thing happened to me (Gary DeMar) when I was doing research for a book project. I wrote to Columbia University and asked them to send a copy of their original seal. They informed me that they no longer make it available. Instead, they sent their current seal. It is nothing like the original. The original Seal of Columbia University, New York, was adopted in 1755. Over the head of the seated woman is the (Hebrew) Tetragrammaton, YHVH (*Jehovah*); the Latin motto around her head means "In Thy light we see light" (Psalm 36:10); the Hebrew phrase on the ribbon is *Uri El* ("God is my light"), an allusion to Psalm 27:1; and at the feet of the woman is the New Testament passage commanding Christians to desire the pure milk of God's word (1 Peter 2:1, 2).

11. William C. Ringenberg, *The Christian College: A History of Protestant Higher Education in America* (Grand Rapids, MI: Eerdmans, 1984), p. 38.

12. "Yale Laws of 1745," in Hofstadter and Smith, eds., *American Higher Education*, p. 54.

issued the first book, THE WHOLE BOOKE OF PSALMES *Faithfully* TRANSLATED *into* ENGLISH *Metre, Whereunto is prefixed a discourse declaring not only the lawfulness, but also the necessity of the heavenly Ordinances of singing Scripture Psalmes in the Churches of God.*[13] In 1661, a translation of the Bible in the language of the Algonquian Indians became the first Bible printed in America. It was the work of John Eliot (1604-1690), a Puritan who dedicated his life to evangelizing and teaching the Indians and who earned the title "Apostle of the Indians."

The establishment of colleges and the setting up of printing presses do not by themselves prove that the Puritans believed that the church would triumph on earth. But these activities do show that the Puritans were not abandoning the world and the future.

"Declension"

Fairly early in New England's history, and even more as the first generation of colonists passed away, the initial vision of the founders was lost to some extent. This was a part of a more general "declension," a decline or crisis of American Puritanism. We are not able to examine the causes, nor all of the effects, of this declension. Instead, we will simply note the effects that this crisis had on the confidence of Puritans in the future of their enterprise.

The crisis produced a more negative tone in Puritan sermons. The preachers increasingly denounced the sins of the people and warned that God would abandon them. A new form of sermon arose, labeled the "jeremiad" by later historians, after the biblical prophet of doom, Jeremiah. New England had broken the covenant, said the preachers, and, as Winthrop had predicted, God was cursing the colony for its sins. As Perry Miller writes, "In the 1640's there commenced in the sermons of New England a lament over the waning of primitive zeal and the consequent atrophy of public morals, which swelled to an incessant chant within forty years. By 1680 there seems to have been hardly any other theme for discourse, and the pulpits rang week after week with lengthen-

---

13. Ahlstrom, *Religious History,* pp. 149-50.

ing jeremiads."[14]

Perhaps no late 17th-century Puritan figure so captured the pessimistic imaginations of his contemporaries as the much-ridiculed poet, Michael Wigglesworth (1631-1705). His "The Day of Doom," a graphic depiction of the Day of Judgment, may have been, according to Miller, "the first American best-seller."[15] And his "God's Controversy with New England," composed during a 1662 drought, traced the decline of Puritan piety as the colony was seduced by material prosperity. In "The Day of Doom," Wigglesworth predicted a sudden appearance of the Judge at a time when men "stopped their ear and would not hear/when mercy warned them,/But took their course without remorse/till God began to pour/Destruction the world upon/in a tempestuous shower."[16]

The same pessimism continued into the early eighteenth century. As in 17th-century England, this dark vision of the future was closely linked to social and political circumstances. During the French and Indian wars, Daniel Rogers warned that

> there is coming a day of wrath and Revelation of the Righteous judgement of God, against such hard hearted impenitent Sinners as despise the riches of God's goodness exercised towards them in the Day of his patience in this world.[17]

Thus, at a surface level, it appears that the Puritans had changed their eschatology. But, if we look deeper, we will see that this pessimism was in many cases based on the old confidence of their forefathers. New Englanders continued to believe that "the lamb would triumph, but not before suffering great tribulations."[18] The fact that New England was not yet destroyed, the colonists' victory in the Indian war known as King Philips' War — these indi-

---

14. Perry Miller, *The New England Mind: The Seventeenth Century* (Cambridge, MA: Harvard University Press, 1939), pp. 471-72.

15. Miller, ed., *The American Puritans*, p. 282.

16. Michael Wigglesworth, "The Day of Doom," in *ibid.*, p. 283.

17. Quoted in Stout, *New England Soul*, p. 239.

18. *Idem.*

cated that God had not abandoned New England. Preachers usually did not predict defeat for the church catholic, only a defeat for the New England churches, if they did not repent. Thus, in the face of these troubles, many American Christians of the late 17th and early 18th centuries continued to express their confidence in the future advancement of the kingdom of Christ, and especially of New England's role in that advance.

One of the major figures of the latter 17th century was Cotton Mather. Kirk House writes that Mather was "[b]orn in 1663, took his M.A. from Harvard at age 18 and joined his father in his Boston pastorate. . . . Widely regarded as the most brilliant man in New England, he wrote 450 books and was a Fellow of the Royal Society. Scientist as well as pastor, he successfully introduced smallpox inoculation during the 1721 epidemic, and had his house bombed for his trouble."[19] One of Mather's numerous books was a history of early New England which he entitled *Magnalia Christi Americana*, or *The Great Achievement of Christ in America*. "The sum of the matter," he explained, "is that from the beginning of the Reformation in the English nation, there had always been a generation of godly men, desirous to pursue the reformation of religion, according to the Word of God." But in England, there were others with "power . . . in their hands" who desired "not only to stop the progress of the desired reformation but also, with innumerable vexation, to persecute those that most heartily wish well unto it." The Puritans were "driven to seek a place for the exercise of the Protestant religion, according to the light of conscience, in the deserts of America." Their purpose was nothing less than to complete the Reformation, believing "that the first reformers never intended that what they did should be the absolute boundary of reformation."[20]

On the future of the kingdom, Mather wrote,

19. Kirk House, *God's Claims on Your Children: Readings in the Last 2000 Years of Christian Education* (Sterling, VA: GAM Printers, 1977), p. 61.

20. Laurel Hicks, ed., *The Modern Age: The History of the World in Christian Perspective* (Pensacola, FL: A Beka Book Publications, 1981), p. 241.

The tidings which I bring unto you are, that there is a REV-
OLUTION and a REFORMATION at the very door, which will
be vastly more wonderful than any of the deliverances yet seen by
the church of God from the beginning of the world. I do not say
that the *next year* will bring on this *happy period*; but this I do say,
the bigger part of this assembly may, in the course of nature, live
to see it.[21]

Millennial expectations peaked during the French and Indian
Wars. Many expected the second coming during their lifetimes.
When it became clear that Armageddon had not occurred, "ministers warned their congregations that the millennium could be far
off in the future."[22] Ezra Stiles said that for the present "God has
great things in design for this [American] vine which his irresistible arm has planted. . . . He purposes to make of us a great people and a pure and glorious church."[23]

Jonathan Edwards and the Great Awakening

These expectations had received renewed impetus from the
Great Awakening that burned through New England from the
1720s to the 1740s. As historian H. Richard Niebuhr said, "It is remarkable how under the influence of the Great Awakening the
millenarian expectation flourished in America."[24]

The views of Jonathan Edwards (1703-1758), one of the leaders of the Awakening and considered by many to have been
America's greatest theologian, are worth examining in some detail. First, Edwards taught that the kingdom had dawned already

---

21. Quoted in De Jong, *As the Waters Cover the Sea: Millennial Expectations in the
Rise of Anglo-American Missions, 1640-1810* (Kampen: J. H. Kok, 1970), p. 92. It is
not clear from this quotation whether Mather believed in a "premillennial" or a
"postmillennial" revolution. In fact, his eschatology was basically "premillennial."
Cf. James West Davidson, *The Logic of Millennial Thought: Eighteenth-Century New
England* (New Haven: Yale, 1977), p. 60. The point of the quotation is that
Mather believed in the earthly victory of Christ's kingdom. It is also significant,
as Davidson shows, that Mather's position was not in ascendancy in his time. His
works are full of detailed argumentation against unnamed opponents.

22. Stout, *New England Soul*, p. 253.

23. Quoted in *idem*.

24. Quoted in De Jong, *As the Waters Cover the Sea*, p. 119.

in the death and resurrection of Christ. The old world is passing away, and the new world is beginning and growing.

> . . . the state of things which is attained by the events of this period [the death, resurrection of Christ, etc.], is what is so often called *the kingdom of heaven*, or *the kingdom of God*.[25]

Second, Edwards believed that there had been several decisive events in the advancement of the kingdom since the time of Christ. These included the destruction of Jerusalem in A.D. 70, the reign of Constantine, the rise of the Papacy, and the Reformation. He expected an even fuller outpouring of the Spirit in the future, so that "the gospel shall be preached to every tongue, and kindred, and nation, and people, before the fall of Antichrist; so we may suppose, that it will be gloriously successful to bring in multitudes from every nation: and shall spread more and more with wonderful swiftness."[26] This great outpouring of the Spirit would be met with vicious opposition. Though Edwards admitted that "we know not particularly in what manner this opposition shall be made," of one thing he was certain: "Christ and his church shall in this battle obtain a complete and *entire victory* over their enemies."[27]

As a result, Satan's kingdom would be fully overthrown. In its place, Christ's kingdom would be "set up on the ruins of it, every where throughout the whole habitable globe."[28] These events would usher in a new era for the church. The church would no longer be under affliction, but would enjoy undiluted success. Edwards believed that "this is most properly the time of the kingdom of *heaven upon earth*." The Old Testament prophecies of the kingdom would be fulfilled in this era. It would be a time of great Spiritual knowledge, holiness, peace, love, orderliness in the church. All of this would be followed by the great apostasy and the second coming of Christ.[29]

---

25. Edwards, "History of Redemption," III.I.IV. In Edward Hickman, ed., *The Works of Jonathan Edwards*, 2 vols. (Edinburgh: Banner of Truth Trust, [1834] 1976), vol. 1, p. 584.

26. *Ibid.*, p. 606.

27. *Ibid.*

28. *Ibid.*, pp. 607-8.

29. *Ibid.*, pp. 609-11.

At times, Edwards used revolutionary language to describe this change: "There are many passages in Scripture which do seem to intend, that as well the civil as the ecclesiastical polities of the nations, shall be overthrown, and a theocracy ensue." But he qualified these statements very carefully.

> Not that civil government shall in any measure be overthrown, or that the world shall be reduced to an anarchical state; but the absolute and despotic power of the kings of the earth shall be taken away, and liberty shall reign throughout the earth.[30]

While we may disagree with certain details of Edwards's interpretations, he clearly and forcefully taught the earthly victory of Christ and His people. Edwards's followers held out the same hope. Samuel Hopkins, in a 1793 "Treatise on the Millennium," attempted to prove from the Scriptures that "the church of Christ is to come to a state of prosperity in this world."[31] The multitude of languages would be replaced by a single, international language, so that "God will be praised in one tongue, as with one voice." In sum,

> The church of Christ will then be formed and regulated, according to his laws and institutions, in the most beautiful and pleasing order. . . . There will then be but one universal, catholic church, comprehending all the inhabitants of the world, formed into numerous particular societies and congregations, as shall be most convenient, to attend on public worship, and the institutions of Christ.[32]

Joseph Bellamy, another of Edwards's disciples, taught that a period of peace and righteousness would be achieved on earth, without any cataclysmic divine intervention.[33]

This renewed optimism fueled the hopes of the generation of

---

30. Quoted in Davidson, *Logic of Millennialism*, pp. 220-21.
31. De Jong, *As the Waters Cover the Sea*, p. 209.
32. Quoted in *ibid.*, p. 211.
33. See Davidson, *Logic of Millennialism*, pp. 221-22.

the American Revolution.[34] Eighteenth-century colonials held many of the same expectations that the 17th-century Puritans had voiced before them. To many American clergymen in particular, "it seemed increasingly likely that the millennial age would arise from this struggle for liberty and Christianity in which the colonists were engaged." One of these, Ebenezer Baldwin, speculated that America might be "the principal Seat of that glorious Kingdom, which Christ shall erect upon Earth in the latter Days."[35] Another New England preacher, Samuel Sherwood, said in 1776 that the government of George III "appears to have many of the features, and much of the temper and character of the image of the beast." He believed that the revolution was essentially an effort to advance the kingdom, and speculated that the war with England "may possibly be some of the last efforts, and dying struggles of the man of sin."[36]

---

34. See Alan Heimert, *Religion and the American Revolution from the Great Awakening to the Revolution* (Cambridge, MA: Harvard University Press, 1966).

35. Quoted in Mark A. Noll, *Christians in the American Revolution* (Washington, D.C.: Christian College Consortium, 1977), p. 58. See also Nathan O. Hatch, *The Sacred Cause of Liberty: Republican Thought and the Millennium in Revolutionary New England* (New Haven: Yale, 1977).

36. Quoted in Stout, *New England Soul*, p. 309.

Throughout this survey, we have discovered that Christians at various times have "nationalized" the prophecies of Scripture, and used prophecy to interpret contemporary events. English Puritans believed that 17th-century England would be the focus of the kingdom. American Revolutionaries believed it would be America. It should be noted that this nationalism is not in any way necessary to the view of the kingdom that we are advocating. In fact, it is a gross distortion of our view. Our point in quoting from these sources is not that we agree with every opinion expressed. Rather, we are simply trying to show that our optimism is not unique in the history of the church.

The United States, for all its historical importance, is not at all a unique people of God. We believe that God deals with nations in the New Covenant, as in the Old, and that nations are blessed insofar as they remain faithful to the Lord. But this does not mean that any nation is the "New Israel." As the New Testament explicitly teaches, we believe that the *church* is the New Israel (Gal. 6:16; 1 Pet. 2:9 with Ex. 19:6). Nations receive blessings through the church. Even the revolutionary clergy, in spite of their apparently blind patriotism, noted this. They claimed that the kingdom would not advance by war or revolution, but only if the people were faithful to God and His covenant law (Stout, p. 310).

The eschatology of the American Revolution often took some unusual, yet strangely familiar, forms. An anonymous writer for the Sons of Liberty claimed that the American Revolution was prophesied in the Book of Revelation. In particular, he believed that the Beast was George Grenville, the British Chancellor of the Exchequer responsible for the Stamp Act. He concluded that the beast's mark in Revelation 13 had been fulfilled by Grenville.

> Here, my beloved brethren, he brings forth the Stamp-Act, that mark of slavery, the perfection and sum total of all his wickedness; he ordained that none amongst us shall buy or sell a piece of land, except his mark be upon the deed, and when it is delivered, the hands of both buyer and seller must infallibly become branded with the odious impression: I beseech you then to beware as good christians and lovers of your country, lest by touching any paper with this impression, you receive the mark of the beast, and become infamous in your country throughout all generations.[37]

This, of course, was a political rather than a theological statement. But it indicates something of the course that American thought was taking during the Revolutionary period. And, it shows that modern dispensationalists are not the first to read their newspapers into the book of Revelation.

Conclusion

We make no pretense that this has been a comprehensive survey of early American eschatology. Yet, we have seen that there was a strong current of eschatological optimism among American Christians throughout the first century and a half of the colonies' existence. It took many different forms, and it waxed and waned with the flow of events. But it cannot be doubted that this was an important part of American religious life in the early years of the settlement of this country. As the newly formed republic entered the next century, this view became increasingly widespread.

---

37. Quoted in Davidson, *Logic*, p. 238.

14

THE ZENITH AND DECLINE OF OPTIMISM

The 19th century saw the widest development of the victorious view of the kingdom that we have described. This was especially true in the United States. As we shall see in this chapter, however, that dominance evaporated rather rapidly toward the end of the century and even more rapidly in the early decades of the present century.

The Century of Triumphalism

By the early 19th century, the idea that the kingdom of God would be victorious on earth and in history had penetrated much of American Protestantism, permeating all the major denominations, whether Congregationalist, Baptist, Presbyterian, Anglican, or Reformed.[1] This emphasis continued to dominate American Christianity into the later decades of the century. As one historian has put it, "During the first three quarters of the nineteenth century, this view was what one clergyman called in 1859 'the commonly received doctrine' among American Protestants."[2]

---

1. De Jong, *As the Waters Cover the Sea: Millennial Expectations in the Rise of Anglo-American Missions, 1640-1810* (Kampen: J. H. Kok, 1970), p. 216. This was, of course, prior to the great flood of immigration that changed forever the denominational configuration of American Christianity. At this time, the Roman Catholic and Lutheran churches were not as large as they presently are.

2. James H. Moorhead, "Between Progress and Apocalypse: A Reassessment of Millennialism in American Religious Thought, 1800-1880," *The Journal of American History* 71 (December 1984), p. 525. See also James B. Jordan, "A Survey of Southern Presbyterian Millennial Views Before 1930," *Journal of Christian Reconstruction* vol. 3, no. 2 (Winter 1976-77) pp. 106-21. Jordan concludes from a survey

Historian Timothy L. Smith concludes from a detailed study of mid-19th century revivals that "Preachers of all persuasions turned to the belief that their mission was to prepare the world for Christ's coming by reducing it to the lordship of his gospel."[3] Smith adds that the most significant millennial views of the mid-19th century "grew out of Protestantism's crusade to Christianize the land."[4] 19th-century American Christians recognized that this was the dominant view throughout the country. Samuel Harris, a theology professor at Yale, noted in 1870 that "The sublime idea of the conversion of the world to Christ has become so common as to cease to awaken wonder."[5]

Just as the Great Awakening had fueled eschatological hopes a century earlier, so the Second Great Awakening (beginning in the 1790s) renewed the future vision of American Christians. In 1819, the General Assembly of the Presbyterian Church described the state of religion in glowing terms.

> We have the happiness to live in a day, Brethren, when the Captain of our Salvation, in a distinguishing manner, is marshalling his *mighty host*, and preparing for the moral conquest of the *world*. The grand contest that has been so long conducting, is drawing rapidly towards a termination, that shall be infinitely honourable both to our glorious leader, and to those who have fought under his banner. Not a finger shall be lifted, nor shall a devout aspiration heave the bosom of a single son or daughter of man, to contribute to the advancement, or plead for the glory of the kingdom of the Messiah, that shall not be met with the smiles and crowned with the blessing of God.[6]

A similar note was sounded by the bishops of the Episcopal church.

---

of theological journals, theology textbooks, and the views of ministers, that the postmillennial position "apparently was indeed the common view of Southern Presbyterianism up until the 1930's" (p. 121).

3. Timothy L. Smith, *Revivalism and Social Reform: American Protestantism on the Eve of the Civil War* (New York: Harper and Row, [1957] 1965), p. 228.

4. *Ibid.*, p. 236.

5. Quoted in Robert T. Handy, *A Christian America: Protestant Hopes and Historical Realities*, (rev. ed.; New York: Oxford University Press, 1984), p. 85.

6. Quoted in *ibid.*, p. 30.

The advancement of our holy religion will probably continue, as it has been heretofore, gradual, but sure. Ages may roll away, and empires may rise and fall, before there shall come the promised era, when "all the kingdoms of this world shall be the kingdoms of the Lord and of his Christ." But, as we rest our expectations of that event on the rock of his never failing promise, we have reason to rejoice in whatever promotes the accomplishment of it, by extending the profession of Christianity over the immeasurable wilds of this immense continent.[7]

This view was voiced by figures across the spectrum of American Christianity. The revivalist Edward Beecher believed that the churches were "aroused as never before," and he expected "a glorious advent of the kingdom of God."[8] The anti-revivalist theologian and historian Philip Schaff

> told a Berlin audience that the growing hold of Protestantism upon the American people made Christ's triumph sure. Their missions, he said, both to the uncivilized and "the nominal Christians of the Old World," and their colonization of Christianized slaves in Africa were hastening the day when the whole earth would be filled with his glory and "all nations walk in the light of eternal truth and love."[9]

This view of the kingdom was adopted by many of the leading 19th-century theologians in the United States, especially those in Reformed seminaries. Princeton's Charles Hodge (1797-1878) wrote that "before the second coming of Christ there is to be a time of great and long continued prosperity." Hodge referred to one theory that claimed that this period would last 365,000 years, but he remained cautious: "During this period, be it longer or shorter, the Church is to enjoy a season of peace, purity, and blessedness as it has never yet experienced." Hodge claimed that "the prophets predict a glorious state of the Church prior to the second advent" because "they represent the Church as being thus

---

7. Quoted in *ibid.*, p. 31.
8. Quoted in Timothy Smith, *Revivalism and Social Reform*, p. 225.
9. *Ibid.*, p. 227.

prosperous and glorious on earth."[10]

The great Southern theologian Robert L. Dabney (1820-1898) concurred with Hodge's views. Before the second coming, Dabney taught, the church would preach the gospel to all nations and would see "the general triumph of Christianity over all false religions, in all nations."[11] Benjamin Breckinridge Warfield (1851-1921), the last great conservative theologian of Princeton, echoed the same themes of victory. Commenting on Revelation 19, he wrote,

> The section opens with a vision of the victory of the Word of God, the King of Kings and Lord of Lords over all His enemies. We see Him come forth from heaven girt for war, followed by the armies of heaven. . . . What we have here, in effect, is a picture of the whole period between the first and second advents, seen from the point of view of heaven. It is the period of advancing victory of the Son of God over the world.[12]

Even as the fundamentalist controversy hit its peak in the 1920s, the postmillennial vision was not entirely lost. Gary North writes that J. Gresham Machen, the founder of Westminster Theological Seminary in Philadelphia, was a postmillennialist, though "there is no sign in any of his writings that he relied heavily on postmillennialism as a motivating concept in his battle against the modernists."[13]

Thus, through most of the 19th century and into the 20th,

---

10. Charles Hodge, *Systematic Theology*, 3 vols. (Grand Rapids, MI: Eerdmans, 1986 [1871-1873]), vol. 3, pp. 858-59. It is interesting to note how *little* space Hodge uses to explain his position. He apparently assumed it was a widely accepted belief. It is also interesting that Hodge, the most orthodox of the orthodox, did not condemn those who taught that Christ's coming would be delayed for many millennia.

11. R. L. Dabney, *Lectures in Systematic Theology* (Grand Rapids, MI: Zondervan, [1878] 1976), p. 838.

12. B. B. Warfield, "The Millennium and the Apocalypse," *Biblical Doctrines* (New York: Oxford University Press, 1929), pp. 647-48.

13. North, *Dominion and Common Grace* (Ft. Worth, TX: Dominion Press, 1987), p. 272. See Machen, *Christianity and Liberalism* (Grand Rapids, MI: Eerdmans, 1923), p. 49, where Machen speaks about the issue between "premillennialism and the opposite view."

American Christians—including pastors, evangelists, theologians, and laymen—expected the church to advance and increase throughout history. They expected the church of Jesus Christ to be victorious over all its enemies.

The Effects of Optimism

The hope of world conquest spurred missionaries to redouble their efforts. Revivals in Britain had stimulated the missionary enterprise.[14] While British missionaries still outdistanced their American counterparts, American missionaries, stimulated by revivals, played an increasingly important role in the extension of Christianity.[15]

Yet, there had been a shift in emphasis since the Great Awakening. Edwards and his followers had placed primary emphasis on the renovation of the world through the preaching of the gospel and the conversion of great multitudes. By contrast, later preachers renewed the old Puritan teaching that social reform was an essential part of the advancement of the kingdom. Charles Finney, for example, "demanded that some kind of relevant social action follow the sinner's conversion." As a result, "His revivals were a powerful force in the rising antislavery impulse and in the rise of urban evangelism."[16]

Similarly, Edward Beecher said that the mission of the church was

> not merely to preach the gospel to every creature, but to reorganize human society in accordance with the law of God. To abolish all corruptions in religion and all abuses in the social system and,

---

14. Kenneth Scott Latourette, *Christianity in a Revolutionary Age: II: The 19th Century in Europe* (Grand Rapids, MI: Zondervan, 1959), p. 254: "To a greater degree than from any other branch of Christianity in the nineteenth century, the Protestantism of the British Isles furthered the geographic extension of the faith."

15. Latourette, *Christianity in a Revolutionary Age: III: The 19th Century Outside Europe* (Grand Rapids, MI: Zondervan, 1961), p. 242.

16. Sidney Ahlstrom, *A Religious History of the American People* (New Haven, CT: Yale University Press, 1972), pp. 460-61. Again, we must emphasize that we do not agree with all of Finney's theology or his revivalistic methods.

so far as it has been erected on false principles, to take it down and erect it anew.[17]

Timothy L. Smith quotes Dutch Reformed pastor Joseph Berg's hope

that, with the termination of injustice and oppression, of cruelty and deceit; with the establishment of righteousness in every statute book, and in every provision of human legislation and human jurisprudence; with art and science sanctified by the truth of God, and holiness to the Lord graven upon the walls of our high places, and the whole earth drinking in the rain of righteousness, . . . this world would be renovated by the power of holiness. . . . Oh! this is the reign of Jesus.[18]

Samuel Harris said that the kingdom of God is "the life which creates the organization, penetrates and purifies also the family and the state, renovates individuals, and blooms and fructifies in Christian civilizations; and these also are its historical manifestations."[19] As Handy writes, "Harris spoke with great confidence of the triumph of the kingdom and the full Christianization of civilization."[20]

The agents of this Christianization were largely the voluntary societies that proliferated during the 19th century. With the churches disestablished in nearly every state by the first decades of the nineteenth century, Christians had to find non-state resources to fund their programs. Local in their origins, these voluntary societies gradually grew to national proportions, and then their efforts were coordinated in a national strategy. Activities ranged from Bible distribution to education to social reform such as the temperance, peace, and abolition campaigns.[21] Winthrup S.

---

17. Quoted in Timothy Smith, *Revivalism and Social Reform*, p. 225.
18. Quoted in *ibid.*, p. 227.
19. Quoted in Handy, *A Christian America*, p. 85.
20. *Ibid.*, p. 86.
21. The best work on the influence of the voluntary societies is C. I. Foster, *An Errand of Mercy: The Evangelical United Front* (Chapel Hill, NC: University of North Carolina, 1958). Foster's work is ably summarized in Winthrup S. Hudson, *Religion in America: An Historical Account of the Development of Religion in America*, (3rd ed.; New York: Charles Scribner's Sons, 1981), pp. 149-154. See also the sections on voluntarism in Handy, *A Christian America*.

Hudson says that "the statistics tell an incredible story of Bibles shipped, tracts distributed, Sunday schools organized, and churches established," not to mention the impact of the various more politically oriented movements.[22] Through these agencies, evangelical Protestants largely succeeded in establishing a "righteous empire."[23] There were other factors in the rise of the voluntary associations, but certainly a victorious view of the kingdom was an important element.

The Eclipse of Optimism

So what happened? If this was the commonly received doctrine into the late 19th century, if it was partly responsible for the large-scale social efforts of 19th-century evangelicals, why is it considered a relic by most 20th-century Christians? Was there a dramatic new insight into Scripture? Was there additional revelation at the beginning of this century? None of these. Several social and theological developments contributed to the decline of a victorious view of the future of the church.

The causes of this decline of optimism are worthy of reflection. Christians are supposed to live by faith, not by sight. Yet, 20th-century Christians argue almost invariably that optimism cannot be sustained in the light of the horrors of the 20th century. We agree that this has been a bloody century, the bloodiest in human history. But we also believe that the Bible teaches that the gospel will eventually triumph. If the Bible teaches this, we should not allow our faith to be undermined by cultural trends.

In examining the reasons for the decline of postmillennialism, we should note first that the doctrine of the kingdom that we have outlined was already on shaky ground when the 19th century began. In particular, the theology of the kingdom had been separated from the sacramental and teaching ministry of the church. Wave after wave of revivals had also weakened the church's theol-

---

22. Hudson, *Religion in America*, p. 154.
23. See Martin Marty, *Righteous Empire* (New York: Dial Press, 1970).

ogy and its governmental structure.[24] Revivalism emphasized "individual decision and personal piety" and "tended to minimize the importance of social structures and practices."[25] Already in the first Great Awakening, numerous schisms occurred, fracturing the church and preventing it from playing a central part in American society. As the church's authority declined and as revivalistic individualism grew, the authority of the states increased. Historian Richard Bushman concluded from a study of the Great Awakening in Connecticut that

> the civil authority was the sole institution binding society [by the 1760s]. The state was the symbol of social coherence, as once the Established churches had been. Group solidarity depended on loyalty to the government. United action in the [French and Indian] wars of 1745 and 1756 restored a society rent with religious schisms. . . . Patriotism helped to heal ecclesiastical wounds.[26]

The voluntary societies filled the social gap left by the decline of the churches, but they were simply not equipped to play the role that God has ordained for the church.

The decline in the authority and social role of the church thus provided an opening for the rise of a nationalistic understanding of the kingdom. In other words, with the churches in decline, the American nation became for many the chief instrument for the advancement of the kingdom of Christ. Jonathan Edwards had suggested that the millennium might begin in America, but Edwards meant that American churches would be the hub of world

---

24. See Peter J. Leithart, "Revivalism and American Protestantism," in James B. Jordan, ed., *The Reconstruction of the Church*, Christianity and Civilization 4 (Tyler, TX: Geneva Ministries, 1985), pp. 46-84; Leithart, "The Great Awakening and American Civil Religion," unpublished paper.

25. Gary Scott Smith, *The Seeds of Secularization: Calvinism, Culture, and Pluralism in America 1870-1915* (Grand Rapids, MI: Eerdmans/Christian University Press, 1985), pp. 50-51.

26. Richard L. Bushman, *From Puritan to Yankee: Character and Social Order in Connecticut, 1690-1765* (Cambridge, MA: Harvard, 1967), p. 208. Marty suggests that the disestablishment of the churches was the most basic change in ecclesiastical administration since Constantine (*Righteous Empire*, pp. 67-68).

evangelization.[27] Later revivalists, during the American Revolution and afterwards, believed that the nation itself was the center of the kingdom's advance. One observer believed that the growth of America showed "the unhasting yet unresting progress of a kingdom ordained ere time began, to be completed when time shall be no more."[28] Josiah Strong wrote in 1885 that the United States was "divinely commissioned to be, in a peculiar sense, his brother's keeper."[29] The distinction between the kingdom of God and the American nation was being blurred. When the nation's flaws became more evident in the early part of this century, people lost confidence not only in America, but in Christ's kingdom. Some identified American culture with Christianity so closely that they "became unwilling or unable to criticize prophetically the society."[30]

The churches had also been weakened by what historian Ann Douglas calls the "feminization of American culture." When the churches were disestablished, they began to adopt "commercial" techniques and modes of operation. They had been forced into competition with one another, and employed methods that would appeal to a wider audience. Because women were the most numerous churchgoers, the clergymen naturally appealed to feminine themes. Thus, from the early 19th century, the churches of America witnessed a declining emphasis on theology and doctrine, a rising influence of women in the church, and a general "sentimentalization" of literature, theology, church life, and culture.[31]

One aspect of 19th-century "sentimental" culture is especially significant for our purposes: what Douglas labels "the escape from history." It was not that 19th-century clergymen and readers dis-

---

27. Nathan O. Hatch, *The Sacred Cause of Liberty: Republican Thought and the Millennium in Revolutionary New England* (New Haven, CT: Yale University Press, 1977), pp. 24, 26, 37ff.

28. Quoted in Timothy Smith, *Revivalism and Social Reform*, p. 227.

29. Quoted in Hudson, *A Christian America*, p. 323.

30. Gary Scott Smith, *Seeds of Secularization*, p. 51.

31. Ann Douglas, *The Feminization of American Culture* (New York: Avon, 1977).

liked history. They read avidly. But they did not read about the great movements and wars of history. Instead, the history they read was concerned with domestic and private life.[32] This reflected a change in the church's posture toward the culture. In the midst of the supercharged revivalist social agenda of the 19th century, parish clergymen and regular churches had, psychologically at least, retreated from the larger cultural issues of the day into a sentimental world of "domesticity." The faith of the regular clergy was an almost completely privatized faith.

As the eschatology of American Christians was gradually nationalized and sentimentalized, it was also secularized.[33] Revivalism emphasized technique. Charles Finney said that a revival was simply the result "of the right use of the constituted means." Finney used various means to bring the sinner to "the moment he thinks he is willing to do anything."[34] As more and more emphasis was placed on the techniques that would hasten the kingdom, the earlier emphasis on the supernatural grace of God was replaced

---

32. *Ibid.*, chapter 5.
33. The relationship of these two processes—nationalization and secularization—is complex. There is no easy cause-and-effect relationship between them. Yet, they are related. First, statism, of which nationalism is a form, is a secular phenomenon. Moreover, in a sense, both grew out of the situation created by revivalism. Revivalism emphasized the experience of the individual believer and employed pragmatic techniques for bringing the crowd to the point of conversion. And, in a sense, both can be traced to a decline in the centrality of the church as God's instrument in history. We have already traced this development with respect to nationalization. Secularization arose in part for the same reasons. The church, centered as it is in the worship of the Transcendent God, and in the real presence of Christ in the sacrament, maintains a supernatural perspective on the advancement of the kingdom. When the sacramental gathering was replaced by the camp meeting, with its techniques of crowd manipulation, the supernatural element of Christianity was jeopardized. Also, insofar as secularism is "the negation of worship," the decline of the church led to a rise of secularism. See Alexander Schmemann, "Worship in a Secular Age," in *For the Life of the World: Sacraments and Orthodoxy* (Crestwood, NY: St. Vladimir's Seminary Press, 1973), pp. 117-134.
34. Charles Grandison Finney, *Lectures on Revivals of Religion*, ed., William G. McLoughlin (Cambridge, MA: Belknap Press of the Harvard University Press, [1835] 1960), pp. 13, 268.

by an emphasis on manipulation and the natural process of moral improvement. It was only a short step from revivalistic optimism to the liberal view that the kingdom was entirely dependent upon human activity. "The building of the Kingdom of God had become as much a matter of technique and program as it was of conversion and religious piety."[35] This shift reached its zenith in the "social gospel" movement. The social gospel maintained the optimism of the 19-century evangelicals, but gradually destroyed its supernatural foundations.[36]

This secular, anti-supernatural emphasis also appeared in the development, first in Europe, of higher critical methods of biblical study. This new scholarship attacked Scriptural optimism, which always relied on faith in the text of Scripture, at its very roots.[37]

The reaction of conservative Christians to the secularism of the social gospel movement was a retreat from social and political action. Historian George Marsden has described this retreat as the "Great Reversal." Evangelical Christians, who had in a sense dominated the national culture of 19th-century America, bowed out of the public arena. Marsden describes several reasons for this reversal, but concludes that

> the factor crucial to understanding the 'Great Reversal,' and especially in explaining its timing and exact shape, is the fundamentalist reaction to the liberal Social Gospel after 1900. Until about 1920 the rise of the Social Gospel and the decline of revivalist social concerns correlate very closely. By the time of World War I, 'social Christianity' was becoming thoroughly identified with liberalism and was viewed with great suspicion by many conservative evangelicals.[38]

35. James H. Moorhead, "The Erosion of Postmillennialism in American Religious Thought, 1865-1925," *Church History,* 53 (1984), p. 75.

36. See Jean B. Quandt, "Religion and Social Thought: The Secularization of Postmillennialism," *American Quarterly* 25 (Oct. 1973), pp. 390-409.

37. Moorhead, "The Erosion of Postmillennialism," pp. 62-67.

38. George M. Marsden, *Fundamentalism and American Culture: The Shaping of Twentieth Century Evangelicalism, 1870-1925* (New York: Oxford University Press, 1980), p. 91.

Because the social gospel was also identified with an optimistic view of the kingdom, this too began to seem "liberal" to many orthodox Christians.

Theological changes on the American scene also contributed to the decline of a confidence in earthly victory for the church. One of these was the rise of dispensational premillennialism. As Marsden notes, the first stage of the "Great Reversal" was marked by a "change from postmillennial to premillennial views of the relation of the kingdom to the present social and political order."[39] By 1875, dispensationalism, first articulated by the English theologian John Darby, began to gain ground in the United States.[40]

Social changes contributed to the decline of confidence in Christ's earthly victory. Industrialization and modernization created social dislocations. People used to rural life moved to the city, where life moved faster and morality was looser. Moreover, the savagery of the late 19th and early 20th century led many to adopt a more pessimistic view of the future. The Civil War, the First World War, the revolution in Russia—all these contributed to a changing mood.[41]

Evangelicals did not retreat all at once. In fact, as Marsden shows, premillennial evangelicals were very active in the period after World War I. Yet, each subsequent tragedy forced evangelicals further and further into the protective walls of their own communities and of a private faith. Each tragedy reminded Americans of man's sinful nature. Thus, each of these setbacks contributed to a climate of pessimism.[42]

Finally, a major blow to the credibility of fundamentalism came with the Scopes trial of 1925. In the wake of this fiasco, Marsden

---

39. *Ibid.*, p. 86.

40. See Timothy P. Weber, *Living in the Shadow of the Second Coming*, (2nd ed.; Grand Rapids, MI: Academie Books/Zondervan, 1983), pp. 16ff.

41. On the civil war's impact, see Douglas W. Frank, *Less Than Conquerors: How Evangelicals Entered the Twentieth Century* (Grand Rapids, MI: Eerdmans, 1986), pp. 66, 138. On World War I, see Marsden, *Fundamentalism and American Culture*, chapter XVI.

42. Marsden, *Fundamentalism and American Culture*, pp. 141-153.

shows, "the strength of the movement in the centers of national life waned precipitously."[43]

In the face of all these tumultuous developments, the hope for cultural victory declined. Late 19th-century and early 20th-century evangelicals continued to speak of victory, but increasingly the victory was personal and individual, not cultural.[44]

Keeping the Flame Alive

Eschatological optimism never died out completely. In fact, we can trace a clear line from the late 19th century postmillennialists to the present day. B. B. Warfield, who taught at Princeton until his death in 1921, was a postmillennialist. The founder of Westminster Theological Seminary, J. Gresham Machen studied at Princeton under Warfield. Westminster was founded in 1929, and Machen taught there until his death in 1937. John Murray, professor of systematic theology at Westminster from 1930-1966, was, at least late in his life, something of a postmillennialist. Outside of the immediate Westminster community, there were also a few postmillennial writers. Roderick Campbell's *Israel and the New Covenant* was published in 1954, and the introduction by Westminster Seminary professor O. T. Allis made clear his own postmillennial convictions. Loraine Boettner studied at Princeton in the late 1920s, and his postmillennial book *The Reformed Doctrine of Predestination* was published in 1932,[45] while his more extended postmillennial study *The Millennium* was first published in 1957. Westminster and Princeton graduate, J. Marcellus Kik, a member of the editorial staff for *Christianity Today*, delivered his postmillennial lectures on Matthew 24 and Revelation 20 at Westminster Seminary in 1961. Kik dedicated one of his books to Roderick Campbell. Thus, the postmillennialism of Princeton Theology was main-

---

43. *Ibid.*, p. 185.

44. See Frank, *Less Than Conquerors*, pp. 123ff.

45. (Nutley, NJ: The Presbyterian and Reformed, [1932] 1987), pp. 130-45. The most recent edition of this book, in 1987, was its twenty-fifth printing. More than 90,000 copies have been published, including translations into several foreign languages. This is not an obscure book.

tained at Westminster and elsewhere, though admittedly as a minority position.

A resurgence of postmillennialism seems to be traceable to the influence of Iain Murray and the Banner of Truth Trust, in Great Britain, and of R. J. Rushdoony, whose first books were published in the late 1950s. Rushdoony has written two books specifically on eschatology, *Thy Kingdom Come* (1970) and *God's Plan for Victory* (1977), and one issue of *The Journal of Christian Reconstrution* was devoted to the millennium. Since then, the number of postmillennial writers has grown rapidly. The most prominent is David Chilton, who has written three major works on eschatology: *Paradise Restored* (1985), *The Days of Vengeance* (1987), and *The Great Tribulation* (1987). Rushdoony's and Chilton's works have sparked a renewal of optimism among many pastors and teachers, and even some seminary professors have reexamined the biblical basis for postmillennialism.

Conclusion

We have seen that the major view of American Christianity in the 19th century was that the kingdom of God would progressively triumph on earth. This hope was shattered in the early 20th century by a series of theological and social movements that splintered the "kingdom theology" that had already been weakened by revivalism, nationalism, secularism, and sentimentalism. The long-range optimism of "reconstructionists," therefore, is no recent development in this country. Instead, it is the pessimistic view of the future that is a relative newcomer on the American theological scene.

15

TURNING THE WORLD RIGHT-SIDE UP

Adam and Eve's descent into sin and judgment brought about a corrupt world. While the image of God was not destroyed by the Fall, the likeness of God was certainly defaced. Now man reflects the attributes of the fallen Adam. Deception and death followed the sin of man. A time came when "the Lord saw that the wickedness of man was great on the earth, and that every intent of the thoughts of his heart was only evil continually" (Gen. 6:5).

The Old Testament is the story of a series of similar judgments. Each time God "recreated" the world, men fell again. God came to dwell with Israel in the wilderness, as He had dwelt with Adam in the Garden, but Israel refused to obey (Num. 14). God enabled Israel to conquer the land (Joshua), but Israel quickly fell (Judges). God established His victorious anointed in Jerusalem (2 Sam. 10), but David's heart led him astray (2 Sam. 11). Solomon built a glorious temple (1 Kings 6), but half of the kingdom was ultimately torn from him (1 Kings 11:29-40).

Jesus' Renewal of This World

Jesus again renewed all things. But, unlike the "recreations" of the Old Testament, *the recreation of the world by Jesus is irreversible.* The resurrection of Christ is the definitive renewal of all things. Even those outside the Christian tradition understood the implications of Jesus' work: "These men who have upset the world have come here also" (Acts 17:6). God, through His Spirit, transforms individuals. But there are societal and global ramifications of the work of Christ just as there were global ramifications of the work

271

of Adam (Gen. 3:14-24). Prior to Jesus' finished work, Israel was confined to a small piece of real estate. Jesus' mission gave a world-wide dimension to the gospel. He came to save "the world" (John 3:16). The Apostle Paul had plans to go on to Spain, no longer bound by the confines of one nation (Rom. 15:24, 28).

The world has changed. It has been transformed, and yet it is still in the *process* of transformation. As we have seen in the chapters on the kingdom, the *definitive renewal* must be followed by *progressive renewal*. Each new generation must appropriate for itself the benefits of Christ's work. Each new generation is faced with personal and cultural crises brought on by sin. The history of Western civilization is evidence that the gospel of Jesus Christ does make a difference both personally and culturally. For example, modern science developed in the Christian West.[1]

But the people of God often forget their "first love" (Rev. 2:4) as Israel did after the death of Joshua. While God's blessings were once regarded as gifts, they come to be seen solely as the products of man. As is too often the case, the people of God forget the working relationship between covenant faithfulness and external blessings that flow from the hand of God. Instead, they begin to say, "My power and the strength of my hand made me this wealth" (Deut. 8:17). God eventually brings them to their senses, showing them that He alone is the One who gives us power to make wealth and anything else (v. 18; cf. Dan. 4:28-37).

Men are still sinners. Does this mean that nothing can be done to change our world? Is God too weak and the devil too strong? Henry Van Til writes:

> To say that culture is now impossible in a sin-sick world is to short-change God, who as Ruler of heaven and earth and the Determiner of man's destiny is causing his purposes to be fulfilled even through man's rebellion, so that the wrath of man is praising God (Ps. 76:10). It is true, of course, that man in his cultural

---

1. R. Hooykaas, *Religion and the Rise of Modern Science* (Grand Rapids, MI: Eerdmans, 1972); Eugene M. Klaaren, *Religious Origins of Modern Science* (Grand Rapids, MI: Eerdmans, 1977).

striving will not reach unto the perfect man in a perfect world while existing in the state of sin. This would be utopianism, of which man as rebel has been guilty repeatedly. Of this, history gives us a long record, as witness Plato's *Republic*, More's *Utopia*, Bacon's *New Atlantis*, Rousseau's return to nature, Saint Simon's social Christianity, Marx's classless society, and, to mention no more, Huxley's *Brave New World* and Orwell's *1984*.[2]

How should the Christian respond to man's propensity to sin? There are at least two ways. First, the church can respond by saying this is the end of all things. We should look for the imminent and final judgment of God. Evil has triumphed over good. Only the physical presence of Jesus Christ can accomplish the task of societal reconstruction. Second, we can repent of our sins, bow in humble submission before the God who made us, and recommit ourselves to covenant faithfulness.

There is certainly truth in the response of judgment. God is not pleased with rebellion. But is it a judgment unto destruction (damnation) or a judgment unto restoration (resurrection)? The history of the world, and especially the history of Israel, shows that judgment is unto restoration for covenant nations. As we shall see, God even holds the door open for the restoration of the church of Laodicea.

Israel as Our Example

God has not left His church without a source of encouragement and instruction. All of the Bible is God's Word to us. All Scripture, including the Old Testament, is "God breathed" and is "profitable for teaching, for reproof, for correction, for training in righteousness; that the man of God may be equipped for every good work" (2 Tim. 3:16-17). Paul had in mind the *Old* Testament when he penned these words. We can learn best by avoiding Israel's mistakes: "Now these things happened to them [the Israel-

---

2. Van Til, *The Calvinistic Concept of Culture* (Grand Rapids, MI: Baker, [1959] 1972), pp. 58-59.

ites in the wilderness] as an example, and they were written for our instruction, upon whom the end of the ages have come" (1 Cor. 10:11).

After the death of Joshua and the generation under His leadership, the moral climate in Israel changed. The people self-consciously rejected Jehovah and served "Baal and the Ashtaroth," gods that were not gods (Judges 2:13):

> There arose another generation after them who did not know the LORD, nor yet the work which He had done for Israel. Then the sons of Israel did evil in the sight of the LORD, and served the Baals, and they forsook the LORD, the God of their fathers, who had brought them out of the land of Egypt, and followed other gods from among the gods of the peoples who were around them, and bowed themselves down to them; thus they provoked the LORD to anger (2:10-12).

Did God forsake them utterly? No! First, God "gave them into the hands of plunderers who plundered them" (v. 14). Second, "He sold them into the hands of their enemies" (v. 14). Third, "the LORD raised up judges who delivered them from the hands of those who plundered them" (v. 16). Fourth, "the LORD was moved to pity by their groaning because of those who oppressed and afflicted them" (v. 18). Fifth, when the judge died, the entire cycle repeated itself (v. 19). But in all of this God did not forsake His people. God raised up another judge each time Israel forsook Him.

Even when God's patience wore thin, He still did not destroy His people. During the 70 years of captivity God gave Israel hope that He would restore them to the land when the period of judgment was complete. The circumstances in Jeremiah's day were little different from the period of the Judges:

> "You too have done evil, even more than your forefathers; for behold, you are each one walking according to the stubbornness of his own evil heart, without listening to Me. So I will hurl you out of this land into the land which you have not known, neither you nor your fathers; and there you will serve other gods day and night, for I shall grant you no favor" (Jer. 16:12-13).

The prophets promised that even through judgment, God would bring restoration: "For I will restore them to their own land which I gave to their fathers" (Jer. 16:15). Even in the midst of captivity, judgment, and hopelessness God was there to give them "a future and a hope" (29:11). Though Israel was under God's judgment, Israel's enemies would be destroyed with no promise of restoration: Egypt (Jer. 46), Philistia (47), Moab (48), Ammon (49), Kedar and Hazor (49:28-33), Elam (49:34-39), and Babylon (50-51). God dramatized Israel's restoration by telling Jeremiah to buy land that would soon be in the hands of the Babylonians (32:24-44). God promised to restore Israel's fortunes. It was hard for them to believe. In fact, "common sense" told them that restoration was hopeless. Seventy years is a long time. Few people, if any, who initially went into captivity returned to see restoration. But Israel was brought back from exile as God had promised to Jeremiah (Ezra 1:1-4).

But you might be saying at this point: "Well, these are promises to *Israel*, God's special people. This special relationship does not exist between God and His church." In the midst of Jeremiah's warning of judgment and promise of restoration, he mentions God's "new covenant": " 'Behold, days are coming,' declares the Lord, 'when I will make a new covenant with the house of Israel and with the house of Judah' " (Jer. 31:31). Is this promise yet to be fulfilled? Not according to the Book of Hebrews. The new covenant began when the Holy Spirit was poured out at Pentecost (Acts 2:9-11). The church, consisting of Jews and Gentiles, partakes of the glories and blessings of the "new covenant" (Heb. 8:7-13). We have a "better covenant" (Heb. 8:6), a "better high priest" (8:1), a "more excellent ministry" (8:6), and a "better sacrifice" (9:1-18). Therefore, the restoration process is multiplied under the better and renewed covenant. If God's people were restored under a covenant that is now obsolete, then God will restore us in greater measure under a covenant that is "better."

Keep in mind that God purchased the church "with His own blood" (Acts 20:28). Jesus "loved the church and gave Himself for her" (Eph. 5:25). Gentiles are no longer "strangers to the covenants of promise" (2:12). Gentile believers "have been brought near by the blood of Christ" (v. 13). There are no longer "two" men but one "new man" in Christ, a man consisting of Jews and Gentiles (v. 15). God reconciled "them both in one body to God through the cross, by it having put to death the enmity" (v. 16).

> So then you [Gentiles; 2:11] are no longer strangers and aliens, but you are fellow-citizens with the saints, and are of God's household, having been built upon the foundation of the apostles [who were Jews] and prophets [who were Jews], Christ Jesus Himself [who was a Jew] being the corner stone, in whom the whole building, being fitted together is growing into a holy temple in the Lord; in whom you also are being built together into a dwelling of God in the Spirit (Eph. 2:19-22).[3]

Why do some say that restoration cannot come today under a better covenant? David Wilkerson states that "America Will Not Repent."[4] How does he know? God always leaves room for repentance. Repentance is always offered to a society. Even a cursory study of America's history will show that America is a covenant nation. Of course, the humanists are trying to deny this, but the evidence is unmistakable.[5] God, if He works like He has done in the past, will leave room for repentance. The church is not perfect. Wilkerson identifies many evils within the church that must be expunged. But this is the repentance process. This is what the grace of God is all about. We deny the gospel if we say that America, or any nation, will not repent. God is sovereign. Even Jonah had doubts about Nineveh. God's grace proved him wrong.

---

3. For those who claim that the "church" was not prophesied in the Old Testament, see Isaiah 57:19, quoted by Paul in Ephesians 2:17. For the dispensationalist, church means "Gentile believers." The Bible describes the "church" as the "congregation of God," something that existed in the Old Testament (Acts 7:38). In the New Testament, the church includes both Jew and Gentile. Gentiles were "grafted in among them" (Jewish believers) to become partakers "with them of the rich root of the olive tree" (Rom. 11:17).

4. Wilkerson, *Set the Trumpet to Thy Mouth* (Lindale, TX: World Challenge, 1985), p. 17.

5. Gary DeMar, *Ruler of the Nations: Biblical Principles for Government* (Atlanta, GA: American Vision, 1987), pp. 203-240.

"The Laodicean Lie!"

One of the pillars of support for the belief that we are indeed living in the "last days" is Jesus' description of the Laodicean church in Revelation 3:14-22. The argument goes something like this. The seven churches listed in Revelation 2 and 3 describe the church throughout history.[6] The church of Laodicea describes the generation of Christians just before Jesus returns to rapture His church. It describes a period of indifference to the things of God. Now, since this is all prophesied in the Bible, there is really nothing that can be done to effect long-term cultural change. The church is "lukewarm" (Rev. 3:16), good for nothing except to be spit out of God's mouth. How could this church impact the world when it is "miserable and poor and blind and naked"? (v. 17).

Those who deny this interpretation are said to "spiritualize everything having to do with Christ's soon return."[7] This is an odd accusation in light of the "seven ages" interpretation of the seven churches described in Revelation 2 and 3. As we will see, there is *nothing* that even hints at the seven churches being seven ages throughout church history. This interpretation must be read into Revelation 2 and 3.

Do the seven churches in Asia represent seven stages in church history? First, there is certainly nothing in the Book of Revelation that would lead one to think so. One would expect some indication that Jesus was describing seven ages of the

---

6. "Some interpreters . . . take the seven letters to the churches as purely a literary device. They see the message as addressed to the church at large, with the division into seven as purely artificial. Others take the churches to stand for periods in history, Ephesus representing the first century, Smyrna the period of persecution, Pergamum the age of Constantine, Thyatira the Middle Ages, Sardis the Reformation era, Philadelphia the time of the modern missionary movement, and Laodicea the apostasy of the last days. . . . Such views are unlikely. It seems much more probable that the letters are letters to real churches, all the more so since each of the messages has relevance to what we know of conditions in the city named." Leon Morris, *The Revelation of St. John* (Grand Rapids, MI: Eerdmans, 1969), p. 57.

7. David Wilkerson, "The Laodicean Lie!" (Lindale, TX: World Challenge, Inc., n.d.), p. 3.

church and not just seven churches in Asia Minor. For those who hold to a literal interpretation of Scripture, seven churches would seem to mean seven churches and not seven ages. Second, each church is mentioned in a specified geographical area: Ephesus, Smyrna, Pergamum, Thyatira, Sardis, Philadelphia, and Laodicea. There is no mention of ages. In fact, John is to write in a book what he sees, and is to "send it to the seven churches" (1:11). Third, in the first chapter of Revelation, John tells us "for the time is *near*" (1:3). What he is about to see "must *shortly* take place" (1:1). The view that these churches extend over 2000 years of church history contradicts these very clear passages that whatever is about to happen will happen in a *short* time frame. "He who testifies to these things says, 'Yes, I am coming *quickly*.' Amen. Come, Lord Jesus" (Rev. 22:20). William Hendriksen comments on the seven churches/seven ages view in his critically acclaimed commentary on the Book of Revelation.

> The notion that these seven churches describe seven successive periods of Church history hardly needs refutation. To say nothing about the almost humorous—if it were not so deplorable —exegesis which, for example, makes the church at Sardis, which was dead, refer to the glorious age of the Reformation; it should be clear to every student of the Bible that there is not one atom of evidence in all the sacred writings which in any way corroborates this thoroughly arbitrary method of cutting up the history of the Church and assigning the resulting pieces to the respective epistles of Revelation 2 and 3.[8]

But there is a further problem with the seven ages interpretation. How do we know when the period of the Laodicean church begins? Some aspect of the church in nearly every generation can be described in some measure as "lukewarm" (Rev. 3:16). If it refers just to a few years prior to the rapture, that's one thing. But if it's made to apply to a long period of time, then the church could be immobilized for centuries because of prophetic miscalculation.

---

8. Hendriksen, *More Than Conquerors: An Interpretation of the Book of Revelation* (Grand Rapids, MI: Baker, [1940] 1982), p. 60. See footnote 6 above.

David Wilkerson and others use the Laodicean church to describe conditions in the church as it exists now. For them, the rapture is just around the corner. But other prophetic teachers have taught the same thing, applying the characteristics of the Laodicean church to their generation.

> Why are there no such saints in Scotland now? Because their wine is mingled with water—their food is debased. It will nourish men no longer, but dwarflings.
>
> Oh, Scotland! oh, Scotland! how I groan over thee, thou and thy children, and thy poverty-stricken Church! Thy Humes are thy Knoxes, thy Thompsons are thy Melvilles, thy public dinners are thy sacraments, and the speeches which attend them are the ministrations of their idol.
>
> And the misfortune is that the scale is falling everywhere in proportion, ministers and people, cities and lonely places; so that it is like going into the Shetland Islands, where, though you have the same plants, they are all dwarfed, and the very animals dwarfed, and the men also.
>
> . . . *How well the state of our Church, nay, of the Christian Church in general, is described by the account of the Laodicean Church. It almost tempts me to think . . . that these seven Churches are emblems of the seven ages of the Christian Church, to the last of which men are now arrived.*[9]

Irving wrote these words in the 1830s, over 150 years ago! Taking David Wilkerson's description of today's church with that of Irving's description of the church in his day, we end up with an impossible situation. Any hope for societal reform is dashed to pieces since the Laodicean church, as Irving and Wilkerson maintain, is an unrepentant church ripe for imminent judgment. Those expecting an imminent judgment have been waiting since Irving's time. The only thing left for the church to do is to wait. All hope is lost for earthly transformation.

Irving's description of the future fueled the fire of prophetic speculation. Prophetic speculation was rampant in Irving's day as

---

9. Edward Irving (1792-1834), cited by Arnold Dallimore, *Forerunner of the Charismatic Movement: The Life of Edward Irving* (Chicago, IL: Moody Press, 1983), p. 100. Emphasis added.

it is in our day. The nearness of judgment was the watch-word. Robert Baxter, a disciple of Irving, used the Laodicean church as the "last days" church to his advantage on January 14, 1832, to predict that the rapture would occur in 1260 days, June 27, 1835.

> Count the days, one thousand three score and two hundred— 1260—the days appointed for a testimony, at the end of which the saints of the Lord should go up to meet the Lord in the air.[10]

Baxter made further predictions until the Irvingite movement believed the return of Christ would probably take place not later than 1835 or 1836. Needless to say, they were mistaken.

The seven churches/seven ages interpretation does not stand up to good Bible interpretation. It is an arbitrary way to divide history, and there is no warrant in Scripture to make such a division. Moreover, it can hinder many people from leading full Christian lives. And it can immobilize the church from being the salt and light that this sin-darkened world needs.

But let's grant for a moment that Irving and Wilkerson are correct in their seven churches/seven ages interpretation. There is nothing in the description of the Laodicean church that closes the door to repentance and future restoration. In fact, Jesus stands at the door knocking, offering to dine with those who have forsaken Him (Rev. 3:20). This is not an abandoned church. *Restoration is found in the life-transforming effects of the gospel and the mercy and grace that God showers on His church "which He purchased with His own blood"* (Acts 20:28). God loves this "lukewarm church" enough to "reprove" and to "discipline" it (Rev. 3:19),

> For those whom the Lord loves He disciplines, and He scourges every son whom He receives. It is for discipline that you endure; God deals with you as with sons; for what son is there whom his father does not discipline? But if you are without disci-

---

10. Baxter, *Narrative of Facts, Characterizing the Supernatural Manifestations, in Members of Mr. Irving's Congregation, and Other Individuals, in England and Scotland, and Formerly in the Writer Himself* (London: James Nisbet, 1833), p. 17. Quoted in *ibid.*, p. 150.

pline, of which all have become partakers, then you are illegitimate children and not sons. . . . All discipline for the moment seems not to be joyful, but sorrowful; yet to those who have been trained by it, afterwards it yields the peaceful fruit of righteousness (Heb. 12:6-8, 11).

We look for the discipline of God for we are legitimate children, heirs according to the promise (Rom. 8:15-17). If there are false doctrines, immorality, coldness, and false pride found in the church, then God will root them out because He loves His church. David Wilkerson is right in his assessment of the church, but this does not mean that *final* judgment is close at hand. He has misinterpreted the seven churches of Revelation 2 and 3, and he has unwittingly forsaken the mercy, grace, love, and patience of God.

Methods of Change

The secularist trusts in the *inherent goodness* of man and the *inevitability of progress* that resides in the evolutionary dogma to bring about change.[11] These two approaches break down into further variations. Bryan R. Wilson classifies seven types of "salvationists" in his book *Magic and the Millennium*:

> The *conversionist* believes that only by changing men can the world be changed. . . . The *revolutionist* is convinced that only the destruction of the world (and usually he means the present social order) will suffice to save men. . . . A third response is to withdraw from the world, since it is so hopelessly evil. The *introversionist* may do this as an individual or as a member of a community. . . . [T]he *manipulationist's* response . . . consists basically of applying religious techniques which allow men to see the world differently and explain evil away. A similar, but narrower type of response is the *thaumaturgical*. Relief from present ills is sought by means of magic. Such salvation is personal and local, and does not as a rule call for any elaborate doctrine. Another response, the *reformist*, is close to the position of secular social reformers, and in

---

11. The *Humanist Manifesto II* triumphantly states: "[N]o deity will save us; we must save ourselves."

fact differs only in positing divine guidance. The intention is to amend the world gradually in the light of supernaturally given insights. Lastly, there is the *utopian* response in which men seek to construct a perfect society, free from evil.[12]

As can be seen, the Christian position is *conversionist*. People must change if there is to be any effective change in the broader society. Any Christian who rejects this fundamental point misses the substance of the gospel.

Optimism is a rejuvenating emotion. The belief that life can change spurs us all on. The hopeless and disenfranchised, when given a ray of hope, can be lifted out of the pit of despair. "A comparable restless certainty that *however good or bad experience is, it can be better*, routinely infects even the most thoroughgoing secularisms."[13] But only the Christian has the elements of real optimism, because only the Christian has the life-transforming gospel of the Lord Jesus Christ to make dead men and women live.

From the Inside Out

The reformation of the world should result from the reformation of the individual. A look at personal salvation will show the relationship between the individual and the world. What happens

---

12. J. F. C. Harrison, *The Second Coming: Popular Millenarianism: 1780-1850* (New Brunswick, NJ: Rutgers University Press, 1979), pp. 8-9. Emphasis added. Wilson's discussion of these "ideal-type constructs" can be found in his *Magic and the Millennium: A Sociological Study of Religious Movements of Protest Among Tribal and Third-World Peoples* (New York: Harper & Row, 1973), pp. 22-26.

13. Lionel Tiger, *Optimism: The Biology of Hope* (New York: Simon and Schuster, 1979), p. 23. While the author is preoccupied with biological evolution as the source of man's optimistic nature ("our huge cerebral cortex [produced] . . . an ever more complex and imaginative stock of optimistic schemes" [p. 16]), he cannot get away from an optimism that finds its reality in the God of the Bible. "Even if the biblical assertion is incorrect that 'where there is no vision, the people perish,' it is difficult to think what could be the engine or stimulus for social behavior in a nihilistic system committed only to the certainty of the passage of time, without any energetic relationship to another principle or purpose" (p. 22). For Tiger, "optimism is a biological phenomenon; since religion is deeply intertwined with optimism, clearly I think religion is a biological phenomenon, rooted in human genes, which is why it keeps cropping up" (p. 40).

when a sinner comes to Christ? The Bible says that "if any man is in Christ, he is a new creature; the old things passed away; behold, new things have come" (2 Cor. 5:17). Now, does this verse teach perfectionism? Is the new Christian without sin? He's not perfect, and he never will be perfect in this life. He must mature in the faith; in fact, this is often what the Bible means when a man is called "perfect" (Job 1:1; AV). A "perfect" man is a mature man. But Christians are not "perfect" in the sense that we usually mean. Christians are not sinless. Yet, we still describe a believer as a Christian. If his Christianity is real, then we should expect, for example, his family to receive the benefits of his new life in Christ. His family is then described as "Christian." As a businessman, his business would be described as "Christian" if it reflected Christian business practices. Now, if there are millions of Christians in a society, each making an impact for Christ in family, church, and community, then why is it impossible to believe that the society could be described as "Christian"?

Would this be a perfect society? No. Even Christians are sinners. Would there still be the need for civil government, the police, and the threat of punishment? Yes. But there would be fewer incidents of crime in such a community. In fact, there are still pockets of righteousness in our country today. The reality of a Christian civilization is only a remnant, however.

Is it possible that the gospel we preach is anemic? Could it be that our gospel does not go far enough? Many evangelists who believe that we cannot build a Christian civilization preach a gospel that has little or no cultural relevance; thus, their preaching against a Christian civilization becomes self-fulfilling. For them, the gospel only has *personal* significance. Yet even Jimmy Swaggart who rightly stresses the gospel's *internal* significance in salvation, has to say that there is also *external* benefit, though only for the believer. He makes his point when he writes that his worldwide preaching of the gospel

> has been *tremendously* productive. *However, you see, it hasn't been our responsibility to reform the world, but to win souls to Him.* What I (and every other preacher of the Gospel) am doing *will* make the world

better—but *only* for those individuals who give their hearts and lives to the Lord Jesus Christ and by so doing become *"the salt of the earth."*[14]

For the most part, we agree with Rev. Swaggart. His emphasis on the gospel is just where it ought to be: Evangelism must come first in any attempt to change anybody or anything. Apart from changed lives no lasting external changes are forthcoming. Without changed lives there will not be a changed society. But the gospel has a benefit for those who do not come under its immediate sway. The world is blessed when the Christian is blessed. This was God's promise to Abraham: "And I will bless you, and make your name great; and so you shall be a blessing; *and I will bless those who bless you*, and the one who curses you I will curse. *And in you all the families of the earth will be blessed"* (Gen. 12:2-3). We are Abraham's spiritual descendants, and thus we reap the benefits of those initial gospel promises to him (Rom. 4:9-25; 9:6-9). As we prosper, that is, as we are blessed by God, the world is blessed. The history of western civilization attests to it. Being salt and light to the world is a blessing to the world. Surely it's a temporal blessing, but it's a blessing nevertheless. So then, the Christian's new life in Christ should benefit the world. If the world is decaying, then it is due to the refusal of Christians to see their new life in Christ as a blessing to the world.

But Rev. Swaggart is inconsistent at one point. He tells us that the world is only made better "for those who give their hearts and lives to the Lord Jesus Christ" and by so doing become *"the salt of the earth."* What about orphanages, charities, homes for unwed mothers, rescue missions, and Christian schools?[15] Do these min-

---

14. Jimmy Swaggart, "The Coming Kingdom," *The Evangelist*, September 1986, p. 9.

15. On a September 12, 1987, television broadcast, Rev. Swaggart told his viewing audience that "Jimmy Swaggart Ministries" has fed 450,000 people in 50 countries, helps to fund 66 medical units around the world, and has helped to build over 300 schools, 110 Bible schools, and 210 churches. This seems to be a benefit beyond salvation. We applaud him and his ministry for their efforts.

istries benefit believers only? Certainly not. In most cases they're established to help *unbelievers*. Does all of this work "make the world better" for non-Christians? Of course. Isn't this the meaning of being "the salt of the earth"? What is our ultimate goal in all of these activities? We do these good works to point the lost to Jesus Christ.

Moreover, Rev. Swaggart is apparently unaware of the great tradition of social reform within evangelical Christianity. Social reform and evangelism went hand-in-hand in the 19th century. John Stott writes about Charles Finney's views on social reform.

> Social involvement was both the child of evangelical religion and the twin sister of evangelism. This is clearly seen in Charles G. Finney, who is best known as the lawyer turned evangelist and author of *Lectures on Revivals of Religion* (1835). Through his preaching of the gospel large numbers were brought to faith in Christ. What is not so well known is that he was concerned for 'reforms' as well as 'revivals.' He was convinced, as Donald W. Dayton has shown in his *Discovering an Evangelical Heritage*, both that the gospel 'releases a mighty impulse toward social reform' and that the church's neglect of social reform grieved the Holy Spirit and hindered revival. It is astonishing to read Finney's statement in his twenty-third lecture on revival that '*the great business of the church is to reform the world. . . . The Church of Christ was originally organised to be a body of reformers. The very profession of Christianity implies the profession and virtually an oath to do all that can be done for the universal reformation of the world.*' [16]

---

16. Stott, *Involvement: Being a Responsible Christian in a Non-Christian Society*, 2 vols. (Old Tappan, NJ: Fleming H. Revell, 1984, 1985), vol. 1, p. 23. Emphasis added. Finney saw no contradiction between gospel and social reform: "The Christian church was designed to make aggressive movements in every direction — to lift up her voice and put forth her energies against iniquity in high and low places— to reform individuals, communities, and government, and never rest until the kingdom . . . shall be given to the people . . . —until every form of iniquity shall be driven from the earth." Finney, quoted from "Letters on Revivals —No. 23," *The Oberlin Evangelist* (n.d.) in Donald Dayton, *Discovering an Evangelical Heritage* (New York: Harper & Row, 1976), p. 21. Quoted in George M. Marsden, *Fundamentalism and American Culture: The Shaping of Twentieth Century Evangelicalism: 1870-1925* (New York: Oxford University Press, 1980), p. 86. In a

The negative reaction to social reform comes from secularized attempts to do what only the gospel can do. This reaction is legitimate, but it should not deter Christians from being truly evangelical in their attempts at reform. Why should we abandon an area of legitimate biblical concern just because humanists have perverted our methods and goals? Christians should strive to be a "light on a hill" to unbelievers.

> See, I have taught you statutes and judgments just as the Lord my God commanded me, that you should do thus in the land where you are entering to possess it. So keep and do them, for that is your wisdom and your understanding in the sight of the peoples who will hear all these statutes and say, "Surely this great nation is a wise and understanding people." For what great nation is there that has a god so near to it as is the Lord our God whenever we call on Him? Or what great nation is there that has statutes and judgments as righteous as this whole law which I am setting before you today? (Deut. 4:5-8).

The statutes and laws that God has given to His people are the standards of reform. Obedience to the law is the "good works" that those outside of Christ are to "see" (Matt. 5:16).

Justification, Sanctification, and Regeneration

One helpful way to look at the relationship between personal renewal and societal renewal and reformation is to study the biblical doctrines of justification, regeneration, and sanctification. When we are united to Christ by faith, we receive these blessings. Christ Himself is our righteousness, our sanctification, and our new life (1 Cor. 1:30; John 1:4; 5:26; 11:25; 14:6), and in Him *we* have righteousness, holiness, and life. Those who believe that societal transformation is impossible concentrate more on regenera-

---

footnote, Marsden tells us that "Letters on Revivals—No. 23" is "left out of modern editions of these letters" (p. 252, note 5). The reader can draw his own conclusions as to why.

tion of individuals than on social activism. Jimmy Swaggart writes that *"it hasn't been our responsibility to reform the world, but to win souls to Him."*[17] Others concentrate on justification to the exclusion of sanctification.

Let's briefly note the differences and the implications for social transformation. Regeneration is the technical theological term for the "new birth." A person is regenerated when he is "born again." Jesus made clear to Nicodemus that the new birth is essential to entering the kingdom: "You must be born again" (John 3:3). Often, however, Christians are so concerned with being born again that they neglect the need for growth in grace and maturity, what the Bible calls "sanctification."

Justification means that God has *declared* the sinner righteous, when the righteousness of Christ is imputed to him. Justification is a legal declaration made by God, whereby God declares the guilty sinner "not guilty" on the merits of Jesus Christ. But justification is more than the forgiveness of sin. God not only forgives the guilt of sin, He actually "imputes" or "attributes" a positive righteousness to the believing, repentant sinner. Thus, God no longer sees a man in his sin, but Jesus in His righteousness.

Justification puts the sinner in a right relationship with God. But this judicial act by itself deals only with one part of man's sinfulness. Justification deals with the *guilt* of sin, but does not change the sinner's disposition to sin. Justification only puts him in a right standing legally before God. This is a central aspect of salvation. As James Buchanan says, guilt "cannot be extinguished by repentance, or even by regeneration; for while these may improve or renew our character, a divine sentence of condemnation can only be reversed by a divine act of remission."[18] But justification is not all there is to the gospel message. Nor is regeneration the entire gospel. We do not want to minimize the importance of

---

17. Swaggart, "The Coming Kingdom," p. 9.
18. James Buchanan, *The Doctrine of Justification*, (Grand Rapids, MI: Baker, [1867] 1977), p. 258.

justification. Without justification, there is no gospel. The justified sinner is no longer condemned by God: "Who will bring a charge against God's elect? God is the one who justifies; who is the one who condemns?" (Rom. 8:33). This is a crucial point. Nor do we wish to minimize the importance of regeneration. The point is that the Christian life is just that, a life; it is not merely a one-time event of "getting saved."

Much of the church today is theologically immature. The basics of the Christian faith are known, but there is little else in their storehouse of theological knowledge. There is no progress in godliness. In fact, the writer to the Hebrew Christians says an astonishing thing. He tells his readers to leave the "elementary teaching about the Christ" behind (Heb. 6:1). They are to "press on to maturity." The foundation has been laid. It's time to build on it.

God does more than justify us. His action is not only judicial and external. It is also recreative and internal. God gives us new life in union with Jesus Christ. The Holy Spirit, through regeneration, brings the dead sinner to life. Prior to regeneration we "were dead in . . . trespasses and sins," but "even when we were dead in our transgressions, [God] made us alive together with Christ" (Eph. 2:1, 5). The results are comprehensive in their effect on the once-dead sinner: He is a "new creation" (2 Cor. 5:17) and a "new man" (Eph. 4:24); he has a "new life" (Eph. 2:1-5) and a "renewed mind" (Rom. 12:2). Regeneration is the "new birth" and makes growth possible (Eph. 4:15; 1 Peter 2:2; 2 Peter 3:18).

The Process of Sanctification

The process by which we are more and more conformed to the image of Christ is *sanctification*. In one sense, sanctification is a definitive, once-for-all act of God.[19] Usually, though, sanctification is described as a process that accompanies the judicial act of justification and the life-transforming power of regeneration. Greg Bahnsen summarizes the relationship between justification and sanctification for us:

---

19. John Murray, "Definitive Sanctification," *Collected Writings of John Murray,* 4 vols. (Edinburgh: Banner of Truth Trust, 1977), vol. 2, chapters 21-22.

[S]alvation continues beyond the *point* of justification into the *process* of sanctification, a process which begins with a *definitive break* with the bondage of sinful depravity and matures by *progressively preparing* the Christian to enjoy eternal life with God by the internal purifying of his moral condition. Because salvation involves accepting Christ as *both* one's Savior and Lord (Acts 16:31), and because the reception of God's Son entails the reception of the Spirit of His Son as well (Rom. 8:9-10), justification cannot be divorced from sanctification.[20]

There is no true justification without sanctification. Christ is our justification *and* our sanctification. To tear these two aspects of salvation asunder is to tear Christ asunder. If we are truly justified by faith, we will be perfected by grace through faith throughout our lives. This is part of James's point when he declares that "faith, if it has no works, is dead, being by itself" (James 2:17). Faith, if it is the true faith that justifies sinners, must express itself in works. B. B. Warfield clearly asserted the interrelatedness of justification and sanctification:

In clear accord with the teaching of Scripture, Protestant theology . . . has never imagined that the sinner could get along with justification alone. It has rather ever insisted that sanctification is so involved in justification that the justification cannot be real unless it be followed by sanctification.[21]

We must now ask a fundamental question: Does the justified, regenerated, and sanctified sinner affect his society? That is, does sanctification spill over into society as Christians work out the implications of their salvation? Are we responsible to reform our lives? Are we responsible to reform our families? Are we responsi-

---

20. *Theonomy in Christian Ethics* (rev. ed.; Phillipsburg, NJ: Presbyterian and Reformed, 1984), p. 161.

21. "On the Biblical Notion of 'Renewal,'" in *Biblical and Theological Studies*, ed., Samuel G. Craig (Philadelphia, PA: Presbyterian and Reformed, 1952), p. 374.

ble to reform our children's education? Should we work to reform our church if it is not following its God-directed mission? As a Christian, should I work to reform a business that I have control over? What if I run for a political office? Should I work to bring righteousness to bear on all the issues of the day? If transformation takes place in the individual, the family, church, business, and the State, doesn't this mean that the world in some manner is being "reformed"? Where do we stop the process? Where do we say "no" to reformation? Where do we draw the line on sanctification's effect on our world?

Can the Christian who has a biblical aversion to abortion sit by and allow the State to fund the murder of the unborn under a legal fiction? In effect, does the Bible-believing Christian say "Thus far and no farther with my sanctification"? Does sanctification only have a *personal* effect? Theodore Roszak has described Christianity as "socially irrelevant, even if privately engaging."[22]

We find instances in Scripture where sanctification does spill over to affect others and the broader culture. The story of the Good Samaritan is ample evidence that this is true (Luke 10:30-37). The self-righteous Levite "passed on the other side" (v. 32), while the Samaritan put his faith into action (vv. 33-37). For the Levite, religion did nothing for the world. The benefit was purely for himself. We should remember at this point that abortion kills a human being. If helping to rescue the Samaritan traveller is the result of a justified and regenerated sinner manifesting his salvation in sanctification, then how can Christians stand by and allow abortion to go on without a protest?

In another example, Zaccheus, the despised tax-collector, expressed his sanctification almost immediately after his conversion: "Behold, Lord, half of my possessions I will give to the poor, and if

---

22. Roszak, *Where the Wasteland Ends* (New York: Doubleday, 1973), p. 449. Quoted in Os Guinness, *The Gravedigger File: Papers on the Subversion of the Modern Church* (Downers Grove, IL: InterVarsity Press, 1983), p. 79.

I have defrauded anyone of anything, I will give back four times as much" (Luke 19:9).

If injustice is operating in the world to hurt others, can we sit by and do nothing like the self-righteous Levite? Isaiah tells us, for example, that tampering with monetary commodities affects orphans and widows, those least able to care for themselves financially (Isa. 1:21-23). Is economics neutral? Apparently not. Notice too that Israel, the people of God, were condemned because they did nothing. In Matthew 23 Jesus indicts the Pharisees, the religious leaders of the day, for using the law to protect their own interests, while ignoring the needs of others.

Marxists Fill the Gap

The Marxists in Central America have attacked the Christian gospel on this very point. Liberation Theologians preach a gospel that has something to do with the here and now. Liberation Theology parades as a biblical system that supposedly brings justice to the masses. We are told that only in Marxism, the heart of much Liberation Theology, is there a reliable struggle for justice.[23] Marxists "try to resolve the situation of exploitation and inequality. The new society they desire and the kingdom of God are the same," one priest said.[24] A person only discovers the meaning of the kingdom of God by making this world a better place. "In 1972 the bishops of two of Nicaragua's largest diocese declared their support for 'a completely new order.' The new order should include the 'preferential option for the poor' and a 'planned economy for the benefit of humankind.' "[25]

This is very attractive to poor people, many of whom do not

---

23. Gary North, *Liberating Planet Earth: An Introduction to Biblical Blueprints* (Ft. Worth, TX: Dominion Press, 1987).

24. Edmund and Julia Robb, *The Betrayal of the Church* (Westchester, IL: Crossway Books, 1986), p. 119.

25. *Ibid.*, p. 124.

know where their next meal is coming from. The terminology of biblical Christianity is used to draw in the nominally religious and usually hopeless. But it's the promise for land, food, housing, and political power *now* that motivates many of them to embrace the Liberationist's gospel.

The gospel of "Christian fatalism" must compete with the Marxist "gospel" of immediate social reform. Many of the evangelical groups doing missionary work in Latin America are "millennialist, preaching Christ's imminent return to earth—and thus favor a passive response to social injustice. 'I've got nothing in the world but a mission in the next,' announces a favorite song."[26] What does this type of thinking do to multi-generational thinking? There is no long-range planning. Planning and building are irrelevant in a world of temporal insignificance. Western civilization was not built using the world view of "I've got nothing in the world but a mission in the next." Rather, it was built with this in mind: "I've got *something* in this world *because* I have a mission in the next."

What does a next-world-only gospel do for the impoverished? It throws them right into the arms of the Marxists. The Marxists stand by and offer (wrong) answers, but for the poor they seem better than what they have. The Christian comes with hope, but a hope that only has meaning when they die. This is not the Christian message. Eternal life begins *now* for the believer. The benefits of heaven are ours *now*. We live heavenly lives *now* (Col. 3:1-4).

The anti-Christian mentality that pervades our world is content to have the church cloistered in its own world of cultural non-engagement. Christians are tolerated as long as they do not make waves, that is, as long as they do not engage the world for Christ. The time has come for Christians to think about what it will take to build a Christian civilization in the next 200 years. That's right. We must begin to think multi-generational. While the next elec-

---

26. "The Protestant Push," *Newsweek* (September 1, 1986), p. 64.

tion is important, the kingdom of God and its extension through the generations is much more important. Let's begin the building process now. Let's get our eyes out of the clouds and on the work at hand (Acts 1:11).

Does Eschatology Make a Difference?

There are a number of pretribulational premillennialists who have a social conscience similar to that of Christian reconstructionists. Believing in the imminent return of Jesus does not deter them from being socially responsible. One Assemblies of God evangelist writes:

> Premillenarians are some of the most active people in the kingdom of God here and now. Most premillenarians are as socially and politically active as any other sector of evangelical Christianity regardless of eschatological views.
>
> I see my premillenarian brothers and sisters at the vanguard of world evangelization, drug rehabilitation, political activism, protest against social evils, feeding and clothing the poor, etc.[27]

Of course, as we've demonstrated throughout this book, this does not square with Mr. Hunt's views. First, Mr. Lewis states that the "kingdom of God" is "here and now." Dave Hunt tells us that the kingdom will appear tangibly only in heaven; it will not even be manifested in the earthly millennium.[28] Second, according to what we've read of Dave Hunt, Jimmy Swaggart, Hal Lindsey, and David Wilkerson, being concerned with such earthly things as "political activism" focuses the eyes of Christians on earthly things.

Then there is a book with the following title: *Christian Reconstruction From a Pretribulational Perspective* by David Schnittger, a

---

27. David A. Lewis, "Premillenarian Rapture Believers: Are They Socially Irresponsible Escapists?," *Pentecostal Evangel*, August 16, 1987, p. 12.

28. Hunt, *Beyond Seduction: A Return to Biblical Christianity* (Eugene, OR: Harvest House Publishers, 1987), p. 250.

publication of the Southwest Radio Church of God.[29] The author wants everything reconstructionists are working for but within the framework of a pretribulational premillennial position. Schnittger criticizes those leaders who hold to "the pretribulational rapture position" and adopt an attitude of cultural pessimism:

> [Gary] North and other postmillennial Christian Reconstructionists label those who hold to the pretribulational rapture position pietists and cultural pessimists. One reason these criticisms are so painful is because I find them to be substantially true. Many in our camp have an all-pervasive negativism regarding the course of society and the impotence of God's people to do anything about it. They will heartily affirm that **Satan is Alive and Well on Planet Earth,** and that this must indeed be **The Terminal Generation**; therefore, any attempt to influence society for Christ is ultimately hopeless. They adopt the pietistic platitude: "*You don't polish brass on a sinking ship.*" Many pessimistic pretribbers cling to the humanists' version of religious freedom; namely Christian social and political impotence, self-imposed, as drowning men cling to a life preserver. Their attitude is: *Just give us the freedom to hand out tracts. Just a few more years, and Jesus will come back to bail us out. Give us a tiny zone of autonomy from the state and we'll be satisfied. Just give us some slack in our chains.*[30]

The Lure of Politics

Of course, the most fundamental question is this: How can either of these men expect any long-term success in their efforts if they believe in the imminent return of Jesus? They might work at reconstruction, but there will be no hope for success during the most trying times. If conditions get worse before they get better, will the belief in cultural transformation or imminent judgment win out? How will the pretribulational premillennialists be

---

29. Southwest Radio Church of God, P.O. Box 1144, Oklahoma City, OK 73101. Ask for publication B-541.
30. *Ibid.*, p. 7.

able to convince others to join a long-term project of Christian reconstruction in the light of Bible prophecy that they believe points to our days as being the "last days"? What will happen when success does not come quickly? Will there be disillusionment, discouragement, and retreat? Some of the most active activists have already dropped out of the battle. Constitutional attorney John Whitehead has noticed that those who once were the most committed are no longer around.

> The great majority of movements come and go, no matter how powerful. Some of the most powerful burn out the fastest. Almost all the activists I began working with are now gone. Some have had mental breakdowns. One is selling ads. One is making movies. Others are pretending to be good Christians by voting and going to church. Burned out.[31]

Whitehead points to "establishment assimilation" as the reason for activistic burn out. At first, activists fight against the system, but in time they become part of the status quo. Among many Christian groups, politics has been suspect. Political finagling gave us abortion, tyrannical laws that threatened to wipe out the growing Christian school movement, and legislation that recognized homosexuality as a legitimate alternative lifestyle. Christians began to awaken in the mid '70s. They were tired of being kicked around. The future was at stake for them and their children.

The year 1976 was the turning point. A supposed champion of Christian ideals came on the scene. Jimmy Carter ran as a nonestablishment candidate for the presidency. Carter claimed to be "born again." This was enough to bring Christians to the polls. Carter won, but his four years in Washington turned out to be a disaster for Christian ideals.

He adopted the born-again image but ignored the born-again Christians who helped put him into office. His presidency was one

---

31. Whitehead, "ACTIVISM: Has the Light Gone Out?," *The Rutherford Institute Magazine*, Vol. 4, No. 2 (March-June 1987), p. 3.

of the most liberal and anti-Christian on record. Little if anything was done to stop the slaughter of the unborn. He packed the courts with liberal judges, a place where real political battles are won and lost. As Carter's presidency drew to a close, disillusionment turned to anger. Carter was rejected for another self-avowed born-again president, Ronald Reagan. His presidency was reconfirmed in 1984 with a landslide victory over Walter Mondale, the last remnant of the Carter presidency. Some battles have been won under Reagan's presidency. A number of Christians secured cabinet posts, and others found their way into places of influence. But while we have made some progress, there is still disappointment. Abortion is still the law of the land. The growing deficit threatens to push our nation into bankruptcy. We should not forget that it was under the Reagan administration that churches were brought under the taxing structure of the Social Security system. Under the latest tax law, all children over 5 years of age will have to have a Social Security number in order for parents to claim them as exemptions on their 1040 forms.

Many Christians feel that they have been used solely for political purposes, and they are right. There was the promise of change with little that actually did change. The established political order "recognized" these vocal Christian activists as a strong political force. But instead of changing the face of politics, the face of activism changed. Activists became "respectful" and compromised.

What happened to the influential born again movement of the '70s and '80s? There was an unhealthy reliance on short-term political solutions to our nation's problems. Politics was seen as the immediate savior. Activist lawyer John Whitehead again writes: "The most alluring reason activist movements are absorbed by the establishment is immersion in politics, to the extent that politics becomes an all-consuming religion. This has essentially wiped out the leftist movement of the '60s, and it will all but destroy the Christian activism of the '80s."[32]

---

32. *Ibid.*

The Psychology of Pessimism

Politics is the "quick fix" approach to cultural transformation. "The next presidential election will turn the tide. A change in the Supreme Court will bring our nation back to righteousness. If we could only get more conservatives elected to office." None of this will do it. Only a long-term effort to change all facets of society will bring about significant and lasting transformation. This means changing the hearts and minds of millions of people. All this takes time, time that is not on the side of the pretribulational premillennialist.

There is a psychology to pessimism. A belief in impending judgment influences the development of a strategy for building. Where should our efforts go? If you have a vision for an earthly future that includes reconstruction, then your efforts will be multifaceted. While it will include politics, there will be more emphasis on building churches and schools and universities. Our children will be trained to be doctors and lawyers as well as medical missionaries and engineers, two of the best ways to get into countries usually closed to missionaries. The design will be to reconstruct the world from the bottom up. All facets of life will come under the sway of the gospel and biblical law.

The short-term solution will be to change things at the top and hope and pray that change will first come through the legislative process. While legislative change is certainly important, especially in the case of abortion, it will not be lasting if the people who put legislators into office do not hold biblical views. A new generation needs to be retaught the things of God. This will take time, more time than the present prophetic time table will give it.

We should also keep in mind that influence for change comes from influential professions. Christians have finally started to develop Christian schools. This is a sign of activism and obedience. But the greatest threat to the Christian school movement is the legal establishment, made up of lawyers and judges who hold a world view in conflict with the Christian world view. There is also a large lobbying group, the NEA, that has a vested interest in seeing parent-funded education kept to a minimum. School systems also have a vested interest. Public school systems receive funds from various governmental jurisdictions to finance their schools.[33] If there are fewer students, then there is less funding. Private educational institutions threaten the financial base of statist education because a student in a private school means decreased tax dollars to the school system. Should Christians expect to have their views expressed in a fair and impartial way in newspapers, on radio, and on television? There are additional areas where Christians have little influence.[34]

It is time that Christians see every area of life as spiritual and ripe for reformation and reconstruction. You can't change just some things. Suppose a church sets up a Christian school, and the state says that it must meet "minimum requirements" established by the legislature in conjunction with the educational establishment. So the church hires a lawyer to fight the requirements. He goes before a judge who was appointed by the state's liberal governor. He rules in favor of the state. Let's suppose you want to fight abortion. A group from your local church decides to picket your town's abortion mill. You're arrested for interfering with the traffic flow of a "legitimate" business. Again you face lawyers and judges who are part of the governmental process. The solution? Christians must become lawyers and judges as well as legislators. But where will these Christians get their training? Most law schools are not very sympathetic to the Christian world view. There are only a handful of good Christian colleges and even fewer Christian law schools. So another facet of our agenda is the building of Christian colleges, universities, and law schools. But all this takes *time*.

---

33. The average cost in the United States is $3,970 per student per school year with a graduation rate of only 70.6%. These figures for spending are for the 1986-87 school year; graduation rates are for 1985. New York spends $6,299 per student with a graduation rate of only 62.7%. *U.S. News & World Report* (Sept. 7, 1987), p. 67.

34. S. Robert Lichter, Stanley Rothman, and Linda S. Lichter, *The Media Elite: America's New Powerbrokers* (Bethesda, MD: Adler & Adler, 1986).

Will our premillennial brethren give these needed areas of reconstruction the required time and attention? Are they willing to keep up the fight in the face of seemingly insurmountable odds? Will they trust God for success and not forfeit this world as prophetic speculators grow in their insistence that the end is near? We welcome all who join in the process of Christian reconstruction. God will not demand anything less, even if He returns by the time you finish reading this.

Conclusion

The devil wants us to remain passive in the face of hostile opposition to the Christian faith. And, when we do get involved, he directs us to follow only defensive measures. The devil isn't too concerned if we battle humanism. He knows that in time we'll go home. For most Christians, there's no long-term strategy to implement. What angers, frustrates, and motivates the devil is when we start building to supplant humanism. When we start building schools, the devil-inspired humanists who have succeeded in claiming the seats of judicial power swoop down on us to try to shut us down.

You see, as long as Christians have remained in their churches, they have been free to criticize the prevailing humanistic world view. The humanists have now seen some of their guarded turf taken over by Christians who maintain that the earth is the Lord's and the fullness thereof. A growing number of Christians have taken the cultural implications of this truth very seriously. As "fellow-heirs" with Christ, Christians are now exercising dominion in His name and under His authority (Rom. 8:17).

But the devil has not quit. His goal is to get Christians to believe the lie that they should keep their religion private, that there's no hope in changing the world. Preachers teach it, and millions of Christians believe it. As we near the close of the 20th century, we see that the humanists and apocalyptic Christians are saying the same thing for different reasons but with the same results. It is time that both extremes were rejected.

16

BUILDING A CHRISTIAN CIVILIZATION

Some belief system, some prevailing ideology makes up the warp and woof of every civilization. Civilizations are not neutral. An analysis of any nation at any point in time will tell us what gives meaning to the people and their institutions. A nation's religious foundation can be determined by looking at its economic system, judicial pronouncements, educational goals, and taxing policy. Culture is "religion externalized." Look at a nation's art and music, and there you will find its religion. Read its books and newspapers. Watch its television programs. The outgrowth of civilization will be present on every page and in every program. The habits of individuals and families are also indicators of a nation's religious commitments. The sum of all these expressions will lead us to a nation's religious commitments. While it might be beneficial to look at the creeds of the churches, the actions of the people who subscribe to the creeds are a more accurate barometer of what the people really believe.[1] In all of this a nation's religion shines bright.

---

1. "This behavioral approach can be extremely helpful for the student of the history of Christianity. The Christian faith has always been a curious blend of belief and behavior, doctrine and duty, profession and practice. The New Testament abounds with behavioral directives. Christians in the apostolic age were often told to 'be doers of the word and not hearers only' (James 1:22). The Apostle Paul repeatedly urged his readers to let their conduct conform to their convictions about Jesus Christ and the new life they had found in him.

"Christians, therefore, have always been expected to live out the implications of their faith. Naturally, Christians have not always done so, and sometimes they have not even been certain of what was expected of them. But few would deny that daily or personal behavior was supposed to be a direct reflection of theological beliefs. Too often historians of Christianity have studied the cognitive or theo-

For man, in the deepest reaches of his being, is religious; he is determined by his relationship to God. Religion, to paraphrase the poet's expressive phrase, is not of life a thing apart, it is man's whole existence. [John A. Hutchison in *Faith, Reason and Existence*], indeed, comes to the same conclusion when he says, "For religion is not one aspect or department of life beside the others, as modern secular thought likes to believe; it consists rather in the orientation of all human life to the absolute."[2]

In the Soviet Union, for example, a Marxist-Leninist ideology defines the society, both in philosophy and policy.[3] The prevailing ideology directs the nation. In Iran, an extreme form of Islamic tyranny dominates the nation.

Some societies are in transition. China has broken with many of its Maoist policies and is now experimenting with Western economic practices, still, however, under the strict oversight and con-

---

logical aspects of the church's history to the neglect of how beliefs were translated into daily life.

"This behavioral approach has already been applied to the study of American religion, with some interesting results. Dr. Martin E. Marty, church historian at the University of Chicago, demonstrated in his *A Nation of Behavers* that it makes more sense to classify religious people in contemporary America by their religious behavior than by the more traditional denominational or even theological labels." Timothy P. Weber, *Living in the Shadow of the Second Coming: American Premillennialism, 1875-1982* (2nd ed.; Grand Rapids, MI: Academie Books/Zondervan, 1983), pp. 7-8.

2. Henry R. Van Til, *The Calvinistic Concept of Culture* (Grand Rapids, MI: Baker, [1959] 1972), p. 37.

3. It's very important to understand that ideology defines culture and thus gives rise to civilizations. Without understanding the underlying ideology of a civilization, words can, and often do, mean different things to different people. The Soviet Union wants "peace" as well as "democracy." Can the once-Christian West work with the non-Christian East since their goals are the same? "[T]here is the problem of logomachy, or the communist device of deceiving their opponents through the subtle use of words which deliberately lead the non-communist to understand the words used by communists in a different way to that in which communists themselves understand them. Classic examples of this are the much used words 'peace' and 'democracy.' For by 'peace,' the communists mean 'world conquest by communism, preferable without (communists') bloodshed,' and by 'democracy' they mean 'the dictatorship of the Communist Party' (which they again misleadingly call 'the dictatorship of the Proletariat')." Francis Nigel Lee, *Communist Eschatology: A Christian Philosophical Analysis of the Post-Capitalistic Views of Marx, Engels, and Lenin* (Nutley, NJ: Craig Press, 1974), p. 16.

trol of the communist State. The State still dominates the nation. Families are limited to one child. Forced abortions are a State policy.[4] As with the Soviet Union, the State is supreme. The State is god. The State directs the nation, and, thus, civilization develops or dies as the statist god mandates.

What of the United States? The United States was at one time Christian.[5] A survey of the religious commitments of the people, its public declarations, and the evaluation from abroad will give us at least some indication of what the impetus was behind our nation's civilization.

The United States: A Christian Nation

In 1892, the United States Supreme Court in the case of *Church of the Holy Trinity* vs. *United States*,[6] determined that the United

---

4. Steven W. Mosher, *Broken Earth: The Rural Chinese* (New York: Free Press/Macmillan, 1983).

5. There is a tremendous amount of debate over this assertion. We do not maintain that everyone was a Christian or that those who professed to be Christians were consistent in their beliefs. A Christian world view prevailed in the colonies and later in the states. In time, however, this Christian base eroded. A natural law ethic was substituted for revealed religion. The Bible was still the nation's Book, but so was a "Common Sense" philosophy.

We believe that the issue of a "Christian America" must be argued in two ways. First, the Christian must set forth the case that our founders had no intention of secularizing the nation. It was not their desire to eradicate religion. The liberal and secularized courts, media, civil libertarians, and public (government) school educators must be confronted with the facts.

Second, Christians must be brought back to reality. Our nation's founders were not perfect. Many of them brought a compromised Christianity into government. The appeal of natural law was alluring to many of them. To equate "Christian America" with a "perfect America" is a mistake.

For a healthy discussion of the issue see: Jerry S. Herbert, *America, Christian or Secular?* (Portland, OR: Multnomah Press, 1984); Mark A. Noll, et al., *The Search for Christian America* (Westchester, IL: Crossway Books, 1983); Robert T. Handy, *A Christian America: Protestant Hopes and Historical Realities* (2nd ed.; New York: Oxford University Press, 1984); Nathan O. Hatch and Mark A. Noll, *The Bible in America* (New York: Oxford University Press, 1982). Also see, Gary DeMar, *Ruler of the Nations* (Atlanta, GA: American Vision, 1987), and Gary DeMar, "Response to Dr. William Edgar and National Confession," Geneva College Consultation on the Bible and Civil Government, June 2-3, 1987. Available from American Vision, P.O. Box 720515, Atlanta, Georgia 30328 ($6.00).

6. 143 US 226 (1892).

States had been a Christian nation from its earliest days. The court opinion, delivered by Justice David Josiah Brewer, was an exhaustive study of the historical and legal evidence for America's Christian heritage. After examining hundreds of court cases, state constitutions, and other historical documents, the court came to the following conclusion: "There is a universal language pervading them all, having one meaning; they affirm and reaffirm that this is a religious nation. These are not individual sayings, declarations of private individuals: they are organic utterances; they speak the language of the entire people."

Then, after citing various American social customs, Brewer added, "These and many other matters which might be noticed, add a volume of unofficial declarations to the mass of organic utterances that is a Christian nation." In 1931, Justice George Sutherland reviewed the 1892 decision of Brewer and reaffirmed that Americans are a "Christian people."

In 1831 Alexis de Tocqueville and Gustave de Beaumont, commissioned by the French government, came to the United States "to examine the various prisons in our country, and make a report on their return to France." On their return to France, and after their prison report was complete, Tocqueville began what was to be his two volume work *Democracy in America* (1834, 1840). What did Tocqueville see? What made America the civilization that it was? Tocqueville writes:

> On my arrival in the United States the religious aspect of the country was the first thing that struck my attention; and the longer I stayed there, the more I perceived the great political consequences resulting from this new state of things. In France I had almost always seen the spirit of religion and the spirit of freedom marching in opposite directions. But in America I found they were intimately united and that they reigned in common over the same country.[7]

---

7. Alexis de Tocqueville, *Democracy in America*, 2 vols. (New York: Alfred A.

But all of this doesn't make a nation or a civilization Christian. A Christian civilization will have as its foundation the basics of the Christian faith. The majority of the people will be professing Christians. They will adhere to their faith in a self-conscious manner and will practice it with little hypocrisy. Those who do not embrace the tenets of the Christian religion will still benefit by its effects on the culture. Tocqueville points out:

> It may fairly be believed that a certain number of Americans pursue a peculiar form of worship from habit more than from conviction. In the United States the sovereign authority is religious, and consequently hypocrisy must be common; but there is no country in the world where the Christian religion retains a greater influence over the souls of men than in America; and there can be no greater proof of its utility and of its conformity to human nature than that its influence is powerfully felt over the most enlightened and free nation on the earth.[8]

Notice that Tocqueville states that "the sovereign authority is religious." What did he mean? Religion, and here we mean Christianity, permeated and pervaded all aspects of the society, though no one ecclesiastical institution did. Neither the church nor the State was sovereign, but religion, Christianity, was the foundation for both. While a man might not belong to a church or profess the Christian faith, he would have been considered an outcast if he did not at least follow the rules laid down by the "sovereign authority" of religion.

The "sovereign authority" of religion ought to prevail today. As Christians, we're not looking for a church/state or a state/church. The prevailing set of presuppositions, however, should be Christian.

Knopf, [1834, 1840] 1960), vol. 1, p. 308. In a footnote, Tocqueville writes: "The New York *Spectator* of August 23, 1831 relates the fact in the following terms: 'The Court of Common Pleas of Chester County (New York) a few days since rejected a witness who declared his disbelief in the existence of God. The presiding judge remarked, that he had not before been aware that there was a man living who did not believe in the existence of God; that this belief constituted the sanction of all testimony in a court of justice; and that he knew of no cause in a Christian country where a witness had been permitted to testify without such belief'" (p. 306).

8. *Ibid.*, pp. 303-4.

Kingdom Aberrations

At least six mistaken approaches come to mind when talk shifts to how Christians ought to go about building a "Christian Civilization": Political Pyramidism, spiritual kingdomism, millennial hope-ism, social gospelism, ecclesiocracy, and blind utopianism. This chapter will deal with only the first five since utopianism has been dealt with elsewhere in this book.

Political Pyramidism

The Pyramid Society is a culture in which a majority of the people spend most of their time transforming the civil government to the near exclusion of themselves, their families, churches, schools, businesses, and local civil governments. By changing the powers at the top, we are led to believe that there will be a trickle-down effect of cultural transformation that will blossom into a better society. The problems that a nation faces, as this approach sees it, are solely political. Change the State, and all of society will change with it. This has been the vision of pagan empires since the building of the tower of Babel.

The Last of the Seven Wonders

Decaying symbols of top-down political systems are a constant reminder that the State cannot save. The Great Pyramid of Cheops or Khufu, at Gizeh near Cairo, is the only surviving edifice of the Seven Wonders of the World. The Great Pyramid and the smaller pyramids are a lasting testimony to the building prowess of the Egyptians. They are also evidence of the religion and political theory of Egypt. The very shape of the pyramids tells us something about Egypt's political philosophy. Egypt had a top-down system of total control. The Pharaohs believed in political centralization. All of life was controlled through the Pharaoh's decree. Their silent witness in the desert kingdom of Egypt should remind us that any top-down political structure is doomed to fail.

In the pyramid society the State controls everything. The ruler is both priest and king. He "is the person who has contact with the gods."[9] In modern pyramid societies the State is god, and politics is its priesthood.

The Pharaohs were not incorporating a new idea in the development of their political philosophy. All those who reject the true God want to be "like God" (Gen. 3:5). God is the controller of all things. Rebels against God want to control, to manipulate, and eventually to enslave. This is the dream of all empire-builders. Given enough power and authority, these power merchants believe that all of life can be controlled by man and for man.

Decentralization: The Essence of Freedom

There is a great danger in following the political model of Egypt, no matter how good the intentions. Political centralization creates a society of potentially endless political controls. The Bible outlines a decentralized social order where power is diffused and the potential for corruption and tyranny are minimized. Freedom is enhanced because of the diluted strength of the one by the maintenance of the many.

> *The biblical social order is utterly hostile to the pyramid society.* The biblical social order is characterized by the following features. *First*, it is made up of multiple institutional arrangements, each with its own legitimate, limited, and derivative sovereignty under God's universal law. *Second*, each institution possesses a hierarchical chain of command, but these chains of command are essentially *appeals courts* — "bottom-up" institutions — with the primary duty of responsible action placed on people occupying the lower rungs of authority. *Third*, no single institution has absolute and final authority in any instance; appeal can be made to other sovereign agents of godly judgment. Since no society can attain perfection, there will be instances of injustice, but the social goal is harmony under biblical law, in terms of an orthodox creed. God will judge all men perfectly. The State need not seek perfect

9. R. J. Rushdoony, *The One and the Many: Studies in the Philosophy of Order and Ultimacy* (Nutley, NJ: Craig Press, 1971), p. 41.

justice, nor should citizens be taxed at the astronomical rates necessary to sustain the quest for perfect justice.[10]

Constantine, it is said, imposed a top-down State religion on the disintegrating Roman Empire. The Edict of Milan (A.D. 313) "secure[d] for Christianity the privileges of a 'licensed cult' (*religio licita*)," and, thus "guaranteed the right of all to profess the faith, and removed any legal disabilities which they might suffer in consequence."[11] Numerous freedoms were granted to Christians, including the restoration of status lost because of a conscientious objection to certain pagan practices; freedom of assembly and worship; restitution for the confiscation of land and other property. The Church was also recognized as a corporation; it was authorized to own property.[12]

Constantine's reign, however, came on the heels of an already established Christian revival throughout the Empire. Even persecutions could not stop the growth of God's kingdom. "[D]espite persecutions, Christianity had grown to such a degree that it was now considered a threat to the State."[13] In time Constantine went beyond these basic freedoms and set the stage for Theodosius and a State-imposed pyramid society. Rushdoony writes:

> Christianity represented strength, and Constantine believed in strength; it represented the power of God, and Constantine believed in the power of God *as a Roman*. As Constantine saw it, the function and calling of the church was to revivify the Roman Empire and to establish on a sound basis the genius of the emperor. Constantine was respectful, kindly, and patient with the church, but in all this he saw the church still as an aspect of the empire, however central a bulwark. The evidence indicates that he saw himself somewhat as Eusebius of Caesarea saw him. Even

10. Gary North, *Moses and Pharaoh: Dominion Religion Versus Power Religion* (Tyler, TX: Institute for Christian Economics, 1985), pp. 211-12.

11. Charles Norris Cochrane, *Christianity and Classical Culture* (New York: Oxford University Press, [1940] 1980), p. 178.

12. *Idem.*

13. Marcellus Kik, *Church and State: The Story of Two Kingdoms* (New York: Thomas Nelson & Sons, 1963), p. 34.

as God was sovereign and monarch over all in heaven, so Constantine was sovereign and monarch on earth. Eusebius wrote, "Thus, as he was the first to proclaim to all the sole sovereignty of God, so he himself, as sole sovereign of the Roman world, extended his authority over the whole human race."[14]

In time, the Eastern church "gladly surrendered herself to the care and protection"[15] of the State. While the State should have a protective function regarding the church, the church does not "surrender herself" to the State, giving up jurisdiction. The church has its own courts, rulers, and jurisdiction. The Western church maintained its own courts because of rampant paganism in the legal system. Administratively and institutionally the Eastern church "merged with the empire to form with it but one politico-ecclesiastical organism and acknowledged the emperor's right to administer her."[16]

Even when the State is Christian and its courts function on a Christian base, the church must maintain itself as a complimentary government. The church's courts should function regardless of the spiritual condition of the State.[17] When the courts are Christian, the church still has jurisdiction over its members. In fact, the church has *primary* jurisdiction. When the State courts are corrupt, the church offers a refuge for those seeking justice.

A Christian civilization means more than converting the State so that it will follow the dictates of God's law. All institutions must be guided by biblical law. Individuals, families, and churches are

---

14. Rushdoony, *The One and the Many*, p. 149.

15. Alexander Schmemann, *Church, World, Mission* (Crestwood, NY: St. Vladimir's Seminary Press, 1979), p. 37.

16. *Idem*.

17. "When Christianity became the religion of the empire [under Constantine], the church gladly closed down her own courts and gave everything over to the transformed Christian courts of the state. Thus, the check and balance of church courts and state courts was lost in the East, and this led in practice to a social monism that eventually became stifling. In the West, because the church continued to exist in a pagan environment, the church maintained her own courts, and these continually discipled and checked the actions of the state courts." James B. Jordan, "Workshop on Church Law and Government," Supplement to *The Geneva Review*, Tyler, Texas, February, 1985.

not to turn jurisdiction over to the State for security. The church does not relax its duties in society because the State becomes more Christian. There is always the danger of accommodation by the church, becoming part of the status quo because Christians have won some political battles. The church historian Philip Schaff warns us by mentioning the corrupting influences of pagan Rome on the church:

> But the elevation of Christianity as the religion of the state presents also an opposite aspect to our contemplation. It involved great risk of degeneracy to the church. The Roman state, with its laws, institutions, and usages, was still deeply rooted in heathenism, and could not be transformed by a magical stroke. The christianizing of the state amounted therefore in great measure to a paganizing and secularizing of the church. The world overcame the church, as much as the church overcame the world, and the temporal gain of Christianity was in many respects cancelled by spiritual loss. The mass of the Roman empire was baptized only with water, not with the Spirit and fire of the gospel, and it smuggled heathen manners and practices into the sanctuary under a new name.[18]

Christians should not expect too much from involvement in politics. God has designed the State to do only so much. Its power is great, but its jurisdiction is limited. The State is often seen as a cure-all for the nation's ills. For example, while changing the Supreme Court to reflect a Christian world view would be welcomed, the nation as a whole would probably rebel at many pro-Christian pronouncements. The abortion issue is a case in point. By the indifference shown by the American public, Christians included, it seems that most Americans prefer abortion. They might not accept convenience abortions, but they want some limited right to abortion: family planning, population control, the mother's "mental health," teenage pregnancy, and "defective children."

---

18. *History of the Christian Church: Nicene and Post-Nicene Christianity: From Constantine the Great to Gregory the Great, A.D. 311-600*, 8 vols. (Grand Rapids, MI: Eerdmans, [1910] 1981), vol. 3, p. 93.

All of society must be transformed. We have not arrived when we can say that we now have a Christian President, a Christian Supreme Court, a majority of Christian Congressmen, and other Christian politicians. In fact, we will not have a Christian nation if we do not have Christian Christians, Christian families, and Christian churches. Humanism continues to march forward because our nation is basically humanistic.

Spiritual Kingdomism

Building a Christian civilization is looked upon with suspicion by those who consider the kingdom of God to be purely spiritual in nature. For them, the kingdom of God is personal and only has a spiritual dimension. The passage in Luke 17:21 restricts the kingdom to the heart: "The kingdom of God is within you."[19] There is no external manifestation of the kingdom, and therefore there can be no Christian civilization. The church is the domain of Christian activity. The world is the devil's kingdom.

The kingdom is certainly spiritual, but confusion arises over the term "spiritual." To be "spiritual" means to be governed by the Holy Spirit. For many, spirituality means to be preoccupied with non-physical reality. Therefore, in this view to be spiritual means *not* to be involved with the material things of this world. Biblically this is not the case. The devil and his demons are spiritual (non-physical) and evil: "And I saw coming out of the mouth of the dragon and out of the mouth of the beast and out of the mouth of the false prophet, three *unclean spirits* like frogs; for they are *spirits of demons*, performing signs, which go out to the kings of the whole world, to gather them together for the war of the great day of God Almighty" (Rev. 16:13-14). There are "deceitful spirits" (1 Tim.

---

19. The preposition *entos* in Luke 17:21 can be translated two ways: the "kingdom of God is *among* you" or the "kingdom of God is *within* you." If the kingdom is among us it is certainly in us. If the kingdom is within us it has an external effect as well. If the kingdom of God is *within* the believer, it ought to energize him to action in building a civilization that will bring honor and glory to God.

4:1), "unclean spirits" (Rev. 18:2), and spirits of "error" (1 John 4:6). There is even "spiritual wickedness" (Eph. 6:12).

On the other hand, Jesus has a body (physical reality), and He is good. Jesus was raised with His body. Scripture tells us that Jesus shared in "flesh and blood" (Heb. 2:14). He who denies that Jesus Christ has come in the flesh "is the deceiver and the antichrist" (2 John 7; cf. 1 John 4:1-3). Man's body is not inherently sinful. If so, then Jesus would have been a sinner just because He had a body. We will have bodies in the resurrection, as Jesus does (John 20:24-27). In the resurrection, we will be "raised imperishable" (1 Cor. 15:52).

"Spiritual" does not stand alone. We should use the term as a description of something. There is the "Holy Spirit" (e.g., Acts 13:2), a "spirit of truth" (1 John 4:6), "spiritual things" (1 Cor. 9:11), "spiritual food" (10:3), a "spiritual body" (15:44), "spiritual sacrifices" (1 Peter 2:5), "spiritual wisdom and understanding" (Col. 1:9), and "ministering spirits, sent out to render service for the sake of those who will inherit salvation" (Heb. 1:14). Spiritual is not opposed to material.

The Bible does not support the belief that Christians should abandon the world because it is not "spiritual." Rather, Christians are to transform the world through the power of the Spirit, using the spiritual law[20] as the standard of righteousness for appraising (judging) where regeneration and restoration are needed. If there are two spiritual forces, then we should expect civilization to be governed by either "spiritual wickedness" or "spiritual wisdom and understanding." So then, the question is not: Does civilization

---

20. "For we know that the Law is spiritual . . ." (Rom. 7:14). Paul goes on to state that he is "of flesh, sold into bondage to sin." The flesh, or body, is nothing until God breathes "into his nostrils the breath of life" (Gen. 2:7). It is only then that he becomes a "living soul." Because we are "dead in trespasses and sins" (Eph. 2:1), a new life-giving Spirit must be imparted. The body, the flesh, is not inherently evil; it is only evil because it is "sold into bondage to sin" (Rom. 7:14b). The regenerating work of the Holy Spirit resurrects the dead sinner. His flesh is no longer devoid of spiritual guidance.

have a spiritual dimension? The question is: *What spirit* is trans-forming civilization?

Civilization, therefore, is the reflection of a chosen spirit, whether Christ or Satan. The Christian, therefore, is to be in the world, but not of the world (John 17:14-16). Civilization is not to squeeze him into the world's mold (Rom. 12:2). The spirituality of the Christian is to make a difference in the world.

The Christian is to keep himself "unstained by the world" (James 1:27). He is warned not to get entangled in the "defilements of the world" (2 Peter 2:20). Nowhere are Christians told to abandon the world because of its unspiritual character (Matt. 28:18-20; John 3:16), to hand the world over to the spirits of darkness.

The "world" is corrupt because people are corrupt. Where corrupt people control certain aspects of the world, we can expect defilement. But the world does not have to remain in decay. When individuals are redeemed, the effects of their redemption should spread to the society in which they live and conduct their affairs. In this case, the effects of regeneration are manifested outwardly.

The world of pagan thinking and practice is to be replaced by Christian thinking and practice. It is a perversion of the gospel to maintain that the world, as the domain where evil exists, is inherently corrupt. We should remember that Jesus came to this *world* to give His life for the *world's* redemption (John 3:16). Jesus' redemptive work is comprehensive enough to affect all aspects of life, not just individuals *in* the world.

By denying the spirituality of God's created order, we neglect its importance and give it by default to those who deny Christ. *Worldliness* is to be avoided, not the world. The Bible warns us

against worldliness *wherever* it is found [James 1:27], certainly in the church, and he is emphasizing here precisely the importance of Christian involvement in *social* issues. Regrettably, we tend to read the Scriptures as though their rejection of a "worldly" lifestyle entails a recommendation of an "otherworldly" one.

This approach has led many Christians to abandon the "secular" realm to the trends and forces of secularism. Indeed, because of their two-realm theory, to a large degree, Christians have themselves to blame for the rapid secularization of the West. If political, industrial, artistic, and journalistic life, to mention only these areas, are branded as essentially "worldly," "secular," "profane," and part of the "natural domain of creaturely life," then is it surprising that Christians have not more effectively stemmed the tide of humanism in our culture?[21]

God created everything wholly good (Gen. 1:31). Man, through the fall, became profane, defiled by sin. Redemption restores all things in Christ. Peter failed to understand the gospel's comprehensive cleansing effects. He could not believe the Gentiles were "clean": "What God has cleansed, no longer consider unholy" (Acts 10:15; Matt. 15:11; Rom. 14:14, 20). The fall did not nullify God's pronouncement that the created order "was very good" (Gen. 1:31). The New Testament reinforces the goodness of God's creation: "For everything created by God is good, and nothing is to be rejected, if it is received with gratitude; for it is sanctified by means of the word of God and prayer" (1 Tim. 4:4, 5).

Scripture is our guide, not the Platonic view of matter as something less good than the "spiritual" world. God "became flesh and dwelt among us" (John 1:14). Jesus worked in his earthly father's shop as a carpenter, affirming the goodness of the created order and the value of physical labor.

A Christian civilization should be built out of conviction, not solely out of reaction to a dominant secularism.

Millennial Hope-ism

One way to have a Christian civilization is to wait until Jesus returns to earth to establish one. In the meantime, Christians are to wait. Evil is inevitable. There is little if anything the Christian can do to stop evil's advance. In fact, the Christian is living in the "last days" of man's attempts to build any type of civilization.

History is filled with examples of generations of Christians awaiting a cataclysmic eschatological event that would transform

---

21. Albert M. Wolters, *Creation Regained: Biblical Basics for a Reformational Worldview* (Grand Rapids, MI: Eerdmans, 1984), p. 54.

the world. "[F]or a long time great numbers of Christians were convinced not only that Christ would soon return in power and majesty but also that when he did return it would be to establish a messianic kingdom on earth. And they confidently expected that kingdom to last, whether for a thousand years or for an indefinite period."[22] The Montanists of the second century went to Phrygia to await the "imminent coming of the Kingdom" where the "New Jerusalem was about to descend from the heavens on to Phrygian soil, where it would become the habitation of the Saints."[23]

It seems that every generation has those who believe that Jesus will return "in their lifetime" to set up His millennial reign. While such a belief can encourage, it can also debilitate. The Millerites[24] of the 19th century are an extreme case in point:

> Utterly convinced that Jesus Christ would appear on October 22, 1844, many Millerites took decisive action. Some left their jobs, boarded up their businesses, confessed to unsolved crimes, sold their farms and everything they owned, and let their crops go unharvested so that they could spread the word of Christ's coming and meet him with clean consciences and free of debt. As the expected day approached, thousands of people found it difficult if not impossible to live normal lives.[25]

The beliefs of the Millerites fortunately are no longer widely held. But, while the extremism of the Millerites is gone, some of the passivity remains. There is little interest in long-term civilization-building. If the world cannot be saved in a month, maybe a

---

22. Norman Cohn, *The Pursuit of the Millennium* (London: Secker & Warburg, 1957), pp. 6-7.

23. *Ibid.*, pp. 8-9.

24. William Miller (1782-1849), founder of Adventism, was converted from Deism in 1816. After fourteen years of Bible study, he decided that Jesus would return in 1843, at the outside, October 22, 1844. His book, *Evidence from Scripture and History of the Second Coming of Christ, About the Year 1843*, published in 1836, was instrumental in winning many to his views.

25. Timothy Weber, *Living in the Shadow of the Second Coming*, p. 43.

year, the effort is not really worthwhile. Universities and law schools, for example, are institutions where tangible results of building them take too long to see. Why put millions into training Christians for "secular" or "worldly" occupations? The money could better be spent on evangelism. Anyway, Jesus is coming back soon.

So what has happened? We have evangelized, and we're still here. Evangelism, witnessing for Christ, is the first step in a comprehensive discipleship program. We save people from hell and for the glory of God. Evangelism has been seen as an end in itself, however, designed to prepare people for the imminent return of Jesus.[26] In the interim, our children need to go to school. Where do they go? The government (public) schools were the only choice we had. It has only been in the last 20 years that many fundamentalist Christian schools have been started. But even here the primary purpose is reactionary. Many Christian schools are little more than baptized public schools with Bible courses taught. Few schools train young people to take dominion in the name of the Lord Jesus.

Where do we send them after high school? Harvard? Yale? Princeton? What if they want to go to graduate school? If Christians send their children to non-Christian colleges, we should expect a percentage of them to lose their faith, or at least to have it severely rattled. Why? There are few Christian instructors. Why are there few Christian instructors? Because, for the most part, Christians have not prepared for the educational future. The time-is-running-out gospel has been preached since the turn of the century. Why spend time and energy building what will soon

---

26. This is the healthiest feature of millennial hope-ism. The goal of reaching the world for Christ has produced tremendous missionary enterprises that are thriving today. The emphasis, however, was simply to "save souls." Little was and is done to redeem the culture. The effects of the gospel rarely go beyond individuals. There is little need to work toward building a Christian civilization because the impetus of evangelism is "not to keep the ship afloat" but to "rescue a few of the passengers." With this view, "Christians, therefore, must be content with their minority status and with the apparent failure of their cause. The lack of overwhelming success was not due to the church's lack of faith or discipline; it was ultimately the preordained will of God for this age." *Ibid.*, p. 70.

perish? Why put our money and effort in such worldly enterprises as schools of higher education?

Most Christian colleges are similarly short-sighted. They cannot compete with secular institutions. They were never designed to compete. Christian colleges are "Bible-oriented."[27] Their purpose is to equip young people for "full-time Christian service." Most consider "full-time Christian service" as exclusively missionary work or the pastorate. Why can't "full-time Christian service" include journalism, economics, law, education, and politics? All of these endeavors have a religious base. A journalist must tell the truth in his reporting. An economist must deal in "just weights and measures." Laws are assumed to have a religious foundation. Education also deals with truth telling. Politics—civil government—is ordained by God as a *ministry* to promote the good and punish evil (Rom. 13:4). Any Christian desiring to enter any of these fields would be in "full-time Christian service."

What happens when the scare tactics no longer work? What happens if 1988 passes and Jesus has not raptured His church?[28] Of course, it can be said that He *will*. But let's suppose He doesn't and the timetable is off. Many prophetic Bible teachers have made predictions. History has proved them wrong. The Millerites are a case in point. The imminent return of Jesus has been an inducement for evangelism for some time now. It is wearing a bit thin,[29]

---

27. All colleges ought to be Bible-oriented, that is, the Bible should be the foundation upon which every other discipline is taught. Unfortunately, the Bible courses are often separate from the general curriculum. Political science, economics (if it's even taught), foreign affairs, journalism, and science usually are taught from a supposed "neutral" perspective, using non-Christian textbooks. What's really sad is that there are few if any Christian textbooks on these subjects.

28. A generation is supposed to witness the events leading up to the coming of Jesus. Forty years, a biblical generation, must pass from the time Israel became a nation again in 1948. The year 1988 is central to the millennial hope-ism scenario.

29. The Jehovah's Witnesses relied heavily on prophetic speculation to increase their numbers. Numerous times the leadership predicted significant "kingdom events": "Be not surprised, then, when in subsequent chapters we present proofs that the setting up of the Kingdom of God is already begun, that it is pointed out in prophecy as due to begin the exercise of power in A.D. 1878, and

seeing that the same prophetic texts have been used for nearly three generations. Millennial hope-ism can debilitate the church, rendering it ineffective to speak a prophetic word to the world.

> Though not all premillennialists have accepted the extreme position on the futility of reform activities, one must finally conclude that in many cases premillennialism broke the spirit of social concern that had played such a prominent role in historic evangelicalism. Its hopeless view of the present order left little room for God or for themselves to work in it. The world and the present age belonged to Satan, and lasting reform was impossible until Jesus returned to destroy Satan's power and set up the perfect kingdom. As Martin Marty has said, premillennialists often give up on the world before God does. And that refusal to get involved in social issues has frequently kept them from fulfilling the biblical mandate to do good and practice justice in the world. Consequently, though there have been significant exceptions, many premillennialists have turned their backs on social reform movements. As a result, the social conscience of an important part of American evangelicalism has atrophied and died. In that regard, at least, premillennialism broke faith with the evangelical spirit that it fought so hard to preserve.[30]

Thankfully, many millennial hope-ists have not abandoned the world. Though their participation in civilization is highly discriminatory and certainly short-term, many are involved in stemming the tide of a militant humanism.

Social Gospelism

The Social Gospel was greatly influenced by the man-centered philosophies of Immanuel Kant, Georg Hegel, and Darwinian evolution. Karl Marx used the phrase in his *Communist Manifesto* (1848).[31]

---

that the 'battle of the great day of God Almighty' (Rev. 16:14), which will end in A.D. 1915, with the complete overthrow of earth's present rulership, is already commenced. The gathering of the armies is plainly visible from the standpoint of God's Word." Quoted in Robert A. Morey, *How to Answer a Jehovah's Witness* (Minneapolis, MN: Bethany Fellowship, 1980), p. 44.

30. Weber, *Living in the Shadow of the Second Coming*, p. 234.

31. ". . . to pave the way for the new social Gospel." *Communist Manifesto* (1848), in Karl Marx and Friedrich Engels, *Selected Works*, 3 vols. (Moscow: Progress Publishers, 1969), vol. 1, p. 135. He rejected the idea because it was peaceful rather than revolutionary.

In this view, society will change because something "inherent in nature drives man to build a rational, international, civil order."[32] Changing society is inevitable because changing man is inevitable. Evolution makes it so.[33] Moreover, with the effects of higher criticism ravaging the church, the Bible was no longer seen as a reliable standard for personal and social ethics. The Bible could be used as the *impetus* for change, but it could not give specific steps to bring about change. Morality was determined outside the boundaries of biblical revelation.[34]

Obviously, the Social Gospel is no gospel. Man's basic problem is no longer sin. Natural forces are at work to keep him from reaching his full potential. In time, through the evolutionary process, change will come. Through technology,[35] science, education,[36] and a taxing policy guided by an omnipotent State, the slowness of evolutionary change can be accelerated.

> Walter Rauschenbusch, for example, in his *A Theology for the Social Gospel*, spoke of the "millennium" coming through natural development as an ideal society expressing the communal brotherhood of man. Shirley Jackson Case's *The Millennial Hope* spoke of the long process of humanity evolving and rising higher in the scale of civilization and attainment; the world is constantly growing better, society's ills are to be remedied by education and

---

32. Greg L. Bahnsen, "The *Prima Facie* Acceptability of Postmillennialism," *Journal of Christian Reconstruction*, Symposium on the Millennium, ed., Gary North, Vol. III, No. 2, (Winter, 1976-77), p. 49.

33. Some manifestations of the Social Gospel "reflected the optimism which was widespread in the latter part of the [19th] century in Western Europe as well as in the United States and which was associated with the older theory of progress reinforced by current interpretations of the theory of evolution." Kenneth Scott Latourette, *Christianity in a Revolutionary Age: The 19th Century Outside Europe*, 5 vols. (Grand Rapids, MI: Zondervan, 1961), vol. 3, p. 224.

34. Even conservative Christians have fallen into the trap set by the higher critics. The Bible no longer is seen as a reliable standard for ethics since civilization building seems to be confined to the Old Testament. Many believe that as "New Testament Christians" our social ethic must come from natural law.

35. The movie *Ghostbusters* is an example of how technology will win over evil. The Rabbis and Catholic clergy are helpless. A fabricated nuclear energizer puts evil in its place.

36. Rousas J. Rushdoony, *The Messianic Character of American Education* (Nutley, NJ: Craig Press, 1963).

legislation, and the responsibility for bringing in the millennium is man's own—to be produced in his own strength.[37]

The State plays a large role in the Social Gospel approach to building a Christian civilization. Advocates of the Social Gospel see "a one undivided realm, the state, as the true order of God and man. The state is given the overall jurisdiction and sovereignty over church, school, family, business, farming, and all things else which belong only to God. The essential function of the social gospel is to render all things unto Caesar and nothing to God."[38]

It should be remembered that evangelicals who opposed the Social Gospel believed that Christians should influence society.[39] Their animosity was toward those who put all of their emphasis on the public and political side of Christian activity. The evangelicals believed that the first step in societal transformation must come through repentance for sin and total dependence on God's grace supplied to us in the sacrificial death of Jesus. The Social Gospel had degenerated into "religious morality,"[40] that is, morality without Christ. "The antisupernaturalism and the radical emphasis upon the social and political application of Christianity which often accompanied the Social Gospel dimmed enthusiasm for political action among fundamentalists; it even stigmatized

---

37. Bahnsen, "The *Prima Facie* Acceptability of Postmillennialism," p. 50.

38. R. J. Rushdoony, *The Foundations of Social Order: Studies in the Creeds and Councils of the Early Church* (Nutley, NJ: Presbyterian and Reformed, 1968), pp. 134-35.

39. Even John Dewey acknowledged that Christianity was a beneficent force in society: ". . . the church-going classes, those who have come under the influence of evangelical Christianity . . . form the backbone of philanthropic social interest, of social reform through political action, of pacifism, of popular education. They embody and express the spirit of kindly goodwill towards classes which are at an economic disadvantage and towards other nations. . . ." "The American Frontier," *The New Republic*, May 10, 1922. Quoted by Paul Johnson, *Modern Times* (New York: Harper & Row, 1983), p. 209.

40. "Following the lead of philosophical pragmatism, proponents of the Social Gospel held that the only test of truth was action. 'Religious morality,' said Walter Rauschenbusch, is 'the only thing God cares about.'" George M. Marsden, *Fundamentalism and American Culture: The Shaping of Twentieth Century Evangelicalism: 1870-1925* (New York: Oxford University Press, 1980), pp. 91-92.

private expressions of social concern."[41]

Once Christ is left out of the transformation of society, a new change-agent must arise. The state becomes the new civilization builder, and we're back to political pyramidism without the gospel. All that is wrong with the world must be cured by the omnipotent state. God is no longer seen as the Provider. Only the state can provide. The church is impotent. Wealth redistribution can effectively restructure society so that justice prevails. The poor will be better off. Our children will receive better education. The idea of a Christian civilization is abandoned.

The ideals of the Social Gospel are still with us. Christ is abandoned. Let's consider poverty. Here is what one Christian advocates:

> It seems obvious that private charitable institutions and local governments cannot handle today's poverty problems. It is even more evident that the churches cannot effectively alleviate the situation. . . . The federal government appears to be the only institution in the society which has the capability to act in a way that will eventually solve the problem of poverty. Why, then, does it not act to do so? According to [Michael] Harrington, "At precisely that moment in history where for the first time a people have the material ability to end poverty, they lack the will to do so." The will of the people is lacking![42]

Obviously, the "material ability to end poverty" is available. What is the best way to help the poor? Social gospel advocates believe that only the State can adequately distribute wealth. We're told that the "churches cannot effectively alleviate the situation." Why not? We're not told. Is it because the "will of the people is lacking"? Who or what will change the will of the people? The State must take an active role in imposing its will on the people.

---

41. James A. Speer, "The New Christian Right and its Parent Company: A Study in Political Contrasts," in *New Christian Politics*, eds., David G. Bromley and Anson Shupe (Macon, GA: Mercer University Press, 1984), p. 30.

42. Robert G. Clouse, et al., *The Cross and the Flag* (Carol Stream, IL: Creation House, 1972), p. 170.

Coercion is used to bring about a good social end.[43]

Is it any wonder that the Social Gospel was rejected? Unfortunately, the church was not ready with a solution to the changes that were taking place in the 19th century. An eschatological pessimism had emerged along with numerous attacks to the foundation of the Christian faith. The policies of the Social Gospel have come home to roost. Is the church ready, willing, and able to pick up the pieces to build a Christian civilization based on the sure foundation of God's Word? Or will the church retreat and allow the bankrupt ideology of humanism to win by default? If our generation does not do it, we will die in the wilderness. Our children's children will judge our efforts. Let us pray that they will not find us wanting.

Ecclesiocracy

Many people are confused over three terms, all of which are related: theocracy (the rule of God), *c*hurch (individual Christians who make up the body of Christ as distinct from the *C*hurch as a government), and *C*hurch (local jurisdictional and governing bodies as distinct from the *c*hurch comprised of individual Christians). We find that critics of dominion theology and Christian re-

---

43. Charles Murray has made it abundantly clear that the social policies of 1950 through 1980 have been a dismal failure. The poor actually have been hurt by "war on poverty" programs. See Charles Murray, *Losing Ground: American Social Policy, 1950-1980* (New York: Basic Books, 1984). Writing from a similar perspective, Walter E. Williams maintains "(1) that social benevolence is not a *necessary* condition for minority socioeconomic progress (2) that political power is not a necessary condition for economic advance." *The State Against Blacks* (New York: McGraw-Hill, 1982), p. 17.

Thomas Sowell makes the same point in *Ethnic America: A History* (New York: Basic Books, 1981) and *The Economics and Politics of Race: An Economic Perspective* (New York: William Morrow, 1983). David Chilton shows that a State-directed economy leads to tyranny and the subjection of the poor to a supposed benevolent State. Their eyes are turned to Washington for salvation while the saving effects of the gospel are repudiated. *Productive Christians in an Age of Guilt-Manipulators* (3rd rev. ed., Tyler, TX: Institute for Christian Economics, 1985). George Grant writes that the church can effectively alleviate the situation of poverty if biblical principles are consistently applied. *Bringing in the Sheaves: Transforming Poverty into Productivity* (Atlanta, GA: American Vision, 1985).

construction confuse the institutional Church with the church as the body of Christ made up of individual believers. The Church as a government has a very limited jurisdiction. It does not rule over the State, business, education, and the civil courts. But individual Christians, who are the body of Christ, the church, should exercise dominion at every level of society. They do not rule as an institution—a government—but as individuals. So then, when Christian reconstructionists talk about the church taking dominion, they do not mean the institutional Church. They have in mind individual Christians as they serve God faithfully in the areas where God has granted them a calling.

Recent articles have used the term "theocracy" to describe those who want to see Christians involved in every area of life. In their minds, a theocracy is what Iran is experiencing—religious leaders (Mullahs) who rule the nation. For these, "theocracy" places the Church over the State and every other institution. This is an improper definition. A more correct term to describe the Church ruling in society with religious leaders (ministers or priests) as the governmental officials would be "ecclesiocracy." Ecclesiocracy is made up of two Greek words: *ekklesia* (church) and *kratos* (power, strength, rule).

An ecclesiocracy means that the Church (a single local body or a network of Churches like a denomination) is the sole governing institution in society. There would be no jurisdictional separation between Church and State. We know of no group advocating an ecclesiocracy. A recent critic of Christian reconstruction makes the mistake of identifying his view of ecclesiocracy with a decentralized biblical moral order advocated by reconstructionists:

> [A] theocracy administered without the benefit of Jesus' physical presence begs for subjective reasoning based on the intellectual whims of man's faulty wisdom.
>
> Yes, the Holy Spirit can keep such a theocratic rule in line. But He won't if it exists apart from the will of God. And based on His Word, no such theocracy will be established by God without Jesus present. *Should any such theocracy be established, it would not be a true theocracy, but a totalitarian state of man's own making.*[44]

---

44. Albert James Dager, "Kingdom Theology: Part II," *Media Spotlight* (July-December 1986), p. 18. Emphasis added.

The author raises a number of unsupported points that need direct answers. First, we now have the Holy Spirit, who is God, operating in the hearts of Christians. God is now in the world. Second, subjective reasoning as a substitute for an objective standard is doomed to fail whether now or in the millennium. What standard will Jesus use in the millennium? Will His law be different from the Bible? What standard should Christians use now? If the Bible is good enough to show a sinner how to get to heaven, can we say that it is not adequate to build a civilization? (2 Tim. 3:16-17). Third, who proposes that dominion theology operates "apart from the will of God"? Reconstructionists insist that the will of God is being denied by those who say the kingdom of God is not now operating and that it cannot expand as Christians obey God and get to work to disciple the nations. God's will is that His kingdom come, that His will be done on *earth* as it is in heaven (Matt. 6:10).[45] Fourth, totalitarianism arises when all power is invested in an individual, a powerful elite, or a single government like the Church or the State. Christian reconstructionists hold to a very decentralized view of government. Government for them is more than the State. Government includes the family, Church, and various levels of civil jurisdiction. Rushdoony writes:

> [W]e do not equate government with the state. To do so is to-
> talitarianism. Government is first of all the self-government of
> man; it is also the family, the church, the school, our vocation,
> society and its institutions, and finally, civil government. Our
> problem today is that government is equated with the state, an
> anti-Christian view.[46]

---

45. All the petitions in the Lord's Prayer refer to earthly *present* benefits. Some of the aspects of the kingdom are that God provides our "daily bread," that He "forgives our debts," and that He "delivers us from temptation." Some want to maintain that the Lord's Prayer is a millennial prayer, that we should not pray it now. Of course, there is *no support* for this in Scripture. It is a kingdom prayer, and we are in the kingdom!

46. Response to Ed Dobson and Ed Hindson, "Apocalypse Now?: What Fundamentalists believe About the End of the World," *Policy Review*, Fall 1986, pp. 6, 17-22. Rushdoony's response appears in the Winter 1987 issue, p. 88. See DeMar, *Ruler of the Nations* (Atlanta, GA: American Vision, 1987), pp. 3-38 and *God and Government: A Biblical and Historical Study* (Atlanta, GA: American Vision, 1982).

What then is a "theocracy"? Like ecclesiocracy, theocracy is made up of two Greek words: *theos* (God) and *kratos* (power, strength, rule). Simply, it means the "rule of God." The word is not found in the Bible, although the concept is certainly present. The word was coined by Josephus, the Jewish historian for the Romans in the first century, and appears in his writings only once, in *Against Apion* 2.164-165.

"Theocracy" describes the rule of God over all His creation, including the angels, Christians and non-Christians, the family, local Church governments, business, economics, civil government at all levels, and every other conceivable created thing. Jesus is said to be "the ruler of the kings of the earth" (Rev. 1:5). The Triune God is described as "He who is the blessed and only Sovereign, the King of kings and Lord of lords" (1 Tim. 6:15).

Theocracy doesn't refer to the Church as God's sole government in society. In a theocracy, law is not administered by a priestly order as God's ministers and agents. While the Church is under the rule of God in a theocracy, the Church is not the sole agent of the theocracy. This would be an ecclesiocracy, a church-state. Theocracy is *God's* government in, of, and over the universe. It is synonymous with the kingdom of God. The Church is not the kingdom of God. The State is not the kingdom of God. The Church is under God's kingdom. The State too is under God's kingdom.

Lex, Rex

These concepts are not new. They are not unique to Christian reconstruction. The church was founded on these ideals. For centuries, Reformed churches lived by these concepts. Samuel Rutherford, author of *Lex, Rex* and participant in the drafting of the Westminster Confession of Faith (1646) wrote the following:

> Kings and magistrates are God's, and God's deputies and lieutenants upon earth (Psalm 82:1, 6, 7; Ex. 22:8; 4:16) . . . and their throne is the throne of God, 1 Chron. 22:10.[47]

---

47. Samuel Rutherford, *Lex, Rex, or, The Law and the Prince* (Harrisonburg, VA: Sprinkle Publications [1644] 1980), p. 4. Quoted in Gary North and David Chilton, "Apologetics and Strategy," in North, ed., *Tactics of Christian Resistance*. Christianity and Civilization, No. 3 (Tyler, TX: Geneva Ministries, 1983), p. 123.

Magistrates (not the king only but all the princes of the land) and judges are *to maintain religion by their commandments* (Deut. 1:16; 2 Chron. 1:2; Deut. 16:19; Eccles. 5:8; Hab. 1:4; Mic. 3:9; Zech. 7:9; Hos. 5:10-11), and to take care of religion.[48]

The king may not dispose of men as men, as he pleaseth; nor of laws as he pleaseth; nor governing men, killing or keeping alive, punishing and rewarding, as he pleaseth. . . . Therefore, *he hath the trust of life and religion, and hath both tables of the law in his custody.*[49]

This is the very office or official power which the King of kings hath given to all kings under him, and this is a power of the royal office of a king, *to govern for the Lord his Maker.*[50]

When men deny God's rule, they implement their own. So then, the question is not, "Theocracy or no theocracy?" but, rather, "*Whose* theocracy?" Theocracy is an "inescapable concept." The humanists who deny God's government over all of life work to implement man's government over all of life. Since man sees himself as god, we may legitimately say that humanism is "theocratic." The *Humanist Manifest II* states: "No deity will save us; we must save ourselves." How do humanists hope to save us? Well, they want humanist laws, humanist schools, humanist courts, a humanist civil government, and humanist economics. In fact, they want the world to be humanistic. And who do you suppose they believe ought to run the world? Humanists, of course.

Remember, theocracy is simply the "rule of God in the world." If you believe in the lordship of Jesus Christ then you believe in theocracy as defined above. This does not mean, however, that you believe in a Church-State or a State-Church.

A Forgotten Legacy

"The Battle of Britain," said Winston Churchill on the 18th of June 1940, "is about to begin. Upon this battle depends the survival of Christian civilization."[51] It would be difficult to learn how

---

48. *Ibid.*, p. 55.

49. *Ibid.*, p. 72; cf. p. 142.

50. *Ibid.*, p. 72; cf. p. 232.

51. John Baillie, *What is Christian Civilization?* (London: Oxford University Press, 1945), p. 5.

Winston Churchill would have defined "Christian civilization." But he did see something that made him connect Christianity with the preservation and advance of civilization. England had a long history of Christian influence that resulted in the advance of civilization around the world. America's earliest founders did not break from their English heritage. In fact, they sought to establish old England in *New* England.

> New England was founded consciously, and in no fit of absence of mind. Patriots seeking the glory of England first called the attention of their countrymen to these shores. Commercial enterprise made the first attempts at settlement. Puritanism overlaid these feeble beginnings by a proud self-governing commonwealth, dedicated to the glory of God and the happiness of a peculiar people. These three main streams in the life of old England, the patriotic, the commercial, and the religious, mingled their waters on every slope.[52]

The colonial colleges of Harvard (1636), William and Mary (1693), and Yale (1701) were founded upon the university system in England. Oxford and Cambridge were their models. There was a disproportionate number of university men who came to New England in relation to the population. This does not include those who received a comprehensive and sound classical education in the English grammar schools. Of course, the university graduates had a cultural impact far greater than their numbers. They were not concentrated in a single geographic area but were "scattered all over the country."[53] These were mainly clergymen who did not serve in the political ruling class. But their influence was great because they were nearly the exclusive source of information for the colonists.[54] William Bradford, John Cotton, John

---

52. Samuel Eliot Morison, *Builders of the Bay Colony* (Boston, MA: Northeastern University Press, [1930] 1981), p. 3.

53. Samuel Eliot Morison, *The Intellectual Life of Colonial New England* (2nd ed.; Ithaca, NY: Cornell University Press, [1956] 1965), p. 18.

54. Harry S. Stout, *The New England Soul* (New York: Oxford University Press, 1986). See "When God Had No Competition," *Newsweek* (October 20, 1986), p. 23.

Wilson, Thomas Hooker, and John Eliot, who entered the University of Cambridge at fourteen, were educated in old England.

> The University of Cambridge as they knew it, not as it has since become, was the standard which the New England puritans attempted, however imperfectly, to attain. . . . And the intellectual life of Cambridge set the pace for the intellectual life of New England.
>
> The English universities, in 1630 as in 1230, were regarded primarily as feeders to the church. Every holder of a college fellowship had to be in holy orders, the ambitious young men looked forward to becoming prelates; most of the students who took degrees intended to be clergymen.[55]

Of course, Churchill could have had in mind the anti-Christian practices of Adolf Hitler and how they compared to English society. Nazism was antithetical to an English society that was nurtured on the Christian world view. Nazi Germany was vehemently opposed to Christianity. Under the leadership of Alfred Rosenberg, an outspoken pagan, "the Nazi regime intended eventually to destroy Christianity in Germany, if it could, and substitute the old paganism of the early tribal Germanic gods and the new paganism of the Nazi extremists. As Bormann, one of the men closest to Hitler, said publicly in 1941, 'National Socialism and Christianity are irreconcilable.' "[56] William L. Shirer would

---

55. Morison, *The Intellectual Life of Colonial New England*, p. 20.

56. William L. Shirer, *The Rise and Fall of the Third Reich* (New York: Simon and Schuster, 1960), p. 240. "By the end of 1933, a sizeable minority of Protestant clergymen, convinced that the regime's support of the German Christians would corrupt pure Lutheran doctrine, had become critical of National Socialism. Within a few months these pastors had met together and formed the Confessing Church (*Bekennende Kirche*).

"The way of the Confessing Church was by no means easy. The regime arrested leaders, closed special pastoral training centers, conscripted a disproportionately large number of members, and made public attacks through the news media. . . .

"An excellent, and a generally neglected source, for examining the activities of the churches in Germany during the war is the reports of the *Sicherheitsdienst* (S.D.), the internal intelligence agency of the S.S. . . .

"Ordinarily, the S.D. was precise in designating religious groups and individ-

later write that "what Hitler envisioned for the German Christians [was] the utter suppression of their religion."[57]

In comparison, English society showed no militaristic intention to dominate the world. Churchill simply compared the fruit of each society and the ideology that brought them into being. For England, it was Christianity. For Nazi Germany, still Christian in form and certainly with a rich Christian tradition, it was tyranny.

Is there such a thing as a "Christian civilization"? Winston Churchill thought so. Was there ever a time when to talk about civilization one had to describe it as Christian? As we have seen, there was. Of course, there are other questions. Does the Bible give the command that a Christian civilization should be built? This is the fundamental question. Without a biblical mandate there really is no need to talk about the necessity of building a Christian civilization.[58] Is the development of a Christian civilization a natural development of Christianity itself, that is, should we expect a Christian civilization to mature if Christians are only consistent with the Word of God at a personal level? What would a Christian civilization look like? Would a Christian civilization be built by coercion, either ecclesiastical or statist, or would it be

---

ual clergymen. Catholics are mentioned far more often than any other group. Protestants receive some attention, but the Confessing Church is specifically mentioned only once. What is said of the free churches and sects is negligible. Sometimes the agents wrote simply of 'the church' or 'confessional circles.' *Whatever the designation, the S.D. clearly regarded organized Christianity as one of the major obstacles to the establishment of a truly totalitarian state. Implicit or explicit in all S.D. reports on religious affairs was the belief that the regime's most implacable internal enemy was growing stronger as the war progressed."* Donald D. Wall, "The Lutheran Response to the Hitler Regime in Germany," ed., Robert D. Linder, *God and Caesar: Case Studies in the Relationship Between Christianity and the State* (Longview, TX: The Conference on Faith and History, 1971), pp. 86-88.

57. William L. Shirer, *The Nightmare Years: 1930-1940* (New York: Little, Brown and Company, 1984), p. 156.

58. Of course, one could suppose that if there is no prohibition, then Christians are free to build any type of civilization they desire. It seems, however, that for many people any type of civilization can be built *except* a Christian civilization. This is the ploy of modern humanism. If a law comes from the Bible then it is expressly religious and therefore it cannot be implemented into our present "pluralistic" legal system.

built outside the parameters of established political power structures and yet still impact them?[59]

For some a Christian civilization is possible only with the return of Jesus Christ to earth to set up a kingdom and rule from Jerusalem. It is certainly proper to define this as a "Christian civilization," but it avoids the issue of how Christians should define civilization prior to His return. Of course, it says nothing about what Christians ought to do in the meantime. For some, the responsibility in this life for building anything is non-existent. But this is not the historical view of the church. Christians in the earliest centuries used the gospel and the law of God to engage a collapsing classical culture. The Christian message

came into Classical Civilization from Semitic society. In its origin it was a this-worldly religion, believing that the world and the flesh were basically good, or at least filled with good potentialities, because both were made by God; the body was made in the image of God; God became man in this world with a human body, to save men as individuals, and to establish "Peace on earth.". . .

This optimistic, "this-worldly" religion was taken into Classical Civilization at a time when the philosophic outlook of that society was quite incompatible with the religious outlook of

---

59. "In Rome, in Byzantium, and in Russia, law was regarded as an enactment of a supreme power. In the West, when no supreme power existed, it was discovered that law still existed as the body of rules which govern social life. Thus law was found by observation in the West, not enacted by autocracy as in the East. This meant that authority was established by law and under the law in the West, while authority was established by power and above the law in the East. The West felt that the rules of economic life were found and not enacted; that individuals had rights independent of, and even opposed to, public authority; that groups could exist, as the Church existed, by right and not by privilege, and without the need to have any charter of incorporation entitling them to exist as a group or act as a group; that groups or individuals could own property as a right and not as a privilege and that such property could not be taken by force but must be taken by established process of law. It was emphasized in the West that the way a thing was done was more important than what was done, while in the East what was done was far more significant than the way in which it was done." Carroll Quigley, *Tragedy and Hope: A History of the World in Our Time* (New York: Macmillan, 1965), p. 83.

Christianity. The Classical philosophical outlook, which we might call Neoplatonic, was derived from the teachings of Persian Zoroastrianism, Pythagorean rationalism, and Platonism. It was dualistic, dividing the universe into two *opposed* worlds, the world of matter and flesh and the world of spirit and ideas. The former world was changeable, unknowable, illusionary, and evil; the latter world was eternal, knowable, real, and good. . . .

Thus the Classical world into which Christianity came about A.D. 60 believed that the world and the body were unreal, unknowable, corrupt, and hopeless and that no truth or success could be found by the use of the body, the senses, or matter. A small minority, derived from Democritus and the early Ionian scientists through Aristotle, Epicurus, and Lucretius, rejected the Platonic dualism, preferring materialism as an explanation of reality. These materialists were equally incompatible with the new Christian religion. Moreover, even the ordinary citizen of Rome had an outlook whose implications were not compatible with the Christian religion.[60]

Times have not changed. We have the same gospel and the same powerful Holy Spirit. Will we adopt the disintegrating world view of humanism or will we work to replace its rotting corpse? Our early Christian brethren recognized the opportunity when they saw it. They changed Western civilization for the better. It is our turn to learn by their example without repeating their mistakes.

Conclusion

Christians are becoming more and more consistent with their theological positions. As we should expect, a shakeup is in the making. As the hard questions begin to surface, the viability of one's theological stance becomes evident. Can your theology really an-

---

60. *Ibid.*, pp. 83-84. Much of the today's church has adopted the religion of Classical Civilization: (1) Christianity is thought of as an exclusively otherworldly religion; (2) the body is often depreciated; (3) the present world is "evil" and is in the grip of the devil; (4) much of the church is nostalgic, looking for ethical absolutes in "traditional values" rather than in the absolutes of biblical law.

swer the tough questions? We are being asked to choose a number of theological options.

The first is retreatism. A number of prominent Christian leaders are calling on the people of God to forget their earthly future. There's no hope, they say. For generations, self-proclaimed prophets of gloom and doom have predicted the end of the world "in their generation." History has proved them wrong.

Another ideological group would like to build for the future. New Agers, some conservative groups, and a number of Christian leaders have emphasized the future dimension of civilization building. They all have one thing in common: Natural law is the standard by which we ought to build. Can natural law be the bridge that will unite us all? We do not think so. Unfortunately, many Christians are getting themselves trapped by the advocates of a Natural Law ethic. They are being told that it has a rich Christian history. As usually happens, the Bible becomes a second-class standard.

It's time that Christians begin to understand what's at stake. There is a battle going on. In many cases, the fire is coming from within the camp. Millions of Christians say they believe the Bible is the word of God, inerrant and infallible. But when it comes to using the Bible as a blueprint for living, they begin to take out their scissors. You've heard the objections:

- The Old Testament doesn't apply in the church age.
- You can't put a non-Christian under Biblical law.
- Since the Christian is under grace, the law is irrelevant.

These objections are myths. Just try to understand the New Testament without the Old Testament. Paul writes that pastors are to be paid, and he supports this from an obscure verse from the Old Testament: "For the Scripture says, 'You shall not muzzle the ox while he is threshing,' and 'The laborer is worthy of his wages'" (1 Tim. 5:18; cf. Deut. 25:4; Lev. 19:13).

Read what the Bible says about the alien in Israel. The alien was required to keep the law just like the covenant-bound Israelite: "There shall be one standard for you; it shall be for the stranger as well as the native, for I am the LORD your God" (Lev. 24:22; cf. Ex. 12:49). The alien was given "equal protection under the law." Aliens could acquire property and accumulate wealth (Lev. 25:47). They were protected from wrong-doing and treated like the "native" Israelite (Lev. 19:33-34). A native-born Israelite could "not wrong a stranger or oppress him" (Ex. 22:21; 23:9). If the alien was bound to keep the law of God, then the law of God was the standard for protecting him against injustice as well (Deut. 1:16; cf. 24:16; 27:19). John the Baptist saw no restriction attached to him when he confronted King Herod and his adulterous relationship with Herodias, the wife of his brother Philip: "For John had been saying to Herod, 'It is not lawful for you to have your brother's wife'" (Mark 6:18; cf. Ex. 20:14).

At a time when the world is looking for firm ground, Christians should be ready, willing, and able to turn people to the Bible as the blueprint by which we can build a Christian civilization.

CONCLUSION

Christianity is a revolutionary religion. This does not mean that Christianity advocates violence or rebellion against authority. Christianity is revolutionary in the most profound and basic sense, because it destroys idols from the inside out, because it brings idols, like Dagon of the Philistines, to fall on their faces before the Living Word. As Herbert Schlossberg has written, Christianity's

> continual willingness to stand against culturally approved evil in the name of Christ . . . makes of the church a revolutionary force. Christian revolution begins with the individual and has its concrete effect in the culture. Whether or not it exercises control, it always takes its stand with the eternal requirements of God against the idolatrous attractions of the moment. . . . All orders, old and new, are subject to the same eternal law that the church serves, and therefore are judged by the same standard.[1]

This is the kind of Christian revolution that we have been defending throughout this book. It is this kind of revolution that Dave Hunt and others believe to be either impossible or undesirable. But we believe that this is precisely what the Lord has called us to.

Eschatology and Orthodoxy

We have tried to show that Dave Hunt's insinuations about "Christian reconstruction" are entirely unfounded. The distinctive

---

1. Schlossberg, *Idols for Destruction: Christian faith and its Confrontation with American Culture* (Nashville, TN: Thomas Nelson, 1983), p. 325.

333

positions of these writers have deep roots in the history of the church, particularly in American church history. Those who advocate these positions are far from being New Age sympathizers. Most importantly, we have tried to show that these teachings are based on the Bible.

The most visible issue between Mr. Hunt and "reconstructionists" is eschatology. "Reconstructionists" are postmillennialists; that is, they believe that the gospel of Christ will triumph in history over all idolatries, and that men and societies will be transformed as the gospel penetrates the world. Mr. Hunt is a premillennialist. He believes that Christ will return soon, and that He will not defeat His enemies in history. Instead, Hunt believes that Christ will come to rescue His people from destruction, and reign on earth for a thousand years. Only after the millennium ends (in failure) will the kingdom be established in any tangible way. Though Hunt believes that Christ presently reigns in the hearts of Christians, He will establish the kingdom only in the new heavens and new earth in which righteousness dwells.

We have written this book to clarify the debate. Mr. Hunt's books have raised questions in many people's minds about the orthodoxy of some "dominion" teachers. Whether or not Hunt intended to raise such questions, we do not know. Whatever his intentions, his books have had that effect. Other premillennial writers, David Wilkerson in particular, have been more explicit, calling the "reconstructionist" position on the timing of Christ's return the "final apostasy."[2]

As we have stressed throughout this book, millennial positions have never been tests of orthodoxy. Certain doctrines of eschatology—the Second Coming, the resurrection of the dead, and the life everlasting—have been included in the creeds, but throughout the history of the church, various millennial positions have coexisted within Christ's church. Christians have always differed on the timing of Christ's return. While we believe that one's millennial position is important, and while we should not be indifferent

---

2. *Omega-Letter* 2 (April 1987), p. 1.

to these differences, we do not label Hunt, Wilkerson, Jimmy Swaggart, Peter Lalonde, Hal Lindsey, or anyone else a heretic simply because he has a different view of the details of eschatology. We consider these men to be brothers in the Lord, because, as Richard B. Gaffin, Jr., has put it, what we share is more important than what divides us: We share Christ, and Christ is not divided.[3]

There are some teachers, prominent in certain charismatic circles, whose teaching is contrary to creedal orthodoxy. There are some teachers, as we have already noted, whose statements about the Christian's status in Christ seem to violate central elements of Christianity. These men should be called to account, as Hunt and others have done. But what happens now? What do Christian churches do when teachers are charged with heresy?

In the case of those whose teaching is contrary to creedal orthodoxy, we think that the debate needs to move beyond a battle of books or public debates on radio and television. It is important, first, for critics of these teachers to determine precisely what they mean. If the problem is *merely* semantic, the charismatic teachers will gladly drop confusing terms. If the problem is doctrinal, the debate should move into the process that Jesus outlined in Matthew 18. The teachers in question should be admonished individually. If they do not repent, they should be admonished by a small delegation. If they continue in their heresy, a church trial should follow. If a church court finds them guilty of heresy, they should be dealt with accordingly. In other words, some kind of judicial process should ensue.

But it is important to make a distinction between these charismatic "kingdom theologians" and non-charismatic "Christian reconstructionists." Neither Hunt nor anyone else has shown that "reconstructionists" have abandoned a single article of the creeds. On the contrary, "Christian reconstructionists" are devoted champions of creedal orthodoxy. Hunt has noted, correctly, that "recon-

---

3. Lectures on "Doctrine of the Word of God," Westminster Theological Seminary, Fall 1984.

structionists" do not share his view of the millennium. But this
issue is not a matter of heresy, but of doctrinal difference within
the orthodox faith. Thus, our plea is that Hunt and others refrain
from labeling "Christian reconstructionists" as heretics or apos-
tates, or, even unintentionally, implying that this is the case. Only
then will it be possible to discuss these issues, and even disagree,
in the loving manner that should characterize members of the
One Body.

In short, we are calling on Dave Hunt, David Wilkerson, Jimmy
Swaggart, Earl Paulk, Robert Tilton, Gary North, R. J. Rushdoony, and everyone else involved in this debate to line up with
the creeds of Christ's church. This must be the starting point of
any discussion, because only in this way can borderline between
heresy and orthodoxy be determined.

Utopian Dream or Historical Reality?

We do not wish to respond to charges and insinuations of
heresy and complicity with the New Age Movement by making
unfounded counter-charges of our own. Still, we believe that it is
enormously important for Christians like Mr. Hunt, who are not
inclined to work for changes in modern society, to ask whether
they themselves might be aiding New Age and other forms of humanism. Herbert Schlossberg writes:

> Christians who resist acknowledging any close correspond-
> ence between their faith and the direction that history takes
> strangely echo the position taken by the reigning humanist estab-
> lishment. As Richard Neuhaus has pointed out, their stand is
> precisely that of the modern secularists who wish to banish Chris-
> tian ideas from influencing public policy. This understanding of
> Christian action aids its enemies by reinforcing the notion of the
> supposed irrelevance of Christian faith.[4]

By (perhaps unintentionally) encouraging Christians to abandon

---

4. Schlossberg, *Idols for Destruction*, p. 324.

cultural involvement, Hunt has aided the humanists who want precisely the same thing.

This danger is not of merely theoretical importance. The Russian Orthodox Church, for example, has found itself in precisely this position within the Soviet regime. The Russian church faces external pressures that cannot be imagined by Americans. One would think that these pressures would be strongly resisted by Christian leaders. On the contrary, as Soviet dissident Evgeny Barabanov has noted, the surprising fact is that "the external limitations on the life of the [Russian] Church correspond to the secret desires of many ecclesiastics."[5] Russian churchmen have adopted the belief that "the Mass itself *is* Christianity," and accept a view of the church in which "there is of course no room for the problems of the Christianization of Russia."[6] For many Russian Christians, Christianity has been reduced "from being a teaching about the new *life* to a mere caring for one's own soul. As a result of this, the earthly aspect of life and the whole structure of social relations turned out to be empty and immune to the influence of the truth."[7] Instead of balancing heavenly and earthly concerns, "heavenward aspirations often went hand in hand with execration of the earth."[8] In other words, in the Soviet Union, the reduction of Christianity has gone hand in hand with the advance of totalitarianism.

Not only have "reconstructionists" been called theological upstarts, they have also been labeled utopians. It would take another volume fully to refute this charge. Another quotation from Herbert Schlossberg's superb *Idols for Destruction* must suffice for the moment:

> To expect a transformation of society that results from changed people is not an idealistic hope that can never come to pass; it is a

---

5. Barabanov, "The Schism between the Church and the World," in *From Under the Rubble*, Alexander Solzhenitsyn, et al. (Boston: Little, Brown and Company, [1974] 1975), p. 179. This entire essay is a moving and profound discussion of the dangers of the reduction of Christianity, and as such it is highly recommended.

6. *Ibid.*, pp. 179-180.

7. *Ibid.*, p. 181.

8. *Ibid.*, p. 182.

matter of historical record. In the midst of the nature worship of
the second millennium before Christ, Israel introduced the dyna-
mism of a people who worshiped the God beyond nature. As long
as Israel maintained the distinctiveness of this heritage, it alone
among its neighbors built a society based on justice, one that recognized that there was an objectively understood ethic beyond
the exigencies of power. Much later the new Christian church in-
fused the Mediterranean world with the same vision. This social
transformation made Western civilization what it was. Love became the central idea in the dominant ethic, so much so that idolatry adopted its language and actions and was thereby made tol-
erable for a time.[9]

Far from being utopian, we are simply urging the church to do
what it has done in many ages and in many nations.

Premillennial Christian Reconstruction

Though we have stressed the eschatological issue in this book,
this is really on the surface of a deeper issue. If eschatology were
the only or even the central issue, we would not find, as we do,
some premillennial writers adopting a "Christian reconstruction"
agenda. David Schnittger, for example, has recently written a
small book entitled, *Christian Reconstruction from a Pretribulational
Perspective*, distributed by the Southwest Radio Church of Oklahoma City. Schnittger rejects postmillennialism because "it is built
upon a figurative system of interpretation in great areas of Bible
prophecy."[10] But he adds

> . . . apart from this defect, I find the term Christian reconstruc-
> tion to be a valid one; and certainly this concept is not the exclu-
> sive property of postmillennialists. The Bible *does* apply to all of
> life. Christ *is* Lord of all the earth, and it *is* a valid task of all
> Bible-believing Christians to seek to bring every area of personal
> and corporate life into obedience to the Word of God. Rather

---

9. Schlossberg, *Idols for Destruction*, p. 325.
10. David Schnittger, *Christian Reconstruction from a Pretribulational Perspective*
(Oklahoma City, OK: Southwest Radio Church, 1986), p. 9.

than desert a good concept simply because it is misused, we should seek to be reconstructionists within the biblical [i.e., premillennial] eschatological framework.[11]

Schnittger supports his conclusions by arguing that the phrase "last days" does not refer merely to the end of the world. Rather he believes the events of the "last days" are "general conditions that characterize the entire church age."[12] Though evil will not be progressively eradicated, there is still "the possibility of a progressive growth in strength and influence of the true church."[13] He even presents statistics to show how the church has grown through the centuries. His interpretations of the parables of Matthew 13 are very much the same as our interpretations.[14]

From this theological basis, Schnittger outlines a "Christian Reconstruction Agenda for the End of the Twentieth Century," including pro-life activism, the building of strong Christian homes, Christian schools, and Christian involvement in law and politics.[15] In addition to this kind of activism, he emphasizes that Christians should always be at work building strong and loving churches, supporting evangelism and missions, and engaging in individual discipleship.[16]

Here is a *pre*tribulation premillennialist who thinks that Christians need to be involved in Christian reconstruction. In eschatology, he believes that Christ will come to rapture His saints *before* the tribulation begins. In other words, Christ's people will escape the worst period of history. It would seem that Christians have little reason to be concerned about the state of the world; after all, they will escape the terrors of the tribulation. Moreover, he believes that this tribulation period is inevitable. The most logical question in the world seems to be, "Why polish brass on a sinking ship?" Yet, Schnittger criticizes the pessimism of most pretrib pre-

---

11. *Idem.*
12. *Ibid.*, pp. 10-12.
13. *Idem.*
14. *Ibid.*, pp. 12-14.
15. *Ibid.*, chapter 4.
16. *Ibid.*, p. 24.

millennialists, and encourages them to get involved.

Thus, we have at least one premillennialist writer who is also a "Christian reconstructionist," and there may well be more like Mr. Schnittger. When we recognize this fact, it becomes clear that the fundamental and distinctive element of "Christian reconstruction" is not eschatology. It is perhaps difficult to sustain a "reconstructionist" position without a long-term time frame. Yet, Schnittger's book indicates that it is at least possible for Christians to be both premillennial and "reconstructionist."

The Centrality of Ethics

The millennial issue, then, is not the deepest issue. The deepest issue is ethics. David Schnittger is a Christian "reconstructionist" because he believes that Christians should live in obedience to the Word of God in every area of life. He advocates "Christian reconstruction" because he realizes that Christ is Lord and King of all things. We believe he is mistaken in one fundamental point. God is pleased with obedience, and He demonstrates His pleasure by blessing His faithful people. Thus, as Christians live in obedience to the Word, they will prosper. A community of faithful Christians will also prosper: "Righteousness exalts a nation" (Prov. 14:34; cf. Deut. 28).[17] A reliance on

---

17. We are not, however, teaching a "prosperity gospel." Suffering is an inevitable part of the Christian life, and we repudiate the current tendency to emphasize self-fulfillment rather than self-denial. If we are to follow Christ, we must, as He did, deny ourselves for the benefit of others, and for the advancement of His kingdom. Job was a "perfect" man, yet suffered grievous trials. Nehemiah and his fellow workers were faithful, but suffered constant persecution at the hands of Sanballat and Tobiah. Christians are *daily* to take up their cross to follow the Lord. We are to count it as joy when we encounter trials, and we exult in our tribulations.

On the other hand, the Bible also teaches that faithful men and women will enjoy success. Both the books of Leviticus and Deuteronomy contain chapters that promise prosperity to righteous nations (Lev. 26; Deut. 28). The righteous man of Psalm 1 prospers in everything he sets his hand to do. The Proverbs are replete with promises that righteousness leads to contentment and success.

Now, which of these should we teach? Obviously, if we are Christians, we

biblical ethics leads to an optimistic eschatology. Aside from this flaw, however, Schnittger is on the right track.

The reason why Hunt and others object to "Christian reconstruction" is not merely that they have a different eschatological position. A more significant underlying reason is that "reconstructionists" advocate the application of biblical law to every area of life.[18] Hunt himself, to his credit, emphasizes obedience:

> Being a Christian does not come about through superficial belief in the existence of a historical Person named Jesus of Nazareth who did miracles and taught sublime truths. It involves personally receiving Him into one's heart and life as Savior and Lord and believing that He died for one's sins and rose from the dead. This is the gospel (good news) which, if truly believed, will transform one's life. Genuine faith is based upon *understanding* and results in *obedience*. Acts 6:7 tells us that a "great company of the priests were *obedient* to the faith." Paul preached *"obedience* to the faith among all nations" (Romans 1:5; 16:26) and warned of the judgment that would one day come upon all who *"know* not

---

cannot choose what we want to teach from Scripture. We must teach everything that Scripture teaches. These two strains of biblical teaching seem contradictory to us, but they are not. We can reconcile these two emphases in a variety of ways. First, biblical prosperity, as Hunt often points out, is not the same as worldly prosperity. A Christian can be successful without being considered successful by the world. Success in the Christian life is not judged by our economic or social status, but by our holiness, by how pleasing we are to the Lord. Second, we gain success through suffering, after the pattern of our Lord (cf. Phil. 2). Thus, when we say that God's people prosper, we are not adopting a worldly perspective. We are simply trying to live and think by every word that proceeds from the mouth of the Lord.

18. We cannot enter fully into this discussion here, but allow us to make our position a bit clearer. We believe that the Bible applies to all of life. We also believe that it is impossible to understand any area of life or thought properly apart from the special revelation of Scripture. Finally, we believe that the whole Bible is relevant to us in the New Covenant. As Rev. Ted Lester, pastor of Cherokee Presbyterian Church, puts it, we are not Old Covenant Christians, nor are we New Testament Christians; rather, we are New Covenant and whole-Bible Christians. This does not mean that everything in the Old Testament applies in the same way as it did under the Old Covenant. We do not even profess to understand *how* the Old Testament applies in every instance. We do insist that, in every sphere of individual and corporate life, the Bible must be the primary authority.

God and that *obey* not the gospel of our Lord Jesus Christ"
(2 Thessalonians 1:8).[19]

Hunt insists, "If we are to be biblical Christians, God's Word must
be our guide in all we say and do, no matter how unpopular that
makes us."[20]

We agree wholeheartedly with that statement. We cannot
stress too strongly our agreement with Hunt's principle. As Christians, we are governed by Scripture in every area of life and
thought. Though we are in agreement with Hunt on this principle, he is inconsistent, we believe, in applying it. In an interview
with Peter Waldron, for example, Hunt said that, if he were to become a congressman, he could not enforce his Christian beliefs,
because he would have to represent people who did not share
those beliefs. He would witness to his colleagues, but he would
not "impose" Christian morality on a non-Christian populace.[21]

In one sense, we agree with Hunt fully. We do not believe that
Christianity can be imposed from the top down. As we have
pointed out previously, we are not "political pyramidists." We believe that Christianity will transform society as people are transformed by the gospel. In another sense, all law is imposed morality. Every law is involved with ethics. The question is not ethical
law versus unethical law. The question is which ethical system will
provide the foundation for law. We believe that the Bible should
provide the moral foundations for law. There are, for example,
clear standards in Scripture for civil government. The Bible gives
the State authority to punish with the sword (Gen. 9; Rom. 13).
The State has the authority to punish murder and other crimes.
Hunt seems to agree in principle that the Bible should be the
foundation of civil law, yet when it comes to passing laws in congress, Hunt indicates that he would not impose biblical morality.

Given the biblical requirements for the State, what would

---

19. Hunt, *Beyond Seduction: A Return to Biblical Christianity* (Eugene, OR:
Harvest House, 1987), p. 259.

20. *Ibid.*, p. 249.

21. Interview with Dave Hunt, "Contact America," August 12, 1987.

"obedience" mean for a congressman? What would Congressman Hunt, for example, do about abortion? Would he work for legislation to change the existing laws? What if the majority of Americans liked abortion? Would Hunt "impose" a law against murdering unborn children on an unwilling populace? What about homosexuality? Would Congressman Hunt work to prohibit this perversion that is explicitly condemned in Scripture? What if he were representing San Francisco? Would he represent his constituency by working for gay rights?

We must emphasize again that we are not obsessed with the political sphere. Christians should promote good politics because, to paraphrase C. S. Lewis, there is bad politics all around us. But politics is not the answer to our cultural dilemmas. We focus on Hunt's view of politics because it illustrates the centrality of ethics, and indicates, we think, his confusion about Christian ethics in general. Hunt's comments on law and morality illustrate that he does not consistently apply his basic, very sound premise about the place of obedience to the Bible in the Christian's life.

We admit that there are many complexities and ambiguities in political life. But we believe that the issues we have referred to and many others finally come down to simple obedience to the Lord. We cannot imagine a Christian justification for legalized abortion on demand, nor for legitimized sodomy. We believe that Hunt shares our opinions on these issues. The problem is implementing biblical principles in society. Obedience is, for Hunt, an essential part of the Christian life. Yet, he tends to restrict the realm of obedience to the personal and individual sphere. Witnessing to other Congressmen would be a fine thing to do. It is the most important thing Congressman Hunt could do. But we suspect that Congressman Hunt would also seek to change the abortion laws. We suspect that he would do what he could to limit homosexual activity, and to prevent it from being an accepted, legal "life-style." Such activity would be consistent with Hunt's principle of obedience. But it would be inconsistent with Hunt's public statements about morality and politics. We hope that Hunt would be consistent to his principle.

Hunt is not opposed to the application of the Bible, but he tends to apply it within certain limited areas of life. We believe that it would be more consistent with his own strong and commendable emphasis on obedience for Hunt to insist that obedience extends to every area of life. And, we believe that his inconsistency on this point accounts for much of his opposition to "dominion" Christianity.

Conclusion

Christianity has triumphed over idolatry before, and it can do so again. Christianity has brought peace to warring tribes, transformed barbarians into champions of justice and mercy, brigands into servants of the poor, and rapists into defenders of women. But a triumphant Christianity must be a complete Christianity. We cannot take every thought captive without adequate ammunition. We cannot fight giants and dragons with a pocket-knife; we must wield a double-edged sword. We cannot satisfy the world's hunger with a diet of milk; men and women must have bread and meat. If we are to fill the earth with the knowledge of the Lord, we must have a full message. If we are to transform the whole world through the gospel of Christ, we must preach the whole gospel. If we are to reduce the world to the lordship of Jesus, we must be done with the reduction of Christianity.

Appendix A

THE NICENE CREED[1]

I believe in one God the Father Almighty, Maker of heaven and earth, And of all things visible and invisible:

And in one Lord Jesus Christ, the only-begotten Son of God; Begotten of His Father before all worlds, God of God, Light of Light, Very God of Very God; Begotten, not made; Being of one substance with the Father; by whom all things were made: Who for us men and for our salvation came down from heaven, And was incarnate by the Holy Ghost of the Virgin Mary, And was made man: And was crucified also for us under Pontius Pilate; He suffered and was buried: And the third day he rose again according to the Scriptures: And ascended into heaven, And sitteth on the right hand of the Father: And he shall come again, with glory, to judge both the quick and the dead; Whose kingdom shall have no end.

And I believe in the Holy Ghost, the Lord and Giver of Life, Who proceedeth from the Father and the Son; Who with the Father and the Son together is worshipped and glorified; Who spake by the Prophets: And I believe one Catholic and Apostolic Church: I acknowledge one Baptism for the remission of sins: And I look for the Resurrection of the dead: And the Life of the world to come. Amen.

---

1. Quoted in R. J. Rushdoony, *The Foundations of Social Order* (Fairfax, VA: Thoburn Press, [1968] 1978), p. 16. The Western version of the creed is quoted here.

Appendix B

WESTMINSTER CONFESSION OF FAITH, CHAPTERS XXXII-XXXIII[1]

CHAPTER XXXII
Of the State of Men after Death, and of the Resurrection of the Dead

I. The bodies of men, after death, return to dust, and see corruption: but their souls, which neither die nor sleep, having an immortal subsistence, immediately return to God who gave them: the souls of the righteous, being then made perfect in holiness, are received into the highest heavens, where they behold the face of God, in light and glory, waiting for the full redemption of their bodies. And the souls of the wicked are cast into hell, where they remain in torments and utter darkness, reserved to the judgment of the great day. Beside these two places, for souls separated from their bodies, the Scripture acknowledgeth none.

II. At the last day, such as are found alive shall not die, but be changed: and all the dead shall be raised up, with the selfsame bodies, and none other (although with different qualities), which shall be united again to their souls forever.

III. The bodies of the unjust shall, by the power of Christ, be raised to dishonor: the bodies of the just, by his Spirit, unto honor; and be made conformable to his own glorious body.

---

1. The Westminster Standards (Philadelphia, PA: Great Commission Publications, n.d.), pp. 32-33. Available from Great Commission Publications, 7401 Old York Road, Philadelphia, PA, 19126.

CHAPTER XXXIII
Of the Last Judgment

I. God hath appointed a day, wherein he will judge the world, in righteousness, by Jesus Christ, to whom all power and judgment is given of the Father. In which day, not only the apostate angels shall be judged, but likewise all persons that have lived upon earth shall appear before the tribunal of Christ, to give an account of their thoughts, words, and deeds; and to receive according to what they have done in the body, whether good or evil.

II. The end of God's appointing this day is for the manifestation of the glory of his mercy, in the eternal salvation of the elect; and of his justice, in the damnation of the reprobate, who are wicked and disobedient. For then shall the righteous go into everlasting life, and receive that fulness of joy and refreshing, which shall come from the presence of the Lord; but the wicked who know not God, and obey not the gospel of Jesus Christ, shall be cast into eternal torments, and be punished with everlasting destruction from the presence of the Lord, and from the glory of his power.

III. As Christ would have us to be certainly persuaded that there shall be a day of judgment, both to deter all men from sin; and for the greater consolation of the godly in their adversity: so will he have that day unknown to men, that they may shake off all carnal security, and be always watchful, because they know not at what hour the Lord will come; and may be ever prepared to say, Come Lord Jesus, come quickly, Amen.

Appendix C

THE ATHANASIAN CREED[1]

1. Whosoever will be saved: before all things it is necessary that he hold the Catholic Faith:

2. Which Faith except every one do keep whole and undefiled: without doubt he shall perish everlastingly.

3. And the Catholic Faith is this: That we worship one God in Trinity, and Trinity in Unity;

4. Neither confounding the Persons: nor dividing the Substance [Essence].

5. For there is one Person of the Father: another of the Son: and another of the Holy Ghost.

6. But the Godhead of the Father, of the Son, and of the Holy Ghost, is all one: the Glory equal, the Majesty coeternal.

7. Such as the Father is: such is the Son: and such is the Holy Ghost.

8. The Father uncreate [uncreated]: the Son uncreate [uncreated]: and the Holy Ghost uncreate [uncreated].

9. The Father incomprehensible [unlimited]: the Son incomprehensible [unlimited]: and the Holy Ghost incomprehensible [unlimited, or infinite].

10. The Father eternal: the Son eternal: and the Holy Ghost eternal.

11. And yet they are not three eternals: but one eternal.

12. As also there are not three uncreated: nor three incompre-

---

1. Source: Phillip Schaff, *The Creeds of Christendom*, 3 vols. (Grand Rapids, MI: Baker [1931] 1983), vol. 3, pp. 66-70. The explanatory words in brackets were added by Dr. Schaff.

hensibles [infinites], but one uncreated: and one incomprehensible [infinite].

13. So likewise the Father is Almighty: the Son Almighty: and the Holy Ghost Almighty.

14. And yet they are not three Almighties: but one Almighty.

15. So the Father is God: the Son is God: and the Holy Ghost is God.

16. And yet they are not three Gods: but one God.

17. So likewise the Father is Lord: the Son Lord: and the Holy Ghost Lord.

18. And yet not three Lords: but one Lord.

19. For like as we are compelled by the Christian verity: to acknowledge every Person by himself to be God and Lord:

20. So are we forbidden by the Catholic Religion: to say, There be [are] three Gods, or three Lords.

21. The Father is made of none: neither created, nor begotten.

22. The Son is of the Father alone: not made, nor created: but begotten.

23. The Holy Ghost is of the Father and of the Son: neither made, nor created, nor begotten: but proceeding.

24. So there is one Father, not three Fathers: one Son, not three Sons: one Holy Ghost, not three Holy Ghosts.

25. And in this Trinity none is afore, or after another: none is greater, or less than another [there is nothing before, or after: nothing greater or less].

26. But the whole three Persons are coeternal, and coequal.

27. So that in all things, as aforesaid: the Unity in Trinity, and the Trinity in Unity, is to be worshiped.

28. He therefore that will be saved, must [let him] thus think of the Trinity.

* * * * *

29. Furthermore it is necessary to everlasting salvation: that he also believe rightly [faithfully] the Incarnation of our Lord Jesus Christ.

30. For the right Faith is, that we believe and confess: that our Lord Jesus Christ, the Son of God, is God and Man;

31. God, of the Substance [Essence] of the Father; begotten before the worlds: and Man, of the Substance [Essence] of his Mother, born in the world.

32. Perfect God: and perfect Man, of a reasonable soul and human flesh subsisting.

33. Equal to the Father, as touching his Godhead: and inferior to the Father as touching his Manhood.

34. Who although he be [is] God and Man; yet he is not two, but one Christ.

35. One; not by conversion of the Godhead into flesh: but by taking [assumption] of the Manhood into God.

36. One altogether; not by confusion of Substance [Essence]: but by unity of Person.

37. For as the reasonable soul and flesh is one man: so God and Man is one Christ;

38. Who suffered for our salvation: descended into hell [Hades, spirit-world]: rose again the third day from the dead.

39. He ascended into heaven, he sitteth on the right hand of the Father God [God the Father] Almighty.

40. From whence [thence] he shall come to judge the quick and the dead.

41. At whose coming all men shall rise again with their bodies.

42. And shall give account for their own works.

43. And they that have done good shall go into life everlasting: and they that have done evil, into everlasting fire.

44. This is the Catholic Faith: which except a man believe faithfully [truly and firmly], he can not be saved.

Appendix D

THIS WORLD AND THE KINGDOM OF GOD[1]
by Greg L. Bahnsen, Th.M., Ph.D.

Virtually all Reformed believers maintain that the kingdom of Jesus Christ is (at least) a matter of Christ's spiritually reigning within the hearts of those who are Christians. The *Westminster Larger Catechism* teaches that Christ executes the office of a king by, among other things, "bestowing saving grace upon his elect" (Q. 45), or to use Scriptural language: "Him has God exalted to His right hand to be a Prince and a Savior, to give repentance to Israel and forgiveness of sins" (Acts 5:31).

The internal, spiritual reign of Christ as Savior and Lord must not be overlooked or minimized in importance. One cannot enter into the kingdom of God apart from spiritual rebirth: "Truly, truly I say unto you, except one be born from above, he cannot see the kingdom of God" (John 3:3). Those who are redeemed have already been transferred into the kingdom of God's beloved Son (Colossians 1:13) and as such appreciate that "the kingdom of God is . . . righteousness and peace and joy in the Holy Spirit" (Romans 14:17). Postmillennialists have always affirmed this foundational doctrine that the kingdom of God is an internal, spiritual reality. For instance, J. Marcellus Kik, interpreted the "thrones" of Revelation 20:4 in this way: "The thrones stand for the saints spiritual dominion within [themselves] and over the world. Through the grace of Christ they reign in life over the flesh, the world, and the devil" (*An Eschatology of Victory*, 1971, p. 210).

---

1. Published originally in *The Reconstruction Report*, II (Jan. 1982).

Is the Kingdom Merely Internal?

Without in any sense diminishing the tremendous Biblical truth that the kingdom of God is an internal, spiritual reign of Christ within our hearts, we can go on to ask whether this perspective completely expresses all that God's word reveals to us about the nature of God's kingdom. Is it accurate to say that the reign of Christ extends beyond the heart of the believer? Does Christ reign in any external, visible, and this-worldly fashion as well?

Amillennialists are categorically hesitant to affirm that the present reign of the Messiah is visible and this-worldly. Some examples will show this to be the general rule among amillennial writers. Geerhardus Vos taught that other-worldliness ought to be "the dominating attitude of the Christian mind" (*The Pauline Eschatology*, 1930, p. 363). When we think of the kingdom of Christ prior to His return in glory, amillennialists would *not* have us think about "earthly blessedness" (W. J. Grier, *The Momentous Event*, 1945, p. 16) or of "highly visible success of Christ through the church in earthly life and institutions" (Lewis Neilson, *Waiting for His Coming*, 1975, p. 346). Leading amillennial writers explain that they are "opposed to the type of millennium taught by the postmillennialist" (William E. Cox, *Amillennialism Today*, 1966, p. 2). How so? Cox tells us that during "the present church age . . . Jesus Christ reigns in the hearts of his saints" (p. 65), and Meredith G. Kline insists that the present reality is "the Lord's invisible reign on the theocratic throne of David in heaven" (*Westminster Theological Journal* XLI, 1978, p. 180.) Since the postmillennialist does not deny for a second that Christ presently reigns in the hearts of his saints from an invisible throne in heaven, what *distinctive* viewpoint is being claimed by these amillennial teachers?

When one reads authors like Cox, Kline, Neilson, and others, it becomes obvious that what they object to in postmillennial writers is the inclusion of external, visible, this-earthly aspects within the scope of the kingdom of God in this age. The direction of their thought, as indicated in what Vos said above, is almost exclusively "other-worldly" or heavenly. This is clearly manifest in Walter J. Chantry's recent book, *God's Righteous Kingdom* (1980). Chantry claims that "Citizens of the kingdom are oriented to another world, not to this present earth" (p. 16). Indeed, Chantry holds that Christ has set aside the outward aspects of Old Testament religion: "By way of contrast Christ's kingdom is inward" (p. 51), so that "material, social, external blessedness may not be sought in a millennium, but in the consummation of the kingdom at the coming of our Lord" (p. 62). Although Mr. Chantry attempts to qualify his remarks by admitting that the material, external world is not inherently evil, the heart of his theological outlook is revealed when he says that the Fall meant that man "raised animal desires above a longing for spiritual realities" (p. 20) and says that "worship and the winning of souls (are) . . . more important by far than the cultural mandate" (p. 27). Chantry makes himself quite clear:

". . . the kingdom of God is preoccupied with eternal and spiritual realities. It has to do with a presently invisible world. Its focal point is the inward man. . . . The gospel of the kingdom completely absorbs men in the eternal *rather than the temporal*. . . . The gospel of the kingdom absorbs men in *the spiritual rather than the material*" (pp. 15, 19, emphasis in original).

If men like Chantry were only indicating what our priorities should be, if they were only reminding us that internal regeneration is a prerequisite for external obedience in all areas of life, if they were only pointing to the provisional and limited nature of kingdom blessing today in contrast to the eternal and consummated kingdom of God, then there would be little dispute. But their criticism of postmillenialists is concrete proof that much more is at stake in the above quotations.

Amillennialists either claim or tend to exclusively emphasize the other-worldly, invisible, internal nature of Christ's kingdom as a spiritual reality. Our question is whether Scripture—the infallible standard for our doctrinal commitments—does not have something *more* to say than that the kingdom of God is presently expressed in the hearts of men. Is the kingdom merely internal?

Some Necessary Distinctions

Before we attempt an answer to our question, we should be reminded of some theological distinctions which must be made. First, we would differentiate the *providential* kingdom of God (His sovereign reign over every historical event, good or evil) from the *Messianic* kingdom of God (the divine rule which breaks the power of evil and secures redemption for God's elect). God's providential rule is indicated in Daniel 4:17, "The Most High rules in the kingdom of men," whereas Daniel 7:13-14 refers to the redemptive, moral, and victorious reign of the messianic Son of Man: "one like unto a son of man came with the clouds to the Ancient of Days . . . and there was given to him dominion, and glory, and a kingdom so that all the peoples, nations, and languages should serve him."

A second distinction which should not be forgotten is the distinction between "kingdom" and "church" in the Bible. These two words do not have precisely the same sense or meaning; otherwise, when Acts 28:23 tells us that Paul was testifying of the kingdom of God, we could just as well say that Paul was testifying about the church—which would be erroneous, given the context of Old Testament prophecy about the person and work of Jesus. "Kingdom" and "church" do not refer to the same entity either, for Matthew 13:38, 41 informs us that the scope of the kingdom is the world inclusive of the doers of iniquity—which is not true of the church. To be accurate, we should say that it is the kingdom of God which creates the church, and that the church in turn has the "keys of the kingdom" (Matthew 16:18-19). Neither statement would be true if we could not distinguish the two entities.

A third necessary distinction has to do with the Messianic kingdom (which has a broader scope than the church). We need to distinguish between this kingdom in the phase of Old Testament *anticipation* (cf. Matthew 21:43, where it is said to be taken away from the Jews), in the present phase of *established* realization (e.g., Matthew 12:28, where Jesus declares that the kingdom of God "has come upon you"), and in the phase of *consummated* realization at the return of Christ (e.g., Matthew 7:21-23, where entry into the kingdom is contrasted to being sent into everlasting damnation; cf. 3:12).

Christ's Kingdom as This-Worldly

To recapitulate, we have observed that it is a foundational truth that the kingdom of Jesus Christ pertains to the Savior's reign within the hearts of His people—a reign which originates from the Lord's heavenly throne. Our question, to be precise now, asks whether the Messianic reign of Jesus (in contrast to His providential reign, and extending beyond the scope of the church) during the current period of its establishment (in contrast to its Old Testament anticipation and to its future consummation in the new heavens and earth) is exclusively spiritual, other-worldly, invisible, and internal (as amillennialists tend to assert). In short, in this present age is the kingdom of Jesus Christ other-worldly and restricted to man's heart? Is it merely internal?

Our answer, if we are faithful to the full range of Biblical teaching on the subject, must be a definite *No*. The reign of Christ—His Messianic kingdom—is meant to subdue *every* enemy of righteousness, as Paradise is regained for fallen men by the Savior. As Isaac Watts poetically expressed it: "He comes to make His blessings flow, Far as the curse is found." Everything touched by the guilt and pollution of sin is the object of the Messiah's kingly triumph—everything. The kingdom of Christ not only brings forgiveness and new heart-love for God; it also brings concrete obedience to God in all walks of life. Those things which stand in opposition to God and His purposes and His character are to be overthrown by the dynamic reign of the Messianic King. The effects of Christ's dominion are to be evident on earth, among all nations, and throughout the range of human activity.

This all-encompassing perspective is set forth by the Apostle Paul in the first chapter of Colossians, where it is revealed that *all* things were created for Jesus Christ (v. 16), that *all* things are restored by His redemptive word (v. 20), and consequently that in *all* things He should be given the pre-eminence (v. 18). Followers of Christ are exhorted to "be holy in all manner of living" (I Peter 1:15). As Paul puts it, "Whether therefore you eat, or drink, or whatsoever you do, do all to the glory of God" (I Cor. 10:31). The reign of Christ is not restricted to internal matters of the heart — to prayer, meditation, and piety. That is only the beginning. The kingdom of God "brings forth fruit" (see Matthew 13:23; 21:43) such that by means of the visible quality of a person's life his inner state of heart can be discerned: "by their fruits you shall know them" (Matthew 7:16-21). So then, even eating and drinking as external activities are included within the Messiah's reign. The inward reign of the Savior must become manifest in *public* righteousness: genuine hearing of the word, genuine religion, and genuine faith are seen in faithful doing of the law, outward helping of the oppressed, and practical aid of the afflicted (James 1:22-2:26). To restrict the reign of Christ to inward matters is to lose touch with the true character of submission to the King.

Christ does not settle for a part-time or restricted reign as King. He demands obedience in all things from us, and His aim is to subdue all resistance — of any nature (internal or external) — to His rule. Paul teaches, "He must reign until He has put all His enemies under His feet," concluding with the defeat of death itself at the general resurrection (I Cor. 15:25-26). All opposition in all areas will be overcome by the King. And as it is, it will be an indication that the Messianic kingdom is coming. Christ taught His disciples to pray: "Thy kingdom come, thy will be done, *on earth* as it is in heaven" (Matt. 6:10). That prayer is a continual reminder to us that the coming of the kingdom means the doing of God's will, and that the reign of Christ (His kingdom) through our obedience comes precisely here on earth. The kingdom of Christ is undeniably *this*-worldly in its effects and manifestation. To be sure, Christ's kingdom does not spring "out of this world" (John 18:36), meaning (as the end of the verse interprets matters for us) that the *source* of Christ's reign is not "from here." Nevertheless, His reign, as originating from God Himself, pertains to this present world. The resurrected, victorious Savior said it Himself: "all authority in heaven *and on earth* has been granted to Me" (Matt. 28:18).

We must admit, therefore, that the kingdom of Christ is not merely internal and other-worldly. It has *external* expression *on earth* at the *present* time. "The kingdom of God and His righteousness" makes provision for every detail of life (Matt. 6:31-33). It is, as Paul taught, "profitable for all things, holding promise for the life that now is, as well as for that which is to come" (I Timothy 4:8). In a famous kingdom-parable, Christ authoritatively explained that the field (the kingdom) is *the world* (Matt. 13:38). In the perspective of Scripture, God's redeemed kingdom of priests — the church (I Peter 2:9) — presently "reigns upon the earth" (Revelation 5:9). Our confidence, calling, and prospect is encapsuled in the wonderful song, that "the kingdom of the world has become the kingdom of our Lord and of His Christ; and He shall reign for ever and ever" (Revelation 11:15). The Messianic kingdom must be seen, then, as this-worldly, external, and visible — *not merely* internal to man's heart and other worldly.

A CHRISTIAN RECONSTRUCTION LIBRARY

For anyone who wants to discover the extent to which modern humanism qualifies as a dying world-and-life view, the best book available is Herbert Schlossberg's *Idols for Destruction: Christian Faith and Its Confrontation with American Society,* published by Thomas Nelson Publishers in 1983. But knowing that your opponent is philosophically doomed is not enough to give you a victory over him in history. Goliath was doomed from the beginning, but David needed a sling and a stone to demonstrate just how doomed he was. Yet it should be obvious that once a culturally dominant world-and-life view is in philosophical and moral retreat, its days are numbered. It may exert influence for a while longer through the exercise of power, but power will eventually ebb away from those who no longer have moral confidence in what they are doing. Humanism has collapsed philosophically and morally.

Schlossberg's book provides evidence that humanism's moral collapse will eventually lead to its institutional collapse. Therefore, the book raises a key question: If humanism is going to collapse institutionally, what will replace it? He thinks it has to be Christianity, but what kind of Christianity? He does not say. But he does say this much: Whatever kind of Christian civilization will triumph, it will not be able to survive if it displays a schizophrenic division between word and deed. It will have to be consistent.

> Straight teaching combined with straight living, in the biblical vision, is to dominate all of life. There will be no exempt corners in which one conducts business as usual while making perfunctory gestures toward religious observances (p. 299).

Whatever replaces humanism must be comprehensive—a world-and-life view that addresses every area of life. Its recommended alternative programs must also be philosophically consistent with its declared world-and-life view. If it is to survive over long periods of time, its recommended programs must also be practical. The programs must *work*, meaning that they must be consistent with the way the world really works, as well as consistent with its own presuppositions. A world-transforming gospel is not one that offers a religious way of life whose visible positive effects are strictly confined to family and church—hearth and sanctuary—because people demand more from a world-and-life view than the promise of a safe place of temporary retreat when the work day or work week is done. What people insist on is a system for their life's work that really does work. What they demand, in short, is a system for *dominion*.

There is an old political slogan, "You can't beat something with nothing." For almost thirty years, Christian Reconstructionists have been publishing books, articles, and newsletters in an attempt to provide the Christian world with a positive, Bible-based program, an alternative to today's collapsing humanist civilization. Without a workable, biblical alternative to humanism, Christians cannot legitimately hope to succeed in pressing the claims of Christ in every area of life. This is why Christians need a comprehensive world-and-life view.

Turning Away Means Turning Toward

Wherever there is sin, there will always be a need for the healing power of the gospel, and there will always be a need for *repentance*—a turning away from sin. But turning away from one way of life necessarily requires turning toward a different way of life. Without a positive alternative world-and-life view to offer sinners, and without positive programs in every area of life that are consistent with this different world-and-life view, Christians will always find it difficult to persuade sinners to turn away from what they have come to love and cherish: sin and a civilization built on sin. A few people in any generation will be willing to abandon their dreams of success in this world in exchange for a promise of pie in the sky by and by, but most people instinctively realize that any religion that promises hope beyond the grave should also be able to demonstrate its future ability to "deliver the heavenly goods" beyond the final judgment by delivering a substantial *down payment* in history, or as the King James translators called it, an "earnest" (Eph. 1:14). Christian Reconstructionists have argued that consistent, biblical Christianity can and does "deliver the goods" in history, yet it is precisely this claim that has outraged the critics, both humanistic and pietistic.

Christian Reconstructionists have presented a detailed, comprehensive, Bible-based program which people should turn to and then work toward when they repent. Christian Reconstructionists argue that the gospel message of redemption is as comprehensive as the effects of Adam's rebellion. Every area of life was affected by Adam's fall; therefore, every area of life was in principle restored by the death, resurrection, and ascension of Jesus Christ. To argue that Christian principles do not apply in a particular area of life is necessarily to argue that this particular area of life is somehow ethically neutral, that God does not intend to bring it under His judgment because He has set forth no laws in His revealed Word for governing it.

Christian Reconstructionists deny that any such ethical "free zone" exists, can exist, or ever has existed. Our critics necessarily believe that such neutral areas do exist, governed by neutral law rather than biblical law. Yet at the same time, most of them insist that they do not believe in the myth of neutrality. In this sense, they suffer from a malady that Rushdoony has called intellectual schizophrenia. They both affirm and deny neutrality. To the extent that Christians adopt the idea that anything is an authority equal to the Bible, they have in fact adopted the view that some idea of man's sits in judgment of the Bible. There has to be a final authority in thought and culture. If it is not the Bible, then it must be something else.

When Christians adopt any version of neutrality — natural law, natural rights, or natural anything else — they inevitably face the same old problem: how to beat something with nothing. They are trying to overcome the collapsing civilization built by natural man by using the religion of natural man. If we Christians say that nothing is neutral, then we should not rely on God-hating philosophers to supply us with our first principles—in politics, economics, psychology, education, or anywhere else. We must offer something better, meaning something self-consciously biblical. This is what Christian Reconstructionists have been doing for over a quarter of a century. This is also why Reconstructionists are so deeply resented.

The Literature of Christian Reconstruction

The amount of Christian Reconstruction literature is large and growing rapidly. It will continue to grow. Anyone who reads published criticisms of the Christian Reconstruction position should carefully examine these criticisms to see whether the particular critic offers evidence that he or she has read the basic literature of the movement and has quoted from large sections of it, word for word. Has the critic provided accurate footnotes to Reconstructionism's books, articles, and newsletters? If not, then the reader should be initially skeptical of the critic's accusations. Perhaps the critic has not really mastered the literature that is being criticized. Perhaps it is a case of bearing false witness. Critics are responsible for doing their homework carefully; they should not rush into print with a lot of wild and unsubstantiated accusations. Their books should offer evidence that they have done their homework. If you have read any of these published criticisms and have believed them, you should go back to the books and ask yourself: "Do these critics provide evidence that they have really done their homework?" If the answer is "no," then you owe it to yourself to re-examine your negative conclusions regarding Christian Reconstruction.

What are the Reconstructionist books that the critics should read before going into print? What are the books that an inquiring reader who is searching for specific answers to real-world problems ought to read? While the following list is not complete, it will provide the reader with a basic introduction to the teachings of the Christian Reconstruction movement. Basically, Christian Reconstruction rests on five theological doctrines: the absolute sovereignty of God (predestination), the covenant, biblical law (theonomy), the self-attesting reliability of the Bible (presuppositionalism), and optimism regarding the earthly future of Christianity (postmillennialism). We have included at least three books in each division, in alphabetical order by author. There are many more books available in each division, but these are basic. The categories are: General Introduction, Dominion, Biblical Law, Eschatology, Government, Politics, Economics, Social Welfare, Education, Philosophy, and Conspiracies, plus Journals and Newsletters.

After you have looked over this list, ask yourself three questions. First, does any other infallible Bible-affirming, six-day creation-affirming, evolution-denying Christian intellectual movement offer an equally comprehensive alternative to humanism? (Answer: no.) Second, is there any Christian college, university, or seminary anywhere in the world that presents to its students an equally comprehensive biblical program to challenge today's humanist civilization? (If you can't think of any, join the club; neither can we.) Third, if it is true that we can't beat something with nothing (and it is!), then what self-consciously Christian movement is most likely to challenge successfully the dominant humanism of our day? (We think we know.)

These are not trick questions. They are real questions that demand serious answers. Critics of Christian Reconstruction abound, but they do not offer answers to these three crucial questions. Ask yourself this question: What are the critics of Christian Reconstructionism offering as a Bible-based, *practical*, alternative theological system? What precisely are their recommended alternative programs—world-transforming programs that follow consistently from their theological system?

We can't expect to beat something with nothing. The humanists have something, and they have it in abundance: power, money, the media, the universities, the law schools, and experience. Humanism's Roman Empire had something, too. But where is the Roman Empire today? The Church overcame it, century by century. The Church had something even better to offer. The Church had *the foundations of social order,* as Rushdoony has titled his book on the social impact of the Christian creeds. It still has these foundations, and *only* the Church has them. Nevertheless, there are millions of Christians today who have been taught, implicitly or explicitly, that Christianity has nothing as good as humanism to offer society, outside of the individual heart, the family, and the local church. Because their teachers recognize that you can't beat something with nothing, they have long recommend that Christians stop fighting. They would rather have Christians surrender, losing by default. They recommend that Christians cease devoting scarce economic resources—time, money, and effort—to challenging humanist civilization, and instead adopt a program of "tract-passing." (And even this tool is gone. When was the last time you passed a tract, or even saw one? Not since the early 1960s, probably.) In short, they teach that we just can't win.

But we *can* win! Christianity has a better program for the world than Satan does. It has always had a better program. The trouble is, Christians have forgotten their own history. They have been taught history by Humanists. They have allowed their enemies to teach them just about everything, but with Christians paying the compulsory tuition fees (tax-supported schools). It is time for Christians to relearn their history.

To do this, they will have to start reading serious books. They should start with the following list.

1. General Introduction

Gary North, *Liberating Planet Earth: An Introduction to Biblical Blueprints.* Ft. Worth, Texas: Dominion Press, 1987. This is the first volume in the multi-volume Biblical Blueprints Series, edited by Dr. North. It was written originally for use by Latin American pastors who are confronting the Marxist and socialist movement known as liberation theology. It provides a full-scale alternative to liberation theology. There are chapters on Christ and liberation, the God of liberation, the enemies of liberation, the covenant of liberation, plus individual chapters on the liberation of the individual, the family, the church, the state, and the economy. It concludes with a chapter on the inevitability of liberation.

Gary North, *Unconditional Surrender: God's Program for Victory.* Revised edition; Tyler, Texas: Institute for Christian Economics, (1981) 1987. This inexpensive paperback book is filled with Bible verses, is simply written, and covers the many of the basic issues of Christian Reconstructionism, with chapters on: God, man, law, and time; family, church, state, and economy; the kingdom of God and a strategy for dominion.

Gary North, *75 Bible Questions Your Instructors Pray You Won't Ask.* Revised edition; Ft. Worth, Texas: Dominion Press, (1984) 1988. This little book covers three areas: predestination, biblical law, and eschatology. Each section contains 25 one-page questions, each tied to a Bible verse, and 25 one-page responses to familiar (and questionable) responses to these questions. The book is aimed at students who attend Christian colleges.

Rousas John Rushdoony, *The Institutes of Biblical Law.* Phillipsburg, New Jersey: Presbyterian & Reformed Publishing Co., 1973. This is the central document of Christian Reconstruction. It is almost 900 pages long. It covers all of the themes of Christian Reconstruction, but it focuses on what the Ten Commandments teach and how they can be applied and should be applied in the modern world. This book was the first to present the Christian Reconstruction position in its entirety.

2. Dominion

Abraham Kuyper, *Lectures on Calvinism.* Grand Rapids, Michigan: Eerdmans, (1898) 1961. This book has gone through many editions. Kuyper served as Prime Minister of the Netherlands at the turn of the century. He was a distinguished theologian and the founder of several Christian newspapers. He was also the founder of the (now liberal) Free University of Amsterdam. There has never been anyone quite like him in the history of Christianity. His book contains chapters on: Calvinism as a life-system, Calvinism and religion, Calvinism and politics, Calvinism and science, Calvinism and art, and Calvinism and the future. He was very influential in the thinking of Cornelius Van Til. Obviously, he was writing long before Christian Reconstructionism appeared.

Gary North, *Backward, Christian Soldiers?: An Action Manual for Christian Reconstruction*. Tyler, Texas: Institute for Christian Economics, 1984. This popularly written paperback book is divided into five sections: the war, the enemy, strategy, tactics, and the duration. It summarizes the issues dividing humanists from Christians and then goes on to demonstrate the nature of the conflict. Christians need a vision of victory and a specifically biblical concept of law in order to replace the humanists in the driver's seat of society. The section on tactics offers practical suggestions on how to operate a newsletter ministry, a cassette tape ministry, and the use of personal computers in Christian social action.

Gary North, *Dominion and Common Grace: The Biblical Basis of Progress*. Tyler, Texas: Institute for Christian Economics, 1987. This easily read book deals with one fundamental question: If things are going to get better as the gospel spreads and serves as the foundation of a Christian civilization, why will there be a massive rebellion by Satan's human followers at the end of a millennium of peace? North answers that in order for a successful satanic revolt to take place, there first has to be a Christian civilization to revolt against. The book answers numerous other questions, such as: Why are non-Christians able to be productive? What is the relationship between biblical law and progress? What went wrong in Van Til's version of common grace? Why can't there be a "secret Rapture of the saints" before Christ returns in final judgment?

Gary North, *The Dominion Covenant: Genesis.* 2nd ed.; Tyler, Texas: Institute for Christian Economics, (1982) 1987. This is the first volume of North's multi-volume economic commentary on the Bible. It explains every verse in Genesis that relates to economics. He begins with Genesis 1 and shows how the concept of man's exercise of dominion over the earth is inescapable; man is a dominion agent under God, either as a covenant-keeper or as a covenant-breaker. The book contains several lengthy appendixes, including North's critique of Darwinism in modern thought, "From Cosmic Purposeless to Humanistic Sovereignty," which North regards as his most important single essay.

Ray R. Sutton, *That You May Prosper: Dominion By Covenant.* Tyler, Texas: Institute for Christian Economics, 1987. This book was the first to present the five-point biblical covenant model: transcendence/presence, hierarchy, law, judgment, and inheritance. It then applies this model to the three covenantal institutions: family, church, and state. It includes detailed appendixes showing how this five-point model serves as the model for the Ten Commandments, Psalms, Matthew, Romans, Revelation, and Hebrews 8.

3. Biblical Law

Greg L. Bahnsen, *By This Standard: The Authority of God's Law Today.* Tyler, Texas: Institute for Christian Economics, 1985. In this easily read paperback book, Bahnsen presents the case for the continuing validity of Old Testament law in New Testament times. Chapters include God's word as our norm, the entire Bible as today's standard, the covenant's uniform standard of right and wrong, the categories of God's law, the political implications of the comprehensive gospel, law and politics in Old Testament Israel, and law and politics in the nations around ancient Israel. This book presents the apologetic case for Rushdoony's position in *The Institutes of Biblical Law,* but in a more easily digested form than in Bahnsen's much larger work, *Theonomy in Christian Ethics* (Phillipsburg, New Jersey: Presbyterian & Reformed, [1977] 1984).

James B. Jordan, *The Law of the Covenant: An Exposition of Exodus 21-23*. Tyler, Texas: Institute for Christian Economics, 1984. This book takes the long-ignored case laws found immediately following the Ten Commandments and explains how they worked in Israel and how their principles can still be used in the modern world. Chapters include the law as God-centered, the Bible as covenantal, the uses of the law, the unchanging law, the Bible as a book of life, laws regulating the state; plus, sections dealing with slavery, violence, stewardship, marriage, witness-bearing, and time and rest.

Gary North, *Tools of Dominion: The Case Laws of Exodus*. Tyler, Texas: Institute for Christian Reconstruction, 1988. This is North's largest and most comprehensive book to date. It is part of his multi-volume economic commentary on the Bible. It takes up where Jordan's *Law of the Covenant* leaves off. It considers in great detail the case laws of Exodus—how they worked in Israel, how they could be applied today, how some of them have been fulfilled by Christ, how others have long operated in the history of Western law, and how the case laws could and should serve as the standard of a reconstructed civilization.

R. J. Rushdoony, *Law and Liberty*. Vallecito, California: Ross House Books, (1971) 1986. This book is a collection of 32 brief, easily read essays on the relationship between biblical law and civilization. Chapters include law and nature, the future, authority, chaos, evolution, alchemy, academic freedom, magic, government, property, inheritance, and the family. This book is the best introduction to the practical implications of biblical law for society.

4. Eschatology

Roderick Campbell, *Israel and the New Covenant*. Tyler, Texas: Geneva Divinity School Press, (1954) 1981. This is a reprint of a pre-Christian Reconstruction book on prophecy. For many years, it served Christian Reconstructionists as their primary book on eschatology. It is easy to read. It contains 35 chapters, each about

10 pages long, on such topics as: Judaism and Christianity, theocracy and revelation, the historical covenants, the heavenly army, the new age, the new heavens and new earth, the new kingdom, covenant law, and the assurance of victory.

David Chilton, *Paradise Restored: A Biblical Theology of Dominion*. Ft. Worth, Texas: Dominion Press, 1985. This book presents the Bible's case for long-term earthly optimism before the second coming of Christ in final judgment. It is filled with Bible verses. Chilton has allowed the Bible to comment on itself. He provides the extensive Old Testament background to Jesus' prophecies concerning the future of Israel and the church.

David Chilton, *The Days of Vengeance: An Exposition of the Book of Revelation*. Ft. Worth, Texas: Dominion Press, 1987. This is a large, detailed commentary that presents the case that the prophecies of Jesus regarding Israel were almost all fulfilled with the Romans' destruction of Jerusalem in A.D. 70. This is an ancient interpretation in church history, but Chilton argues it more forcefully and with greater attention to detail than previous commentators. He also goes into great detail explaining some of the most difficult prophetic passages in the Bible, including the dragon, the beast, 666, and the harlot.

David Chilton, *The Great Tribulation*. Ft. Worth, Texas: Dominion Press, 1987. This little paperback book presents the case that the prophesied great tribulation was in fact the fall of Jerusalem in A.D. 70. It is a simplified introduction to the primary theme of his book, *The Days of Vengeance*. He argues that all of church history since A.D. 70 is post-tribulational. There will be no future great tribulation to threaten the church.

5. Government

Gary DeMar, *God and Government*. 3 volumes; Atlanta, Georgia: American Vision, 1982-86. These books are workbooks designed to introduce people to the concept of God's system of government, beginning with self-government under God's law. They present the case that all government is God's government. They present the case against the idea of neutrality in law and government. They are suitable for Bible study classes and Sunday school classes.

Gary DeMar, *Ruler of the Nations: Biblical Blueprints for Government*. Ft. Worth, Texas: Dominion Press, 1987. This is volume 2 of the Biblical Blueprints Series. It presents the case for the world under God's law. It is structured in terms of the five-point biblical covenant model. It includes chapters on: the sovereignty of God, the bottom-up biblical hierarchy, plural law systems and plural gods, God judges the nations, the myth of neutrality, and rebuilding takes time. It then applies biblical principles of government to family, church, and state.

6. Politics

George Grant, *The Changing of the Guard: Biblical Blueprints for Political Action*. Ft. Worth, Texas: Dominion Press, 1987. This 8th volume of the Biblical Blueprints Series takes the five-point covenant model and applies it to politics. Then it applies the conclusions to church, family, and personal action. It begins with this presupposition: the earth is the Lord's. Then is continues with chapters on: render unto Him, sins of commission, sins of omission, reclaiming the land, honorable opposition, and prayer and precept. All of life is under God's law; if Christians refuse to press the crown rights of King Jesus in politics, then humanists will win by default. This book shows that Jesus died for politics, too, for there are political ramifications in Christ's redemptive program.

R. J. Rushdoony, *The One and the Many: Studies in the Philosophy of Order and Ultimacy*. Fairfax, Virginia: Thoburn Press, [1971] 1978. This is Rushdoony's history of Western man's social and political thought. He examines the history of humanist tyranny from the point of view of the doctrine of the Trinity: the equal ultimacy of unity and plurality in the Godhead. It includes chapters on: the ancient tyrannical states, Greece, Rome, the early church, medieval thought, and the rise of the modern power state.

R. J. Rushdoony, *Politics of Guilt and Pity.* Fairfax, Virginia: Thoburn Press, (1970) 1978. In this collection of 34 essays, Rushdoony shows how Christianity is at war with humanism in the field of politics and civil government. Humanism teaches that man can save himself through political action; Christianity teaches that only God can save man, and politics is only one of many spheres of action and responsibility for the redeemed man. The book is divided into four sections: the politics of guilt, the politics of pity, the politics of money, and the sociology of justification. Its most important essay is "Calvin in Geneva," first published in 1954. It also includes, "The United Nations: A Religious Dream," one of three important essays he has written on the U.N.

7. Economics

David Chilton, *Productive Christians in an Age of Guilt-Manipulators: A Biblical Response to Ronald J. Sider.* 4th ed.; Tyler, Texas: Institute for Christian Economics, 1986. This is a detailed answer to Ronald Sider's case for government intervention in the name of Jesus. Chilton presents a positive case for the free market in terms of fundamental biblical principles. He then shows that Sider's more socialistic position is based on anti-Bible standards. Sider refused to respond to Chilton in the second edition of his book in 1984. Chilton then rewrote his own book to include answers to Sider's second edition. Sider has remained silent.

Ian Hodge, *Baptized Inflation: A Critique of "Christian" Keynesianism.* Tyler, Texas: Institute for Christian Economics, 1986. This book is similar to Chilton's *Productive Christians.* It singles out a particular economist who has offered modern economic interventionism in the name of Jesus and attacks his system, line by line. At the same time, this strategy of negative criticism offers Hodge an opportunity to present the positive biblical case for economic liberty. His target is the Keynesian economist Douglas Vickers, who has publicly proclaimed himself as a follower of Cornelius Van Til. Gary North's Preface to the book is an uncompromising attack on the self-conscious mixing of biblical phrases and political liberalism that goes on daily in Christian college classrooms. Tenured liberal professors will not appreciate his characterization of them as "epistemological child molesters."

Gary North, *An Introduction to Christian Economics*. Nutley, New Jersey: Craig Press, 1973. Unfortunately out of print, this book was published the same year as Rushdoony's *Institutes of Biblical Law*. It is a collection of 31 essays on the relationship between the Bible and free market economics. Chapters include: the biblical critique of inflation, repressed depression, downward price flexibility and economic growth, statist bureaucracy in the modern economy, the mythology of spaceship earth, the teacher glut, tariff war, and stewardship and usury. Many of these essays were published originally in *The Freeman* in the late 1960s, when North was a graduate student.

Gary North, *Honest Money: The Biblical Blueprint for Money and Banking*. Ft. Worth, Texas: Dominion Press, 1986. Volume 5 of the Biblical Blueprints Series. Not many people recognize that the Federal Reserve System is the institutional source of today's monetary problems. Fewer know why: fractional reserve banking. Fewer still know that the Bible establishes rules that would make fractional reserve banking illegal. North presents the Bible's case for honest money, and it is not the case for Social Credit's government-printed paper money, nor is it the case for a government-operated gold standard. It is the case for responsible liberty under law: free coinage and 100% reserve banking.

Gary North, *Inherit the Earth: The Biblical Blueprint for Economics*. Ft. Worth, Texas: Dominion Press, 1987. Volume 7 of the Biblical Blueprints Series. This is one of the Biblical Blueprints Series. It presents the case for free market economics in terms of the five-point biblical covenant model. It deals with such topics as scarcity, theft, debt, exchange, profit and loss, and dominion. It then applies these economic principles to family, church, and state.

8. Social Welfare

George Grant, *Bringing in the Sheaves: Transforming Poverty into Productivity.* Atlanta, Georgia: American Vision, 1985. This was George Grant's first book on Christian charity. He established his HELP program in a church of 35 people in the early 1980s in Humble, Texas, just north of Houston. Both the church and the program then grew rapidly. The book demonstrates that tax-financed poverty programs are part of a massive war on the poor, for they keep people in poverty, generation after generation. The biblical answer is not more of the same; the answer is private Christian charity, coupled with a gospel that transforms individuals, families, and institutions.

George Grant, *In the Shadow of Plenty: The Biblical Blueprint for Welfare.* Ft. Worth, Texas: Dominion Press, 1986. Volume 4 of the Biblical Blueprints Series. In this book, Grant presents the biblical principles that undergird a comprehensive program of redemption out of poverty. He argues that evangelism must be word-and-deed evangelism: putting our money where our mouths are. Dominion is by service, and then by hard work. God does not randomly make people poor; He gives them blessings or cursings in terms of their obedience to His word. The way out of poverty is by obedience to God. After sketching ten principles of welfare, he applies them to civil government, the church, and the family.

George Grant, *The Dispossessed: Homelessness in America.* Ft. Worth, Texas: Dominion Press, 1986. Grant continues his criticisms of taxpayer-financed government welfare with a detailed study of the poverty that government programs have created. He shows how the divorce revolution has vastly increased the poverty of broken families, how the United Nations is getting ready to leap into the fray with compulsory international wealth-transfer programs, how unemployment and the farm crisis offer looming problems. Most of all, he shows how a return to biblical Christianity will solve these problems. Twenty-five pages of footnotes lead the serious reader into the literature of poverty.

Ray R. Sutton, *Second Chance: Biblical Blueprints for Divorce and Remarriage*. Ft. Worth, Texas: Dominion Press, 1987. Volume 10 of the Biblical Blueprints Series. Pastor Sutton takes the five-point biblical covenant model and applies it first to divorce and second to remarriage. He argues that lawful divorce is always by death: primarily by covenantal death, and secondarily (where societies enforce biblical civil law) by execution. Remarriage is based on covenantal adoption. Because no major Christian counseling approach has fully understood that the covenant is the basis of marriage, none has seen that the Bible's rules regarding covenant-breaking govern divorce and remarriage. This is a revolutionary book, one which truly does offer a guilt-free second chance to the innocent victims of covenant-breaking marriage partners.

9. Education

David Chilton (editor), *The Biblical Educator*. Tyler, Texas: Institute for Christian Economics. This is the assembled collection of the ICE newsletter, *The Biblical Educator*, published from 1979 to 1982. It includes essays on education theory, teaching methods, and other issues related to the war between Christian day school education and the public school system.

Gary North (editor), *Foundations of Christian Scholarship: Essays in the Van Til Perspective*. Vallecito, California: Ross House Books, 1976. This is a compilation of scholarly essays that expose the myth of neutrality in several academic disciplines: education, psychology, history, mathematics, economics, politics, sociology, and philosophy. It is written at the level of an upper division college student. There is no other book quite like it. It is mandatory reading for all college students. The authors include Gary North, R. J. Rushdoony, Greg Bahnsen, Vern Poythress, William Blake, Larry Pratt, and John Frame, whose concluding essay on Van Til is regarded by many of Van Til's followers as the classic summary of Van Til's position.

R. J. Rushdoony, *The Messianic Character of American Education: Studies in the History of the Philosophy of Education.* Phillipsburg, New Jersey: Presbyterian & Reformed, 1963. This book surveys the humanist philosophies of education of 21 major American educators, plus includes chapters on such topics as a liberal education, the "divine rights" of education, the kindergarten as a model for a new Eden, education as religion, and the lowest common denominator. The chapters include detailed references to the primary sources of progressive education. This book has been the "bible" of the Christian school movement in the United States for a generation. It exposes as no other book ever has the myth of neutrality in modern humanist education.

Robert L. Thoburn, *The Children Trap: The Biblical Blueprint for Education.* Ft. Worth, Texas: Dominion Press, 1986. Volume 6 of the Biblical Blueprints Series. Christian school founder, state legislator, and real estate entrepreneur Robert Thoburn presents the case for Christian day school education and against public (government) schools. He asks the fundamental question: Who owns the child? He concludes that God does, and he then shows that the Bible teaches that God has delegated to families (not to the state and not to the church) the responsibility of educating their children. His final chapter on the state presents a comprehensive program for hamstringing the public schools politically.

10. Philosophy

Richard Pratt, *Every Thought Captive: A Study Manual for the Defense of Christian Truth.* Phillipsburg, New Jersey: Presbyterian & Reformed, 1979. This book is an easy to read introduction to the philosophy of Cornelius Van Til. It was originally designed as a course for high school students.

R. J. Rushdoony, *By What Standard? An Analysis of the Philosophy of Cornelius Van Til.* Tyler, Texas: Thoburn Press, (1959) 1983. This was Rushdoony's first book. It presents a tightly written (and not particularly easy to read) presentation of Van Til's presuppositionalist approach to the philosophical defense of Christianity. Van Til's work is the philosophical foundation of Christian Reconstructionism, although Van Til was not himself a Christian Reconstructionist. No one has presented the case against the myth of neutrality more forcefully than Van Til. He shows that all philosophies are presuppositional. There are really only two systems: those that presuppose that the God of the Bible created everything and that His word is therefore the standard of truth, and those that presuppose that man is ultimately autonomous and that his word is the standard of truth. Van Til taught philosophy to the late Francis Schaeffer in the mid-1930s.

Cornelius Van Til, *The Defense of the Faith*. 2nd ed.; Phillipsburg, New Jersey: Presbyterian & Reformed, 1963. This is Van Til's most famous book on apologetics (the philosophical defense of Christianity). The difficulty with reading Van Til is that he approached every topic by refuting what is wrong in his opponent's system. This makes for hard reading. But his basic theme is always present: without presupposing the Creator God of the Bible, man's thinking is always incomplete and inconsistent. Autonomous man, he said, is like a child that must sit on his father's lap in order to slap his face.

11. Conspiracies

Douglas R. Grothuis, *Unmasking the New Age*. Downers Grove, Illinois: InterVarsity Press, 1986. A calm, scholarly look at the New Age movement, with chapters on its philosophical roots (pantheism, monism), the counterculture, holistic health, the human potential movement in psychology, and New Age spirituality. It shows how close New Age ideas are to modern humanism. This book demonstrates that it is possible for Christians to examine critically a rival religious movement without becoming hysterical and without falling for Satan's lie that he and his cohorts will inevitably win in history, making Christians historical losers.

Gary North, *Conspiracy: A Biblical View.* Ft. Worth, Texas: Dominion Press, 1986. North demonstrates that Satan's preferred approach to social change is conspiratorial. Satan is in rebellion to God; his earthly followers are also in rebellion. They seek to overturn God's rule in history. Thus, all history is intensely personal. History is not the product of impersonal forces. He lists two kinds of conspiracy: revolutionary and murderous (Marxism, Nazism) and deal-doing and compromising (Council on Foreign Relations, Trilateral Commission). Both are equally opposed to Christianity. The deal-doers are pressing for "convergence" with the Communists; the Communists agree, but only on their terms. What Christianity offers is an open, non-conspiratorial alternative, as North demonstrates (John 18:19-20).

Gary North, *Unholy Spirits: Occultism and New Age Humanism.* Ft. Worth, Texas: Dominion Press, 1986. This is the updated version of his 1976 book, *None Dare Call It Witchcraft.* In the original book, North exposed the "higher consciousness — New Age movement," the first book by a Christian to deal in detail with this topic, published seven years before Constance Cumbey's *Hidden Dangers of the Rainbow.* In it, he shows the connections between modern humanistic philosophy and ancient occultism. The two are being fused by the New Age movement. The updated version adds chapters on "flying saucers" (UFO'S) and on eschatology.

R. J. Rushdoony, *The Nature of the American System.* Fairfax, Virginia: Thoburn Press, (1965) 1978. This collection of historical essays includes his path-breaking chapter on the relationship between Unitarian Humanism and revolution ("The Religion of Humanity"). It also includes a chapter on the United Nations and another on "The Conspiracy View of History." This is the companion volume to Rushdoony's *This Independent Republic: Studies in the Nature and Meaning of American History* (Fairfax, Virginia: Thoburn Press, [1964] 1978).

12. Journals

The Journal of Christian Reconstruction. Published by the Chalcedon Foundation, P.O. Box 158, Vallecito, California. This scholarly journal has been published since 1974. Gary North was its editor until 1981.

Christianity and Civilization. Published by Geneva Ministries, P.O. Box 131300, Tyler, TX 75713. Only four volumes of this journal appeared, 1982-85: two edited by Gary North and two edited by James Jordan.

13. Newsletters

Newsletters covering many topics are available from the following organizations. As time goes on, many organizations continue to adopt elements of the Christian Reconstruction position, and the first thing they do is start a newsletter. These four organizations have been around the longest.

American Vision
P.O. Box 720515
Atlanta, GA 30328

Chalcedon Foundation
P.O. Box 158
Vallecito, CA 95251

Geneva Ministries
P.O. Box 131300
Tyler, TX 75713

Institute for Christian Economics
P.O. Box 8000
Tyler, TX 75711

SCRIPTURE INDEX

OLD TESTAMENT

NEW TESTAMENT

NAME INDEX

391

SUBJECT INDEX

Who Owns the Family: God or the State?
Rev. Ray R. Sutton

Does the Bible have answers for the problems facing today's families? Yes, absolutely. Our families are under siege. Divorce is rampant. Parental rights are eroding. Social welfare coercion is on the rise. Governmental intervention has become commonplace. Many social analysts and Christian counselors fear that if the basic family structures continue to sustain such destructive attacks, they will not survive—and the very foundations of Western civilization will crumble. They don't know what to do. They don't have the answers. But the Bible does.

Who Owns the Family? outlines what those answers are. Rev. Sutton shows how the bombs can be diffused. He assures us that families can be saved from the ravages of this revolutionary siege if only we would obey Scripture's clear commands. As Rev. Sutton states, the Bible tells us what to do, when, where, how, and why. It offers us blueprints for victory.

228 pp.
ISBN 0-930462-16-5
$6.95

Present this discount coupon to your local Christian bookstore and save $2 off the suggested retail price. If they do not have it available you may order directly from the publisher by sending $4.95, plus $1 postage, and this coupon, to:

Dominion Press
Post Office Box 8204
Fort Worth, Texas

(*Attention Bookseller*: Dominion Press will refund you $2.50 for honoring this discount coupon.)

Bookseller's Signature _____